Public Policy and Poli...
Series Editors: Colin Fudge . ...bin ... ...on

PUBLISHED

Danny Burns, Robin Hambleton and ... ...ggett, / ...Politics of Decentralisation:
  Revitalising Local Democracy
Stephen Glaister, June Burnham, Handley Stevens and Tony Travers, Transport Policy
  in Britain (second edition)
Christopher Ham, Health Policy in Britain (sixth edition)
Ian Henry, The Politics of Leisure Policy (second edition)
Christopher C. Hood and Helen Z. Margetts, The Tools of Government in the Digital
  Age
Peter Malpass and Alan Murie, Housing Policy and Practice (fifth edition)
Robin Means, Sally Richards and Randall Smith, Community Care: Policy and Practice
  (fourth edition)
David Mullins and Alan Murie, Housing Policy in the UK
Gerry Stoker, The Politics of Local Government (second edition)
Marilyn Taylor, Public Policy in the Community
Keiron Walsh, Public Services and Market Mechanisms: Competition, Contracting and
  the New Public Management

Public Policy and Politics
Series Standing Order
ISBN 0–333–71705–8 hardcover
ISBN 0–333–69349–3 paperback

(outside North America only)

You can receive future titles in this series as they are published by placing a standing order. Please contact your
bookseller or, in case of difficulty, write to us at the address below with your name and address, the title of the
series and the ISBN quoted above.

Customer Services Department, Macmillan Distribution Ltd
Houndmills, Basingstoke, Hampshire RG21 6XS, England

Also by Christopher Ham

Policy Making in the NHS: A Case Study of the Leeds Regional Hospital Board

The Policy Process in the Modern Capitalist State (with M. J. Hill)

Managing Health Services: Health Authority Members in Search of a Role

Handbook for CHC Members (with R. Levitt)

Health Check: Health Care Reforms in an International Context (with R. Robinson and M. Benzeval)

The New NHS: Organisation and Management

The NHS Guide (with S. Haywood)

NHS Handbook

Management and Competition in the New NHS

Priority Setting Processes for Healthcare (with F. Honigsbaum, J. Calltorp and S. Holmström)

Priority Setting in Healthcare: Lessons for General Practice

Public, Private or Community: What Next for the NHS?

Health Care Reform: Learning from International Experience

Tragic Choices in Health Care: The Case of Child B (with S. Pickard)

The Global Challenge of Health Care Rationing (with A. Coulter)

The Politics of NHS Reform 1988–97: Metaphor or Reality?

Contested Decisions (with S. McIver)

Reasonable Rationing (with G. Robert)

NHS Mutual (with J. Ellins)

Health Policy in Britain

Sixth edition

Christopher Ham

First edition 1982
Second edition 1985
Third edition 1992
Fourth edition 1999
Fifth edition 2004

Published 2009 by
PALGRAVE MACMILLAN

Palgrave Macmillan in the UK is an imprint of Macmillan Publishers Limited,
registered in England, company number 785998, of Houndmills, Basingstoke,
Hampshire RG21 6XS.

Palgrave Macmillan in the US is a division of St Martin's Press LLC,
175 Fifth Avenue, New York, NY 10010.

Palgrave Macmillan is the global academic imprint of the above companies
and has companies and representatives throughout the world.

Palgrave® and Macmillan® are registered trademarks in the United States,
the United Kingdom, Europe and other countries.

ISBN-13: 978–0–230–50756–2   hardback
ISBN-13: 978–0–230–50757–9   paperback

This book is printed on paper suitable for recycling and made from fully
managed and sustained forest sources. Logging, pulping and manufacturing
processes are expected to conform to the environmental regulations of the
country of origin.

A catalogue record for this book is available from the British Library.

A catalog record for this book is available from the Library of Congress.

10 9 8 7 6 5 4 3 2 1
18 17 16 15 14 13 12 11 10 09

Printed and bound in Great Britain by
CPI Antony Rowe, Chippenham and Eastbourne

To Ioanna

Contents

List of Figures and Tables

Acknowledgements

The author and publishers would like to thank the following who have kindly given permission for the use of copyright material: The King's Fund Institute for Figure 2.1 taken from *Health Finance: Assessing the Options*, 1988; Radcliffe Medical Press, Oxford for Figure 2.2 taken from C. J. Ham, *Management and Competition in the NHS*, 2nd edn, 1997. Reproduced with the permission of the copyright holder; Crown Copyright material is reproduced with the permission of the Controller of Her Majesty's Stationery Office under click licence C2009000462: Figure 3.1 taken from Secretary of State for Health, *The New NHS: Modern, Dependable*, 1997; Figure 3.4 taken from Department of Health, *Health Reform in England: Update and Next Steps*, 2005; Figure 4.4 taken from Department of Health, *Departmental Report 2006*; Figure 10.2 taken from M. Bajekal and A. Prescott, *Disability. The Health Survey for England 2001*, 2003; and Figure 12.1 from the Commonwealth Fund's report, *Mirror, Mirror on the Wall: An International Update on the Comparative Performance of American Health Care*, 2007.

Every effort has been made to contact all the copyright holders, but if any have been inadvertently overlooked the publishers will be pleased to make the necessary arrangements at the first opportunity.

Preface to the Sixth Edition

This book was originally based on undergraduate and postgraduate courses I taught at Bristol University. The first edition benefited from the comments and suggestions of the students who followed those courses. I am particularly grateful to Laurie McMahon and Andrew Wall for their insights, gained during the first intake of the MSc in Public Policy Studies run by the School for Advanced Urban Studies at Bristol. I would also like to thank former colleagues at the School who commented on draft chapters, most notably Robin Hambleton, Michael Hill, Robin Means, Randall Smith and David Towell. Special mention should also be made of Ken Judge, with whom I jointly taught an undergraduate course in health policy. As editor of the series, 'Studies in Social Policy', in which the first two editions appeared, Ken encouraged me to write *Health Policy in Britain*, and as always was a constructive and critical collaborator.

The sixth edition is based on the same structure as earlier editions but has been completely revised and updated to take account of developments in health services and health policy since the previous edition appeared in 2004. These developments have resulted in a much more extended discussion of policy issues, resulting in the division of the chapter previously devoted to funding health services and setting priorities into two new chapters. The first new chapter (Chapter 4) focuses on financing health services and the rediscovery of public health, and the second (Chapter 5) on policy and priorities in the NHS. The final chapter of the previous edition, the current Chapter 12, has been rewritten to encompass discussion of the performance of the NHS in the international context, reforms to the delivery of health care, debates on the role of markets, options for the future funding of health care, the challenges of priority-setting or rationing, and the proposals of the main political parties in Westminster.

A new concluding chapter has been added to provide some personal reflections on the reform of the NHS in the past decade, drawing on my experience as director of the Department of Health's strategy unit between 2000 and 2004, and my work as a researcher and adviser to NHS bodies and national organisations involved with health and health care. Throughout this new edition I have extended the analysis of the policy-making process by using more extensively than in the previous edition the insights I gained while working as a civil servant. There are two reasons for this: first, a reviewer of the previous edition identified this as an important omission from the book (Thornton, 2004), and I felt it important to respond; and second, my perspective on the period under review is clearer five years on than it was at the time the fifth edition was being written. Alongside my own reflections and insights, I have also drawn on the writings of a number of advisers and civil servants who held senior roles in the Blair government. I hope that as a result of these changes the sixth edition provides both a comprehensive and up-to-date introduction to the subject, and a unique outsider/insider perspective on the issues discussed.

In updating the book, I have benefited from advice and comments from a number of colleagues at the University of Birmingham and elsewhere. I would like to thank Steve Allen, John Appleby, Angela Coulter, Jennifer Dixon, Ian Dodge, Steve Dunn, Derek Feeley, Jon Glasby, Alan Hall, Andrew McCormick, Elias Mossialos, Mike Ponton, Nick Timmins and Kieran Walshe who helped in this way. I also received valuable support from Rachel Posaner and colleagues in the library of the Health Services Management Centre and Jackie Francis, who came to the rescue when my word processing skills were tested beyond their limits.

Once again, I am pleased to dedicate the book to Ioanna Burnell for her continuing support and for wonderful help in commenting on draft chapters and helping me to improve the text. I would also like to thank our daughter, Jessica, for helping with the proofreading.

I alone am responsible for the final text.

CHRISTOPHER HAM

Abbreviations

AHA	Area Health Authority
ASH	Action on Smoking and Health
BMA	British Medical Association
BUPA	British United Provident Association
CHC	Community Health Council
CHI	Commission for Health Improvement
CPRS	Central Policy Review Staff
CSR	Comprehensive Spending Review
DGH	District General Hospital
DH	Department of Health
DHA	District Health Authority
DHSS	Department of Health and Social Security
DMT	District Management Team
EMS	Emergency Medical Service
ENT	Ear, Nose and Throat
EU	European Union
FHSA	Family Health Services Authority
FPC	Family Practitioner Committee
GMC	General Medical Council
GP	General Practitioner
HAS	Health Advisory Service
HImP	Health Improvement Programme
HMC	Hospital Management Committee
ICT	Information and Communication Technology
IPPR	Institute for Public Policy Research
ISTC	Independent Sector Treatment Centre
JCC	Joint Consultative Committee
LIFT	Local Improvement Finance Trust
ME	Management Executive (of the National Health Service)
MPC	Medical Practices Committee
NAHA	National Association of Health Authorities
NAO	National Audit Office
NHS	National Health Service
NICE	National Institute for Health and Clinical Excellence
NPSA	National Patient Safety Agency
OECD	Organisation for Economic Cooperation and Development
ONS	Office for National Statistics

PAC	Public Accounts Committee
PAF	Performance Assessment Framework
PCGs	Primary Care Groups
PCTs	Primary Care Trusts
PEC	Professional Executive Committee
PESC	Public Expenditure Survey Committee
PFI	Private Finance Initiative
PROMs	Patient Reported Outcome Measures
QOF	Quality and Outcomes Framework
RAWP	Resource Allocation Working Party
RCP	Royal College of Physicians
RHA	Regional Health Authority
RHB	Regional Hospital Board
SARS	Sudden Acute Respiratory Syndrome
SHA	Strategic Health Authority
SMR	Standardised Mortality Ratio
WHO	World Health Organization

Introduction

This book provides an introduction to health policy in the United Kingdom covering both the substance of health policy and the process of health policy-making and implementation. Its aim is to offer an introduction to the organisation of the National Health Service (NHS), its history and development and to the way in which policies for NHS services are made and implemented in central government and in NHS bodies. The book also examines the auditing and evaluation of health policy, and considers which groups have power over policy-making. The main concern of what follows, then, is the politics of health care: who decides, who benefits and who controls health services.

In examining health policy, the focus is not just central government, important as government is in accounting for what happens in the NHS. Rather, the book examines both the macro politics of health policy and the micro politics by reviewing the dynamics of policy-making in health bodies as well as in Westminster and Whitehall. Attention is also given to the influence of the health professions in policy-making, especially doctors, both through their involvement in committees and boards and through the power available to health professionals by virtue of their training and clinical autonomy. Put another way, if formal accounts of the organisation of government and the administration of the NHS provide the starting point of analysis, we seek to test the reality of these accounts by drawing on a wide range of studies and research evidence in the search for a fuller understanding of what actually happens in practice.

One of the characteristics of contemporary debates about health policy is the strength of the views of those who participate in those debates. Controversy is the norm and opinions on what government should do to tackle the problems of the NHS are two a penny. This book endeavours to stand above these debates, reflecting the variety of views that exist in the health policy community but resisting the temptation to take sides. For readers new to this field it is important to be led into the issues that give rise to dispute as dispassionately as possible while not ignoring the conflict that exists. This is therefore not a textbook for those wanting to be persuaded of a particular point of view. Rather, it will have succeeded if the reader is better informed about the terms of the debate about health policy and in a position to make up his or her mind on the issues. Only in the final chapter do I venture some personal reflections on the reform of the NHS.

As well as students of health services in the United Kingdom, the book is aimed at those working in the health services and readers from outside the United Kingdom seeking to understand the dynamics of the NHS and health policy. Recognising that an introductory textbook is likely to raise as many questions as it provides answers, suggestions for further reading are offered at the end.

The structure of the analysis

The book is organised into 13 chapters. Chapter 1 examines the way in which the state has increasingly become involved in providing health services in the United Kingdom. Starting with state involvement in public health in the nineteenth century, the chapter traces the development of health insurance measures in the first part of the twentieth century and the establishment of the NHS in 1948. Particular attention is given to events after 1948, including the reorganisation of the NHS in 1974, and its subsequent restructuring in 1982.

Chapter 2 focuses on the development of health policy in the 1980s and 1990s. The chapter begins by describing the efficiency initiatives taken by the Thatcher government during the 1980s and this is followed by an account of the Ministerial Review of the NHS and the White Paper, *Working for Patients*. The process by which the White Paper was translated into law is reviewed, and the impact of the reforms is assessed. The chapter also considers the policies that were developed when John Major became Prime Minister.

Chapter 3 examines the policies pursued by the Blair and Brown governments since 1997. The chapter begins with a review of the government's inheritance and goes on to outline the proposals in the White Paper, *The New NHS*. This leads into a discussion of *The NHS Plan* and the subsequent changes to the organisation of the NHS in England that followed from *Delivering the NHS Plan* and *The NHS Improvement Plan*. The chapter concludes by reviewing Gordon Brown's impact on health policy when he became Prime Minister, and assesses the effects of the reforms pursued under the Labour government.

Chapter 4 explores the financing of health services and the rediscovery of public health. The growth of NHS expenditure is reviewed and this is followed by a description of the Wanless review into the long-term funding of health care and its outcome. The way in which NHS funds are used is then discussed and this leads into a review of public health policies since the 1970s and the impact of these policies.

Chapter 5 focuses on policy issues in health care and priority-setting. A wide range of issues is discussed including access and standards, primary care, acute hospital services and policies covered by national service frameworks such as cancer, heart disease and stroke, mental health and services for older people. The challenge of setting priorities in the NHS is considered in the context of the large number of targets and objectives promoted by government.

Chapter 6 considers the policy-making process in Westminster and Whitehall. The functions and powers of Parliament, the Cabinet, the Prime Minister, ministers, civil servants and outside interests are outlined, in order to establish the political context of health policy-making. The development of a number of theoretical approaches to interpret the role of different institutions is also discussed.

Chapter 7 explains differences between England, Wales, Scotland and Northern Ireland in health and health services before and after political devolution. The impact of devolved government on the structure of the NHS in each country is discussed and emerging divergences in health policy are described. The possible implications of regional government for the NHS in England are also explored, as is the impact of the European Union.

Chapter 8 concentrates on the workings of the Department of Health (DH). The way in which the Department is organised is described, and this is followed by an examination of the various influences on health policy-making within central government. The role of pressure groups and other interests is considered, and the chapter concludes with a discussion of attempts within the DH to introduce a greater measure of analysis into the policy process.

Chapter 9 looks at the implementation of health policy, and the local influences on policy-making. A key issue here is the relationship between the DH and NHS bodies. Also significant is the position of the medical profession in the structure of management and as major resource controllers at the local level. These issues are analysed, and the extent to which national policies are implemented is discussed. The chapter also considers the ability of NHS bodies to engage in independent policy-making.

Chapter 10 focuses on audit and evaluation. The development of interest in this area is described and the current arrangements for audit and evaluation are outlined. This includes discussion of the performance assessment framework and the use of performance ratings, and an analysis of the role of bodies such as the Audit Commission, the Care Quality Commission and the National Audit Office. The extension of audit into the quality of medical care is described and the importance of the Kennedy Inquiry into heart surgery in Bristol is emphasised. This is followed by an assessment of the performance of the NHS in relation to health improvement and access to health care.

Chapter 11 examines the distribution of power in the NHS. Through a discussion of different theories of power, the chapter asks whose interests are served by health services. The relevance of pluralist, structuralist and Marxist theories is assessed, and issues for further research are identified. The chapter seeks to stand back from the detailed discussion of health policy in earlier chapters in order to explore the variety of overarching approaches to understanding the development of health services and power relationships in health care.

Chapter 12 looks to the future. It does so by first examining the performance of the NHS in the international context. This is followed by a review of reforms to the organisation of the NHS and an analysis of the role of hierarchies, networks and markets in health care. The pressures to increase health care funding are then discussed, as is the balance between public and private funding. This leads into a discussion of efficiency within the NHS and rationing or priority-setting. The chapter concludes by examining the policies of the main political parties in Westminster on the future of the NHS.

Chapter 13 offers some personal reflections on the reform of the NHS and identifies 11 lessons for policy-makers.

Chapter 1

The Development of Health Services and Health Policy

Health policy in Britain today is a legacy of decisions taken by public and private agencies over many hundreds of years. These decisions have shaped the organisation and financing of health care and the part played by government, voluntary or third sector organisations and private interests. The aim of this chapter is to trace the development of health services and health policy in the period leading up to the establishment of the National Health Service, and in the first 30 years of its existence. As well as providing a context for the rest of the book, the chapter illustrates the dynamics of health policy formulation and raises a number of questions explored in more detail in subsequent chapters.

The National Health Service came into existence on 5 July 1948 with the aim of providing a comprehensive range of health services to all in need. One hundred years earlier the first Public Health Act was placed on the statute book, paving the way for improvements in environmental health which were to have a significant effect in reducing deaths from infectious diseases. The name of Aneurin Bevan is usually associated with the founding of the NHS, and that of Edwin Chadwick with the public health movement. However, legislation and policy are not made only or mainly by outstanding individuals. It has been said of Bevan that he was 'less of an innovator than often credited; he was at the end, albeit the important and conclusive end, of a series of earlier plans. He "created" the National Health Service but his debts to what went before were enormous' (Willcocks, 1967, p. 104). Much the same applies to other health policy decisions. Individuals may have an impact, but under conditions not of their own making. What is more, most decisions in their final form result from bargaining and negotiation among a complex constellation of interests, and most changes do not go through unopposed. These points can be illustrated through the examples already cited.

Take the 1848 Public Health Act, for example. The main aim of the Act was to provide powers to enable the construction of water supply and sewerage systems as a means of controlling some of the conditions in which infectious diseases were able to thrive and spread. On the face of it, this was a laudable aim which might have been expected to win general public support. In fact, the Act was opposed by commercial interests who were able to make money out of insanitary conditions; and by anxious ratepayers, who were afraid of the public expense which would be involved. It was therefore only after a lengthy struggle that the Act was passed.

Again, consider the establishment of the NHS. The shape taken by the NHS was the outcome of discussions and compromise between ministers and civil servants on the one hand, and a range of pressure groups on the other. These groups included the medical profession, the organisations representing the hospital service, and the insurance committees with their responsibility for general practitioner services. Willcocks has shown how, among these groups, the medical profession was the most successful in achieving its objectives, while the organisations representing the hospital service were the least successful. A considerable part too was played by civil servants and ministers. In turn, all of these interests were influenced by what had gone before. They were not in a position to start with a blank sheet and proceed to design an ideal administrative structure. Thus history, as well as the strength of established interests, may be important in shaping decisions. Let us then consider the historical background to the NHS.

The origins of hospitals and medicine

The origins of hospitals in Britain can be traced back to medieval times when religious foundations established institutions such as St Bartholomew's in 1123 and St Thomas's in 1215. Hospital building took off in the thirteenth century alongside the establishment of universities across Europe and formal medical training. Even at this early stage, three types of doctor began to emerge: physicians, barber-surgeons and apothecaries, the forerunners of general practitioners. Physicians were the elite doctors and their training was based in the universities. In contrast, surgeons served an apprenticeship organised through guilds. Apothecaries were originally shopkeepers who provided basic medical care and administered drugs. Like physicians and surgeons, apothecaries were limited in their ability to offer help to patients by the rudimentary understanding of the causes of disease that existed at that time. Midwives played the major part in childbirth, and childbirth was dominated by women until the eighteenth century.

It was not until 1518 that the College of Physicians of London was formed to exercise control over the licensing and examination of physicians. Subsequently, surgeons separated from barbers and established the London Company of Surgeons in 1745 and this became the College of Surgeons in 1800. The Society of Apothecaries was involved in regulating general practitioners in London, although the extent to which it was effective in this role has been questioned (Porter, 1997). The nature and content of medical education in the eighteenth century was highly variable and many doctors practised without formal qualifications. Only in the nineteenth century with the passage of the Apothecaries Act in 1815 and, more importantly, the Medical Act in 1858, did the state act to regulate medicine.

The Apothecaries Act required apothecaries to have the Licence of the Society of Apothecaries, the receipt of which rested on a combination of training and clinical experience. The Medical Act created the forerunner of the General Medical Council (GMC) with responsibility for licensing doctors and overseeing education and disciplinary matters. In place of a variety of forms of local regulation, a single national register of qualified medical practitioners was created for the first time. Although ostensibly intended to protect the public, the Medical Act also served the interests of doctors by enabling controls to be exercised over the number of doctors in practice. At a time when medical practice was almost entirely private practice, control over entry helped to maintain medical incomes and exclusivity (Stacey, 1992). This was particularly important for general practitioners who were the biggest group of doctors at that time and who sought protection from the unqualified. The important point about the Medical Act was that it led to a system of state-sanctioned self-regulation that has persisted with minor modifications until this day.

The development of hospitals was set back by the dissolution of the monasteries by Henry VIII and the impact this had on institutions for the sick that had had their origins in religious foundations. In London, only St Bartholomew's, St Thomas's and the Bethlem survived until the resurgence of hospitals in the eighteenth century. In parallel there grew up the dispensaries as an early form of outpatient care that also provided drugs for the sick. The role of hospitals developed further in the nineteenth century when specialisation among doctors led to the establishment of specialist hospitals. By 1860 there were at least 66 special hospitals and dispensaries in London concerned with children's health, nervous diseases, orthopaedics and other needs (Porter, 1997). In the second half of the nineteenth century, public infirmaries were created separate from the workhouses that provided relief for the poor, and in this way the basis for state involvement in hospital provision was laid down (see below). Another important development was increasing separation between specialists who controlled care in hospitals and general practitioners who worked in the community. The end of the nineteenth century saw the emergence of the referral system under which specialists became consultants to general practitioners. This division of labour among doctors was to have long-lasting implications for the practice of British medicine and the organisation of health services.

Public health services

While the Medical Act of 1858 was a landmark in the development of the medical profession, the most important area of state involvement in the provision of health services during the nineteenth century, in terms of the impact on people's health, was the enactment of public health legislation. Infectious diseases like cholera and typhoid posed the main threat to health at the time. The precise causes of these diseases remained imperfectly understood for much of the century, and the medical profession was largely powerless to intervene. In any event, the main reason for the decline in infectious diseases was not to be advances in medical science, but developments in the system of public health. It was these developments which provided an effective counterweight to the sorts of urban living conditions created by the industrial revolution and within which infectious diseases could flourish.

The 1848 Public Health Act provided the basis for the provision of adequate water supplies and sewerage systems. Behind the Act lay several years of struggle by Edwin Chadwick and his supporters. As Secretary to the Poor Law Commission, Chadwick played a major part in preparing the Commission's *Report of an Inquiry into the Sanitary Conditions of the Labouring Population of Great Britain*, published in 1842. The report, and the ever-present threat of cholera, created the conditions for the Act, which led to the establishment of the General Board of Health. Subsequent progress was variable, with some local authorities keen to take action, while others held back. In practice, a great deal depended on the attitude of local interests, as the Act was permissive rather than mandatory, and the General Board of Health was only an advisory body.

Chadwick's campaign was taken forward by John Simon, first as Medical Officer to the General Board of Health, and later as Medical Officer to the Medical Department of the Privy Council, which succeeded the Board in 1858. Simon's work and the report of the Royal Sanitary Commission, which sat from 1869 to 1871, eventually bore fruit in the establishment of the Local Government Board in 1871, and the Public Health Acts of 1872 and 1875. The 1875 Act brought together existing legislation rather than providing new powers, while the 1872 Act created sanitary authorities who were obliged to provide public health services. One of the key provisions of the 1872 Act was that local sanitary authorities should appoint a medical officer of health. These officers – whose origins can be traced back to Liverpool in 1847 – were significant figures, both in the fight against infectious diseases, and in the campaign for better health. It was mainly as a result of their activities at the local level that more concerted action was pursued.

Mothers and young children

From the beginning of the twentieth century, the sphere of concern of medical officers of health extended into the area of personal health services as the result of increasing state concern with the health of mothers and young children. One of the immediate causes was the discovery of the poor standards of health and fitness of army recruits for the Boer War. This led to the establishment by government of an Interdepartmental Committee on Physical Deterioration, whose report, published in 1904, made a series of recommendations aimed at improving child health. Two of the outcomes were the 1906 Education (Provision of Meals) Act, which provided the basis for the school meals service, and the 1907 Education (Administrative Provision) Act, which led to the development of the school medical service. It has been argued that these Acts 'marked the beginning of the construction of the welfare state' (Gilbert, 1966, p. 102). Both pieces of legislation were promoted by the reforming Liberal government elected in 1906, and the government was also active in other areas of social policy reform, including the provision of retirement pensions.

At the same time action was taken in relation to the midwifery and health visiting services. The 1902 Midwives Act made it necessary to certify midwives as fit to practise, and established a Central Midwives Board to oversee registration. The Act stemmed in part from the belief that one of the explanations for the high rates of maternal and infant mortality lay in the lack of skills of women practising as midwives. Local supervision of registration was the responsibility of the medical officer of health, whose office was becoming increasingly powerful. This trend was reinforced by the 1907 Notification of Births Act, one of whose aims was to develop health visiting as a local authority service. The origins of health visiting are usually traced back to Manchester and Salford in the 1860s, when women began visiting mothers to encourage higher standards of childcare. The state's interest in providing health visiting as a statutory service mirrored its concern to regulate midwives and provide medical inspection in schools, and the importance of health visiting was emphasised by the Interdepartmental Committee on Physical Deterioration. The 1907 Act helped the development of health visiting by enabling local authorities to insist on the compulsory notification of births. An Act of 1915 placed a duty on local authorities to ensure compulsory notification.

Arising out of these developments, and spurred on by the 1918 Maternity and Child Welfare Act, local authorities came to provide a further range of child welfare services. These services included not only the employment of health visitors and the registration of midwives, but also the provision of infant welfare centres and, in some areas, maternity homes for mothers who required institutional confinements. However, the Ministry of Health, which had been established in 1919, continued to be concerned at the high rate of maternal deaths, as the publication in 1930 and 1932 of the reports of the Departmental Committee on Maternal Mortality and Morbidity demonstrated. Particular importance was placed on the provision of adequate antenatal care. This led to an expansion of antenatal clinics, and, after the 1936 Midwives Act, to the development of a salaried midwifery service.

Health insurance

The 1911 National Insurance Act was concerned with the provision of general practitioner (GP) services. The Act was an important element in the Liberal government's programme of social policy reform, and it provided for free care from GPs for certain groups of working people earning under £160 per annum. Income during sickness and unemployment was also made available, and the scheme was based on contributions by the worker, the employer and the state.

Like other major pieces of social legislation, the Act was not introduced without a struggle. As Gilbert (1966, p. 290) has noted, 'The story of the growth of national health insurance is to a great extent the story of lobby influence and pressure groups'. Gilbert has shown how Lloyd George pushed through the Act to come into operation in 1913, but only after considerable opposition from the medical profession. The doctors were fearful of state control of their work, and of the possible financial consequences. They were persuaded into the scheme when the government agreed that payment should be based on the number of patients on a doctor's list – the capitation system – rather than on a salary, thereby preserving GPs' independence. Also, it was decided that the scheme should be administered not by local authorities, but by independent insurance committees or 'panels'. The insurance companies and friendly societies that had previously played a major part in providing cover against ill health were given a central role on the panels. The professional freedom of doctors was further safeguarded by allowing them the choice of whether to join the scheme, and whether to accept patients. Finally, the financial fears of the profession were assuaged by the generous level of payments that were negotiated, and by the exclusion of higher income groups from the scheme. The exclusion of these groups created a valuable source of extra income for GPs. By the mid-1940s around 21 million people or about half the population of Great Britain were insured under the Act. Also, about two-thirds of GPs were taking part. Nevertheless, the scheme had important limitations: it was only the insured workers who were covered, and not their families; and no hospital care was provided, only the services of GPs. Despite these drawbacks, the Act represented a major step forward in the involvement of the state in the provision of health services.

Hospital services

As we noted earlier, public provision of hospitals developed out of the workhouses provided under the Poor Law. The voluntary hospital system had a much longer history, being based at first on the monasteries and later on charitable contributions by the benevolent rich. Of the two types of institution, it was the voluntary hospitals that provided the higher standards of care. As the nineteenth century progressed, and as medicine developed as a science, the voluntary hospitals became increasingly selective in their choice of patients, paying more and more attention to the needs of the acutely ill to the exclusion of the chronic sick and people with infectious diseases. Consequently, it was left to the workhouses to care for the groups that the voluntary hospitals would not accept, and workhouse conditions were often overcrowded and unhygienic. Some of the vestiges of this dual system of hospital care can still be observed in the NHS today.

It was not, perhaps, surprising that workhouse standards should be so low, since one of the aims of the Poor Law was to act as a deterrent. The 'less eligibility' principle underpinning the 1834 Poor Law Amendment Act depended on the creation of workhouse conditions so unattractive that they would discourage the working and sick poor from seeking relief. The Act was also intended to limit outdoor relief: that is, relief provided outside the workhouses. In the case of medical care, this was provided by district medical officers under contract to the Boards of Guardians who administered the Poor Law. Vaccination against smallpox was one of the services for which medical officers were responsible, beginning with the introduction of free vaccination for children in 1840.

There was some improvement in Poor Law hospital services in London after the passing of the 1867 Metropolitan Poor Act. The Act provided the stimulus for the development of infirmaries separate from workhouses, and the London example was subsequently followed in the rest of the country through powers granted by the 1868 Poor Law Amendment Act. However, the establishment of separate infirmaries coincided with a further campaign against outdoor relief. This was despite the fact that in some areas public dispensaries, equivalent to rudimentary health centres, were provided for the first time. Nevertheless, the legislation which encouraged the development of Poor Law infirmaries has been described as 'an important step in English social history. It was the first explicit acknowledgement that it was the duty of the state to provide hospitals for the poor. It therefore represented an important step towards the NHS Act which followed some eighty years later' (Abel-Smith, 1964, p. 82). And as Fraser has commented, 'through the medical officers and the workhouse infirmaries the Poor Law had become an embryo state medical authority providing in effect general practitioners and state hospitals for the poor' (Fraser, 1973, p. 87).

The 1929 Local Government Act marked the beginning of the end of the Poor Law, and was a further step on the road to the NHS. The importance of the Act was that it resulted in the transfer of workhouses and infirmaries to local authorities. County councils and county borough councils were required to set up public assistance committees to administer these institutions, and were empowered to appropriate from them accommodation for the care of the sick. The intention was that this accommodation should then be developed into a local authority hospital service. Although uneven progress in this direction was made before the outbreak of the Second World War, the 1929 Act was important in placing the Poor Law infirmaries in the same hands as the other public health services which were under the control of medical officers of health. These services included not only those already mentioned, but also the provision of specialised hospitals – for example for infectious diseases and tuberculosis – which local authorities had developed rapidly from the last decades of the nineteenth century. In addition, local authorities had a duty to provide hospitals for people with mental illness and learning disabilities. Local magistrates had been given the power to erect asylums under the 1808 County Asylums Act, but fear of the cost meant that the power was not widely used. The legislation was made mandatory in 1845, leading to a rapid growth in asylums thereafter. By 1930 there were 98 public asylums in England and Wales accommodating about 120,000 patients (Jones, 1972, p. 357).

Accordingly, at the outbreak of the Second World War, local authorities were responsible for a wide range of hospitals. As part of the war effort, public hospitals joined the voluntary hospitals in the Emergency Medical Service (EMS), set up to cope with military and civilian casualties and to provide some coordination of a disparate range of institutions and services. The EMS, with its regional form of organisation, provided a framework for the administration of hospital services after the war. More important, it resulted in senior members of the medical profession seeing at first hand the poor state of local authority hospitals and the smaller voluntary hospitals. At the same time, regional hospital surveys were carried out by the Nuffield Provincial Hospitals Trust, a voluntary body concerned with the quality and organisation of hospital services, and with a particular interest in the regionalisation of hospitals. The surveys were conducted in conjunction with the Ministry of Health, and provided thorough documentation of the widely varying standards which existed (hospitals for the mentally ill and mentally handicapped were not included in the surveys). The summary report of the surveys, published in 1946 as *The Hospital Surveys: The Domesday Book of the Hospital Services*, pointed to considerable inequalities in the distribution of beds and staff between different parts of the country, as well as to the lack of organisation of the service as a whole (Nuffield Provincial Hospitals Trust, 1946). It was in this sense, then, that the experience of war may be said to have created pressure for change, although what form the change should take was very much an issue for debate.

The establishment of the National Health Service

We have seen how, in a variety of ways, responsibility for the provision of health care was increasingly taken over by the state. The key legislative developments were the 1808 County Asylums Act, the 1867 Metropolitan Poor Act and the 1929 Local Government Act, all emphasising the importance of public provision of hospital services; the Public Health Acts and the legislation relating to maternal and child welfare, placing on local authorities a duty to develop environmental and, later, some personal health services; the 1911 National Insurance Act, recognising the state's responsibility in relation to primary health care; and the Medical Act of 1858 with its provisions on the regulation of the medical profession.

Given the ad hoc manner in which these developments occurred, it was not surprising that there should be calls for the coordination and consolidation of service provision. Thus the report of the Dawson Committee, set up in 1919 after the establishment of the Ministry of Health to make proposals for improving health services, recommended the provision of a comprehensive scheme of hospital and primary health care. Later reports from the Royal Commission on National Health Insurance in 1926, the Sankey Commission on Voluntary Hospitals in 1937, and the British Medical Association (BMA) in 1930 and 1938, all pointed to shortcomings in the existing pattern of services, and made various suggestions for change. These included the need for greater coordination of hospitals, and for the extension of health insurance to other groups in the population. The Royal Commission's report also suggested that health service funding might eventually be derived from general taxation instead of being based on the insurance principle.

This view was not shared by the BMA, which, in an important report from its Medical Planning Commission published in 1942, advocated the extension of state involvement in the provision of health services. The BMA suggested that health insurance should be extended to cover most of the population and that the items covered by insurance should encompass the services of hospital specialists and examinations. The same year as the BMA's report appeared saw publication of an even more influential document, the Beveridge Report on Social Insurance and Allied Services. This report made wide-ranging recommendations for the reform and extension of the social security system, together with proposals for a national health service. Coming a year after the government had announced its intention to develop a national *hospital* service at the end of the war, the Beveridge Report added impetus to the movement for change.

The movement gathered momentum in subsequent years, leading to a White Paper containing proposals for a national health service in 1944, the National Health Service Act in 1946, and the establishment of the Service itself in 1948. Prolonged negotiations accompanied the birth of the Service, and these negotiations at times seemed likely to prevent the birth taking place at all (Webster, 1988). Certainly, the medical profession, as in 1911, fought strongly for its own objectives, and was successful in winning many concessions: retention of the independent contractor system for GPs; the option of private practice and access to pay beds in NHS hospitals for hospital consultants; a system of distinction awards for consultants, carrying with it large increases in salary for those receiving awards; a major role in the administration of the Service at all levels; and success in resisting local government control. The concessions made to hospital doctors led Aneurin Bevan to say that he had 'stuffed their mouths with gold' (Abel-Smith, 1964, p. 480). In fact, Bevan cleverly divided the medical profession, winning the support of hospital consultants and specialists with generous financial payments, and thereby isolating and reducing the power of GPs, who were nevertheless successful in achieving many of their aims.

Far less successful were the local authorities, who lost control of their hospitals, despite the advocacy by Herbert Morrison in the Labour Cabinet of the local government point of view. The main reason for this, apart from the opposition of the doctors, was the unsuitability of local government areas for the administration of the hospital service. As a result, Bevan – and this was one of his personal contributions to the organisation of the NHS – decided to appropriate both the local authority hospitals and the voluntary hospitals and place them under a single system of administration. Another major personal contribution made by Bevan was to persuade the medical profession that the Service should cover all of the population and not just 90 per cent as many doctors wished. Furthermore, the Service was to be funded mainly out of general taxation, with insurance contributions making up only a small part of the total finance.

This, then, is a very brief summary of the debate surrounding the establishment of the NHS. One point to note is the relative unimportance of Parliament in the debate. The policy in this case was more strongly influenced by extra-Parliamentary forces, in particular by the major pressure groups with an interest in health services. As we shall argue later, these forces can be seen to comprise a health policy community within which many issues are settled and agreed, either without or with only token reference to Parliament. In this sense, legislation is often little more than a record of the bargains struck in the health policy community. There are exceptions, and Parliamentary influence can be important, but to recognise the importance of other factors is a useful corrective to conventional views of British government and politics.

The structure of the National Health Service

The administrative structure of the NHS which came into being in 1948 was the product of the bargaining and negotiation that had taken place in the health policy community in the preceding years. It was therefore a representation of what was possible rather than what might have been desirable. The structure was also shaped by the historical antecedents which have been discussed, with the result that the Service was organised into three parts. First, representing the closest link with what had gone before, general practitioner services, along with the services of dentists, opticians and pharmacists, were administered by *executive councils*, which took over from the old insurance committees. Executive councils were appointed partly by local professionals, partly by local authorities and partly by the Ministry of Health, and they were funded directly by the Ministry. In no sense were executive councils management bodies. They simply administered the contracts of family practitioners (the generic term for GPs, dentists, opticians and pharmacists), maintained lists of local practitioners and handled complaints by patients.

Second, and again closely linked with the previous system of administration, responsibility for a range of environmental and personal health services was vested in *local authorities*. These services included maternity and child welfare clinics, health visitors, midwives, health education, vaccination and immunisation, and ambulances. The key local officer continued to be the medical officer of health, and funding of the services was provided partly by central government grants and partly by revenues raised by local authorities. A number of other services previously administered by local authorities, most notably, hospitals, tuberculosis services and cancer schemes, were removed from their control, representing a substantial reduction in the role of public health departments (Lewis, 1986).

Figure 1.1 *The structure of the NHS in England, 1948–74*

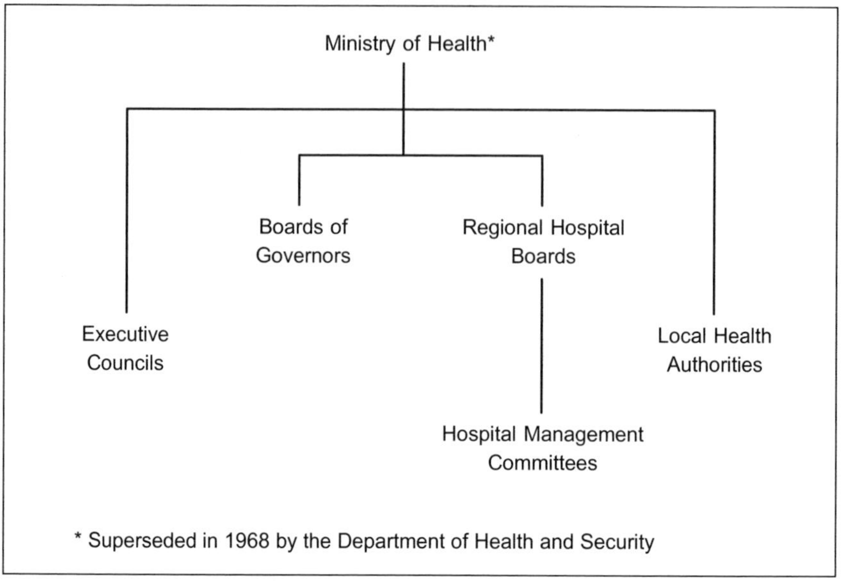

```
                        Ministry of Health*


              Boards of          Regional Hospital
              Governors              Boards

   Executive                                          Local Health
   Councils                                            Authorities

                          Hospital Management
                              Committees


      * Superseded in 1968 by the Department of Health and Security
```

Third, hospitals were administered by completely new bodies – Regional Hospital Boards (RHBs), Hospital Management Committees (HMCs), and boards of governors. Special status was given to the teaching hospitals – the elite members of the old voluntary hospital system – which were organised under boards of governors in direct contact with the Ministry of Health. This was one of the concessions Aneurin Bevan made to the medical profession. The vast majority of hospitals, though, came under the RHBs, of which there were 14 in England and Wales at first, and 15 later, and HMCs, numbering some 400 in total. RHBs were appointed by the Minister of Health, and they in turn appointed HMCs. Finance for the hospital service was passed down from the Ministry of Health through RHBs and on to HMCs. In the case of teaching hospitals, money was allocated straight from the Ministry to boards of governors. The tripartite structure of the NHS is illustrated in Figure 1.1.

The NHS between 1948 and 1974

One of the assumptions that lay behind the NHS, and which had been made in the Beveridge Report, was that there was a fixed quantity of illness in the community which the introduction of a health service, free at the point of consumption, would gradually reduce. It was therefore expected that expenditure would soon level off and even decline as people became healthier. In fact, the reverse happened. Health service spending in the years immediately after 1948 was much greater than Parliamentary estimates had allowed, and supplementary funding was necessary. Concern at the cost of the Service was reflected in the appointment of the Guillebaud Committee of Enquiry in 1953:

> to review the present and prospective cost of the National Health Service; to suggest means, whether by modifications in organisation or otherwise, of ensuring the most effective control and efficient use of such Exchequer funds as may be made available; to advise how, in view of the burdens on the Exchequer, a rising charge upon it can be avoided while providing for the maintenance of an adequate Service; and to make recommendations. (Guillebaud Committee, 1956)

The Committee's report, published in 1956, concluded that there was no evidence of extravagance or inefficiency in the NHS. Indeed, using research carried out by Richard Titmuss and Brian Abel-Smith, the Committee showed that, expressed as a proportion of the gross national product, the cost of the Service had actually fallen from 3.75 per cent in 1949–50 to 3.25 per cent in 1953–54. If anything, the Committee felt that more money, not less, should be allocated to the NHS, particularly to make up for the backlog of capital building works needing to be under-taken. The Committee also considered that more could be done to strengthen the links between the three branches of the Service, although it was not prepared to recommend any major organisational change.

The call for extra resources was echoed by a number of individuals and organisations, and it is not difficult to see why. The 1950s have been characterised aptly as the years of 'make do and mend' in the hospital service, with capital expenditure during the decade amounting to only £100 million. Within this budget, no new hospitals could be built and critics maintained that doctors were having to practise twentieth-century medicine in nineteenth-century buildings. This was the argument of two hospital consultants, Abel and Lewin, who, in a study commissioned by the BMA and published in 1959, argued for greatly increased expenditure (Abel and Lewin, 1959). The response came in the form of the 1962 Hospital Plan, providing for an expenditure of £500 million in England and Wales in the ten years up to 1971. The key concept behind the plan was the District General Hospital (DGH), a hospital of between 600 and 800 beds providing specialist facilities for all but the rarest illnesses for a population of 100,000 to 150,000. Several completely new DGHs were to be built during the decade, while many more existing hospitals were to be upgraded to DGH standard. Thus, after a number of years of restraint, the hospital building programme witnessed a significant expansion.

The 1950s were not, however, wasted years in the hospital service. The amalgamation of local authority and voluntary hospitals soon brought results in terms of a better use of resources. The grouping of hospitals on a district basis under the control of a Hospital Management Committee, and the introduction of a system of regional planning, helped to eliminate some of the shortages and overlaps that had existed before 1948. A good example was the rationalisation of infectious diseases hospitals and the release of beds for alternative uses. Also, there was an increase in the number of medical staff employed, and the services of hospital consultants became much more widely available. Before the establishment of the NHS, most consultants worked in urban areas where there were plentiful opportunities for private practice. After 1948, the introduction of a salaried service for hospital doctors, with national salary scales and conditions of service, assisted in bringing about a more even distribution of staff. At the same time, the hospital outpatient service was further developed. These were some of the advantages to accrue from a national hospital service (see Ham, 1981).

As far as general practitioners were concerned, it has been argued that 'it was general practice, sustained for 37 years by National Health Insurance and gaining substantial additional support from the new system, which really carried the National Health Service at its inception' (Godber, 1975, p. 5). A cause of concern, though, was the increasing gulf that developed between GPs and their consultant colleagues, a gulf that had its origins in the referral system established at the end of the nineteenth century (see above). Contact was maintained between the two branches of medical practice through a variety of mechanisms, including part-time hospital appointments for some GPs and allowing GPs direct access to hospital diagnostic facilities. But on the whole, the division between general practice and specialist practice widened, despite recommendations from bodies like the Guillebaud Committee that bridges should be built between the two branches of the NHS.

The most significant developments in general practice did not occur until almost 20 years after the creation of the NHS. These developments stemmed largely from the BMA's Charter for the Family Doctor Service published in 1965 which resulted in a new contract for GPs being introduced in 1966 (Loudon et al., 1998), discussed in more detail below. The terms of the new contract helped in the expansion of health centres, and the emergence of the primary health care team. Equally important was the distribution of GPs between different parts of the country, which was overseen by the Medical Practices Committee, set up under the 1946 NHS Act. The Committee could not direct doctors to work in particular places, but it could designate areas so that well-provided areas did not improve their position at the expense of less well-provided areas. A study carried out in 1971 concluded that:

> the broad pattern of staffing needs have not changed dramatically over the last twenty to thirty years. Areas which are currently facing the most serious shortages seem to have a fairly long history of manpower difficulties, whilst those which are today relatively well supplied with family doctors have generally had no difficulty in past years in attracting and keeping an adequate number of practitioners. (Butler et al., 1973, p. 42)

In 1966 a financial inducement, a designated area allowance, was introduced to try to attract doctors to less well-provided areas, and by the 1980s the average list size of doctors practising in designated areas had steadily fallen and the proportion of the population living in such areas had also fallen significantly (Office of Health Economics, 1989). There were, however, a number of outstanding problems in relation to the quality and coverage of general practitioner services, and these are discussed further in Chapter 5.

The third branch of the Service, that provided by local authorities, developed slowly after 1948, with ambulances comprising the main element of expenditure. Care of mothers and young children, home helps and home nurses were the other major items in the local authority health budget. At the opposite end of the scale came vaccination and immunisation, and, until the second half of the 1960s, health centres, which local authorities were responsible for building. It is relevant to note that under the 1948 National Assistance Act and other legislation, local authorities also provided a range of welfare services, including old people's homes and social workers. The division of responsibility for these services and health services became a matter of increasing concern, particularly as long-term plans for both sets of services were developed in the 1960s.

The significance of the 1962 Hospital Plan has already been mentioned. A year later, the Ministry of Health published a parallel document, *Health and Welfare: The Development of Community Care*, setting out proposals for the development of local authority health and welfare services. This was much less of a national plan than the Hospital Plan. It was essentially the bringing together of the ideas of local authorities for the growth of their health and welfare services. The difference between the two documents was a reflection of the greater measure of autonomy enjoyed by local authorities as compared with Regional Hospital Boards and Hospital Management Committees. Nevertheless, the Health and Welfare Plan was important in displaying publicly the directions in which local authority services were intended to develop. One point to emerge was the considerable variation in the plans of authorities, and it was hoped that comparisons would lead to the revision of plans and greater uniformity between areas. This happened to some extent, but the second revision of the Health and Welfare Plan, published in 1966, illustrated that wide differences still existed.

Both Health and Welfare Plans outlined developments in relation to four main client groups: mothers and young children, the elderly, the physically handicapped, and the mentally ill and handicapped (as they were called at the time). As far as the mentally ill and handicapped were concerned, a greater onus was placed on local authorities by the 1959 Mental Health Act, which, among other provisions, heralded a shift from hospital care to community care. The intention was that a range of community services should be developed, including homes and hostels, social clubs, sheltered workshops and social work support. The Health and Welfare Plans indicated what authorities were proposing to provide, and demonstrated that the commitment in central government to the community care policy was not always shared at the local level. Indeed, in a policy document published in 1975, the government noted that 'By and large the non-hospital community resources are still minimal ... The failure ... to develop anything approaching adequate social services is perhaps the greatest disappointment of the last 15 years' (DHSS, 1975a, p. 14).

A further set of ten-year plans for local authority services was prepared in 1972. In this case, the plans covered the newly established social services departments, which were created in 1971 following the report of the Seebohm Committee. The main effect of the Seebohm reforms was to divorce those local authority health services deemed to involve mainly medical skills – such as vaccination and immunisation, and health education – from those services deemed to involve mainly social work skills – such as home helps and residential care. The former were retained by the health departments of local authorities under the control of the medical officer of health, while the latter were transferred to the new social services departments under the director of social services. The new departments comprised a range of services previously provided by the local authority welfare and children's departments, as well as some of those previously administered by the health departments. The main aims of the reforms were to integrate services which had been administered separately in the past, and to provide for the development of a comprehensive family service through the new departments.

One of the points to emerge from the Health and Welfare Plans was the commitment of local authorities to the building of health centres. For a variety of reasons, including the shortage of money and hesitancy among the medical profession, health centres did not develop in the 1950s in the way that had been envisaged by the architects of the NHS.

However, local interest in health centres revived in the early 1960s, and was matched by central government attaching greater priority to health centre building. The consequence was that whereas in 1965 in England and Wales there were only 28 health centres from which 215 GPs worked, by 1989 there were 1320 in operation, with almost 8000 GPs. As a result, 29 per cent of all GPs worked in health centres, and many more worked in group practices.

Simultaneously, a greater emphasis was placed on the primary health care team, rather than on the GP working in isolation. This development was very much in line with the thinking behind the Gillie Report on *The Field of Work of the Family Doctor*, published in 1963. Although much less ambitious than either the Hospital Plan or the Health and Welfare Plan, the Gillie Report can to some extent be seen as the GPs' counterpart to these documents. The report argued for more ancillary help to be made available to GPs, and for a closer integration between GPs and other health services, particularly hospitals. The BMA took up the cause of GPs in 1965 with publication of the *Charter for the Family Doctor Service*. Negotiations with government followed and resulted in the first major changes to the GPs' contract since the inception of the NHS. The most important of these changes were direct reimbursement of the costs of ancillary staff, payment of the costs of practice premises, incentives to encourage doctors to work in areas short of GPs, a postgraduate training allowance, and the provision of loans to enable GPs to work in more modern buildings. The new contract also resulted in a large increase in the pay of GPs.

The theme of integration was taken up in a number of reports as the problem of securing coordination between the three different parts of the NHS gained increasing importance in the 1960s. The nature of the problem could be seen clearly with older people, who might need a short hospital stay followed by a period of convalescence and care in a local authority home, and subsequent assistance at home from the GP, home help and meals-on-wheels service. In a case such as this, there was a need not only to secure close collaboration between the different professional staff involved, but also to ensure the appropriate joint planning of services. The development of long-term plans for the respective services in the early 1960s heightened this, and again pointed to the difficulty of providing a comprehensive and coordinated range of facilities within the existing system of administration, despite exhortations from central government that hospital authorities, local authorities and executive councils should plan and work together.

A second problem which had become apparent by the late 1960s was the poor quality of care provided to certain patient groups. Public attention was drawn to this issue in 1967 with publication of allegations of low standards of service provision and even the ill-treatment of elderly patients at a number of hospitals in different parts of the country (Robb, 1967). This was followed two years later by the report of the official committee which enquired into conditions at Ely Hospital, Cardiff. Ely was a mental handicap hospital, and the committee of enquiry found there had been staff cruelty to patients at the hospital. The committee made a series of recommendations for improving conditions at Ely and for preventing a similar situation arising elsewhere. Subsequently, the Department of Health and Social Security (DHSS), which had been created in 1968 through the amalgamation of the Ministry of Health and the Ministry of Social Security, set aside special money to be spent on mental handicap hospitals, and this was later extended to hospitals for the mentally ill and older people. In addition, the Hospital Advisory Service (in 1976 made the Health Advisory Service) was established to visit and report on conditions at these hospitals. A review of policies was also put in hand, leading to the publication of White Papers on services for the mentally handicapped in 1971, and the mentally ill in 1975. Despite these initiatives, the Ely Hospital 'scandal' was followed by further reports on conditions at other long-stay hospitals, including Whittingham, South Ockenden, Farleigh, Napsbury, St Augustine's and Normansfield, demonstrating that the process of change in what came to be known as the 'Cinderella' services was often slow, and that significant improvements were difficult to achieve (Martin, 1984).

A third problem, related to the first two, concerned the system of administrative control in the NHS. The neglect of long-stay services was not new, and had been recognised by successive Ministers of Health from the early 1950s onwards. Equally, the need for authorities to work in collaboration had been endorsed and advocated by the Ministry since the establishment of the NHS. The difficulty was in achieving and implementing these policy intentions at the local level. A variety of means of control was available to the Ministry, including circulars, earmarking funds for particular purposes, and setting up special agencies like the Hospital Advisory Service. At the same time, the bodies that were responsible locally for the administration of health services were not just ciphers through which national policies were implemented. They had their own aims and objectives, and, equally significant, they were responsible for providing services where professional involvement was strong. Doctors constitute the key professional group in the NHS, and within the medical profession some interests are stronger than others. In the hospital service it is the consultants in the acute specialties such as surgery and general medicine who have traditionally been most influential. In contrast, consultant psychiatrists and geriatricians have wielded less influence. This helps to explain why it has been difficult to shift resources in favour of services for groups like older people and the mentally ill.

The reorganisation of the NHS

These were some of the problems which had emerged in the NHS some 20 years after its establishment. Suggestions on the best way of tackling the problems varied, but increasingly a change in the tripartite structure of the Service came to be seen as a significant part of the solution. This was the view of the Porritt Committee, a high-status body representing the medical profession, which in a report published in 1962 suggested that health services should be unified and placed under the control of area boards. The first statement of government intentions came in 1968, when the Labour government published a Green Paper which echoed the Porritt Committee's suggestion, and asked for comments on the proposal that 40 to 50 area health boards should be responsible for administering the health services in England and Wales.

One possibility was that a reorganised NHS would be administered by local government, which was itself undergoing reform at the same time. However, this was discounted in the second Green Paper, published by the Labour government in 1970. The second Green Paper put forward the idea that there should be around 90 area health authorities as the main units of local administration, together with regional health councils carrying out planning functions, and some 200 district committees as a means of local participation. These proposals were developed further in the following year by the Conservative government in *National Health Service Reorganization: Consultative Document*, which strengthened the role of the regional tier of administration and provided a separate channel for local participation in the form of community health councils. The *Consultative Document*, and the subsequent White Paper, also emphasised the importance of improving management efficiency in the NHS. These proposals were enshrined in the 1973 National Health Service Act and came into operation on 1 April 1974. The reorganised structure in England is illustrated in Figure 1.2.

Reorganisation had three main aims. First, it was intended to *unify* health services by bringing under one authority all of the services previously administered by Regional Hospital Boards, Hospital Management Committees, boards of governors, executive councils and local health authorities. Unification was not, however, achieved in full because general practitioners remained independent contractors, with the functions of executive councils being taken over by family practitioner committees.

Figure 1.2 *The structure of the NHS in England, 1974–82*

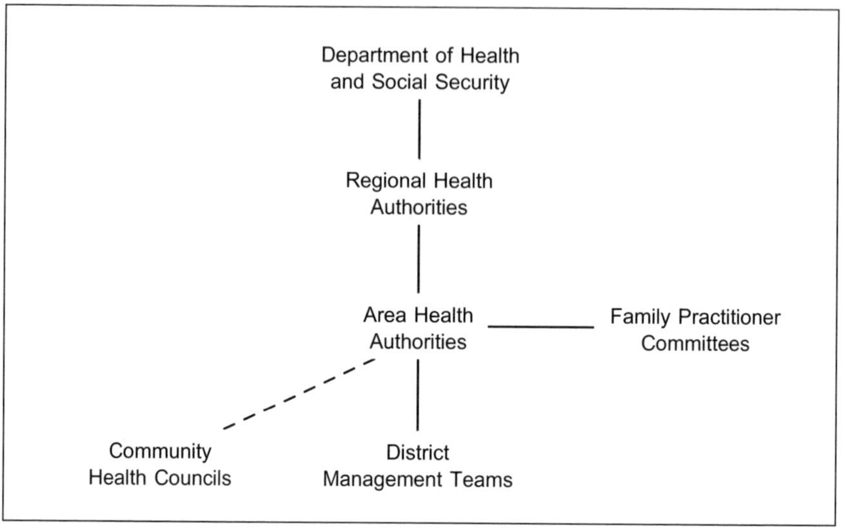

```
                    Department of Health
                    and Social Security
                            |
                            |
                    Regional Health
                    Authorities
                            |
                            |
                    Area Health  _____  Family Practitioner
                    Authorities              Committees
                       -  -                     |
                  -  -                          |
             - -                                |
    Community                 District
    Health Councils           Management Teams
```

Also, a small number of postgraduate teaching hospitals retained separate boards of governors.

Second, reorganisation was intended to lead to better *coordination* between health authorities and related local government services. To achieve this, the boundaries of the new Area Health Authorities were, in most parts of the country, made the same as those of one or more of the local authorities providing personal social services – the county councils in shire areas, the metropolitan district councils and the London boroughs. In addition, the two types of authority were required to set up joint consultative committees (JCCs) to facilitate the collaborative development of services.

A third stated aim of reorganisation was to introduce *better management*. In fact, important changes in the management of the hospital service had already taken place as a result of the Salmon Report on nursing staff structure, the 'cogwheel' reports on the organisation of medical staff (so called because of the design on the cover of the reports), and the Farquharson Lang Report on the administrative practices of hospital authorities. The Conservative government particularly stressed the need to build on these changes, and one of the outcomes was *Management Arrangements for the Reorganised NHS*, popularly known as the 'Grey Book', which set out in considerable detail the functions of each of the tiers in the new structure, as well as providing job descriptions for health authority officers. Key concepts included multidisciplinary team working and consensus management, and the medical profession was given an explicit role in the management system.

The DHSS also referred to the principle of 'maximum delegation downwards, matched by accountability upwards' to illustrate the spirit behind the new structure. Another significant aspect of the concern to improve management efficiency was the introduction of a national planning system in 1976, two years after the structural reforms (DHSS, 1976c). All of these measures were part of a wider interest within government to borrow ideas from the private sector in the hope of improving performance. It was therefore no coincidence that the new arrangements were devised with the assistance of the management consultants, McKinsey. But the changes also reflected the particular concern in the NHS, discussed earlier, to find a more effective means of pursuing national priorities at the local level, and of shifting resources in favour of neglected groups.

The reorganised National Health Service

Thus, after almost 26 years, the NHS underwent a major organisational change. Within the new structure, Regional Health Authorities (RHAs) took over from Regional Hospital Boards, with somewhat wider responsibilities and slightly modified boundaries. The members of RHAs were appointed by the Secretary of State for Social Services, and their main function was the planning of health services. Beneath RHAs there were 90 Area Health Authorities (AHAs) in England, and their members were appointed partly by RHAs, partly by local authorities, and partly by members of the non-medical and nursing staff. The AHA chairman was appointed by the Secretary of State. Some AHAs contained a university medical school and teaching hospital facilities, and were designated as teaching areas. AHAs had planning and management duties, but one of their most important functions was to develop services jointly with their matching local authorities. Both RHAs and AHAs were supported by multidisciplinary teams of officers. Alongside each AHA was a Family Practitioner Committee (FPC) which administered the contracts of GPs, dentists, pharmacists and opticians. FPC members were appointed by the AHA, local professionals and local authorities. Finance for health authorities and FPCs was provided by the Department of Health and Social Security. Most areas were themselves split into health districts, each of which was administered by a district management team, which in practice became the lowest tier of the Service. At district level were located Community Health Councils (CHCs), introduced as part of the reorganised structure to represent the views of the public to health authorities. There were around 200 CHCs in England.

It is pertinent to note that somewhat different arrangements were made in Wales, Scotland and Northern Ireland, which until reorganisation had had similar structures to those existing in England. The Welsh reorganisation bore the closest resemblance to that of England, the main exception being the absence of RHAs in Wales, where the Welsh Office combined the functions of a central government department and a regional authority. The differences were rather greater in Scotland, where again there was no regional tier of administration. Instead, the Scottish Office dealt directly with 15 health boards, a majority of which were divided into districts. There was no separate system of administration for family practitioner services, and the Scottish equivalent of CHCs were called Local Health Councils. In Northern Ireland, there were four health and social services boards, in direct contact with the DHSS (Northern Ireland), and each of the boards was split into a number of districts. As their name indicated, these boards were responsible for personal social services as well as health services. What is more, as in Scotland, there was no separate system of administration for family practitioner services. District Committees performed the function of CHCs.

These, then, were the administrative changes brought into being in 1974. However, almost before the new system had had a chance to settle down, the reorganised structure became the subject of attack from a number of quarters (Webster, 1996). Criticism centred on delays in taking decisions, the difficulty of establishing good relationships between administrative tiers, and the widespread feeling that there were too many tiers and too many administrators. In fact, the DHSS acknowledged in evidence to the House of Commons Public Accounts Committee that there had been an increase of 16,400 administrative and clerical staff as a result of reorganisation, although some of these staff had previously worked in local authority health services, while others were recruited to the new CHCs (Public Accounts Committee, 1977, p. xvii).

Research on the operation of the new structure pointed to other problems, including the unexpectedly high cost of reorganisation, both in terms of finance and, more particularly, of the impact on staff morale (Brown, 1979; Haywood and Alaszewski, 1980). These issues were the subject of analysis and review by the Royal Commission on the NHS, which was established in 1976 at a time of considerable unrest in the NHS. The unrest stemmed from industrial action by various groups of health service workers, and discontent in the medical profession with the government's policy of phasing out private beds in NHS hospitals. The Commission was asked '[t]o consider in the interests both of the patients and of those who work in the National Health Service the best use and management of the financial and manpower resources of the National Health Service' (Royal Commission on the NHS, 1979), and it reported in 1979. In its report, the Commission endorsed the view that there was one tier of administration too many, and recommended that there should be only one level of authority beneath the region. A flexible approach to change was advocated, and the Commission pointed out that structural reform was no panacea for all of the administrative problems facing the NHS. Other conclusions in a wide-ranging survey were that Family Practitioner Committees should be abolished, and Community Health Councils should be strengthened.

It fell to the Conservative government which took office in May 1979 to respond to the report. In *Patients First*, a consultative paper published at the end of 1979, the government announced its agreement with the proposal that one tier of administration should be removed, and suggested that District Health Authorities should be established to combine the functions of the existing areas and districts. *Patients First* also stated that Family Practitioner Committees would be retained, and that views would be welcomed on whether Community Health Councils would still be needed when the new District Health Authorities were set up (DHSS, 1979). The government's final decisions on the main aspects of reorganisation were published in July 1980 (DHSS, 1980a). In large part, they endorsed the *Patients First* proposals and in addition announced that Community Health Councils would remain in existence, though their functions would be reviewed.

The result was the creation of 192 District Health Authorities (DHAs) in England. DHAs came into operation on 1 April 1982, and within districts emphasis was placed on the delegation of power to units of management. Detailed management arrangements varied considerably, with some units covering services in districts as a whole, such as psychiatric services, while others were limited to a single large hospital. Health authorities were expected to establish management structures within overall cost limits set by the DHSS, and in 1983 it was estimated that the amount spent on management in the NHS had fallen from 5.12 per cent of the total budget in 1979–80 to 4.44 per cent in 1982–83, representing a saving of £64 million. Apart from the reduction in administration, the main change wrought by the reorganisation was the loss in many parts of the country of the principle of coterminosity between health authorities and local authorities. Equally significant was the announcement in November 1981 that Family Practitioner Committees (FPCs) were to be further separated from the mainstream of NHS administration and given the status of employing authorities in their own right. This change was brought into effect by the Health and Social Security Act 1984 and FPCs achieved their independent status on 1 April 1985. In addition, a number of Special Health Authorities were established. Their main responsibility was to run the postgraduate teaching hospitals in London. The structure of the NHS in England after 1982 is shown in Figure 1.3.

Figure 1.3 *The structure of the NHS in England, 1982–91*

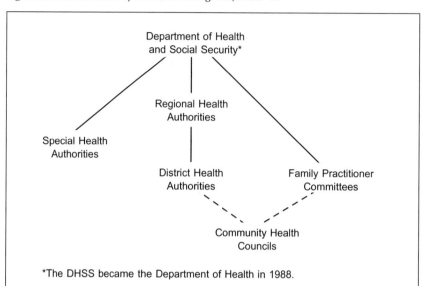

In the rest of the United Kingdom different changes were made, reflecting the different administrative structures existing in Scotland, Wales and Northern Ireland. In Wales the main change was the abolition of the district level of management, and the establishment in its place of a system of unit management on a similar basis to that developed in England. In Scotland, a varied approach was pursued initially, some health boards deciding to abolish the district tier, others opting to retain it. However, in 1983 the Secretary of State for Scotland announced that all districts would be abolished and that they would be replaced by a system of unit management from 1 April 1984. As in England and Wales, the importance of delegating power to the local level was stressed. The same principle of delegation applied in Northern Ireland, where the basic structure of health and social services boards was retained. Within boards, district teams were superseded by unit management arrangements.

Conclusion

This chapter has provided an overview of the development of state involvement in the provision of health services in the United Kingdom. It has set out the historical context for discussions in the rest of the book on the dynamics of health policy formulation. Already, however, some key questions about health policy have been raised, if not answered, and they can be summarised as follows:

- First, we have noted the importance of focusing on negotiation and bargaining in the policy community in seeking to understand and explain the detailed processes of health policy-making. In particular, our preliminary analysis has highlighted the significance of identifying the key pressure groups and of examining their interaction with policy-makers. This issue is discussed further in Chapter 8.
- Second, we have noted that there may sometimes be a gap between the intentions of policy-makers and what happens in practice. This was considered in relation to the continued neglect of 'Cinderella' services, and the failure to develop adequate community-based services for the mentally ill. These examples draw attention to the importance of policy implementation, which is examined further in Chapter 9.
- A third question concerns the relationship between policy-makers and service providers. A factor of major significance in the NHS is the position occupied by doctors as service providers and their concern to retain control over their own work. We have seen how the medical profession has fought strenuously to keep its independence, most especially in the campaign by GPs to be independent contractors rather than salaried employees. Hospital doctors have been equally concerned to maintain their autonomy even though they are in a salaried service. As the DHSS acknowledged in evidence to the House of Commons Expenditure Committee, 'the existence of clinical freedom undoubtedly reduces the ability of the central authorities to determine objectives and priorities and to control individual facets of expenditure' (Expenditure Committee, 1971). The concept of clinical freedom therefore poses peculiar difficulties for policy-makers seeking to change patterns of resource allocation. It also raises central questions about the power structure in the NHS, questions to which we return in later chapters.
- Related to this, a fourth issue, not addressed directly so far but of crucial importance, concerns the relationship between health services and society. In other words, what purposes are served by health services, and what is the significance of the dominant position occupied by the medical profession? These issues are rarely discussed explicitly in books on health services and health policy. Instead, implicit assumptions are often made about the benevolent motives underlying state involvement in the provision of health services. Thus, the NHS is viewed as a great social experiment, and as a concrete expression of the development of more humane attitudes to disadvantaged groups in society. In short, the Service is seen as one of the main planks in the welfare state. These are key issues which are considered further in Chapter 11.

Chapter 2

Health Policy under Thatcher and Major

If health policy between 1948 and 1982 was characterised by successive adjustments to the original design of the NHS and a focus on fine tuning its administrative structure, in the following 15 years events took a different turn. The election of the Conservative government under Margaret Thatcher in 1979, coupled with the emergence of major funding pressures, led to the consideration of more radical alternatives. Of particular importance was the introduction of the reforms set out in the White Paper, *Working for Patients*, published in 1989 (Secretary of State for Health and others, 1989a). These reforms in turn followed from the introduction of general management and the implementation of a range of efficiency initiatives. The aim of this chapter is to trace the development of health policy under Thatcher and Major, and in the process to examine the various influences on policy-making and implementation.

Increasing NHS efficiency

In reviewing the evolution of health policy in the 1980s and 1990s, it is essential to understand the economic and political context in which the NHS developed. The oil crises of the mid-1970s brought to a halt the rapid expansion of public services and public expenditure that had characterised the post-war era. The Labour government in power at the time was forced to introduce much tighter economic policies bringing it into conflict with its traditional support base in the trade unions and marking the beginning of the end of the corporatist style of politics that had dominated British government in the 1960s and 1970s. These changes were accelerated by the Conservative government elected in 1979 which challenged the prevailing Keynesian orthodoxy and pursued a programme involving the privatisation of state-owned enterprises, reductions in some forms of taxation and controls over public spending. One of the consequences for the NHS was that budgets grew much more slowly than had previously been the case, and attention shifted from the use of increases in resources made available by government to ways of deploying existing budgets more efficiently. As the 1980s wore on, the consensus that had prevailed on health policy broke down and bargaining between government and pressure groups gave way to conflict over plans to introduce market principles into the NHS.

During the first half of the 1980s the main focus of government policy was how to make the NHS more businesslike and efficient. In this respect, health policy illustrated the emergence of what came to be known as the new public management (Hood, 1991) and the priority attached by the Thatcher government to achieving value for money in the use of public resources. In the case of the NHS, the Thatcher government did not come to power in 1979 with a comprehensive and coherent programme of reform. Rather, it introduced a series of policies intended to increase efficiency, and the relationship between these policies was not always apparent. Although the effect was to bring to an end the period of incremental adaptation that had been characteristic of the post-war consensus on the NHS, it was difficult to detect at any stage a clear plan guiding the changes that were made. As Webster has commented:

> The Thatcher reforms represented a long-drawn-out sequence of changes, amounting to a process of continuous revolution, in which the end result was not predictable at the beginning, and indeed the whole process of policy-making was akin to a journey through a minefield, advances being made in an erratic manner, as dictated by the exigencies of political opportunism. (Webster, 1998, pp. 143–4)

Nowhere was this better illustrated than in relation to the wide range of efficiency initiatives launched during the 1980s. One such initiative was a requirement that health authorities should generate efficiency savings every year, which was intended to release funds from existing budgets to support new service developments. Efficiency savings were renamed 'cost improvement programmes' in 1984, and by the end of the decade it was estimated that these programmes had achieved annual savings of almost £1 billion in the hospital and community health services in England. Second, a series of Rayner scrutinies were conducted along the lines of those carried out in the civil service by Sir Derek (later Lord) Rayner and his staff. Rayner was brought in from the retail chain Marks & Spencer to advise the government in 1979 and the approach which bears his name was first applied to the NHS in 1982. The scrutinies were carried out by NHS managers and areas examined included transport services, recruitment advertising and the collection of payments due to health authorities under the provisions of the Road Traffic Act.

Third, performance indicators were developed during 1982 and were first published in the following year. The indicators covered clinical services, finance, manpower and estate management and enabled health authorities to compare their performance with what was being achieved elsewhere. The information used readily available statistics and included variables such as cost per case, length of stay and waiting lists. Fourth, in 1983 health authorities were asked to test the cost-effectiveness of catering, domestic and laundry services by inviting tenders for the provision of these services from their own staff and from outside contractors. It was estimated that the first round of competitive tendering achieved annual savings of £110 million with most of these savings deriving from contracts won in-house by health authority staff (Social Services Committee, 1990). Fifth, in 1988 the income-generation initiative was launched to explore ways in which health authorities could generate additional resources. A total of £10 million was yielded in the first year through schemes such as income from private patients, car parking charges and the use of hospital premises for retail developments.

Making the NHS businesslike

Of all the policies pursued during this period, the introduction of general management following the Griffiths Report of 1983 had the most significance in the longer term. This report was produced by a small team led by Roy Griffiths, deputy chairman and managing director of the Sainsbury's supermarket chain, and it offered a fundamental critique of NHS management and its failure to ensure that resources were used either efficiently or with the needs of patients in mind. Specifically, the report identified the absence of a clearly defined general management function as the main weakness of the NHS, commenting:

> Absence of this general management support means that there is no driving force seeking and accepting direct and personal responsibility for developing management plans, securing their implementation and monitoring actual achievement. It means that the process of devolution of responsibility, including discharging responsibility to the Units, is far too slow. (Griffiths Report, 1983, p. 12)

Accordingly, the report recommended that general managers should be appointed at all levels in the NHS to provide leadership, introduce a continual search for change and cost improvement, motivate staff and develop a more dynamic management approach. At the same time, the report stated that hospital doctors 'must accept the management responsibility which goes with clinical freedom' (p. 18) and participate fully in decisions about priorities. Another key proposal was that the management of the NHS at the centre should be streamlined and strengthened through the establishment of a Health Services Supervisory Board and an NHS Management Board, with the Chairman of the Management Board being drawn from outside the NHS and the civil service. The report did not attempt to offer a comprehensive analysis of management arrangements in the NHS but rather a series of recommendations for immediate action. As the team concluded:

> action is now badly needed and the Health Service can ill afford to indulge in any lengthy self-imposed Hamlet-like soliloquy as a precursor or alternative to the required action. (p. 24)

This advice was heeded by the Secretary of State who, in welcoming the report, announced that he accepted the general thrust of what the team had to say. Subsequently, the Supervisory Board and Management Board were established within the DHSS, and the government asked health authorities to appoint general managers at all levels in the Service. A phased programme of implementation was planned, beginning with the identification of regional general managers followed by general managers at unit and district levels. Table 2.1 shows the background of general managers appointed in the first round and illustrates that the majority at all levels were administrators from within the NHS. The government also endorsed the Griffiths Report's view that doctors should be involved in management and that they should be given responsibility for management budgets. To this end a number of demonstration projects were established and in 1986 management budgeting was superseded by the resource management initiative. The change in terminology signalled a shift in emphasis away from the development of a budgeting system in isolation towards an approach in which doctors and nurses took on more responsibility for the management of resources as a whole.

Table 2.1 *Background of general managers, 1986*

	Administrators	Doctors	Nurses NHS	Other NHS	Outside	Total
Regional general managers	9	1	1	1	2	14
District general managers	113	15	5	17	38	188
Unit general managers	322	97	63	16	44	542

Source: Hansard (1986).

Research evidence indicates that the impact of these changes was mixed. In the DHSS, the Management Board led the implementation of general management and resource management. However, its role initially excluded involvement in the development of policy and its first chairman, Victor Paige, became increasingly frustrated at political interference in his work, resigning from his post in 1986. Griffiths' own assessment was that the changes made at the centre were 'half hearted in their implementation' (Griffiths, 1992, p. 65) and did not succeed in introducing the clarity he and his team had sought (see Chapter 8). At a local level, the impact of general management varied with some studies arguing that managers had gained influence in relation to doctors and others maintaining that change had been minimal (Harrison, 1994). In relation to resource management, an evaluation indicated that some progress had been made in involving doctors and nurses in management but much remained to be done and the process of change could not be rushed (Packwood et al., 1991). The most important effect of the Griffiths Report was to lay the foundations for the introduction of the internal market in 1991 through the appointment of a cadre of chief executives within the NHS who were largely receptive to the policies that were being pursued.

Dealing with the funding crisis

As the 1980s wore on, a widening gap emerged between the money provided by the government for the NHS and the funding needed to meet increasing demands. This is illustrated in Figure 2.1 which compares actual spending, spending adjusted to include cash-releasing cost improvements, and target spending based on the government's own estimate of the resources needed to fund the demands of an ageing population, advances in medical technology, and rising patient expectations. By 1987/88, the cumulative shortfall in the hospital and community health services since 1981/82 amounted to £1.8 billion, even after allowing for the recurrent savings from cost improvement programmes. For 1987/88 alone, expenditure was almost £400 million below its target level (King's Fund Institute, 1988).

The impact of cumulative underfunding became particularly apparent during the course of 1987. In the autumn of that year, many health authorities had to take urgent action to keep expenditure within cash limits. A survey conducted by the National Association of Health Authorities reported that authorities were cancelling non-urgent admissions, closing wards on a temporary basis, and not filling staff vacancies in order to cope with financial pressures (NAHA, 1987). In the face of a developing crisis in the funding of hospital services, the British Medical Associa-

Figure 2.1 *Hospital and community health services: trends in spending, targets and shortfalls*

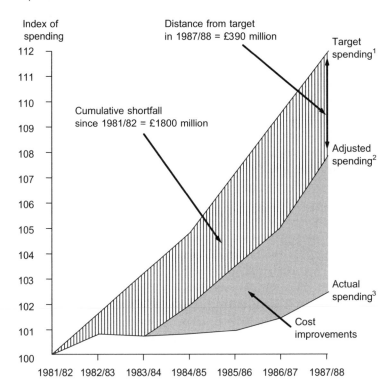

Index of spending

Distance from target in 1987/88 = £390 million

Target spending[1]

Cumulative shortfall since 1981/82 = £1800 million

Adjusted spending[2]

Actual spending[3]

Cost improvements

1981/82 1982/83 1983/84 1984/85 1985/86 1986/87 1987/88

Notes
1. Increase over base spending necessary for demography, technology and service improvements: 1.3 to 2.3 per cent per year.
2. Actual spending plus cash-releasing cost improvements at 1987/88 purchasing power prices.
3. Actual spending at 1987/88 purchasing power prices.

Source: King's Fund Institute (1988).

tion (BMA) called for additional resources to help meet the funding shortfall. And in an unprecedented move, the presidents of the Royal Colleges of Surgeons, Physicians and Obstetricians and Gynaecologists issued a joint statement claiming that the NHS had almost reached breaking point and that additional and alternative financing had to be provided (Ham et al., 1990).

The government responded in two ways. First, in December 1987, ministers announced that an additional £101 million was to be made available in the United Kingdom to help tackle some of the immediate difficulties that had arisen. Second, Prime Minister Thatcher decided to initiate a far-reaching review of the future of the NHS. The decision was revealed in an interview on the BBC TV programme *Panorama* in January 1988 and it was made clear that the results would be published within a year. The Prime Minister established a small committee of senior ministers chaired by herself to undertake the review and the committee was supported by a group of civil servants and political advisers (Timmins, 1995). In a departure from established consultative processes, groups like the BMA were not involved and the analysis of options for change was confined to a small group at the core of government. The leaders of the BMA at the time have subsequently described their exclusion from the policy process (Lee-Potter, 1997).

As the review progressed, it became clear that there was little enthusiasm for a major change in how the NHS was financed. The reasons for this included support for taxation as the principal method of funding and recognition that the alternatives all had drawbacks and might not help in addressing the problems that gave rise to the review. In other words, the same factors identified by Norman Fowler as precluding a move to private insurance in the early 1980s again served to maintain the status quo (Fowler, 1991). This was confirmed by the Chancellor of the Exchequer at the time of the review who has recalled in his memoirs:

> we looked ... at other countries to see what we could learn from them; but it was soon clear that every country we looked at was having problems with its provision of medical care. All of them – France, the United States, Germany – had different systems; but each of them had acute problems which none of them had solved. They were all in at least as much difficulty as we were, and it did not take long to conclude that there was surprisingly little that we could learn from any of the other systems. To try to change from the Health Service to any of the other sorts of systems in use overseas would simply be out of the frying pan into the fire. (Lawson, 1992, p. 616)

With the financing debate taking a back seat, greater attention was paid to how resources could be used more efficiently through changes to the delivery of health services. Of particular importance was the proposal that hospitals should compete for resources in an internal market. This proposal had originally been advocated by Alain Enthoven in 1985 (Enthoven, 1985) and it was taken up and developed by right-wing think tanks such as the Adam Smith Institute and the Centre for Policy Studies. The debate about delivery also included proposals to make doctors more accountable for their performance and to involve doctors more effectively in management. In parallel, suggestions were put forward for strengthening the management of health services by building on the introduction of general management.

During the review, the Prime Minister decided to split the DHSS into two and to move the Secretary of State John Moore to the Department of Social Security. This decision was prompted by the difficulty experienced by Moore in managing one of the biggest government departments, and the need to ensure that health issues received the undivided attention of a senior minister at a time of critical importance for the government. Before his departure, Moore indicated that he intended to pursue a path of evolutionary reform, and this was reinforced by the appointment of Kenneth Clarke as the new Secretary of State for Health. Clarke took up his post in July 1988, and he played a major part in the preparation of the White Paper, *Working for Patients*, which was published in January 1989 (Secretary of State for Health and others, 1989a).

Working for Patients

In the White Paper, the government announced that the basic principles on which the NHS was founded would be preserved. Funding would continue to be provided mainly out of taxation and there were no proposals to extend patient charges. Tax relief on private insurance premiums was to be made available to those aged over 60, apparently at the Prime Minister's insistence (Lawson, 1992), but the significance of this was more symbolic than real. For the vast majority of the population, access to health care was to be based on need and not ability to pay. The main changes in the White Paper concerned the delivery of health services. These changes were intended to create the conditions for competition between hospitals and other service providers, through the separation of purchaser and provider responsibilities and the establishment of self-governing NHS trusts and GP fundholders.

As well as these changes, the White Paper aimed to strengthen management arrangements. In the new Department of Health (DH), this was to be achieved by appointing a Policy Board and NHS Management Executive in place of the Supervisory Board and NHS Management Board. At a local level, the composition of health authorities was to be revised along business lines. Managers would sit as members of authorities for the first time and would be joined by a small number of non-executive directors appointed for their personal contribution and not because they were drawn from designated organisations. Similar changes were planned for the family practitioner services, involving the replacement of Family Practitioner Committees by Family Health Services Authorities (FHSAs).

Another important aim of the White Paper was to make doctors more accountable for their performance. This was to be achieved by general managers playing a bigger part in the management of clinical activity, including participating in the appointment of consultants, drawing up job plans for each consultant, and deciding which consultants should receive distinction awards (increases in salary intended to reward clinical excellence). In addition, new disciplinary procedures were introduced for hospital doctors to enable disciplinary matters to be dealt with expeditiously. Considerable emphasis was also placed on the involvement of doctors and nurses in management through an extension of the resource management initiative, and on making medical audit a routine part of clinical work in both general practice and hospitals.

The reform of primary care and community care

In parallel with the review, the government developed equally far-reaching proposals for the future of primary care and community care. The primary care changes stemmed from a consultative document issued in 1986 and a White Paper, *Promoting Better Health*, published in 1987 (Secretary of State for Social Services and others, 1987). The stated aims of the changes were to raise standards of health and health care, to place greater emphasis on health promotion and disease prevention, and to offer wider choice and information to patients. A key element in the changes was the introduction of new contracts for GPs and dentists.

The contract for GPs, which was published at the same time as *Working for Patients*, included provision for health checks for new patients, three-yearly checks for patients not otherwise seen by a GP, and annual checks of patients aged 75 or over. In addition, targets were set for vaccination, immunisation and cervical cancer screening, encouragement was given to the development of health promotion clinics and the provision of minor surgery, and GPs were expected to become more closely involved in child health surveillance. Other features of the new GP contract included extra payments for doctors practising in deprived areas, additional money to employ practice staff and improve practice premises, and a request that practices produce an annual report and information leaflets for patients. The procedure through which patients changed their doctors was also simplified. Overall, the proportion of a GP's income that derived from capitation payments was increased from 46 per cent to 60 per cent. This was designed to act as an incentive to GPs to provide services demanded by patients. The new contract came into operation in April 1990.

In the case of family dentists, the new contract emphasised the need for dental care to include preventative work as well as restorative treatment. Regular patients would be entitled to more information about their treatment in a treatment plan, emergency cover arrangements, and replacement of certain restorations which failed within a year. As far as children were concerned, dentists were to receive a capitation payment for each child instead of being paid by item of service for treatment given. Part of the cost of these changes was met by introducing a charge for adult dental examinations and by removing most adult eye tests from the NHS. The new contract for dentists came into operation in October 1990.

The government's plans for the future of community care were developed in response to a report prepared by Sir Roy Griffiths in 1988 (Griffiths Report, 1988). The community care White Paper *Caring for People*, published in 1989, contained the government's proposals (Secretary of State for Health and others, 1989b) which in large part endorsed the recommendations of the Griffiths Report. Local authorities were given the lead responsibility in the planning of community care and were required to prepare community care plans in association with NHS authorities and other agencies. It was expected that local authorities would become enablers and purchasers, coordinating the provision of care in different sectors, and providing some services directly themselves. These changes went hand in hand with new funding arrangements. Under these arrangements, the income support available to people in need of assistance from public funds was to be the same whether they lived at home or in voluntary or private sector residential care. In this way, it was hoped to target more effectively public support of people in residential care.

Implementing the reforms

The proposals set out in *Working for Patients* aroused strong feelings on all sides. Opposition to the government's proposals was led by the medical profession. The BMA launched a fierce campaign, and this was directed as much against the new contract for GPs as against the programme set out in the White Paper. Organisations representing patients shared many of the concerns of the medical profession as did bodies speaking for other staff groups. There was more support for the reforms from managers and health authorities, although the timetable for implementing some of the changes was widely perceived to be unrealistic. Despite opposition, the government's large majority in Parliament meant that the NHS and Community Care Bill received the Royal Assent in June 1990. The determination of the Secretary of State Kenneth Clarke was particularly important in this process.

In comparison with the NHS reforms, the discussion of the changes to community care provoked much less controversy. The Griffiths Report had attracted considerable support at the time of its publication and the fact that the government accepted most of the recommendations of the Report helped to smooth the process of reform. The one major concern about the changes was whether local authorities would be allocated enough money to develop adequate services in the community. This issue was complicated by the reform of local government finance with the community charge or poll tax replacing domestic rates in 1990. Mainly because of this, the government decided to delay implementation of the changes to community care until 1993.

The structure of the NHS in England as it emerged from these changes is illustrated in Figure 2.2. In the rest of the United Kingdom similar changes were implemented, although the timetable for reform in both Scotland and Northern Ireland was somewhat slower than in England

Figure 2.2 *The structure of the NHS in England, 1991–96*

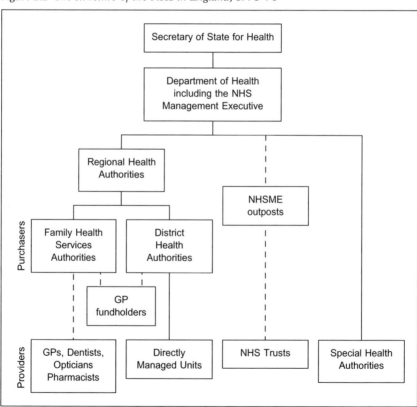

Source: Ham (1997a).

and Wales. There were also detailed differences in the composition of health authorities in each country.

At the heart of the NHS reforms was a shift from an integrated system in which District Health Authorities (DHAs) both held the budget for health care and managed hospital and community health services, to a contract system in which responsibility for purchasing and provision was separated. This was achieved by the creation of entirely new organisations – self-governing NHS trusts – to manage services thereby enabling DHAs to focus on purchasing health care for the populations they served. Alongside DHAs, GP fundholders purchased a limited range of services for their patients, the budgets they received being deducted from the resources allocated to DHAs. Under these arrangements, DHAs and GP fundholders negotiated contracts with NHS trusts to provide services, and these contracts (or service agreements as they were often known) specified the cost, quantity and quality of care expected by purchasers. One of the purposes of separating responsibility for purchasing and provision was to stimulate competition between providers in what was often referred to as an 'internal market'.

Implementation of *Working for Patients* differed from previous reorganisations in that the reformed structure was not put in place on a single appointed day. Rather, in recognition of the complexity of the changes and political anxieties about their feasibility, implementation was phased in. This was particularly apparent in the case of the two major organisational innovations contained within the reforms, NHS trusts and GP fundholders, whose numbers increased every year between 1991 and 1996 (see Table 2.2).

At the outset, there was some uncertainty about the degree of interest there would be in NHS trusts and fundholding in view of the strength of opposition to *Working for Patients* on the part of the medical profession.

Table 2.2 *The implementation of GP fundholding and NHS trusts*

	NHS trusts	GP fundholders
1991	57	306
1992	99	288
1993	136	600
1994	140	800
1995	21	560
1996	–	1200

Note: Figures are for number of new entrants each year in England.

In the event, a combination of commitment by general managers, the leadership provided by the NHS Management Executive, and financial incentives that made it attractive for managers and doctors to put themselves forward meant that support for these innovations was greater than expected. In the course of implementation, the proposals in *Working for Patients* were progressively modified to enable all NHS providers to seek trust status (not just acute hospitals with over 250 beds as the White Paper had specified) and to encourage smaller as well as bigger general practices into fundholding. These developments were possible because the broad framework set out in the White Paper omitted many of the details of how the internal market would operate in practice, and what details there were changed in the light of debate and experience.

The lack of detail reflected the speed with which *Working for Patients* was produced, the absence of any coherent proposals on the part of those involved in the Ministerial Review, and a concern to avoid more radical alternatives because of the risk of unpopularity. The consequence of these gaps in the government's thinking was an impression that ministers and civil servants were 'making it up as they went along' (Timmins, 1995, p. 467). It also meant that managers and health service professionals were left to discover the importance of the separation of purchaser and provider roles, NHS trusts, GP fundholding and contracts in the process of implementation. In some respects, therefore, national policy was shaped by the local response as well as vice versa. To be sure, on certain issues the Department of Health did publish prescriptive guidance which appeared at odds with the emphasis on the devolution of responsibility within the internal market, but in many areas policy was made on the hoof as part of an emergent strategy (Ham, 1997a).

Alongside the phased approach to change and the emphasis on an emergent strategy, implementation was affected by the changing political context. In recognition of the radicalism of the reforms and the risks associated with their implementation, ministers and civil servants emphasised the need for a 'steady state' and a 'smooth take off' for the reforms in order to avoid hospitals running into financial difficulties as a result of the operation of the internal market in the run up to the election. The risks were perceived to be particularly great in London where purchasers had an incentive to move contracts and resources from relatively expensive teaching hospitals in inner London to providers with lower costs. Partly in anticipation of problems arising, in 1991 the government appointed Professor Sir Bernard Tomlinson to lead an inquiry into the future of health services in London and to make recommendations. Outside London these issues were handled less through Tomlinson-style inquiries than by health authorities working with each other and with providers to plan the changes in provision that the market necessitated. Whatever the preferred approach, the outcome was the same: the internal market became a *managed* market in which competition and planning went hand in hand.

By intervening to determine the future of health care in London and other areas, ministers were acknowledging the realities of a health service in which the ultimate responsibility for decisions rested with them. Yet, in so doing, they ran the risk of weakening the competitive incentives designed to drive down costs and raise standards. This applied particularly to NHS trusts whose freedoms as self-governing organisations were increasingly constrained by central guidance from the Department of Health. As one of the civil servants most closely involved in this process has observed:

> ministers and the centre are finding it difficult to reconcile devolved accountability with the demand for detailed monitoring created by parliamentary interest in operational issues. In consequence, the centre is drawn into a whole range of issues, from hospital catering standards to the freedom of speech of hospital staff that it once expected to leave to the discretion of local management. The dilemma is that without substantial operating freedom, Trust management cannot be expected to produce a better performance than the old directly managed units, but that with such freedom there is bound to be a diversity of behaviours and performance. The existence of outliers is then seen – by the press, auditors and politicians – as a cause for central regulation. (Smee, 1995, p. 190)

In practice, market management and regulation developed in an ad hoc manner and it was not until the end of 1994 that national guidance was published (DH, 1994). The guidance had little influence in practice, coming too late to change ways of working that were already established and to alter the imperatives facing politicians in circumstances where providers were threatened with closure or major change of use. It was partly for this reason that ministers altered their approach to the presentation of their policies, describing them as a programme of *management reforms* and not an internal market.

The impact of the reforms

In assessing the impact of the reforms, it is as well to remember the title of the White Paper from which they derive. *Working for Patients* may have been a response to the funding problems facing the NHS at the end of the 1980s, but its declared purpose was to improve services to patients. The emphasis on patients was maintained after John Major replaced Margaret

Thatcher as Prime Minister in 1990 with the publication of the *Patient's Charter* (DH, 1991) which set out a range of rights and standards and provided the basis for the development of performance tables showing how NHS trusts compared in areas such as waiting times and cancelled operations. Ministers maintained that increases in the number of patients treated provided a clear indication that patients were benefiting from the reforms, although independent analysts pointed out that these increases were probably the result of substantial increases in funding for the NHS between 1990 and 1993 rather than due to the reforms per se. Ministers also used reductions in the longest waiting times for treatment to argue that the NHS was becoming more responsive.

While the evidence on waiting times was stronger than that in relation to the number of patients treated, critics contended that patients waiting under a year for their operations were waiting longer to enable the government to deliver its promise in the *Patient's Charter* that no patient should wait longer than two years. Other assessments were equally inconclusive with the British Social Attitudes' survey reporting in 1994 that levels of dissatisfaction with the NHS had fallen at the same time as the Health Services Commissioner or Ombudsman criticised the record of the NHS in responding to patient complaints and argued that the more fragmented structure introduced as a consequence of the reforms had made it more difficult to coordinate the provision of care. Later evidence from the British Social Attitudes' Survey confirmed the concerns of the Health Services Commissioner with figures from 1996 indicating the highest ever level of reported dissatisfaction with the NHS (Judge et al., 1997).

Researchers have offered a variety of judgements on the impact of the internal market experiment. The most comprehensive early assessment detected relatively few changes in the first stages of implementation and argued that more time was needed to reach an informed judgement (Robinson and Le Grand, 1994). Studies by economists underline the difficulty of demonstrating productivity or efficiency gains as a consequence of the internal market. For example, Soderlund and colleagues concluded that competition between hospitals had no significant effect on productivity (Soderlund et al., 1997), whereas Propper (1996) found some evidence that the degree of competition was related to the prices charged by trusts. In a later analysis, Propper and colleagues examined the impact of competition on the quality of care (Propper et al., 2003). Using data on hospital death rates after heart attack within 30 days of admission, this analysis reported that hospitals in competitive areas had poorer outcomes than hospitals in areas with little or no competition.

The most thorough analysis of the evidence concluded that overall little change – positive or negative – could be detected (Le Grand et al., 1998). This analysis systematically reviewed the findings from a large number of research studies, seeking to assess the impact of the reforms under five broad headings: efficiency, equity, quality, choice and responsiveness, and accountability. Like other researchers, these authors emphasised the difficulty of separating the effects of the reforms from other changes in policy occurring at the same time and from increases in NHS funding. Given this caveat, they noted some evidence of improvements in efficiency, indications that equity was affected adversely by the differential access achieved by GP fundholders, no evidence that trust status had an impact on quality, minimal change to choice and responsiveness, and no real difference in accountability arrangements.

The main explanation of the findings offered by these authors is that the incentives contained within the internal market were too weak. Le Grand and colleagues emphasised that their analysis was concerned primarily with *measurable* change, and they added that there was some evidence of cultural change as a result of the reforms which may not have been adequately captured in the research studies they reviewed. In relation to cultural change, the findings of Ferlie and colleagues lend support to the argument that *Working for Patients* did have an impact on roles and relationships within the NHS (Ferlie et al., 1996). Among the changes reported by these researchers was a reorientation of hospital specialists towards GPs and some evidence that the influence of managers and of clinicians in management roles was increasing. These findings echo the author's own assessment based both on research into the reforms and experience of working with a wide range of NHS bodies throughout this period (Ham 1996, 1997a).

Streamlining the structure

As implementation of the reforms progressed, it became apparent that a contract-based system was more expensive to administer than the integrated system it replaced. The scale of increase in management costs was difficult to quantify with precision, although one estimate suggested that the reforms had resulted in an additional expenditure of £1.5 billion on management. Much of this increase derived from the need to employ staff to negotiate and monitor contracts and to supply information to purchasers and providers. Ministers responded by establishing a review of functions and manpower in 1992 which started as an examination of the respective roles of Regional Health Authorities (RHAs) and NHS Management Executive regional outposts in England, but turned into a comprehensive assessment of management arrangements at all levels.

The outcome was a decision to merge the functions of RHAs and the regional outposts in eight regional offices of the renamed NHS Executive.

In addition, the roles of District Health Authorities and Family Health Services Authorities were combined in unified health authorities and action was taken to reduce management costs. Taken together, these changes amounted to nothing less than a further reorganisation of the NHS, and the new structure is illustrated in Figure 2.3. Subsequently, an efficiency scrutiny set out a number of ways in which paperwork and regulation could be reduced, including moving towards longer term contracts or service agreements (NHS Executive, 1996). In making this proposal, the scrutiny was reflecting developments already occurring within the NHS, illustrating once again the extent to which national policy was shaped during the course of implementation.

To return to the starting point of this chapter, the reorganisation of the NHS that took place in 1996 and the organic nature of the reforms lend support to Webster's observation that developments in health policy under Margaret Thatcher and John Major involved a continuous revolution. Yet, unlike Webster, it is not necessary to subscribe to the view that ideological imperatives were the main driving force behind the reforms to explain what happened (Webster, 1998, pp. 142–8). As Klein (1995, p. 176) has suggested, there are many different ways of telling the story of *Working for Patients* and its aftermath, ranging from a response to the changing state of

Figure 2.3 *The structure of the NHS in England, 1996–99*

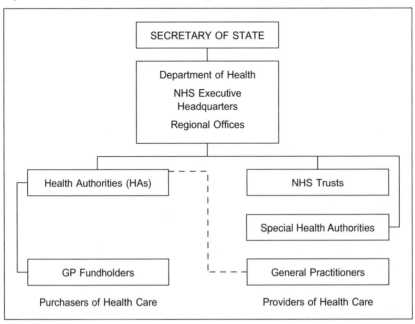

Source: NHSE.

the economy to an exercise in policy learning. All versions of the story put politicians at the heart of the reform of the NHS, but other influences were also at work. What is clear is that the evolution of health policy in the 1980s and 1990s sheds further light on the dynamics of the policy process and in the Conclusion we draw out the main lessons.

Conclusion

In this chapter we have seen how changes in the economic context in which the NHS functions and in political debate exerted a significant influence on health policy. The election of a Conservative government under Margaret Thatcher and the adoption by the government of policies to control public expenditure and achieve greater efficiency in public services led to radical reforms to the NHS. The incremental pattern of policy development that dominated the first 30 years of the NHS was replaced by the implementation of changes that were neither the product of political consensus nor the outcome of bargaining between government and pressure groups. This is a reminder of the need to seek explanations of the development of health policy beyond the health sector, a theme we return to in later chapters.

One of the most striking observations on health policy in this period is that a government with a parliamentary majority was able to drive through changes in the face of strong opposition. This testifies to the power of the executive in the British system of government and shows that even unpopular policies can be promulgated if the government has the political will to do so. The involvement of Prime Minister Thatcher in the most radical of these policies undoubtedly contributed to this as did her adherence to the school of conviction politics. Yet Margaret Thatcher was not alone in this regard as the determination of Kenneth Clarke to face down the medical profession amply demonstrated. To this extent, health policy during the 1980s and 1990s showed that ministers matter and make a difference.

The corollary is that the power of even the most well-placed pressure groups may not always be sufficient to defeat proposals put forward by ministers. This lesson emerges not just from the failure of the BMA and other groups to stop the government proceeding with the implementation of *Working for Patients*, but also from the inability of doctors to prevent the imposition of a new contract for GPs in 1990. In both instances, ministers overcame resistance to their policies and were not afraid to risk unpopularity in the process. The established rules of conduct in the health policy community were suspended (although not abandoned), and in place of bargaining and negotiation with key groups ministers decided among themselves what they wanted to do and acted accordingly. Notwith-standing this, pressure groups were closely involved in the implementation of policy and on many issues apart from *Working for Patients* and the new contract for GPs they continued to exert influence.

Finally, it is clear that the implementation of policy feeds back into policy-making, making it difficult to draw hard and fast distinctions between these activities. This is particularly evident from experience in the 1990s when doctors and managers in the NHS shaped the implemen-tation of *Working for Patients* and in so doing influenced how national policy itself developed. A number of examples of this have been identified in this chapter, indicating how the broad framework set out in *Working for Patients* was adapted and refined in practice. In this respect, the impact of political ideology was modified by managerial pragmatism and judge-ment of what was likely to be acceptable to the public and the health professions. And as we note in later chapters, the need to secure the coop-eration of the medical profession to ensure effective implementation of policy meant that the BMA was excluded from the corridors of power for only a short period.

Chapter 3

Health Policy under Blair and Brown

The election of a Labour government under Tony Blair in 1997 brought to an end 18 years of Conservative government under Margaret Thatcher and John Major and appeared to offer the prospect of a return to quieter times for the NHS. In practice, this was not to be as the Blair government developed its own policies for the reform of the NHS and in the process published proposals which were just as radical as those contained in *Working for Patients*. These proposals centred on what ministers described as a 'third way' of reform, different from both the internal market of the Thatcher government and the application of centralised planning by previous Labour governments. The process of reform continued when Gordon Brown succeeded Tony Blair as Prime Minister in 2007. The aim of this chapter is to analyse this third way under Blair and Brown and to explore its evolution.

The inheritance

The way in which successive Conservative Health Ministers changed the language used to present their reforms by placing less emphasis on competition was noted in the previous chapter. This change was initiated as early as 1991 when the Secretary of State for Health, William Walde-grave, explained in an interview that the NHS market:

> isn't a market in a real sense ... it's competition in the sense that there will be comparative information available. It's not a market in that people don't go bust and make profits and all that, but it's using market-like mechanisms to provide better information. (quoted in Smith, 1991, p. 712)

Waldegrave's comments were echoed by his successor Virginia Bottomley in a 1995 speech reviewing the development of the reforms. Like Waldegrave, Bottomley emphasised the importance of competition by comparison and she argued for:

[a] long-term and strategic view. A great deal can and will be achieved through the purchaser/provider system. As that relationship matures, I want to see greater use of longer term contracts between health authorities, fundholders and NHS Trusts ... The new NHS requires a strategic oversight ... There are many issues ... where it is important to take a broad view. The implementation of our strategy for developing cancer services is just one example of where we shall achieve a long-term goal by working together within the framework offered by the new NHS. (Bottomley, 1995, p. 7)

Bottomley's replacement, Stephen Dorrell, also played down the role of markets in health care and focused instead on using what he described as the *management reforms* to increase efficiency and raise standards. In his view, there was a need to encourage collaboration between purchasers and providers and long-term relationships, in part because of the policy of reducing management costs. Dorrell's position was expressed most clearly in a White Paper on the NHS published in 1996, restating the government's commitment to the founding principles of the NHS, and outlining a future in which priority would be given not to the development of the market but to information and information technology, professional development and managing for quality (Secretary of State for Health, 1996). The White Paper was an important stepping stone between the application of market principles in the early 1990s and the explicit rejection of these principles at the end of the decade.

With competition out of favour among ministers, a new policy agenda began to emerge in the latter stages of the Major government. This owed less to a belief in market forces than a desire to use the organisational changes brought about by *Working for Patients* to achieve other objectives. Specifically, the separation of purchaser and provider roles refocused attention on the public health agenda as health authorities developed strategies for meeting the needs of the populations they served in line with the national health strategy published by the government (see Chapter 4). There was also increasing interest in primary care as the shift in the balance of power that resulted from *Working for Patients* turned the spotlight on services in the community and ways in which these services might be strengthened. The other main strand in the new policy agenda was the establishment of a research and development programme for the NHS, including the encouragement given within the programme to evidence-based health care. None of these policies was in place at the time *Working for Patients* was published, but all rose to prominence as a consequence of the reforms.

The emphasis placed on public health, primary care and evidence-based health care and the shift away from competition had the effect of narrowing the differences between the Thatcher government and the

Labour Party. In reality, the common ground between the Conservatives and Labour became larger as a result of movement on both sides. From a position of outright opposition to the internal market in 1989, the Labour Party came to acknowledge that there had been some benefits from the changes contained within *Working for Patients* while promising to reverse those elements of the changes which it disliked. The willingness of the Labour Party to accept some of the policies initiated by its political opponents was symptomatic of the changes to Labour's approach that occurred throughout the 1990s. Having lost four general elections in succession, the Labour Party undertook a fundamental review of its programme and developed a series of proposals in different areas of public policy designed to make it more attractive to the electorate. These proposals drew on the philosophy of leaders like Tony Blair and were distinctive both in the acceptance that some of the changes made under the Thatcher and Major governments should be supported and in the rejection of policies associated with what became known as 'Old Labour'. This helps to explain why the election of the Blair government in 1997 did not entail a return to the status quo ante, but rather a further period of reform in which the organisation of the NHS was altered yet again. Put another way, health policy in the late 1990s was shaped by the changing face of British politics with developments in the NHS paralleling changes made in other sectors such as education and social care.

The New NHS

On its arrival in office the Blair government had developed the outlines of its approach to the NHS but this approach was much stronger in relation to the principles that should guide change than the detail of how to convert these principles into practice. It was also the case that the new government was clearer about what it was opposed to – the fragmentation of the NHS market – than what it was for. The government's position reflected frequent changes among Labour Party shadow Health Ministers and continuing internal debates between the so-called modernisers who were willing to accept some of the changes initiated by the Thatcher government and the traditionalists who were much more sceptical and whose influence was still important. The appointment of a traditionalist, Frank Dobson, as Secretary of State for Health, and a moderniser, Alan Milburn, as Minister of State, had the effect of internalising this debate within the Department of Health.

The first six months of the new government were therefore taken up with elaboration of the policy position articulated by the Labour Party in opposition, and it was not until December 1997 that the government's proposals were published. The White Paper setting out these proposals, *The New NHS*, identified six principles behind the government's plans:

- to renew the NHS as a genuinely national service;
- to make the delivery of health care against these new national standards a matter of local responsibility;
- to get the NHS to work in partnership;
- to drive efficiency through a more rigorous approach to performance and by cutting bureaucracy;
- to shift the focus on to quality of care so that excellence is guaranteed to all patients;
- to rebuild public confidence in the NHS.

The White Paper went on to state:

In paving the way for the new NHS the Government is committed to building on what has worked but discarding what has failed. There will be no return to the old centralised command and control system of the 1970s ... But nor will there be a continuation of the divisive internal market system of the 1990s ... Instead there will be a 'third way' of running the NHS – a system based on partnership and driven by performance. (Secretary of State for Health, 1997, p. 10)

This statement and others in the White Paper indicated that the Blair government was at pains to distance itself from both Conservative policies towards the NHS and the approach of previous Labour governments. In this respect, developments in health policy mirrored those across government as a whole, with 'New Labour' seeking to carve out a niche in the marketplace of political ideas that was both distinctive and electorally attractive. The 'third way' was used to describe the position.

The central and recurrent description of the government's stance in *The New NHS* White Paper was 'new', with the 'modernisation' of the NHS identified as the main objective. Ministers emphasised that they were adopting a pragmatic approach based on the belief that 'what counts is what works' (ibid. p. 11). It was for this reason that the White Paper included a commitment to retain what it described as 'the separation between the planning of hospital care and its provision' (ibid. p. 12) as well as the decentralisation of responsibility for operational management to NHS trusts and the priority attached to primary care. Indeed, in relation to primary care, the government announced that while fundholding per se would be abolished, it wanted to extend the principles of fundholding to all family doctors and community nurses through a system of primary care groups (PCGs). Equally important, the White Paper included a clear commitment to bring an end to what was left of the market and to promote collaboration and partnership. In this sense it was seeking to 'go with the grain' (ibid. p. 11) of developments already under way, for example by moving towards longer term service agreements and further reducing the paperwork and bureaucracy associated with annual contracting.

The Blair government's approach was eclectic as well as being pragmatic. Whereas the Thatcher government's reforms were based on a single core idea – the use of the market to improve NHS performance – the White Paper included a number of different mechanisms to increase efficiency and to enhance responsiveness (Ham, 1999). For example, there was a return to greater central involvement in the NHS in the aspiration to develop a 'one nation NHS' (Secretary of State for Health, 1997, p. 55), and to reduce variations in performance through the development of national service frameworks and the creation of agencies like the National Institute for Clinical Excellence (NICE). In parallel, the White Paper placed considerable emphasis on the freedom available to GPs and others in the new PCGs to make decisions on the use of resources at a local level and to bring about improvements in services for patients.

Similarly, ministers pointed out that their plans included a wide range of incentives for NHS staff to increase efficiency and raise standards alongside the use of sanctions to penalise poor performance. The incentives focused on the flexibilities available to PCGs to move resources around and to redeploy savings; the sanctions on new arrangements for visiting hospitals and other providers through the proposed Commission for Health Improvement (CHI); and the threat of intervention by ministers and civil servants in the event of performance failures. The eclectic nature of the government's approach was particularly apparent in the framework for performance management set out in the White Paper which demonstrated that in future performance would be assessed not only in relation to efficiency (the preoccupation of the Thatcher and Major governments), but also health improvement, fair access, effective delivery, patient experience and health outcome. In putting forward these proposals, ministers explained that they represented a ten-year programme for the modernisation of the NHS. The aim was to encourage 'evolutionary change rather than organisational upheaval' (ibid. p. 5) and in the process to address weaknesses in the system the government had inherited.

The new structure

Figure 3.1 illustrates the structure of the NHS in England as it emerged from *The New NHS* White Paper. The White Paper emphasised that health authorities would give strategic leadership at a local level with a

Figure 3.1 *The structure of the NHS in England, 1999–2002*

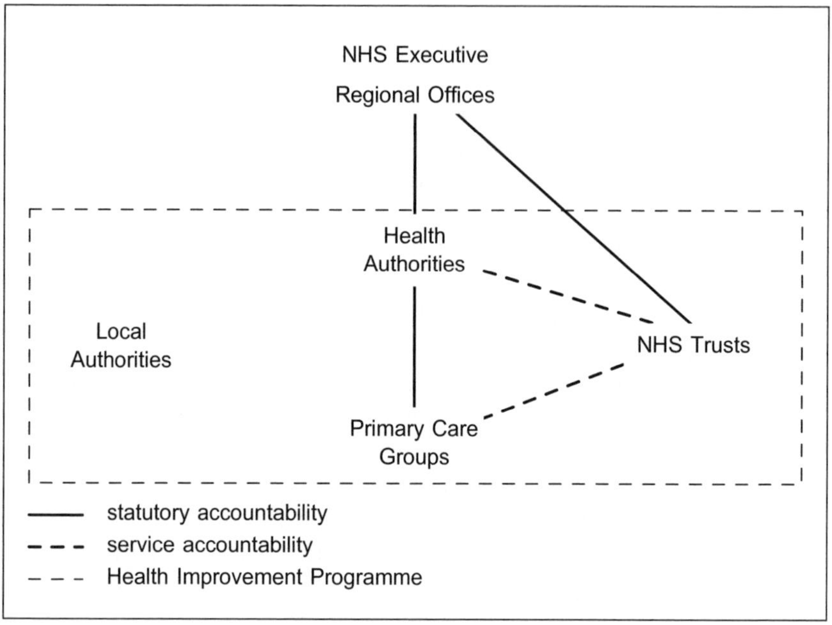

NHS Executive
Regional Offices

Health
Authorities

Local
Authorities

NHS Trusts

Primary Care
Groups

────── statutory accountability
─ ─ ─ service accountability
─ ─ ─ Health Improvement Programme

Source: Secretary of State for Health (1997).

particular focus on public health, for example by developing health improvement programmes (HImPs) in conjunction with NHS bodies, local authorities and other partner organisations. HImPs were intended to be local health strategies and a means of translating national targets for the improvement of health and health services into practice. Health authorities were also given a major role in the development and support of PCGs. This included establishing groups and helping them take on more responsibility for commissioning and service provision, thereby freeing up health authorities to concentrate on their strategic functions. PCGs were held to account by health authorities through annual accountability agreements which provided the framework for monitoring and performance review.

The number and configuration of PCGs was determined locally by health authorities in discussion with GPs and others involved in primary care, subject to the approval of regional offices. In the event, 481 groups were set up in England in April 1999 serving populations ranging from 46,000 to 257,000. Each PCG was run by a board comprising four to seven GPs, one or two community or practice nurses, one social services nominee, one lay member, one health authority non-executive, and the group's chief executive. PCG chairs were almost invariably GPs and were supported by a small management team. While membership of PCGs was a requirement for all GPs, there was flexibility over the degree of respon-sibility they wished to assume. All PCGs were initially established as advi-sory bodies and it was envisaged that over time they would take on a wider range of functions, including becoming primary care trusts account-able for commissioning care and providing community services for the population. This was confirmed in *Shifting the Balance of Power* in 2001 (DH, 2001a) (see below).

NHS trusts were the other main organisations in the structure that was developed by the Blair government. While many of the responsibili-ties of trusts continued as before, the government underlined its expec-tation that trusts would work in partnership with health authorities in the spirit of collaboration that lay behind the changes. To this end, health authorities were expected to involve trusts fully in the prepara-tion of HImPs and they were given reserve powers to ensure that capital investment and new consultant medical staffing decisions of trusts did not cut across the strategy set out in HImPs. In parallel, new statutory duties for partnership and quality were created, the latter finding expres-sion in the emphasis placed on clinical governance. Under these duties, chief executives of trusts were held accountable for the quality of the services they provided, and the White Paper proposed that each trust should establish a sub-committee chaired by a senior clinician to lead work on quality.

It was significant that the structure set out in the White Paper illus-trated in Figure 3.1 included local authorities alongside NHS bodies. This reflected the concern in the government's plans to break down barriers between agencies and to encourage partnerships not only within the NHS but more widely. The consultative document on public health published in 1998 (see Chapter 4) underlined this concern with its proposal that HImPs should be the means of translating national health targets into action, and that health action zones should be established in which NHS bodies would come together with local authorities and others to tackle the root causes of ill-health and develop new ways of involving local people (Secretary of State for Health, 1998a). The consultative document on public health also announced that the government intended to place a duty on local authorities to promote the economic, social and environ-mental well-being of their area.

Implementation

Taken together, these proposals amounted to a further period of radical change within the NHS. Although ministers emphasised that the propos-als were to be implemented gradually over a ten-year period, the continuous revolution initiated by the Thatcher government was perpetuated under the Blair government which showed no wish to slow the process of change. A further similarity with the reforms that followed from *Working for Patients* was that *The New NHS* set out a broad framework rather than a detailed blueprint. The guidance that was issued after publication of the White Paper filled in many of the gaps but, as with the Thatcher reforms, there was scope for NHS bodies to take the framework developed by the government and adapt it in the process of implementation.

The establishment of primary care groups was the most important innovation made by the government and signalled a clear commitment to maintain the move towards a primary-care-led NHS initiated by the Conservatives. Indeed, by involving all GPs in commissioning and offering the opportunity to primary care groups to take on the management of community health services and to become primary care trusts, the government was taking the Conservatives' reforms a good deal further and was holding out the prospect of an NHS in which doctors and nurses in primary care would exercise increasing influence. The decision to give PCGs control of resources and to unify different elements in the budget, thereby allowing resources to be transferred between hospitals and the community, was particularly important, creating an incentive for as much work as possible to be done in primary care and to reduce the use of hospital services. In pursuing this approach, the government was seeking, in the words of the White Paper, to 'align clinical and financial responsibility' (Secretary of State for Health, 1997, p. 9), drawing on the experience of fundholding and extending this to primary care as a whole.

The proposals on public health and health improvement were also significant. Although previous governments had given priority to these issues, the commitment of the Blair government was indicated by the appointment of the first Minister for Public Health and by the focus on the role of health authorities in improving the health of the population and not just developing local health services. The decision to maintain the separation between planning and service provision was motivated by a concern to avoid health authorities being drawn into the management of services, thereby enabling them to concentrate on the public health agenda. Similarly, the proposal to give PCGs responsibility for commissioning most health services for their patients was intended to free up health authorities to assess the health needs of the populations they served and to make a reality of the national health strategy at a local level. In this sense, health authorities were expected to become public health agencies, leading the development of local health strategies and harnessing the contribution of different agencies in so doing.

As far as health services were concerned, the attention given to the quality of care in the government's plans emerged as a particularly high priority. Again, improving quality was not a new policy objective, but the combination of strong political commitment and a series of incidents which highlighted failures of performance meant that the momentum behind this objective was of a different order than under other governments. This was illustrated by publication of a document, *A First Class Service*, setting out the government's plans in detail and explaining the link between the various initiatives that had been set in train (Secretary of State for Health, 1998b). These plans centred on the establishment of clear national standards through NICE and national service frameworks; the introduction of clinical governance to ensure the delivery of these standards at a local level; and the setting up of the CHI to monitor delivery. The significance of these initiatives lay in recognition that self-regulation by the health professions was no longer sufficient to ensure consistently high standards, and that new mechanisms were needed to promote quality within the NHS.

The comprehensive spending review

The New NHS White Paper was published at the mid-point of the comprehensive spending review (CSR) initiated by the Blair government on coming into office. The purpose of the review was to take stock of public expenditure as a whole and the balance between spending programmes in the light of the government's election commitments. In advance of the completion of the review in July 1998, extra resources were allocated to the NHS to deal with winter pressures and to assist in the achievement of the targets that had been set for reducing waiting lists. But it was the CSR that provided the first real indication of the Blair government's approach to public spending in general and NHS spending in particular.

The significance of the CSR was threefold. First, it resulted in education and health receiving substantial increases in expenditure at a time when lower priority was attached to other spending programmes. Second, the CSR was based on plans for three years rather than the usual period of one year. And third, the additional resources allocated by the government were intended to produce specified improvements in performance. The watchwords of the CSR were 'money for modernisation' and 'investment for reform' in recognition that ministers expected public services to become more efficient, equitable and responsive as a result of the commitment made by the government (Chancellor of the Exchequer, 1998). To ensure that this happened, departments were required to negotiate public service agreements with the Treasury setting out performance targets for different services. Public service agreements were the means chosen by Gordon Brown as Chancellor of the Exchequer to influence the use of additional resources agreed during the CSR for the NHS and other public services and they enabled central government to exert considerable control over the NHS.

In the case of the NHS, the CSR led to a planned increase in expenditure of £21 billion between 1999 and 2002. This amounted to an annual increase of 4.7 per cent in real terms. On closer inspection, the priority attached to the NHS was not as impressive as first appeared, in part because the increase of £21 billion was calculated by adding together the extra spending planned over three years, and in part because pay awards made to NHS staff in 1999 eroded the value of the real-terms increase assumed in the CSR White Paper. The targets to be achieved with the increased funding included the reduction of waiting lists by 100,000 to fulfil the promise made by the Prime Minister before the election. The public service agreement subsequently negotiated with the Treasury set out a range of other targets. These included objectives relating to public health, the policy of improving quality and access, and the emphasis on primary care. Consistent with the CSR and the priority attached by the Blair government to partnership working, a number of targets included a commitment to collaboration between the NHS and other agencies. Despite the funding increases, the Blair government ran into difficulties in achieving its target of reducing waiting lists, dealing with the pressures of emergency hospital admissions during the winter months, and finding the resources to pay for new drugs and medical technologies.

These difficulties came to a head in the winter of 1999/2000 when hospitals found themselves under considerable pressure from an outbreak of flu. Media reporting of patients being forced to wait on trolleys for beds to become available brought to public attention the consequences of capacity constraints. The plight of Mavis Skeet, a patient with cancer whose operation was cancelled until the point when her condition was inoperable, came to symbolise the shortcomings of the NHS. Influential figures like Lord Winston, a Labour peer, expressed their dissatisfaction with government policies, with Winston drawing on his mother's experience of using the NHS to compare the United Kingdom unfavourably with other countries. In a television interview in January 2000 the Prime Minister made a commitment to increase spending on health care to bring it up to the average of the European Union. This commitment was reinforced by the decision in the March 2000 budget to increase NHS spending in 2000/01 by £2 billion more than the plans set out in the CSR and by around one-third in real terms in five years. This decision reflected recognition by both the Prime Minister and the Chancellor of the Exchequer that there needed to be a sustained commitment to increase NHS funding to address the pressures it was facing.

The NHS Plan

In responding to its critics, the government emphasised that it would take time to improve the performance of the NHS, and work was put in hand to prepare a ten-year plan for the future of the NHS. A series of Modernisation Action Teams were set up to analyse the challenges facing the NHS and to come up with proposals for reform. The teams comprised a range of stakeholders including NHS staff, patients' representatives, and people drawn from professional associations, the research community and other sectors. The results of the work of the Modernisation Action Teams were brought together with the views of ministers and officials in the Department of Health in *The NHS Plan: a plan for investment, a plan for reform*, published in July 2000 (Secretary of State for Health, 2000). The preface to the Plan set out the core principles of the NHS and contained a commitment from the leaders of 25 national organisations to these principles. The Plan itself described how the resources made available to the NHS would be used to deliver 'a health service designed around the patient' (p. 10).

The emphasis on investment and reform in *The NHS Plan* followed from the analysis undertaken in its preparation. The results of this analysis were presented in Chapter 2 of the Plan which summarised the outcome of consultation with the public and staff. This analysis showed that both the public and staff attached high priority to more and better paid staff. For the public, reduced waiting times for treatment were important, while staff identified the need for more training and 'joined up working' with social care at community and primary care levels. In its analysis, the government highlighted the failure of the NHS to provide services centred around the needs of individual patients, notwithstanding its many achievements. This failure was attributed to an under-invested system, a lack of national standards, demarcations between staff, a lack of clear incentives, barriers between services, a lack of support and intervention, over-centralisation and disempowered patients. The Plan emphasised that the values and principles that lay behind the NHS still held good, but that its practices had to change to meet contemporary expectations.

A major theme of *The NHS Plan* was the need to increase spending on the NHS to enable capacity to be expanded. Specific commitments included the provision of 7000 extra beds in hospitals and intermediate care, over 100 new hospitals by 2010 and 500 new one-stop primary care centres, over 3000 GP premises modernised and 250 new scanners, 7500 more consultants, 2000 more GPs, 20,000 extra nurses and 6500 extra therapists. *The NHS Plan* also reiterated the need for investment to be accompanied by reform. Reform was to be achieved through a new relationship between the Department of Health and the NHS in which local NHS organisations that performed well would be given more freedom to run their own affairs and a Modernisation Agency would be established to spread best practice. The Modernisation Agency would build on existing work to redesign care around patients in order to improve access and raise standards. Its main purpose was to provide advice and external expertise to NHS staff 'to support continuous service improvement' (p. 60). The Modernisation Agency started work in April 2001.

The Plan contained a large number of specific commitments in a wide range of areas. These included the use of additional resources to ensure that hospitals were clean and hospital food was of higher quality; improved pay for NHS staff and a commitment to improve the working lives of staff; the development of intermediate care and part-nership working between the NHS and social care; new contracts for GPs and consultants; the appointment of 'modern matrons' with authority on hospital wards; and changes for patients that included more information, greater choice, and the development of a patient advocacy and liaison service. Of particular importance were the commitments to cut waiting times for treatment, including the estab-lishment of targets to reduce maximum times for outpatient appoint-ments to three months and inpatient treatment to six months by 2005. A waiting-time target was also set for primary care, with patients being guaranteed access to a primary care professional within 24 hours and to a primary care doctor within 48 hours by 2004. These and other key objectives were brought together in the public service agreement included as an annex to the Plan and again this underlined the empha-sis placed on government targets and central control as mechanisms for improving NHS performance.

Throughout *The NHS Plan* there was reference to the need for better systems for improving performance to enable the investment of additional resources to be used to good effect. Although no longer using the 'third way' rhetoric, the Plan echoed the analysis in *The New NHS* White Paper in noting the weakness of the internal market and of the 'top down government model' (p. 57). In place of these approaches, a new delivery model was outlined in which the Department of Health would set national standards and put in place a framework to support delivery of those standards. Arrangements for inspection through the CHI would be strengthened and the performance of NHS organisations would be assessed and made public. High performing organisations would be rewarded with extra funding and greater autonomy. Failing organisations would be given additional support and would be subject to a rising scale of interventions. The Department of Health would change its role to support these developments.

The NHS Plan can be seen both as a restatement of New Labour's commitment to the NHS, and as a declaration of its determination to reform the Service to overcome the weaknesses that had brought it back into the public gaze. The involvement of stakeholders in the development of the Plan, and their support for the core principles on which it was based, was designed to create a coalition to support implementation, although this did not prevent critics expressing scepticism about whether the commitments contained in the Plan could be delivered. In particular, it was argued that the NHS was based on an outdated structure – the post-war nationalised model – that had been superseded in other sectors, and was unlikely to work in health care even with additional investment accompanied by reform. For its part, the government argued that a long-term commitment to increase NHS funding, at levels not achieved in the past, would enable the consequences of under-investment to be addressed, provided that staff were willing to embrace reform. In making this case, ministers emphasised that the changes taking place in the NHS were consistent with the principles of public service reform articulated by the Prime Minister, and applied in other sectors such as education, policing and social care.

Shifting the Balance of Power

Further detail on the new relationship between the Department of Health (DH) and the NHS emerged in 2001 as part of an initiative known as *Shifting the Balance of Power* (DH, 2001a). This initiative set out the organisational changes the government felt were needed to support implementation of *The NHS Plan* and these changes were ostensibly intended to move power and control over budgets to frontline staff and patients. At the heart of the changes was the decision to establish primary care trusts (PCTs) throughout the NHS in place of primary care groups. In addition, the government decided to reduce the number of health authorities from 95 to 28, and replace the eight regional offices of the DH with four Directorates of Health and Social Care. At the centre, the NHS Executive within the DH lost its separate identity as part of a programme to streamline the work of the Department under the leadership of a combined permanent secretary and NHS chief executive.

The new structure of the NHS in England came into effect in 2002 and is illustrated in Figure 3.2. The aim was to give PCTs control over 75 per cent of the NHS budget by 2004 in an effort to ensure that staff in close contact with patients were able to decide on the commissioning of services for the populations they served. This initiative was consistent with the approach set out in *The New NHS* White Paper in 1997 but

Figure 3.2 *The structure of the NHS in England after 2002*

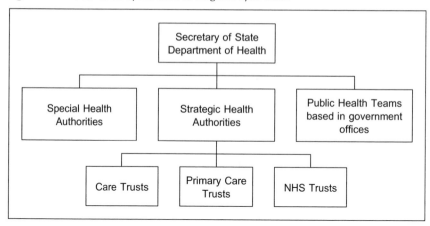

took the development of PCTs further and faster than had been anticipated. The decision to reduce the number of health authorities, focus
their role on strategic issues and replace regional offices was intended to
enable PCTs to assume greater responsibility for commissioning and
service provision. One of the consequences was a period of further structural upheaval at a time when the NHS was in the early stages of implementing *The NHS Plan.*

NHS trusts were not directly affected by these developments but their
future was brought into question by the announcement early in 2002 of
plans to create NHS foundation trusts. The original intention behind
NHS foundation trusts was to give high performing NHS trusts the
opportunity to manage their services with less interference from the DH
and with greater involvement of local communities, staff and other
stakeholders. In the event, the government announced that all NHS
trusts were expected to become NHS foundation trusts in time and a
programme for improving performance in the NHS was put together to
enable this to happen. Even more importantly, ministers decided to
establish NHS foundation trusts as public benefit corporations overseen
by a new regulator rather than line-managed by the DH. The freedoms
available to NHS foundation trusts were more circumscribed than had
been planned by health ministers, largely because of objections by the
Treasury, but nevertheless they represented potentially the most radical
organisational innovation in the history of the NHS since its inception.
Perhaps not surprisingly, the government's plans to establish NHS foundation trusts attracted criticism from some Labour MPs and trade
unions, and these plans were only enacted into law after protracted
negotiations (Shaw, 2007). Both NHS trusts and NHS foundation trusts

negotiated with PCTs the level of funding they needed to deliver services and the range and mix of these services.

Delivering the NHS Plan

The significance of NHS foundation trusts became clear on publication of *Delivering the NHS Plan* in April 2002. (Secretary of State for Health, 2002). *Delivering the NHS Plan* was issued at the time of the 2002 budget and it described how the new relationship between the DH and the NHS was expected to evolve. The main new elements in *Delivering the NHS Plan* were the emphasis on patient choice and the commitment to develop greater plurality of provision. Although patient choice had been mentioned in *The NHS Plan*, it was now identified as a key priority in the reform of the NHS. *Delivering the NHS Plan* invoked experience in Sweden and Denmark to support the argument that choice for patients could be delivered in a tax-funded system. Patient choice was to be supported by a new system of payment by results under which hospitals were to be funded on the basis of the work they undertook.

The policy of developing greater plurality of provision was also foreshadowed in *The NHS Plan* but was taken further in *Delivering the NHS Plan*. The latter document included commitments to maximise the use of spare capacity in private hospitals and develop new public–private partnerships to support the rapid development of diagnostic and treatment centres. Proposals to establish NHS foundation trusts included in *Delivering the NHS Plan* (described in the document as NHS 'Foundation Hospitals') were consistent with the policy of developing greater plurality of provision, and with the drive to shift the balance of power to the front line. Diagnostic and treatment centres became known as independent sector treatment centres (ISTCs) and their development by a Labour government was almost as controversial as the plans to establish NHS foundation trusts (see Chapter 12).

The April 2002 budget was the occasion on which the Chancellor of the Exchequer announced the outcome of the spending review for 2002. The NHS was one of the principal beneficiaries of the spending review, securing increases in funding of over 7 per cent per year in real terms between 2002/03 and 2007/08 as a result of the Wanless Review (see Chapter 4). The plans announced in the budget envisaged expenditure on the NHS in England increasing from £56 million to £90 million over this period. The 2002 spending review was particularly important in making a commitment to increase funding over five years compared with the three year planning period covered in previous spending reviews. And unusually for a budget, taxes were raised to pay for these spending increases through changes to national insurance contribution rates. Although ministers had been concerned about the reaction to tax increases, the immediate reaction from the public was positive.

A return to the market?

Taken together, the policies set out in *Delivering the NHS Plan* were similar in a number of respects to those that lay behind the internal market. This was particularly apparent in the emphasis placed on patient choice, the system of payment by results in which money would follow patients to providers, and the commitment to establish NHS foundation trusts. As in the 1990s, these policies were intended to create stronger incentives to improve performance and to ensure that the NHS really did work for patients. A further similarity was the willingness to use the private sector and to develop new forms of public–private partnerships. The approach displayed in *Delivering the NHS Plan* in this area signalled a marked departure from New Labour's early period in office when the NHS was actively discouraged from working with the private sector. As such, it represented a triumph for the modernisers over the traditionalists, exemplified by the opposition of the former Secretary of State for Health, Frank Dobson, to the policies developed by his former junior minister and successor, Alan Milburn.

At the same time, there were important differences between the policies set out in *Delivering the NHS Plan* and the internal market. To begin with, patient choice, provider diversity and payment by results were introduced in a context in which NHS funding was increasing at a much faster rate than in the 1990s. In addition, the government had started the process of establishing national standards for the NHS through national service frameworks and NICE guidance, and it had established an independent mechanism for inspecting providers in the form of the CHI. These differences meant hospitals were seeking to increase their share of a rapidly rising budget rather than competing in a zero sum game, and they were doing so in an environment where there were safeguards against quality of care being sacrificed as a result of competition. And unlike in the internal market where there was price competition, under the payment by results system the aim was to reimburse hospitals according to a fixed tariff modelled on experience in countries where this method of funding was well developed.

Having made these points, there is no doubt that the wheel had turned, if not full circle, then at least part of the way back to New Labour's 1997 inheritance. The reason for this has to be sought in the limited impact of the policies set out in *The New NHS* White Paper and the recognition in government that other approaches were needed to produce improvements in performance. This did not entail abandoning the commitment to develop PCTs, a more explicit approach to improving quality, and a systematic framework of national standards and inspection. Rather, it meant supplementing these instruments through greater plurality of provision and patient choice. These policies reflected recognition that more emphasis needed to be given to incentives and contestability than had been appreciated in the early phases of New Labour's tenure in government. A further influence was the competition for political ideas with the government pre-empting some of the policies advocated by opposition parties.

Viewed in the wider context, *The NHS Plan* and *Delivering the NHS Plan* can be seen as an attempt to move the NHS from a hierarchically managed to a regulated health care system. It was this that lay behind the commitment in *The NHS Plan* to develop a new relationship between the DH and the NHS. At the heart of this relationship was devolution of power to PCTs and to clinical teams; a more limited role for the Department centred on setting priorities and promulgating standards; and an increasing role for the CHI in inspecting providers and improving quality. One of the changes heralded in *Delivering the NHS Plan* was the establishment of a new Commission for Healthcare Audit and Inspection (known as the Healthcare Commission) to replace the CHI with responsibility for inspecting both the public and private health care sectors. This symbolised the greater emphasis placed on regulation.

One of the drivers of these changes was the high political cost involved in running the NHS as a centralised system. With accountability for NHS performance residing with the Secretary of State, responsibility for failures as well as credit for successes gravitated towards a single point in the system. In an era of ever closer media scrutiny of the NHS, the imperatives confronting the government of the day to respond to reports of performance failures grew stronger, even if the ability of government to address the causes of these failures remained limited. With NHS staff complaining about the adverse consequences of micro management by government, ministers had a strong incentive to find a way of devolving as much responsibility as possible within the NHS, thereby distancing themselves from matters over which in practice they had little control. Strengthening the role of inspectors and placing more emphasis on regulation were a logical consequence of these developments. Reducing (but not eliminating) the role of national targets in the NHS and placing more responsibility on PCTs and NHS foundation trusts arose from the same motivation.

In the debate between Labour's modernisers and traditionalists, the Chancellor of the Exchequer occupied an ambiguous position. Treasury concerns about NHS foundation trusts meant that the radicalism of the DH had to be modified to enable this policy to be pursued. The concerns of the Treasury found expression in a major speech by the Chancellor in which he argued the case for competition as the engine to drive economic prosperity, while emphasising the limits to markets in areas like education and health care (Brown, 2003). Yet in noting the weaknesses of markets in health care, he also gave support to policies designed to decentralise power in the NHS and promote contestability between providers. This included endorsement of the policies set out in *Delivering the NHS Plan*. While the Chancellor's speech seemed to indicate that differences within government on the direction of reform were directed at the detail rather than the principle of reform, in practice it was clear that the occupants of the Treasury remained to be convinced that greater patient choice and plurality of provision could be reconciled with equity and other established NHS values. These suspicions were confirmed when Gordon Brown succeeded Tony Blair as Prime Minister in 2007 and put his own stamp on New Labour's health policy (see below).

The NHS Improvement Plan

The government's plans for the reform of the NHS were developed further in *The NHS Improvement Plan*, published in June 2004 (Secretary of State for Health, 2004a), which listed the progress made in improving health and health services since *The NHS Plan* and identified priorities for the NHS in the period up to 2008. These priorities were to further improve the health of the population by focusing on the prevention of ill-health and tackling health inequalities; to support people with long-term conditions to live healthy lives; and to deliver high quality, personalised care to patients. The major new commitment contained in *The NHS Improvement Plan* was that no one should wait longer than 18 weeks from GP referral to hospital treatment by 2008. In support of this commitment, the government announced that by 2008 patients would have the right to choose from any provider meeting the Healthcare Commission's standards and providing care within the payment by results tariff. The priorities contained in *The NHS Improvement Plan* were important in indicating how the additional funding for the NHS announced in the 2002 spending review would be used in the second half of the five year period covered by the review. With the bulk of this funding going into further reductions in waiting times for treatment and the expansion of patient choice, ministers in effect committed themselves to bring an end to waiting for hospital treatment, thereby transforming patients' experience of NHS care.

The means of achieving the objectives contained in *The NHS Improvement Plan* were those set out in *Delivering the NHS Plan*, albeit with greater emphasis on the role of commissioners in bringing about improvements in performance. Specifically, *The NHS Improvement Plan* highlighted the role of PCTs in commissioning care for their populations, and it also argued that GP practices needed to be closely involved in commissioning services. The importance of commissioners in the health reform programme was underlined in subsequent policy documents, most importantly *Commissioning a Patient-Led NHS* published in July 2005 (Crisp, 2005). This document gave a clear indication that as PCTs focused increasingly on promoting the health of their populations and commissioning care, they should cease being direct providers of services. It also reiterated the need for GP practices to play a major part in commissioning services and stated that PCTs should make arrangements to ensure universal coverage of 'practice based commissioning' by the end of 2006. The interest shown by the government in practice based commissioning, and the strong parallels with GP fundholding in the 1990s, reinforced the feeling that the Blair government was turning the clock back to the internal market reforms of the Thatcher and Major governments. *Commissioning a Patient-Led NHS* identified the need to put in place the right configuration for commissioning, followed by a programme of development support to enable commissioners to do their job effectively. In response, plans were put forward for reconfiguring PCTs, and proposals were also formulated for reducing the number of strategic health authorities (SHAs) to achieve closer alignment with Government Office boundaries.

In the event, the proposal that PCTs should give up their role as direct providers of care met with opposition from trade unions representing NHS staff who feared that it might lead to the privatisation of the services run by PCTs. Ministers responded by dropping this proposal while continuing with the other changes outlined in *Commissioning a Patient-Led NHS*. Following a period of public consultation and advice from an independent review panel, the government decided to reduce the number of SHAs from 28 to 10 from July 2006, and to cut the number of PCTs from 303 to 152 from October 2006. The principal raison d'être for the reconfiguration of PCTs was to create fewer, larger commissioning bodies able to negotiate on equal terms with health care providers. Also important in many parts of the country was the desire to achieve coterminosity between PCTs and local authorities in order to facilitate joint working on issues of common concern. The new structure of the NHS in England is illustrated in Figure 3.3.

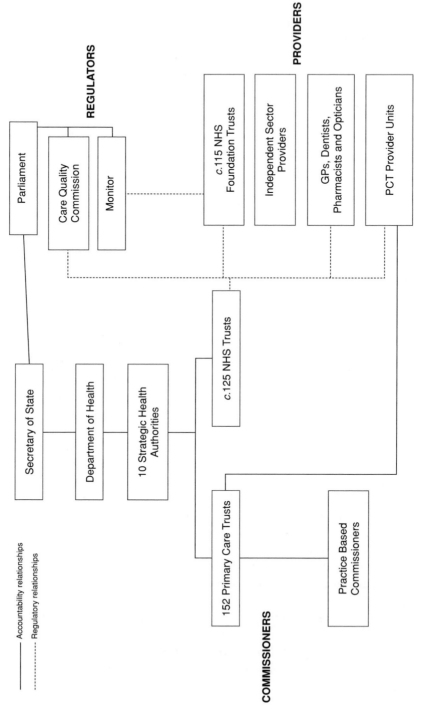

Figure 3.3 *The structure of the NHS in England in 2009*

Accountability relationships
Regulatory relationships

REGULATORS

PROVIDERS

COMMISSIONERS

Parliament

Care Quality Commission

Monitor

Secretary of State

Department of Health

10 Strategic Health Authorities

c.125 NHS Trusts

152 Primary Care Trusts

Practice Based Commissioners

c.115 NHS Foundation Trusts

Independent Sector Providers

GPs, Dentists, Pharmacists and Opticians

PCT Provider Units

The health reform programme

In parallel with changes to the structure of the NHS, ministers sought to clarify the direction of the health reform programme in general and the role of commissioning in particular. Figure 3.4 illustrates the framework developed by the Department of Health to describe the health reform programme and the way in which supply-side reforms, demand-side reforms, transactional reforms and system management reforms were intended to lead to better care, better patient experience and better value for money. Policy documents published in December 2005 and July 2006 (DH, 2005, 2006a) built on the plans originally outlined in *Delivering the NHS Plan* to describe how NHS foundation trusts working alongside providers from the private and voluntary sectors would offer patients a

Figure 3.4 *Framework of the health reforms*

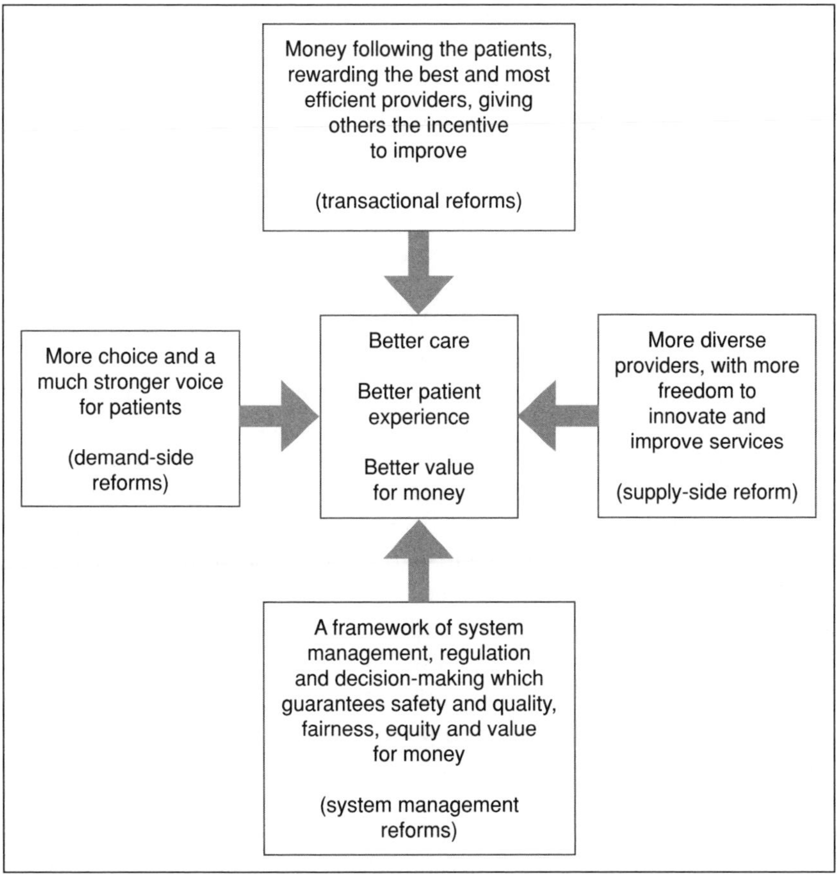

Money following the patients, rewarding the best and most efficient providers, giving others the incentive to improve

(transactional reforms)

More choice and a much stronger voice for patients

(demand-side reforms)

Better care

Better patient experience

Better value for money

More diverse providers, with more freedom to innovate and improve services

(supply-side reform)

A framework of system management, regulation and decision-making which guarantees safety and quality, fairness, equity and value for money

(system management reforms)

Source: DH (2005).

wider range of choices. Patient choice would be supported by a new system of commissioning involving GP practices and PCTs, and by payment by results under which money was intended to follow patients to the best and most efficient providers. These reforms were underpinned by a framework of system management, including arrangements for inspection and regulation.

The guiding philosophy behind the government's plans was to achieve 'a decisive shift from top-down to bottom-up as we develop a devolved and self-improving health service where the main drivers of change are patients, commissioners and clinicians, rather than national targets and performance management' (DH, 2006a, p.5) – a clear echo not only of the ideas set out in *Delivering the NHS Plan* in 2002 but also the proposals contained in *Shifting the Balance of Power* in 2001. The Secretary of State for Health at the time the 2005 and 2006 health reform documents were published, Patricia Hewitt, described the reform programme as being about modern public services rather than markets (Hewitt, 2005), thereby echoing the reluctance of her Conservative predecessors to be explicit about the role of competition in health care (see the beginning of this chapter for similar statements from Conservative politicians).

Guidance on health care commissioning was published as part of the 2006 health reform update. As well as setting out the roles of PCTs and practice based commissioners, and the core functions involved in commissioning, the Department signalled a commitment to make use of the skills of private sector companies with expertise in commissioning to offer the NHS. It also announced that a development programme would be made available to enable the staff involved in commissioning to strengthen their skills. Various sources of support for commissioners were also offered, including a national model contract and an inventory of care and resource utilisation techniques. The main focus of the guidance was commissioning of hospital services and further advice was promised for other areas of care, such as health and well-being. The emphasis placed on commissioning reflected belated recognition that the health reforms had initially concentrated on the development of providers and payment by results, and risked being out of kilter unless commissioners received the same attention. Subsequently, ministers spoke of the need to develop 'world class commissioning' in a further signal that this aspect of the reform programme had risen to the top of the policy agenda.

In parallel with these developments, the government undertook a consultation on the future regulation of health and adult social care in England. The consultation arose out of the shift from a hierarchically managed to a regulated health care system and the need to review the roles of the Healthcare Commission, the Commission for Social Care Inspection, the Mental Health Act Commission, and Monitor, the independent regulator of NHS foundation trusts. In the light of the consultation, the government decided to create an integrated regulator – the Care Quality Commission – bringing together the functions of the Healthcare Commission, the Commission for Social Care Inspection and the Mental Health Act Commission, with effect from April 2009. Monitor's role as the independent regulator of NHS foundation trusts was not affected by this decision.

Gordon Brown and the NHS Next Stage Review

When Gordon Brown succeeded Tony Blair as Prime Minister in June 2007 there was widespread speculation on the direction the health reform programme would take, and in particular whether the market-oriented policies favoured by Blair would be embraced by Brown. Early indications from the government were mixed with the Prime Minister and his new Secretary of State, Alan Johnson, announcing a scaling back of the ISTC programme while at the same time maintaining support for the private sector to offer its expertise to NHS commissioners. The Brown government also signalled its intention to open up primary care provision to a wider range of providers as part of a policy of extending patient choice in primary care.

Further detail emerged at the beginning of 2008 in the Prime Minister's first major speech on the NHS. Key themes in the speech were the need for the benefits of medical advances to be made available in the NHS, the importance of the prevention of illness as well as the treatment of sickness, the increasing significance of long-term medical conditions and the services provided to people with these conditions, the need for patients to recognise their responsibilities alongside their rights, and the value offered by the NHS as 'the best insurance system for the long term' (Ham, 2008a, p. 53). In emphasising these themes, the Prime Minister was adding points of emphasis to existing policies rather than proposing major points of departure. Missing from the speech was any discussion of how these priorities were to be implemented and the extent to which competition or other mechanisms would be used to enable implementation.

Part of the explanation of this omission was that the Prime Minister and the Secretary of State for Health asked one of the new Health Ministers, Lord Darzi, to lead a review of the next stage of reform in July 2007 with the aim of it being published before the 60th anniversary of the NHS on 5 July 2008. The NHS Next Stage Review, as it became known, was based on extensive engagement with staff and patients, and drew on Lord Darzi's experience of conducting a similar review in London. An interim report published in October 2007 endorsed the broad direction of health reform and highlighted a number of new priorities, including improving access to primary care, and building on progress made in improving the NHS to develop a world class service. The final report, *High Quality Care for All* (Secretary of State for Health, 2008a), focused particularly on the need to improve the quality of health care and patient safety. In so doing, it emphasised the need for staff to lead quality and service improvement and to strengthen staff engagement and leadership to enable this to happen. Although *High Quality Care for All* neither endorsed nor rejected the role of competition in health care, a review of the Brown government's approach to public service reform published at the same time sent out a clear signal that the new Prime Minister did not share his predecessor's enthusiasm for market based reform. Rather, like Lord Darzi's NHS Next Stage Review, it argued that changing public services depended on empowering citizens, fostering a new professionalism and providing strong leadership (Cabinet Office Strategy Unit, 2008).

Importantly, during the course of the NHS Next Stage Review, the government announced the outcome of the 2007 comprehensive spending review. The spending review took place in the context of deficits in many NHS organisations and increasing concern in government and the media at the apparent inability of these organisations to balance their books even with the big increases in resources that had been allocated. As had been widely expected, the spending review marked the end of the period of rapid growth in NHS expenditure that started at the beginning of the decade. At a time when public spending increases were constrained by deteriorating economic conditions, the spending review resulted in planned increases in the NHS budget of 4 per cent a year in real terms. The relatively generous settlement for the NHS compared with other public services was interpreted as a sign of Gordon Brown's commitment to strengthening the NHS, albeit using somewhat different instruments of reform than those favoured by his predecessor. At the same time, the government announced that it was initiating a review of funding of long-term care with the aim of publishing a Green Paper setting out options for reform (see Chapter 5).

The impact of the reforms

Early assessments of the impact of New Labour's health reforms, as summarised in the last edition of this book, offered a broadly positive verdict on progress made in the period up to 2003. The most comprehensive and independent of these assessments, commissioned by the Nuffield Trust, concluded that 'Qualitative and quantitative data indicate that mid-term overall performance is trending in the right direction, most particularly in those areas on which attention and effort has been focused by policy mandates, performance-reporting requirements and extrinsic incentives' (Leatherman and Sutherland, 2003, p. 265). Similarly, the King's Fund acknowledged the government's achievements and concluded that 'the direction of travel seems to us to be well judged and much of the detail is admirable. More credit is due than is currently paid (Appleby and Coote, 2002, p. 7). For their part, both the Audit Commission and the CHI offered even handed assessments, noting areas of achievement as well as outstanding challenges (Audit Commission, 2003; CHI, 2003).

Five years on, all of these organisations delivered more cautious and in many ways more critical judgements on the impact of the reforms. The King's Fund's assessment of ten years of the Labour government acknowledged the increases in funding that had occurred and the use of this funding to employ more staff and build new hospitals (Thorlby and Maybin, 2007). Like other reviews of the government's record, the King's Fund particularly highlighted reductions in waiting times for treatment in both hospitals and primary care as one of the government's most significant achievements. On the other side of the balance sheet, the challenge of healthcare associated infection was emphasised. In relation to the management of the NHS, the King's Fund drew attention to the existence of deficits in around one-third of NHS organisations, and it concluded that there was little evidence that successive structural changes to the NHS had brought any benefits. This assessment was explored in greater detail in the King's Fund's review of NHS funding and performance led by Derek Wanless (Wanless et al., 2007). The Wanless review emphasised in particular the high cost of the new contracts for GPs, consultants and other staff introduced by the government, and the failure to bring about improvements in productivity. The implications of the government's mixed record on public health were also highlighted, with the review expressing concerns about widening health inequalities and increasing rates of obesity.

Many of these points were echoed in the Nuffield Trust's assessment of the impact of the reforms on health care quality (Leatherman and Sutherland, 2008). While noting major improvements in the quality of care since 1997, the authors of this assessment argued that these improvements had not been commensurate with the investment that had occurred. A number of explanations were offered for this, including an ideological rift between advocates of central control and supporters of devolution within the NHS; a predisposition to structural change and reorganisation with adverse consequences for staff morale; a tendency to promote new policies as 'flavour of the month'; perennial problems with coordination of care, duplication of effort and territorialism; strong policy conceptualisation that was unmatched by the requisite competence in implementation; and deficiencies in availability of data to report on quality improvement. To address these challenges, the authors called for the establishment of an English National Quality Programme for the NHS to develop a coherent and integrated approach and to refine the reform agenda.

The assessment prepared by the Audit Commission and the Healthcare Commission (2008a) focused particularly on progress with the implementation of the government's health reforms, specifically patient choice, payment by results, NHS foundation trusts, greater NHS use of the private sector, and the development of commissioning. In line with the other reviews summarised here, the Audit Commission and the Healthcare Commission gave the government credit for significant progress in improving the performance of the NHS, as evidenced by much shorter waiting times and other improvements summarised in the Healthcare Commission's annual health check. However, they noted that progress had resulted mainly from increases in funding and the use of national targets, rather than the market-oriented reforms introduced by the Blair government. There was no evidence that patient choice had had a significant impact, the results achieved by NHS foundation trusts were not striking, and commissioning remained a weak link in the reform programme. Although noting that some of the reforms had been implemented too recently to enable a proper assessment to be made, and that the programme as a whole had potential for the future, the Audit Commission and the Healthcare Commission concluded that there were a number of barriers to further progress, including the need to engage staff more effectively in the process of change. As we have noted, this recommendation was addressed in the final report of the NHS Next Stage Review led by Lord Darzi.

Work carried out by the Office for National Statistics (ONS) (2008a) analysed changes in NHS productivity between 1995 and 2006. This work found that productivity fell by an average of 1 per cent a year during this period. The fall in productivity was particularly marked between 2001 and 2005 even after allowing for changes in the quality of care, which have not usually been included in measures of NHS productivity. The findings of the ONS were broadly consistent with those of the King's Fund Review of NHS funding and performance led by Derek Wanless. Factors that helped to explain declining productivity included increases in the number of staff employed in the NHS, following from *The NHS Plan*, high growth in the volume of goods and services purchased, and the cost of the new contracts for GPs, consultants and other staff introduced by the government. These increases in inputs were not matched with commensurate rises in output, although the ONS acknowledged that improvements in quality not included in its assessment might have resulted in bigger increases in output than it had estimated. The analyses undertaken by the ONS contributed to the argument that the NHS reforms had failed to deliver improvements consistent with the scale of the investment that had occurred.

Conclusion

In this chapter we have described the policies of the Blair and Brown governments towards the NHS. In the process we have noted the strong element of continuity between the latter stages of the Conservative government and the approach pursued by the New Labour government. There were of course differences between politicians but these were much less significant than might have been expected in view of the debate that took place on *Working for Patients* a decade earlier. Continuity was born out of convergence which resulted from movement on both sides. The third way pursued by the Blair government incorporated important elements of the reforms initiated by the Thatcher and Major governments and was facilitated by the retreat on the part of Conservative politicians from the pro-market policies of the early 1990s. It also illustrated the extent of the change that had occurred within the Labour Party itself involving the development of policies to modernise public services as a whole and not just the NHS.

The evolution of health policy in the 1990s indicates the influence of learning in the policy process. On the one hand, Conservative ministers adjusted course in the light of experience and feedback on what was working (and what was acceptable) and what was not working in the implementation of *Working for Patients*. On the other hand, Labour politicians were willing to take a pragmatic approach, emphasising that 'what counts is what works' and avoiding the temptation to engage in knee-jerk opposition to policies initiated by their opponents. The scope for learning extended to the implementation of *The New NHS* which, like *Working for Patients*, provided a broad framework only and offered the opportunity for policy to be shaped and remade as it was carried into action, and to *The NHS Plan*. Equally important was the learning that occurred about the effectiveness of national targets and central controls over the management of the NHS, and the shift that started in 2001 towards a more devolved, market-oriented approach.

To make this point is to underline the argument of Heclo (1974) and others that policy-making is both an arena in which there is bargaining between different interests and a focus for puzzling about ways of tackling social problems. The balance between bargaining and puzzling varies between issues and over time. In the case of health policy in Britain, the political struggles of the late 1980s and early 1990s gave way to a greater degree of analysis and reflection as the decade wore on. To be sure, there remained strong disagreements within the government and between government and outside interests about the detail of policy and to some degree the direction of change, as in debates about NHS foundation trusts and ISTCs, but these disagreements need to be seen in the context of the large measure of consensus that existed. Having emphasised the politics of policy-making in the previous chapter, the focus on learning in this chapter draws attention to another important aspect of the policy process.

While the changes to the organisation of the NHS initiated by the Blair and Brown governments were being implemented, the debate about NHS funding and rationing simmered in the background. This debate was not new but it assumed particular intensity in this period as the ability of the NHS to continue providing universal and comprehensive services came under scrutiny. To understand the context of this debate we now go on to review long-term trends in the funding of the NHS and the way in which successive governments have set priorities for public health and health care through White Papers, national service frameworks and other means.

Chapter 4

Financing Health Services and the Rediscovery of Public Health

The aim of this chapter is to describe key issues in the financing of health services and the Wanless reviews of the long-term funding of health care and of public health. The rationale for considering the financing of health services alongside policy on public health derives from the assessment in the Wanless review of the long-term funding of health care that concerted action was needed on public health to ensure the financial sustainability of the NHS. The chapter begins with an analysis of trends in NHS expenditure and an assessment of the sources of funding and its distribution. This leads into a discussion of the Wanless review of the long-term funding of health care and its argument that the NHS spending should increase significantly. Policy on public health since the 1970s is then reviewed including the Wanless review of public health and its impact. The chapter concludes by assessing what has been achieved in the area of public health.

The growth of NHS expenditure

One of the assumptions made in the Beveridge Report was that expenditure on health services would decline once the backlog of ill health which was thought to exist in the community had been eradicated by the introduction of a health service free at the point of use. This assumption turned out to be false and, far from declining, expenditure increased steadily in the years after the establishment of the NHS. Whereas in its first full year of operation the Service cost £447 million to run (as Table 4.1 shows), by 2007 expenditure in the United Kingdom (UK) had risen to an estimated £104 billion. Over the same period the real cost of the NHS increased ninefold, and the NHS share of total public expenditure rose from 11.8 per cent in 1950 to an estimated 18.1 per cent in 2006 (Office of Health Economics, 2008) .

These increases were necessary to enable the NHS to meet the demands created by changes in demography, technology and society. Analysts of health services pointed out that there was not a fixed quantity of disease,

Table 4.1 *NHS expenditure in the UK, 1949–2006*

Calendar year	Total (£m)	Total NHS cost at 1949 prices (£m)
1949	447	447
1955	596	464
1960	883	568
1965	1,306	723
1970	2,046	882
1975	5,358	1,218
1980	11,677	1,341
1985	17,514	1,476
1990	29,178	1,824
1995	42,326	2,251
2000	58,279	2,745
2006	104,672	4,204

as the idea of a backlog of ill health implied, but rather there was potentially infinite demand (Thwaites, 1987). This was because of the greater use of services by older people and their increasing numbers in the population; the opportunities for diagnosis and treatment opened up by developments in medical technology; and the emergence of a new generation of service users with higher expectations of the standard of care to be provided. Although the importance of these factors varied from year to year and was difficult to quantify, taken together they added to the pressures confronting the NHS and helped fuel the increase in expenditure over time. Another way of expressing this increase is shown in Figure 4.1 which illustrates the share of the gross domestic product consumed by the NHS rising from 3.5 per cent in 1949 to over 7 per cent in 2006. In that year, total health expenditure in the UK exceeded 8 per cent and was just below the European Union average.

The size of the NHS budget is shaped by the state of the economy and government decisions on the priority to be attached to different spending programmes. High rates of growth in the 1960s and early 1970s gave way to lower increases in the late 1970s and 1980s. This change was stimulated by escalating oil prices which fuelled inflation and caused successive governments to take action to control public expenditure. One of the mechanisms used was cash limits which capped expenditure in most areas of NHS spending and imposed a strict financial discipline on those responsible for running services. The election of the Thatcher

Figure 4.1 *The cost of the NHS as a percentage of GDP, 1949–2006*

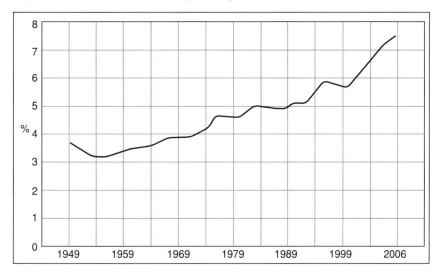

government in 1979 meant that spending continued to be tightly controlled as monetarist policies began to bite. The government gave priority to achieving economic prosperity through privatisation and competition, and social policy expenditure was subjected to close scrutiny. A strong emphasis was placed on using expenditure on public services like the NHS more efficiently, and we noted in Chapter 2 the wide range of efficiency initiatives launched during this period.

The purse strings were subsequently loosened as more money was allocated to the NHS between 1990 and 1993 to ease the introduction of the proposals set out in *Working for Patients*. Growth rates were then much lower until the completion of the comprehensive spending review initiated by the Blair government on its election in 1997. These lower rates of growth reflected the state of the economy and the concern of both Conservative and Labour politicians to be seen to be responsible in their public spending plans. As we noted in Chapter 3, the comprehensive spending review resulted in much higher increases in NHS funding from 1999, but even so these increases did not prevent a crisis emerging during the winter of 1999/2000. It was in response to this crisis that the Prime Minister made his commitment in 2000 to bring health care spending in the UK up to the European Union average, and the Wanless review provided the post hoc justification for the significant increases in spending that then followed (see below). The 2007 comprehensive spending review resulted in the NHS budget being increased by 4 per cent per year in real terms between 2008 and 2011. The global financial crisis that began in 2007 held out the prospect that spending on the NHS would increase much more slowly after 2011, if at all. With the economy in recession, and government using public resources to support commercial banks in difficulty and other economic priorities, the NHS and other public services entered a period of austerity unprecedented in its recent history.

Alongside public expenditure on health care, private spending accounts for around 13 per cent of total health care expenditure (OECD, 2008). Private expenditure is made up of the charges paid by patients for NHS prescriptions, dental care and ophthalmic services, as well as spending on services that are provided privately. The latter may be paid for out of pocket or under the terms of private medical insurance. Around 7.5 million people or 12 per cent of the population are covered by private medical insurance in the UK. The number of people with insurance has increased steadily throughout the lifetime of the NHS and expansion was particularly rapid in the 1980s. The majority of subscribers are in group schemes, especially those offered by companies as fringe benefits, and the main services provided are outpatient appointments with specialists and quicker access to non-urgent surgery than is available within the NHS. Recent trends indicate that the total number of people covered by private medical insurance has remained relatively stable since the early 1990s, although there has been a reduction in the number of individual policyholders from a peak of 1.46 million in 1996 to a low of 1.09 million at the end of 2007. One of the factors that has influenced the uptake of private medical insurance is the high cost of cover and premium increases above the level of inflation. This is despite the entry of new commercial companies into the market in the 1990s to compete with the British United Provident Association (BUPA) and other insurers (Foubister et al., 2006).

International comparisons show that expenditure on health care in the UK as a proportion of gross domestic product has been lower than in many other developed countries in the past, though recent increases in spending on the NHS have narrowed the gap considerably. This is illustrated in Figure 4.2. Analysis of variations in health service expenditure between countries indicates that levels of spending are closely related to levels of national income and that the UK spends about what would be expected given the pattern of economic development in the post-war period. The main difference between the UK and other countries is in the composition of health service spending, with private expenditure making up a smaller proportion of the total in the UK than the average for OECD countries. This has led some commentators to argue that the funding pressures under which the NHS operates should be addressed by encouraging private expenditure to increase to the levels

Figure 4.2 *International comparison of expenditure on health care, 2005*

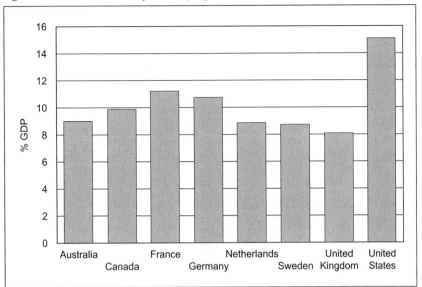

found elsewhere. Recent debates about allowing patients to top up the care provided by the NHS by paying themselves for expensive cancer drugs not yet approved by the National Institute for Health and Clinical Excellence (NICE) suggest that the public/private mix in health care spending will continue to be a focus of controversy, and we discuss this further in Chapter 12.

Whatever the merits of these arguments, it is clear that the NHS is an effective mechanism for controlling expenditure on health care, certainly in comparison with many other countries. The corollary is that this may create problems, as when a series of years of expenditure constraint require staff in the NHS to cut back or delay the provision of services in order to balance their budgets. This is precisely what happened in 1987, and the funding crisis in that year forced the Thatcher government to set up its review of the NHS. These funding pressures reappeared in the late 1990s after several years of low growth in spending and were accompanied by debates about the rationing of health services and the denial of treatment to patients. We noted in the previous chapter the decision of the Blair government to increase NHS funding in response to these pressures and we now discuss the Wanless review set up subsequently to examine the long-term funding requirements of the NHS.

The Wanless review of the long-term funding needs of the NHS

In March 2001 the Chancellor of the Exchequer, Gordon Brown, announced the establishment of a review of the long-term funding needs of health care led by Derek Wanless, former Group Chief Executive of NatWest Bank. The terms of reference of the review were:

1. To examine the technological, demographic and medical trends over the next two decades that may affect the health service in the UK as a whole.
2. In the light of (1), to identify the key factors which will determine the financial and other resources required to ensure that the NHS can provide a publicly funded, comprehensive, high quality service available on the basis of clinical need and not ability to pay.
3. To report to the Chancellor by April 2002, to allow him to consider the possible implications of this analysis for the Government's wider fiscal and economic strategies in the medium term; and to inform decisions in the next spending review in 2002. (Wanless, 2001, p. 1)

The link between the setting up of the Wanless review and the 2002 spending review was important in signalling the intention of using the results of the work undertaken by Wanless to inform future decisions on NHS spending.

Wanless published an interim report in November 2001 as a basis for consultation. In a wide ranging analysis, the report concluded that there was no evidence that tax financing of health care should be replaced either by social insurance or private funding. The interim report went on to note that the UK lagged behind some other countries in health outcomes and argued that this was in part because of the relatively low level of expenditure on health care in the UK. It identified a number of factors likely to increase spending on health care over a 20-year period including rising patient and public expectations and advances in medical technology, although the scale of the increase was not estimated.

The final Wanless report was published in April 2002 and largely confirmed the conclusions of the interim report. The main additional points to arise from consultation on the interim report were the need for stronger links between health and social care, and for greater emphasis on health promotion and disease prevention. Unlike the interim report, the final Wanless report provided estimates of the costs of achieving its vision of a health service better able to meet the public's expectations of accessible, convenient and high quality care. These estimates were based on three alternative scenarios, described as:

scenario 1: *solid progress* – people become more engaged in relation to their health. Life expectancy rises considerably, health status improves and people have confidence in the primary care system and use it more appropriately. The health service becomes more responsive, with high rates of technology uptake, extensive use of ICT and more efficient use of resources;

scenario 2: *slow uptake* – there is no change in the level of public engagement. Life expectancy rises, but by the smallest amount in all three scenarios. The health status of the population is constant or deteriorates. The health service is relatively unresponsive with low rates of technology uptake and low productivity; and

scenario 3: *fully engaged* – levels of public engagement in relation to their health are high. Life expectancy increases go beyond current forecasts, health status improves dramatically and people are confident in the health system and demand high quality care. The health service is responsive with high rates of technology uptake, particularly in relation to disease prevention. Use of resources is more efficient. (Wanless, 2002, p. 9)

Figure 4.3 displays spending estimates for these three scenarios. As the figure shows, the final Wanless report argued for higher rates of spending increases in the first five years of the period reviewed to enable the UK to *catch up* with other countries. Beyond the first five years, lower rates of spending increases were recommended to enable the UK to *keep up* with other countries. In making these recommendations, the report emphasised the importance of resources being used effectively. This included proposals for a role for NICE in examining older technologies and practices that might no longer be appropriate and effective, the extension of national service frameworks to areas not already covered, and a major programme of investment in ICT based on central standards.

The final Wanless report confirmed that 'the current method of funding the NHS through taxation is relatively efficient and equitable' (p. 13) but added that 'there may be some scope to extend charges for non-clinical services. This would potentially help provide more choice for patients' (p. 13). In practice, this recommendation received relatively little attention in the context of the report's main finding that there was a need for a very substantial increase in resources for health care over the long term. This finding was accepted by the government and was reflected in the outcome of the 2002 spending review: an increase in NHS funding averaging over 7 per cent a year in real terms in the period up to 2007/08. The 2002 spending review also resulted in a substantial increase in social care spending, although the increase was

Figure 4.3 *Average annual real growth proposed by Wanless (percentage)*

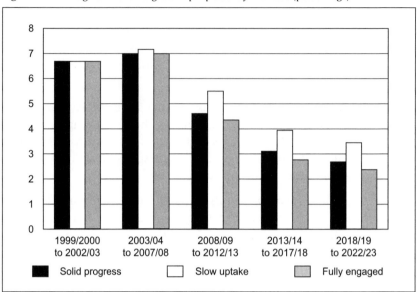

lower than that made available to the NHS. This was in part to compensate for previous spending reviews that had not benefited social care to the same extent as the NHS, and which as a consequence had contributed to the problems of discharging patients from hospital and achieving key targets.

The Wanless review did not break new ground but it did serve an important function in making the case for a sustained increase in health care funding. Although the government's critics argued that Wanless was appointed by the Chancellor to lend legitimacy to decisions announced by the Prime Minister in 2000, the manner in which the review was conducted, including consultation with outside experts and the use of research on international experience of health care financing (Dixon and Mossialos, 2002), meant that Wanless could claim a degree of independence that an internal review could not. In any case, there was little serious dissent from the conclusion that additional resources were required, even if there remained differences as to the rate of increase in spending the NHS could absorb and doubts about the ability of the government to achieve a fundamental change in the performance of the NHS. These doubts were reinforced by evidence published at the time of the Wanless review that appeared to show declining efficiency in the NHS in the late 1990s (Le Grand, 2002).

Raising and spending money in the NHS

NHS funds come from three sources. In 2006/07, over three-quarters of NHS funds derived from taxation, and around one-fifth were raised through national insurance contributions (DH, 2006b). The remainder came from charges and other receipts, including income from land sales and the proceeds of income generation schemes. User charges have always comprised a small proportion of total NHS expenditure and this continues to be the case. Dental charges make up the biggest source of income from patients followed by prescription charges.

How is the NHS budget spent? The biggest proportion is allocated to current expenditure on hospitals, community health services and family health services. The remainder is allocated to capital expenditure on hospitals and community health services, departmental administration and central health and miscellaneous services. A more detailed breakdown of hospital and community health services' current expenditure shows that the largest share of expenditure (63 per cent) goes on acute services, including accident and emergency services, followed by mental health (14 per cent), community health services (12 per cent), learning disability (4 per cent) and maternity (3 per cent) (DH, 2008a, p.155).

In the case of family health services expenditure, the biggest proportion of the budget goes on payments to general practitioners (41 per cent), followed by drugs (39 per cent), dentists (11 per cent), pharmacists (7 per cent) and opticians (2 per cent). Another way of looking at how the money is spent is to analyse expenditure by different age groups. As Figure 4.4 shows, expenditure is particularly high at the time of birth and among older people. The rising trend of expenditure with age explains why the ageing population adds to the demands facing the NHS.

Staff salaries and wages are the largest single item of expenditure in the NHS as a whole, comprising around two-thirds of the total. Approximately 1.3 million people were employed in the NHS in 2007, and around half of these staff were professionally qualified. They included 400,000 nurses, midwives and health visitors, 95,000 hospital and public health doctors, 137,000 scientific, therapeutic and technical support staff, and 17,000 qualified ambulance staff. Around 564,000 staff provided support to professionally qualified staff or worked in managerial or administrative roles. As well as these directly employed staff, there were around 33,000 general practitioners, 21,000 dentists, 10,000 pharmacists and 9000 opticians working as independent contractors. The number of staff working in the NHS has increased as part of the expansion outlined in *The NHS Plan*.

While almost all of the NHS budget is allocated according to a weighted capitation formula, some resources are set aside for specific

Figure 4.4 *Distribution of hospital and community health services expenditure by age group for 2003–04*

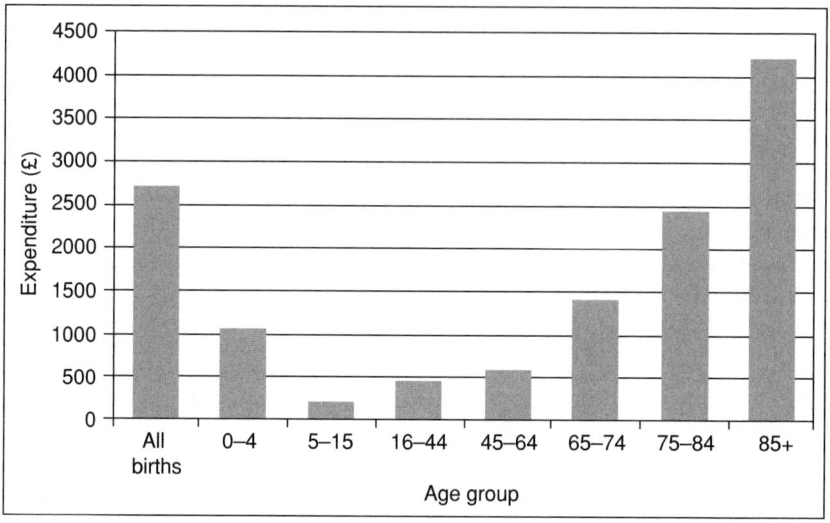

Source: DH (2006b).

purposes. Earmarking funds in this way was used by the Blair government to ensure that priority was given to particular services and needs. Recently there has been a move away from earmarking funds for specific purposes in favour of block allocations to PCTs, leaving them with the discretion to decide how to use these allocations to meet the needs of the populations they serve.

NHS capital expenditure has traditionally been provided and controlled by the Treasury in the same way as revenue expenditure. In the first decade of the NHS, funds for capital development were limited and only on publication of the Hospital Plan in 1962 did this change. More recently, NHS trusts have been encouraged by both Conservative and Labour Governments to seek resources through the private finance initiative (PFI). This is a scheme under which public sector capital projects like new hospitals are paid for via money loaned by banks. Initially, PFI was used for minor NHS schemes such as car parks and incinerators, but it is now applied to major projects including the rebuilding of entire hospitals. Private sector involvement in these projects encompasses not only the provision of capital, but also facilities management and the development of services in partnership with the NHS. *The NHS Plan* made a commitment that 100 hospital building schemes would be delivered by the end of 2010 and the use of PFI together with some continuing capital investment from public sources means that this target will be achieved (DH, 2008a). A sister initiative, the NHS Local Improvement Finance Trust (LIFT), was set up to support the development of public–private partnerships in rela-tion to primary care premises. By 2008 there were 48 NHS LIFT schemes and these had delivered over 160 new primary care premises with a further 50 under construction.

The costs and benefits of both LIFT and PFI have been widely debated. In raising money for new NHS buildings from the private sector, they are attractive for governments seeking to limit public borrowing by appear-ing to take capital expenditure off the public sector balance sheet. On the other hand, the costs of borrowing from the private sector have to be met through annual payments by NHS bodies, and the high level of these payments puts pressure on NHS budgets. The supporters of private finance argue that the costs involved are more than outweighed by the speed with which projects funded in this way are completed and the inno-vation and quality they offer. For their part, critics contend that PFI is a more expensive way of paying for new buildings than public capital, and that the additional costs have resulted in the building of hospitals with insufficient capacity (Gaffney et al., 1999).

These critics also maintain that hospitals built through PFI are forced to seek other sources of income to cover their costs and that the private compa-nies involved in PFI schemes are earning excess profits from the taxpayer (Pollock et al., 1999). A further argument is that PFI locks the NHS into long-term contracts to pay for services and buildings that may not always be appropriate for the duration of these contracts. Partly in recognition of this, the government undertook a review of planned PFI schemes in 2006, and the White Paper, *Our Health, Our Care, Our Say* (Secretary of State for Health, 2006), emphasised that the planning of capital schemes should be consistent with the move of services out of hospitals. In the event, most of the planned schemes went ahead, although some were scaled back. Changes in international accounting rules introduced in 2009 mean that PFI counts as part of government borrowing and this is likely to lessen its attraction as a way of funding public sector capital developments.

There has also been extensive debate about the Blair government's decision to procure additional capacity from the private sector to treat NHS patients on waiting lists as part of the independent sector treatment centre (ISTC) programme (see Chapter 3). As well as providing additional capacity, it was expected that ISTCs would be a source of innovation by introducing more efficient ways of treating patients and delivering serv-ices. This was a major part of the rationale for using the private sector to provide treatment centres for the delivery of care to NHS patients rather than simply creating treatment centres within NHS hospitals, even though this had been the model used at the pioneering Central Middlesex Ambu-latory Care and Diagnostic Centre and that was later adapted in the development of some NHS treatment centres.

A national programme was launched at the end of 2002 to procure a number of ISTCs in different parts of the country at a cost of £1.7 billion in the first wave of procurement, covering a five year period (Health Committee, 2006, p. 10). A second wave of procurement followed in 2005 encompassing both diagnostic and treatment capacity in support of the target of achieving a maximum waiting time of 18 weeks from GP referral to treatment by the end of 2008. The estimated cost of the second wave of procurement was £3.75 billion over five years (Health Committee, 2006, p. 14). In parallel, agreements were reached with existing private hospitals to make use of their spare capacity to treat NHS patients. The first ISTC opened in October 2003 and by 2008 there were around 30 in operation in England, including a number providing mobile diagnostic and treatment services.

An inquiry by the Health Committee that reported in 2006 found there was evidence that ISTCs had helped to reduce the prices paid by the NHS for the treatment of patients in private facilities. This was despite the fact that the prices paid to ISTCs were on average 11 per cent higher than equivalent NHS costs in the first wave and is explained by the very high prices the NHS used to pay when it undertook spot purchasing of spare private sector capacity. The Committee noted too that ISTCs had increased the choices available to patients and had demonstrated good practice, while adding that NHS providers also showed evidence of innovation in the delivery of services. Among the concerns noted by the Committee were the lack of integration of ISTCs with the NHS, and the paucity of data on the quality of care they provided. A similar conclusion was reached by the Healthcare Commission which called for greater consistency and comparability in the data used to compare performance in the NHS and ISTCs (Healthcare Commission, 2007a).

Overall, the Health Committee found it difficult to assess the value for money of the ISTC programme and concluded that other options, such as the development of NHS treatment centres and the use of spare capacity in established private hospitals, might have been preferable. For its part, the Healthcare Commission reported that patient experience of ISTCs was generally positive, while also endorsing the need for closer integration with NHS services. A related concern was the nature of staffing arrangements in ISTCs and the need for these to be strengthened. Other commentators were more critical, drawing on the findings of the Health Committee and the Healthcare Commission to highlight the weaknesses in the government's approach and commenting:

The failure to require independent sector treatment centres – which treat NHS patients – to provide data on the same basis as the NHS raises serious accountability issues. So too does government failure to collect and publish relevant data on the productivity, performance and quality of these centres (Pollock and Godden, 2008, p. 423).

We return to discuss the impact of ISTCs in Chapter 12.

Public health and health improvement

We noted in Chapter 1 the importance of public health measures in the nineteenth century in contributing to improvements in population health. During the twentieth century, more attention was given to the development of hospitals and medical services than to public health as advances in medicine opened up increasing opportunities for diagnosis and treatment. The focus on organised health services was maintained after the establishment of the NHS and not until the 1970s was the importance of public health and prevention rediscovered. Key developments at that time were the analyses of McKeown (1976) and other writers who highlighted both the historical and contemporary contribution of public health to health improvement, and policy documents such as the Lalonde (1974) report in Canada that argued for a reorientation of health services towards prevention. These developments occurred in parallel with growing awareness of the importance of risk factors such as smoking in contributing to ill health, and immediately before a major review that showed the persistence of inequalities in health between socioeconomic groups. We now go on to describe the response of policy-makers and to assess the impact of the rediscovery of public health. After 1999 the governments of Northern Ireland, Scotland and Wales developed their own public health policies and these are discussed in Chapter 7.

Table 4.2 *Key public health policy documents*

1976 *Prevention and Health: Everybody's Business* (consultative document)
1977 *Prevention and Health* (White Paper)
1980 Black Report, *Inequalities in Health* (working group set up to advise government)
1992 *The Health of the Nation* (White Paper)
1998 Acheson Report, *Independent Inquiry into Inequalities and Health* (scientific advisory group set up to advise government)
1999 *Saving Lives: Our Healthier Nation* (White Paper)
2003 *Tackling Health Inequalities: A Programme for Action*
2004 *Securing Good Health for the Whole Population: Final Report* (the Wanless Public Health Review)
2004 *Choosing Health* (White Paper)

Policies in the 1970s and 1980s

The consultative document, *Prevention and Health: Everybody's Business* (DHSS, 1976d), was the first significant policy statement that focused on public health. The document noted that improvements in health in the previous century had resulted largely from the public health movement rather than specific medical interventions, and argued that further gains were dependent on people taking care of themselves by changing their lifestyle. Individuals were urged to stop smoking, take more exercise and adopt an appropriate diet in order to reduce the risk of ill health and death. These views were reiterated in a White Paper on *Prevention and Health*, published a year later (DHSS, 1977a), and a series of other publications gave advice on issues such as safety during pregnancy, eating for health and avoiding heart attacks.

A rather different approach was taken in the Black Report, *Inequalities in Health*, published in 1980. This report resulted from the deliberations of a working group set up to assemble information about differences in health status among the social classes and factors which might contribute to these differences. Following a comprehensive review of the available data, the working group concluded 'we wish to stress the importance of differences in material conditions of life' (Black Report, 1980, p. 357) in explaining social class inequalities in health. On this basis, the working group made a series of recommendations for reducing inequalities, in particular emphasising the importance of factors outside the NHS. The Thatcher government was not persuaded by the analysis and recommendations of the Black Report, and it was not until almost 20 years later that the Report was taken seriously by policy-makers following the Acheson inquiry established by the Blair government (see Chapter 10).

During the 1980s, particular attention was paid to the development of policies to limit the spread of HIV/AIDS. Earmarked funds were set aside to support work in this field with priority being given to preventing HIV/AIDS through changes in behaviour and the provision of information to the public about risk factors. This emphasis on changes in lifestyle was also reflected in the work of the Health Education Authority, the body responsible at the time for campaigns to improve health. The Authority initiated programmes on cigarette smoking, alcohol abuse and healthy eating, including the 1987 'Look After Your Heart' campaign. In parallel, the Thatcher government put forward proposals for preventing illness by strengthening the role of GPs, dentists and other providers of primary care (Secretary of State for Social Services and others, 1987). As we noted in Chapter 2, this included the implementation of new contracts for GPs and dentists which contained incentives to encourage health checks, vaccination and immunisation, screening, health promotion, and preventative dentistry.

The 1990s White Papers

In a White Paper entitled *The Health of the Nation* (Secretary of State for Health, 1992), the Major government set targets for the improvement of health in five key areas including HIV/AIDS. A Cabinet Committee was appointed to oversee implementation of the strategy in government as a whole, while at a local level health authorities through their directors of public health were expected to work with other agencies to counteract the conditions which give rise to ill health and to attach higher priority to prevention within the NHS. *The Health of the Nation* was superseded by the consultation paper, *Our Healthier Nation*, issued by the Blair government shortly after coming into office (Secretary of State for Health, 1998a). Although similar in some respects to *The Health of the Nation*, the consultation paper differed in placing greater emphasis on the social, economic and environmental causes of illness and in explicitly acknowledging the importance of inequalities in health. *Our Healthier Nation* identified two aims of the health strategy, namely:

> To improve the health of the population as a whole by increasing the length of people's lives and the number of years people spend free from illness. To improve the health of the worst off in society and to narrow the health gap. (Secretary of State for Health, 1998a, p. 5)

It went on to propose a national contract for better health in which government, local communities and individuals would work in partnership to improve health. The contract set out action by different agencies and the consultation paper also identified three settings for action: schools, workplaces and neighbourhoods. To signal its commitment to public health, the Blair government appointed the first Minister for Public Health, and it asked health authorities to develop health improvement programmes (HImPs) with partner organisations (see Chapter 3). In support of this initiative, a pilot programme of health action zones was established to develop new approaches to improving health in areas of high need.

Our Healthier Nation suggested the following aims for the year 2010:

- *Heart Disease and Stroke*: to reduce the death rate from heart disease and stroke and related illnesses amongst people aged under 65 years by at least a further third;
- *Accidents*: to reduce accidents by at least a fifth;
- *Cancer*: to reduce the death rate from cancer amongst people aged under 65 years by at least a further fifth;
- *Mental Health*: to reduce the death rate from suicide and undetermined injury by at least a further sixth.

Following consultation, the Blair government published the public health White Paper, *Saving Lives: Our Healthier Nation* (Secretary of State for Health, 1999), together with a report setting out how it was planning to respond to the Acheson inquiry on health inequalities. The White Paper confirmed the four priority areas as those identified in the consultation paper but gave greater emphasis to improving health in later life, for example by setting targets for health improvement in people aged under 75 and not under 65 as in the consultation paper. An overall aim of preventing up to 300,000 untimely and unnecessary deaths was set. The need for action across government was also emphasised in the response to the Acheson inquiry which enumerated actions being taken to address the inquiry's recommendations.

The public health agenda assumed renewed importance in response to the threat of global terrorism and the emergence of new infectious diseases such as sudden acute respiratory syndrome (SARS). The establishment of the Health Protection Agency in 2003 was in part a response to these challenges. The Agency brought together a number of bodies working in the field of health protection and emergency planning to provide a single focus for action in this area of public health. Among other priority areas of work, the Agency is responsible for leading action on improving the UK's preparedness for a future influenza pandemic.

The Wanless public health review and the smoking ban

The challenges involved in giving priority to public health were emphasised in a review undertaken by Derek Wanless at the invitation of the Prime Minister, the Chancellor of the Exchequer and the Secretary of State for Health in April 2003. The review followed directly from the first Wanless report on the long-term funding needs of the NHS and the argument in that report that the population needed to be fully engaged in prevention and health improvement to ensure the financial sustainability of the NHS. The report of the Wanless public health review acknowledged successes in improving the health of the population, as in the campaigns on HIV/AIDS, while also drawing attention to the risks posed by cigarette smoking, rising levels of obesity and overweight and other risk factors (Wanless, 2004). Wanless was particularly critical of the emphasis placed in *The NHS Plan* on improving the performance of the NHS to the neglect of public health issues, adding that rigorous implementation of effective policies was often lacking. To address these weaknesses, the report recommended that the government should develop a conceptual framework to take forward public health in a systematic way, including quantified national objectives and performance management of the NHS and local government to support implementation of these objectives.

Publication of the White Paper, *Choosing Health*, at the end of 2004 provided an opportunity to assess the government's response to the Wanless public health review (Secretary of State for Health, 2004b). The title of the White Paper sent out a clear signal that the government's approach was intended to support people to make healthy choices in a consumer society. Three core principles underpinned this approach, namely informed choice by individuals, support tailored to the realities of people's lives (described as 'personalisation') and partnership working between public and private organisations, coordinated by government. Key priorities identified in the White Paper were reducing the numbers of people who smoke, reducing obesity and improving diet and nutrition, increasing exercise, encouraging and supporting sensible drinking, improving sexual health and improving mental health. *Choosing Health* set out a long list of specific initiatives to be taken in support of these priorities, including proposals to consult and legislate on the introduction of smoke-free public places and workplaces, including restaurants and bars.

These proposals signalled a step change in the government's approach to smoking. A White Paper on smoking published in 1998 had set out a wide range of measures designed to cut the number of people smoking by 2010. Although rejecting a ban on smoking in public places at that time, the White Paper included plans to develop smoking cessation clinics, restrict tobacco advertising and protect young people and children. The Tobacco Advertising and Promotion Act 2002 created powers to ban press, billboard and most internet advertising of tobacco products and to bring an end to the promotion of tobacco products through the sponsorship of sporting and other events. From a public health perspective, action to reduce smoking is important in relation to tackling health inequalities in the light of evidence that differences in smoking rates between socio-economic groups are a major factor explaining the persistence and in some cases widening of health inequalities. Following the commitments included in *Choosing Health* in 2004, the government created powers in The Health Act 2006 to implement a ban on smoking in public places in England with effect from July 2007. Legislation was enacted despite concerns in parts of the government about the risks of unpopularity among core Labour party supporters.

Obesity

Both the Wanless public health review and *Choosing Health* highlighted the challenge posed by rising levels of obesity and overweight in the population. Recognition of this challenge led to a more concerted approach across government as a whole to analyse the actions needed to stem and ultimately reverse the increases that were occurring. Building on the detailed analysis of the Government Office for Science's Foresight report (Government Office for Science, 2007) and its depiction of the 'obesogenic society', a cross-government strategy for England was published in 2008 (Secretary of State for Health and Secretary of State for Children, Schools and Families, 2008). The strategy argued that Britain was in the grip of an obesity epidemic, and included a target (originally announced in September 2007) to reverse the rising tide of obesity and overweight in the population. The initial focus was on children where the aim was to reduce the proportion of overweight and obese children to 2000 levels by 2020. In line with the recommendations of the Foresight report, the strategy identified the need for action in five areas: promoting children's health, promoting healthier food choices, building physical activity into daily lives, supporting health at work, and providing effective treatment and support when people become overweight or obese.

Health inequalities

The Acheson report and the government's response provided the platform for a renewed focus on tackling health inequalities under the Blair government. This included the government setting a target of reducing inequalities in health outcomes by 10 per cent as measured by infant mortality and life expectancy at birth by 2010 in the public service agreement between the Department of Health and the Treasury. The target was underpinned by two more detailed objectives:

- starting with children under one year, by 2010 to reduce by at least 10 per cent the gap in mortality between routine and manual groups and the population as a whole
- starting with local authorities, by 2010 to reduce by at least 10 per cent the gap between the fifth of areas with the lowest life expectancy at birth and the population as a whole. (DH, 2003a, p. 7)

In working towards this target and these objectives, a programme of action to be taken forward across government was published (DH, 2003a) and this focused on four themes. These were supporting mothers, families and children, engaging communities and individuals, preventing illness and providing effective treatment and care, and addressing the underlying determinants of health. The programme of action built on a cross-cutting government review in 2002 and identified 12 cross-government headline indicators where improvements would be sought. Examples included reducing child poverty and smoking prevalence among manual groups. As we discuss in more detail in Chapter 10, a review published in 2008 found that the overall health gap remained even though life expectancy and infant mortality were improving for all groups in the population.

What has been achieved?

Independent analyses of progress in implementing public health poli-cies under the Blair government paint a mixed picture. One of the most critical verdicts was offered by Derek Wanless in a report commis-sioned by the King's Fund (Wanless et al., 2007). The report reviewed progress in the five years that had elapsed since his report on the long-term funding needs of the NHS and found it was impossible to assess whether the fully engaged aspirations for a doubling in public health spending by 2007–08 had been met because no official figures on this were kept. More specifically, the review found solid progress on smoking prevention and on actions to increase physical activity and improve diets, but expressed great concern about rising trends in obesity. The review also noted that no action had been taken on the recommendation in the Wanless public health review that government should develop a conceptual framework to take forward public health in England in a systematic way. Overall, the report found little evidence that the government had attached the same priority to public health as to the improvement of the NHS, not least because public health budgets had been raided in some areas to deal with financial deficits that emerged in the NHS in 2005.

Similar questions about progress were raised in a review conducted by the Audit Commission and the Healthcare Commission of the impact of policy on the delivery of HImPs and services (Audit Commission and Healthcare Commission, 2008b). While commending the government for an ambitious programme to improve health and tackle health inequali-ties, and for the progress made in reducing premature deaths from cancer and heart disease, the review highlighted areas in which little or no progress had been made, and it echoed the Wanless public health review of 2004 in focusing particularly on the need to strengthen implemen-tation and delivery, rather than develop further policies or changes in structure. In this context, the key role of PCTs and local authorities in taking forward national public health policies was emphasised, with local strategic partnerships being identified as having particular promise for the future. As far as government policy was concerned, the Audit Commis-sion and the Healthcare Commission argued that there should be ambi-tious and measurable public health objectives backed up by effective delivery plans, relevant, reliable and up-to-date information, a consistent focus across the NHS and government, further work to identify cost-effective interventions, greater use of economic and other incentives to support the delivery of HImPs, more support for commissioners to priori-tise public health at a local level, and clear accountabilities for commis-sioning and delivery.

In their different ways, both the Wanless review for the King's Fund and the analysis by the Audit Commission and the Healthcare Commission raised major questions about the priority attached to public health by the government, and the capacity to implement the targets and objectives that had been set. As we discuss in Chapter 10, although the health of the population has improved over the longer term and health care has made an increasing contribution to the improvements that have occurred, significant challenges remain, not least in tackling health inequalities and addressing new risks like obesity. In the period reviewed here, the most important public health measure was arguably the use of legislation to ban smoking in public places. The initial reluctance of ministers to promote legislation for fear of adverse reactions among some sections of the public underlines the political nature of health policy-making and contains a distant echo of the debates on public health measures discussed in Chapter 1.

Conclusion

In this chapter we have noted that the size of the NHS budget is shaped by the state of the economy and government decisions on priorities between spending programmes. Periods of growth have been interspersed with years of relative famine as economic imperatives and political bargaining have combined to determine the allocation of resources to different sectors. Since the Prime Minister's commitment in 2000 to bring expenditure up to the European Union average, NHS spending has grown more rapidly and over a longer period of time than at any stage in its history. The prospect of a lengthy economic recession in the UK means that funding will become much tighter after 2011 when the results of the next spending review will take effect. At that time, debate about the relative contribution of public and private funds to total health care expenditure is likely to resurface in a context in which the UK is more dependent on public funding than most OECD countries. We discuss this further in Chapter 12.

The Wanless review of the long-term funding of health care emphasised the importance of action on public health in ensuring the financial sustainability of the NHS. Successive governments since the mid 1970s have developed policies on public health and examination of long-term trends shows there has been progress in a number of areas, including falling premature deaths from major killers like cancer, heart disease and stroke, and reductions in the prevalence of cigarette smoking. At the same time, health inequalities have persisted and new risks such as obesity have emerged. Independent assessments have questioned whether the rhetoric of government policy documents has been matched by the reality of resource allocation as public health budgets have been squeezed and other priorities within government have received greater attention. At a time when public funding for health care is entering a more hostile climate, the failure to give higher priority to public health will only accentuate the challenge of priority-setting in the NHS – a challenge to which we now turn.

Chapter 5

Policy and Priorities in the NHS

The aim of this chapter is to describe the policies that successive governments have adopted in seeking to improve different aspects of the NHS. Issues covered in the chapter include access and standards, primary care, acute hospital services, cancer, heart disease and stroke, mental health, learning disabilities, older people, children's services and maternity care, and health and social care integration. In developing policies for the NHS, ministers have sought to ensure greater consistency in the availability and funding of services in different areas. Sixty years after the establishment of the NHS, there are still wide variations in expenditure on different services between areas, and there is no certainty that government policies will be implemented at a local level. Alongside the challenge of policy implementation, both government and NHS bodies have to determine the priority to be attached to competing claims on resources. The way in which priorities are set is considered in the final section of the chapter in the context of the changing balance between national and local responsibilities. After 1999 the governments of Northern Ireland, Scotland and Wales developed their own policies in relation to a number of the issues covered in this chapter, and the impact of devolution on health policy is discussed further in Chapter 7.

The context

The Department of Health (DH) gives guidance to the NHS on the use of resources in Green Papers or consultative documents, White Papers and related publications. Of particular importance is the annual guidance on planning and priorities set out in the NHS operating framework which brings together advice from different sources to set out priorities for both health and social care. One of the characteristics of the NHS under the Blair and Brown governments was the large number of priorities and targets set for the NHS. Politicians were particularly profligate in the period around the development of *The NHS Plan* (Secretary of State for Health, 2000) both in relation to specific targets, such as those relating to the reduction in waiting times, and in the publication of national service frameworks setting out standards for improving areas of major clinical priority. What then have been the main priorities for the NHS in recent years?

Access and standards

Improving patients' access to health care has been a major concern throughout the history of the NHS because of the existence of delays in patients making an appointment to see a doctor or to undergo a test. Publication of the *Patient's Charter* in 1991 exemplified this concern and was the first attempt since the establishment of the NHS to define the rights of patients and the standards of service they should expect from the NHS (DH, 1991). Table 5.1 summarises the standards and guarantees in the *Patient's Charter*. As this shows, particular emphasis was placed on reducing waiting times for hospital treatment. Performance tables showing how providers were performing on a number of the *Patient's Charter* standards were published from 1994, and over time greater attention was given to measures of clinical performance alongside indicators of access and responsiveness.

Table 5.1 *The* Patient's Charter

Ten rights were included in the *Patient's Charter* published in 1991:
• to receive health care on the basis of clinical need, regardless of ability to pay;
• to be registered with a GP;
• to receive emergency medical care at any time through a GP or through the emergency ambulance service and a hospital accident and emergency department;
• to be referred to a consultant, acceptable to a patient, when a GP thinks this is necessary, and to be referred to a second opinion if a patient and GP agree this to be desirable;
• to be given a clear explanation of any treatment proposed, including any risks or alternatives;
• to have access to health records, and to know that those working for the NHS are under a legal duty to keep their contents confidential;
• to choose whether or not to take part in medical research or medical student training;
• to be given detailed information on local health services, including quality standards and maximum waiting times;
• to be guaranteed admission for treatment by a specific date no later than two years from the day when a patient is placed on a waiting list;
• to have any complaint about NHS services investigated and to receive a full and prompt written reply from the chief executive or general manager.

The updated and enlarged *Patient's Charter* published in 1995 set out new rights and standards including:

- 90 per cent of outpatients to be seen within 13 weeks for their first appointment and everyone within 26 weeks;
- all patients waiting for an operation to be guaranteed admission for treatment no later than 18 months from the day of being placed on a waiting list;
- a three- to four-hour standard for 'trolley waits' in accident and emergency departments, to be reduced to two hours from April 1996;
- urgent home visits by community nurses within four hours and for non-urgent patients within two days.

The policy of raising standards was given added impetus after the election of the Blair government in 1997, particularly as a result of the strategy that was developed in relation to quality of care and clinical performance in the government's consultation document, *A First Class Service* (Secretary of State for Health, 1998b). This policy was developed in response to increasing concerns that the standards of care delivered in the NHS were not as high as patients had a right to expect. *A First Class Service* led to the establishment of two new organisations, the National Institute for Clinical Excellence (NICE) and the Commission for Health Improvement (CHI). The role of NICE (since renamed the National Institute for Health and Clinical Excellence) is to produce authoritative national guidance on the use of new and existing technologies, while the Commission for Health Improvement was given the job of scrutinising standards and advising on action needed to strengthen quality (see Chapter 10 for further discussion).

The work of these institutions is supported by the development of national service frameworks setting out national standards and models for services such as heart disease and mental health. National service frameworks are important policy documents that establish targets and objectives in areas of clinical priority (see Table 5.2), and we discuss a number of these frameworks in the rest of this chapter. In addition, clinical governance was introduced to strengthen existing systems for quality control. Subsequently, the government established the National Patient Safety Agency (NPSA) to run a mandatory reporting system for logging all failures and errors, and the National Clinical Assessment Authority to provide a fast response to concerns about doctors' performance. The priority attached to these issues by the Blair government was in part a response to evidence of failures of clinical performance within the NHS, and a concern to underpin self-regulation within the medical profession with other mechanisms of quality assurance.

Table 5.2 *National service frameworks*

1999 Mental Health
2000 Coronary Heart Disease
2000 NHS Cancer Plan
2001 Older People
2003 Diabetes
2004 Children
2004 Renal Services
2005 Long-term Neurological Conditions
2009 (expected) Chronic Obstructive Pulmonary Disease

The Blair government also gave priority to policies designed to improve access and convenience within the NHS. Of particular significance was the reduction of waiting lists for hospital treatment in the light of the pledge made by the Prime Minister when in opposition to cut the number of people on waiting lists by 100,000. The emphasis on access and convenience was seen too in the establishment of a number of pilot projects to introduce booked admission systems in place of waiting lists and to test out a 24-hour telephone nurse helpline known as NHS Direct. In addition, an annual survey of patient and user experience was set up to provide regular feedback on how well the NHS was serving its customers. Both NHS Direct and the booked admissions pilots soon became part of mainstream policy development and they featured prominently in *The NHS Plan* (Secretary of State for Health, 2000). Achievement of the target of reducing waiting lists by 100,000 led to the establishment of new targets for cutting waiting *times* for treatment as policies to improve access took centre stage.

The focus on access as the government's highest priority in *The NHS Plan* resulted in significant reductions in waiting times for patients. The targets of achieving maximum waiting times of three months for outpatient appointments and six months for inpatient treatment by 2005 were achieved, as was the target of a maximum four hour wait in accident and emergency. Success in these areas led the government to set even more ambitious targets for improving access in *The NHS Improvement Plan* in 2004 (Secretary of State for Health, 2004a), centred on a maximum waiting time of 18 weeks from GP referral to inpatient treatment by the end of 2008 (see Chapter 10). One of the consequences was that much of the increase in resources that went in to the NHS was spent on reducing waiting times and other priority areas did not benefit to the same extent.

As progress was made on access, there were increasing concerns with healthcare associated infections, especially MRSA and *Clostridium difficile*. Healthcare associated infections were first identified as a priority for the NHS in 2004, reflecting growing public, media and political awareness of the nature of the challenge they represented. The government introduced a wide range of measures to support implementation of its targets for reducing these infections and by 2008 there was evidence that these measures were having an impact. Figures from the DH showed that rates of MRSA and *Clostridium difficile* had fallen from their peak, although it was not clear whether the reductions that had occurred could be sustained and extended. The focus on healthcare associated infections was a key part of a wider concern to improve the safety and quality of health care. The final report of Lord Darzi's NHS Next Stage Review, *High Quality Care for All* (Secretary of State for Health, 2008a), emphasised that safety and quality were the most important priorities for the NHS in the next stage of reform, building on and extending the approach that had started with the consultative document, *A First Class Service*, in 1998. Accordingly, the DH announced that health care providers would be required to publish quality accounts from 2010 to provide information to the public on the quality of their services.

Alongside *High Quality Care for All*, the government published its proposals for *The NHS Constitution* (DH, 2008b). In many ways, *The NHS Constitution* was a more modern and more ambitious version of the *Patient's Charter*. It included seven key principles to guide how the NHS should act and make decisions, six core NHS values, and a number of rights and responsibilities for patients and staff, as well as pledges to patients and staff. The core values included a commitment to respect and dignity, quality of care, compassion, improving lives, working together for patients and everyone counts. For patients, rights encompassed access to services, informed choice, and respect, consent and confidentiality, while for staff, rights were those embodied in law relating to the working environment. Patients' responsibilities included to contribute to their own health, register with a GP practice, and treat NHS staff and other patients with respect. Staff responsibilities included to accept professional accountability, take reasonable care of health and safety at work, and act in accordance with the terms of their contract of employment. The pledges in *The NHS Constitution* were commitments made by government that were not rights but were seen as important, like the pledge to patients to make decisions in a clear and transparent way.

Following a period of consultation, the government announced plans in the Queen's Speech in December 2008 to use the Health Bill to require NHS and independent sector organisations to take account of *The NHS Constitution* in performing their functions. Responses to *The NHS Consti-*

tution ranged from a feeling that it was window dressing unsupported by substance to the argument that it was the most far-reaching and interesting idea to emerge from the NHS Next Stage Review (Walshe, 2008).

Primary care

The position of primary care as the first point of contact for patients and the gateway to hospital and specialist services has long been seen as a strength of the NHS, and survey evidence shows that the services of GPs are highly valued by patients. Despite this, there are inequities in the availability of primary care services in different parts of the country. Data for England for 2006 show wide variations in spending on GP services adjusted for need, indicating that areas with the greatest needs still lag behind other parts of the country (Public Accounts Committee, 2008). The quality of primary care provision also varies with examples of excellent services co-existing with poor quality provision, often in areas of greatest need.

The 1997 Primary Care Act created powers to encourage new approaches to primary care provision to be developed. These centred on a series of pilot projects, including the employment of salaried family doctors and nurse-led schemes. The Act emerged from a process of consultation and debate started under the Major government and it was passed into law with the support of opposition parties. Its main significance was in offering greater flexibility and choice in the provision of primary care. This entailed the continuation of independent contractor status for the vast majority of GPs who preferred this option, and the ability to negotiate local personal medical services contracts for GPs who wished to do so. Alongside changes to arrangements for providing cover for GPs in the evenings and at weekends, often involving the creation of cooperatives in which doctors supported each other in delivering services out-of-hours, the personal medical services pilots opened up a new chapter in primary care.

In line with developments in other areas of health policy since 1997, primary care has been under pressure to improve access for patients. This has been pursued in two main ways. First, new forms of primary care provision have been developed alongside the GP practice. The most important new forms have been NHS Direct, discussed earlier, and walk-in centres. Around 90 walk-in centres have been set up in England to deal with minor ailments and they are often located in high street premises. Walk-in centres are staffed by experienced nurses and they provide treatment for minor injuries and illnesses. Second, policies to improve access to primary care have focused on reducing the time patients may have to wait to see a GP. *The NHS Plan* set a target that by 2004 patients should be able to have a GP appointment within 48 hours and to see a primary care professional within 24 hours. A related policy was the encouragement given to the development of GPs with special interests, able to treat patients without referral to hospital.

A report published by the DH in 2004 summarised progress in improving primary care, including increases in the number of GPs and nurses, the provision of a wider range of care in the community, and investment in new buildings (Colin-Thome, 2004). The progress report particularly highlighted the ability of almost all patients to see a GP within 48 hours and a primary health care professional within 24 hours. A national survey of the public conducted in 2007 reported high levels of overall satisfaction with GP services, although in this survey only 86 per cent of respondents said they were able to get an appointment with a GP within 48 hours. The survey also found variations in levels of satisfaction between practices in the same PCT, and variations between age groups. For example, 23 per cent of people aged under 35 were not satisfied with the opening hours of practices compared with 9 per cent of people aged over 65. Evidence of this kind, as well as consultation with the public on what they wanted from primary care, was instrumental in the decision by ministers to argue that practices should extend their opening hours, particularly in the evenings and weekends, to provide more accessible care. By the end of 2008 over one half of practices in England were offering extended weekend and evening opening hours.

The future direction of primary care and other services provided in the community was set out in the White Paper, *Our Health, Our Care, Our Say*, published in 2006 (Secretary of State for Health, 2006). In her foreword to the White Paper, the Secretary of State for Health, Patricia Hewitt, noted that the government had given priority to the reform of hospital services initially, and was now turning its attention to services outside hospital. Four main goals were set out for these services, namely providing better prevention services with earlier intervention, giving people more choice and a louder voice, tackling inequalities and improving access to community services, and offering more support to people with long-term medical conditions. Specifically in relation to general practice, the White Paper signalled the government's commitment to strengthen the incentives available to practices wishing to expand and to encourage new providers to enter the NHS to meet the needs of patients in deprived areas who were often not well served by existing practices. This commitment sent out a clear indication that policies on patient choice and provider competition were being extended to primary care.

The primary and community care strategy that resulted from the NHS Next Stage Review led by Lord Darzi (Secretary of State for Health,

2008b) underlined the importance of choice and competition in primary care and many of the other policies included in *Our Health, Our Care, Our Say*. Additional funds were allocated to support these policies, and some of these funds were used to develop GP-led health centres in every PCT offering walk-in services and bookable appointments from 8 a.m. to 8 p.m. each day of the week. The aim of these health centres is to provide services to any member of the public, in addition to the services they receive from the practice with which they are registered. In parallel, priority was given to the provision of new GP practices in the most deprived PCTs to address concerns about inequities in spending on GP services referred to earlier.

One of the consequences of these developments was to stimulate increasing interest in primary care provision from new providers, including private sector companies from the United Kingdom (UK) and the United States who saw opportunities to play a significant role in this area of care. The British Medical Association expressed its opposition to these developments and to the proposal, originally put forward in Lord Darzi's review of health services in London, that primary care would be strengthened through the establishment of polyclinics bringing together a number of practices with other services to offer patients access to a wider range of care in one location. Despite this opposition, the government pressed on with its plans and the procurement of new primary care capacity, although polyclinics were not referred to by name in the 2008 primary and community care strategy.

The most important development in primary care under the Blair government was the negotiation of a new contract for GPs in 2003. The new contract built on the 1997 Primary Care Act and included four main options: the general medical services contract under which most GPs work, the personal medical services contract negotiated locally between PCTs and practices, the primary care trust medical services contract that enables PCTs to run practices directly; and the alternative provider medical services contract that permits PCTs to contract with providers other than standard GP practices. The alternative provider medical services contract was important in opening up the provision of primary care to commercial companies. The general medical services contract included a quality and outcomes framework (QOF) which offered practices the opportunity to increase their income by around 25 per cent depending on their performance with respect to 146 quality indicators relating to ten chronic diseases, organisation of care and patient experience.

The quality indicators cover conditions such as heart disease, hypertension, diabetes and asthma, and practices earn points for their performance on these indicators. Examples of indicators include the existence of registers of patients with the designated conditions, evidence that the practices have undertaken reviews of these patients, and evidence that practices have achieved specified outcomes, for example control of blood pressure and cholesterol levels. Studies have shown that practices achieved a high level of performance in the first year of the new contract, and that the rate of improvement in performance increased modestly after 2004 in comparison with the historic trend. As well as bringing benefits to patients, the new contract helped increase recruitment into primary care, and was advantageous to GPs whose incomes increased by 58 per cent between 2002/03 and 2005/06. This resulted in greater than expected spending as GPs achieved higher levels of performance than the 75 per cent achievement against indicators estimated at the outset. The size of the income increases raised questions as to whether the contract offered value for money for the taxpayer. In its assessment, the National Audit Office (2008) offered a mixed review, noting progress against objectives in most areas, and highlighting areas where progress had not been demonstrated or where there was room for improvement.

One of the other consequences of the new GP contract was the opportunity for practices to decide not to provide a service out of hours. When this happened, PCTs were responsible for the provision of out-of-hours care. A review carried out by the National Audit Office (2006) found that the costs of out-of-hours care commissioned by PCTs were higher than had been estimated. Also, because PCTs lacked experience in commissioning out-of-hours care, there were shortcomings in the commissioning process. More positively, the National Audit Office reported that out-of-hours providers, who in most cases were GP led, were beginning to deliver a satisfactory level of service, and that the market was starting to mature. Alongside GP providers of out-of-hours care, NHS Direct and private sector companies were competing for contracts, leading to some innovation in the use of staff to provide care. The DH commended the report to PCTs and in so doing underlined the report's conclusion that there was scope to improve value for money through better commissioning of out-of-hours care. The need to strengthen the commissioning of care through PCTs and practice based commissioners was the focus of the world class commissioning programme developed by the Department at this time as a key element in the programme of health reforms.

The new contract for GPs played a major part in the government's policy of giving greater priority to the prevention of long term conditions (the term used to describe chronic diseases), as first announced in *The NHS Improvement Plan* in 2004. Other elements in this policy included the Expert Patient Programme, designed to support people with long term conditions to manage their own diseases; the appointment of specialist nurses, known as community matrons, to offer case management support to people with complex needs; and the use of assistive technologies to enable people to live independently in their own homes. Long term conditions were identified as a priority for three main reasons. The first was recognition of the changing burden of disease in the population and the increasing prevalence of conditions like arthritis and diabetes. Data from the General Household Survey (an annual survey by the ONS that gathers data on a range of topics including people's health) indicate that more than 30 per cent of people report that they have a chronic condition. This group accounts for 52 per cent of all visits to GPs, 65 per cent of all outpatient appointments and 72 per cent of hospital bed days. The DH's best estimate is that the treatment and care of people with long term conditions account for 69 per cent of total health and social care spending in England (DH, 2008c).

The second factor was a perception on the part of policy-makers that there was room for improving chronic care. The importance of this perception was confirmed by later survey evidence showing that UK physicians were particularly concerned about the coordination of care for people with chronic diseases across time and settings (Schoen et al., 2007). The third factor was the progress made in implementing earlier priorities and the opportunity this created to refresh the government's objectives. Specifically, major reductions in waiting times for hospital treatment enabled government to set even more challenging objectives in this area in *The NHS Improvement Plan* (see above), while also permitting new objectives to be set in other areas, including long term conditions.

One of the aims of the long term conditions policy was to reduce emergency hospital bed day use by identifying people at risk and providing care through specialist nurses and others to anticipate their needs and avoid hospital admissions. This aim was included in the public service agreement that the DH negotiated with the Treasury which contained a target of reducing emergency bed day use by 5 per cent by 2008. This target was achieved even though an evaluation of the use of community matrons found no evidence that they reduced the use of hospitals for the patients they served. An assessment of the long term conditions policy found some evidence of progress, as in the new contract for GPs, while emphasising the modest level of increased investment in this area in comparison with objectives like the reduction in waiting times (Ham, 2009).

Diabetes was one of the long term conditions identified as a priority for action in line with the national service framework for diabetes published in 2003. This set 12 national standards aimed at raising quality and reducing variation across the NHS, encompassing prevention, support for self-management and improved treatment. A delivery strategy was published in 2003 and progress in implementing the strategy was reviewed by the DH in 2008. The progress report noted achievements in a number of areas, including better management of diabetes in primary care resulting from the new GP contract, while also noting challenges from rising rates of obesity (which is closely linked with diabetes), and variations in the provision of care, as illustrated in a survey of diabetes patients undertaken by the Healthcare Commission. In its review, the Healthcare Commission reported that there was considerable room for improvement in diabetes care, including more emphasis on care planning and partnerships between people with diabetes and their health care professionals, increasing the number of people with diabetes attending education courses, and reducing avoidable admissions to hospital (Healthcare Commission, 2007a). Some of these ideas were taken forward through the Year of Care programme which involved a number of pilots in different areas testing out care planning and the role of education courses in helping to improve the quality of life for people with diabetes.

Pharmacy and dentistry

Government policies on primary care have sought to give greater priority to pharmacy services in the NHS. The White Paper, *Pharmacy in England: Building on Strengths, Delivering the Future* (Secretary of State for Health, 2008c), together with *Our Health, Our Care, Our Say* and the primary and community care strategy that resulted from the NHS Next Stage Review, envisaged a future in which community pharmacies would be involved not only in advising people on the use of medicines but also playing a bigger part in the treatment of minor ailments, promoting self-care and undertaking screening, including the new programme of screening for vascular diseases announced in 2008. These policies build on the new contractual framework for community pharmacy introduced in 2005 which organises services into three categories: essential services that must be provided by all pharmacies, advanced services such as medicines-use review, and enhanced services commissioned locally by PCTs.

In parallel, the government has introduced changes to NHS dental services designed to improve access to these services, change the system for paying dentists to remove incentives for invasive and complex treatments, and simplify the charges paid by patients. These changes have taken place in a context of improving oral health resulting from the fluoridation of water supplies, the use of fluoride toothpaste, improvements in diets, and access to dental care. A new contract for dentists was implemented in 2006 to give effect to the government's reform and an inquiry undertaken by the House of Commons Health Committee found that patient access to dental services had in fact deteriorated following the introduction of the new contract (Health Committee, 2008a). One of the reasons for this was the decision of some dentists to cease providing care to NHS patients and to concentrate on patients paying for their treatment privately because of concerns about the payments dentists received from the NHS. The longer term trend for dentists to increase their private practices and reduce their NHS commitments has led to the emergence of a mixed public/private system in which the role of privately funded treatment is much greater than in other areas of health care. Concerns about patient access to dental services led the government to set up an independent inquiry into dentistry at the end of 2008.

Acute hospital services

Acute hospital services have come to play an increasingly important part in the NHS. The role of hospitals has expanded as medical advances have opened up new possibilities for diagnosis and treatment. The way in which care is provided in hospitals has also changed through developments in anaesthesia and surgery and through the emergence of new drugs and medical interventions. Much of the work that used to be done in hospitals is now performed in primary care, an example being the routine management of patients with long term conditions. This has resulted in a progressive reduction in the number of acute hospital beds, and debate about the most appropriate way of organising services. At the heart of this debate is the question of which services should be provided in every area and which services should be centralised, as well as how hospitals can work together to provide care that is accessible to patients and of a high standard.

The organisation of acute hospital services was first addressed systematically in the 1962 Hospital Plan which set out a vision of a network of district general hospitals (DGHs) serving populations of 100,000 to 150,000, and each containing between 600 and 800 beds. The programme of hospital building that occurred after the Plan resulted in the construction of many completely new DGHs and the upgrading of several existing hospitals to DGH standard. The Bonham Carter Report of 1969 (Central Health Services Council, 1969) proposed that even larger DGHs should be built to serve bigger populations but these proposals were not accepted. Instead, policy moved in favour of smaller DGHs supported by community hospitals (DHSS, 1980b). Despite this, the changing pattern of medical staffing in hospitals, with junior doctors spending more time undergoing training, consultants playing a bigger part in the delivery of services, and specialisation requiring a larger number of consultants to work together to offer the full range of services to a high standard, threatened the viability of smaller DGHs and led to moves to link and integrate services at adjacent hospitals (Ham et al., 1998).

Changing patterns of use of acute services have resulted in more patients being treated in fewer beds. This has been made possible by advances in medical technology, including the increased use of day surgery, developments in anaesthetics, and the use of new drugs. The average length of stay of patients in acute hospitals has fallen as a consequence and NHS hospitals typically operate with high levels of bed occupancy and little spare capacity. This has caused problems in recent years, especially during the winter months when increases in emergency admissions have put pressure on a system already working close to its limits. In some cases this has meant patients having to wait on trolleys until beds have become available. Policy on acute services has sought to deal with this by allocating additional resources to assist with winter pressures and by encouraging the development of alternatives to hospital care in the community and in nursing homes. The government has also acted to increase the provision of intensive care facilities as rising demands have exposed inadequacies in capacity.

An inquiry into NHS hospital beds was undertaken by the DH and published in 2000 (DH, 2000a). The inquiry found that there was a mismatch between patients' needs and available resources. In particular, it highlighted evidence of significant inappropriate or avoidable use of acute hospital beds and of shortages of service alternatives to hospitals that could reduce admissions and bring care closer to patients' homes. Looking ahead to the next 10 to 20 years, the inquiry developed three scenarios: maintaining the current direction, acute bed focused care, and care closer to home. In the event, the government opted for the third scenario in which the main emphasis was placed on the development of intermediate care services to prevent avoidable admissions to acute care and to facilitate the transition from hospital to home. *The NHS Plan* announced that provision was being made for 5000 extra intermediate care beds and an extra 1700 intermediate care places to support people who did not need to be in acute hospitals but could not live independently at home. Intermediate care includes a range of services such as rapid response, hospital at home and residential rehabilitation, and often involves social care as well as the NHS.

Subsequently, the government carried out a review of the organisation of acute hospitals in the light of trends to centralise some services in fewer, larger facilities. The report of the review (DH, 2003b) challenged the view that 'biggest is best' and argued that it was important to maintain local access to acute hospitals through a greater emphasis on these hospitals operating as part of networks of care. The review argued for a whole systems and integrated approach to service requirements in which hospitals were planned in relation to primary and social care as well as other specialist facilities. It was anticipated that small acute hospitals would have a continuing role, even though they might not provide the full range of services. One of the factors driving change in acute hospital organisation was the European Working Time Directive which made it difficult to maintain 24-hour medical cover in small hospitals. The review argued that networking between hospitals and the development of extended roles for nurses and non-medical practitioners were essential to address these challenges.

The need for hospitals to work more closely in networks and with community services was also emphasised in a report prepared by a project board set up by the National Leadership Network (2006) to review the future of acute hospitals. The report called for a step change in the planning of services, centred on hospitals and community services working as part of a whole system rather than individual hospitals struggling to survive in isolation. The challenge this threw down was how to develop service networks and whole system working when the government's health reform programme was encouraging hospitals to exploit their autonomy as NHS foundation trusts rather than to work collaboratively. Similar tensions were evident in the case of cancer services and heart disease services (see below) where service networks linking providers and commissioners were established to support implementation of national service frameworks in these high priority clinical areas. The sustainability of these networks came into question when the Blair government adopted market based reforms in which individual providers were encouraged to compete for patients rather than work together to improve care.

The organisation of acute hospitals and the location of specialist services were issues addressed during the NHS Next Stage Review led by Lord Darzi in 2008, as well as by the DH's national clinical directors in their reports on the clinical case for change. One of the implications of this work was that there were potential benefits for patients from the provision of some services in specialist centres. A widely cited example was stroke care where there was evidence of better outcomes when patients were transferred to hospitals with the resources and expertise to provide rapid diagnosis and expert treatment. In this case, the DH argued for a hub and spoke model of care in which hospitals worked with each other and with the ambulance service to improve the quality of care provided. Recognising the challenges in changing the role of acute hospitals to strengthen specialist services, Lord Darzi emphasised the need for change to be locally led and clinically driven, and for new services to be in place before existing services were withdrawn.

Cancer

Cancer is a major issue in health policy because of the large numbers of people who are diagnosed with cancer and because of evidence that the quality of cancer care in the UK has fallen behind that of other countries. Policy on cancer services derives from the Calman-Hine report which set out a framework for commissioning high quality cancer care (Calman-Hine, 1995). The central proposal of this report was that care should be organised at three levels – primary care, cancer units and cancer centres – linked together to offer a network of appropriate services to patients. *The NHS Cancer Plan*, published in 2000, built on the Calman-Hine report, announcing significant investment in cancer services and new targets for improving access and raising standards (DH, 2000b). *The NHS Cancer Plan* noted that one-third of the population of England would develop cancer at some stage of their lives and one-quarter would die of cancer. The Plan went on to note that progress had been made in reducing deaths from some cancers but England still lagged behind other European countries, particularly in poorer survival rates from lung, colon, prostate and breast cancer. These differences were attributed in part to delays in diagnosis resulting from waiting times to see a specialist, and decades of under-investment in staff and equipment. The Plan also acknowledged the importance of variations in cancer services and outcomes and the need to address the postcode lottery of cancer care.

Among the challenges set out in the Plan, the need to improve prevention was strongly emphasised. This included further action to tackle smoking and improve diet, and to improve screening. At the heart of the Plan was a commitment to reduce waiting times for diagnosis and treatment to overcome the delays that contributed to poorer outcomes. A series of targets were specified in the Plan including a maximum 31 day wait from diagnosis to treatment for all cancers by 2005, and a maximum 62 day wait from urgent GP referral to treatment for all cancers by 2005. These targets were to be achieved through increased investment in staff and equipment involving the appointment of an extra 1000 cancer specialists by 2006, and the provision of 50 new magnetic resonance imaging scanners and 200 new CT scanners. Consistent with the approach taken in *The NHS Plan*, this extra investment was to be accompanied by reform. Specifically, the Plan announced that the Cancer Services Collaborative would be rolled out across the country as part of the expanding work programme of the Modernisation Agency.

Progress towards the 31 day and 62 day waiting time targets contained in *The NHS Cancer Plan* was slow between 2000 and 2004. This led the DH to establish the National Cancer Waits Project to support the NHS in the delivery of these targets. A review published by the Department showed that progress was much faster during 2005 and by the first quarter of 2006 almost 100% of patients were treated in line with the 31 day target and 93% in line with the 62 day target (Richards, 2006). Achievement of these targets, alongside evidence of other improvements in cancer care, including continuing reductions in mortality rates from cancer and improved survival rates, led the National Audit Office (2005a) and the King's Fund (Rosen et al., 2006) to offer positive endorsements of the government's policies in this area in their assessments of progress. In its report, the National Audit Office recommended that *The NHS Cancer Plan* should be revised and updated to take account of changing circumstances and the views of stakeholders.

The government responded by publishing the *Cancer Reform Strategy* at the end of 2007 (DH, 2007a). The *Cancer Reform Strategy* set out plans for the period until 2012 with the aim of developing world class cancer services in England. These plans were based on recognition of the increasing incidence of cancer resulting from the ageing population, the availability of new opportunities for prevention, early diagnosis and treatment, and the potential to improve patient experience and develop new service models. As the plans noted, England continued to lag behind the best European countries in cancer survival rates, notwithstanding the progress that had been made. Six areas of action were identified in the *Cancer Reform Strategy*. These were to prevent cancer, diagnose cancer earlier, ensure better treatment, help people live with and beyond cancer, reduce cancer inequalities, and deliver care in the appropriate setting. Among the specific proposals included in the strategy was a national vaccination programme for young girls to prevent cervical cancer, the expansion of breast cancer and bowel cancer screening, and an increase in radiotherapy capacity. A report on progress in implementing the strategy in its first year reiterated the importance of GPs diagnosing cancer early to address poor survival rates from cancer in England compared with other countries.

Cancer networks were one of the organisational innovations to result from the Calman-Hine report and *The NHS Cancer Plan*. These networks are responsible for developing and planning all aspects of cancer services and they bring together NHS organisations with the voluntary sector and other sources of expertise. Thirty-four cancer networks were established in England and their contribution to the improvements in care that have occurred was recognised both by the National Audit Office and the King's Fund in their reviews of progress. However, the National Audit Office noted variations in the functioning and effectiveness of cancer networks, while the King's Fund highlighted tensions between the drive to achieve closer integration of care through networks and the policy of giving NHS organisations greater autonomy as NHS foundation trusts. The *Cancer Reform Strategy* emphasised that cancer networks had a continuing role in improving cancer services, acting as agents for commissioning and supporting the development of world class commissioning for cancer.

Heart disease and stroke

Like cancer, heart disease and stroke have been identified as priorities because of the large numbers of people diagnosed with these conditions, and evidence that the UK has not made the same progress as other countries in preventing these conditions and ensuring access to appropriate treatments. In the case of heart disease, a national service framework was published in 2000 (DH, 2000c) This framework noted that heart disease was the commonest cause of premature death in the UK, and that there were wide variations between social classes, ethnic groups, and geographical areas. It went on to argue that timely, effective treatment could reduce the suffering and risk associated with heart disease, and it drew on available evidence to suggest how this might be done. Twelve service standards were identified in the framework encompassing prevention, treatment and rehabilitation. Specific areas for improvement included the provision of smoking cessation clinics and rapid access chest pain clinics, reducing call-to-needle time for clot-busting drug treatment, improving the use of effective medicines after heart attack, and increasing the number of revascularisation procedures undertaken. As in the case of cancer, emphasis was also placed on reform and service redesign, and this was subsequently pursued through the coronary heart disease collaborative which again came under the Modernisation Agency. Particular priority was attached to the reduction of waiting times for heart operations, and a patient choice pilot was launched in 2002 enabling patients who had been waiting for longer than six months to travel to another hospital for surgery.

A review by the Healthcare Commission published in 2005 reported significant progress in implementing the national service framework, noting in particular advances in the treatment of heart attacks, faster diagnosis of angina, reduced waits for revascularisation, and the development of registers of people with heart disease or at risk of heart disease in primary care (Healthcare Commission, 2005a). The review also highlighted areas where more needed to be done, including reducing heart disease in the population through public health initiatives, providing better care for people with heart failure and promoting cardiac rehabilitation. As far as the organisation of services was concerned, the Healthcare

Commission found wide variations in the functioning and effectiveness of cardiac networks, and weak involvement of PCTs and patients in many networks. Around the same time as publication of this review, the DH added to the national service framework a new chapter on cardiac arrhythmias (electrical disorders of the heart), setting out three quality requirements and 20 markers of good practice in this area.

The government's own review of progress in implementing the national service framework published in 2008 reported improvements in all areas of care (Secretary of State for Health, 2008d). In the case of premature deaths from heart disease, the review noted that the government's target of cutting mortality in people under 75 by at least 40 per cent by 2010 was achieved five years ahead of schedule. Access to treatment had improved to the point where no patients waited over three months for heart surgery, the greater use of statins to reduce cholesterol levels was estimated to have contributed to the saving of 10,000 lives, and clot-busting drugs were delivered to 68 per cent of individuals within 60 minutes in 2007 compared with 24 per cent in 2001. Progress had also been made in reducing smoking prevalence among adults and in increasing the consumption of free fruit in school by children. A number of these improvements resulted from increases in spending and capacity, including a 61 per cent increase in cardiologists, a 32 per cent increase in heart surgeons between 1999 and 2006, and investment in new buildings and equipment. A new priority set out in the review was the development of a vascular risk screening programme.

Stroke services did not receive the same attention as cancer and heart disease until the publication of a national stroke strategy in 2007 (Secretary of State for Health, 2007a), even though stroke was identified as an area of concern in the *National Service Framework for Older People* published in 2001 (see below under Older People). An important stimulus behind the development of the stroke strategy was the publication of a critical report by the National Audit Office (2005b) highlighting the opportunity to improve performance through fast emergency response, treatment in a specialised stroke unit, better access to rehabilitation and support services, and greater emphasis on prevention. The National Audit Office's report raised the profile of stroke care and led to joint action with the DH to develop the national stroke strategy. Work on the strategy was informed by a survey of stroke patients undertaken by the Healthcare Commission (2005b) which found high levels of satisfaction among patients while also identifying areas for improvement. The national stroke strategy set out 20 quality markers and a 10 point action plan, and as in the case of cancer and heart disease advocated the development of networks to review and organise the delivery of stroke services across the care pathway.

Mental health

People with mental health problems have a range of needs and account for a large proportion of overall expenditure on health care (Appleby and Gregory, 2008). The nature of care for these people has changed significantly during the lifetime of the NHS, shifting away from services based mainly in psychiatric hospitals to care in the community and services that are more closely integrated with other forms of health care. There have been significant challenges in ensuring that mental health services are properly resourced in relation to the demands placed on them and that new services in the community provide support and protection for both patients and the public.

The 1959 Mental Health Act signalled the intention to develop community-based services, spurred on by developments in the treatment of mental illness and in social attitudes which made it possible to begin the run down of the large old psychiatric hospitals or asylums which had been the main source of care until that point. The White Paper, *Better Services for the Mentally Ill* (DHSS, 1975a), continued this trend and encouraged the integration of hospital services for people with mental illness in DGHs. The White Paper also included norms for the provision of services by local authorities, encompassing day centres, hostels and long-stay accommodation. In practice, public expenditure restrictions served to slow the development of these services, and the availability of comprehensive mental health care remained uneven. This again demonstrated the gap between the intentions of policy and implementation.

The care programme approach developed in the 1990s was intended to ensure that health and social care needs were assessed systematically and agreed services provided. This was supplemented by guidance on the components of care the government expected to be offered to people with mental illness. In view of concerns about patients discharged from hospital without adequate support, supervised discharge was introduced in 1996 to provide more control over certain categories of patients considered to pose risks either to themselves or the community. The rapid succession of policy initiatives in this period culminated in publication of a White Paper, *Modernising Mental Health Services*, in 1998 setting out the Blair government's plans for the future. The White Paper highlighted the failures of the community care policy and indicated that additional resources would be provided not only to address these failures but also to fund extra beds. To this extent, the White Paper recognised the need for a range of services to be available to people with mental illness and it reflected both public and political recognition of the continuing role of hospitals in the treatment of mental illness.

A *National Service Framework for Mental Health* was published in 1999 (DH, 1999). This set standards in five areas: health promotion, primary care and access to services, services for people with severe mental illness, carers, and the prevention of suicide. Additional resources were allocated to mental health services to support implementation of the national service framework. Examples of good practice were included in the framework and the standards that were set were based on a review of the evidence on the effectiveness of different services and interventions. The proposals in the framework on the prevention of suicide were intended to support the achievement of the target set in the public health White Paper, *Saving Lives: Our Healthier Nation* (Secretary of State for Health, 1999), that the suicide rate should be reduced by at least one-fifth by 2010.

A progress report prepared by the DH in 2007 highlighted improvements in a number of areas, including the provision of 700 new mental health teams in the community, large increases in the number of psychiatrists, clinical psychologists and mental health nurses, and a twentyfold increase in the use of modern anti-psychotic drugs. And while the report noted a reduction in suicides in relation to the 1995–97 baseline rate, the achievement of the target of a 20 per cent reduction by 2010 appeared challenging (Appleby, 2007). Despite this, the report quoted with approval the view of the WHO head of mental services in Europe that England had the best mental health services in Europe. A review of acute inpatient mental health services published by the Healthcare Commission in 2008 suggested that the focus on supporting people to live more independent lives in the community may have resulted in lower priority being given to acute services for people with mental illness and it identified actions that needed to be taken to improve acute inpatient services (Healthcare Commission, 2008).

One of the specific challenges identified by the Healthcare Commission, the Commission for Social Care Inspection and the Audit Commission as well as the DH was mental health in old age, including the increasing incidence of dementia. A review of services and support for people with dementia published by the National Audit Office (2007) was critical of the lack of priority attached to these services and concluded that services were not delivering value for money for taxpayers or people with dementia and their families. A series of recommendations were put forward for improving services including early diagnosis and intervention, the more systematic use of care plans and case management to support people with dementia, and a campaign to raise awareness of dementia among older people. The National Audit Office drew on an analysis commissioned by the Alzheimer's Society (2007) to emphasise the scale of the problem presented by dementia now and in the future, and the need for urgent

action. In response, the DH launched a consultation on a national dementia strategy during 2008, and this was published in 2009. As in other
policy areas, the priority attached to improving access by reducing waiting
times for hospital treatment meant that limited resources were available
for developing dementia services.

Learning disabilities

Services for people with learning disabilities have experienced many of
the same changes as those for people with mental health problems and
have encountered similar challenges. One of the differences affecting
people with learning disabilities is that many of their needs relate to the
provision of support outside the NHS. Policy-makers have been slow to
recognise this and to put in place policies that enable these people to live
an ordinary life. Further changes are likely following the recent transfer
of responsibility for commissioning learning disability services from the
NHS to local government.

Policies for people with learning disabilities have undergone significant change following the White Paper, *Better Services for the Mentally
Handicapped*, published in 1971 (DHSS, 1971). The main objective of
the White Paper was to bring about a reduction of about one-half in the
number of hospital beds provided for mentally handicapped people (as
they were known at the time), and to expand local authority services in
the community. Standards in hospital were also to be improved to overcome the deficiencies noted in the *Report of the Committee of Enquiry
into Ely Hospital, Cardiff* (Ely Report, 1969) which found evidence both
of the neglect of patients and their abuse.

A review published in 1980 indicated progress in meeting these objectives and proposed an even greater reduction in hospital provision and
the need for care to be provided in smaller units (DHSS, 1980c). The
review went on to stress the importance of developing local authority
services and integrating these services with those provided by health
authorities. These developments were taken further by the increasing
emphasis placed on enabling people with learning disabilities to live an
ordinary life in the community through supported living programmes and
similar initiatives. In recognition that social care is often more important
for people with learning disabilities than health care, health authorities
and local authorities in some parts of the country have agreed to pool
budgets, with local authorities taking the lead responsibility for the
commissioning of these services.

In 2001 the government published a review of learning disability services in a White Paper, *Valuing People: A New Strategy for Learning Disa-*

bility for the 21st Century (DH, 2001b). The White Paper reviewed the full range of needs of people with learning disabilities, including health care, and set out a vision based on four principles: rights, independence, choice and inclusion. The major problems identified in the White Paper included poorly coordinated services for families with disabled children, insufficient support for carers, limited housing and employment opportunities, and few examples of real partnership between health and social care. Additional funding was announced in the White Paper, including a Learning Disability Development Fund of up to £50 million per annum, and an Implementation Support Fund. Help was also provided for advocacy services and for carers. In the case of the NHS, the White Paper emphasised that people with learning disabilities should have the same right of access to mainstream health services as the rest of the population.

A review published in 2005 summarised progress made in implementing the White Paper, noting signs of progress in many areas while also emphasising variations in what had been achieved both between areas and on different issues. Concerns about the extent and pace of progress were reinforced by investigations carried out by the Healthcare Commission into NHS services for people with learning disabilities and into specific independent health care organisations providing care in this area. Examples included investigations into services in Cornwall and Sutton that found significant gaps in the quality of care provided and evidence of institutional abuse. In response, the government produced a consultation document, *Valuing People Now*, setting out plans for the future focused on five main priorities: personalised care tailored to the needs of individuals, helping people to be properly included in communities, ensuring access to good quality health care, providing housing that people want and need, and making sure that change happens (DH, 2007b). In support of these plans, the government announced that the Learning Disability Development Fund would continue, and that funding for learning disability services would transfer from the NHS to local government. This transfer took effect in April 2009.

Older people

The growing number of older people in the population is testimony to improvements in health that have occurred since the inception of the NHS. With premature deaths from cancer, heart disease and stroke falling, and with long term conditions such as arthritis and diabetes becoming more significant, more people are surviving into retirement, albeit with continuing health care needs. This presents a challenge to the NHS and to adult social care services in reorienting their focus and particularly working in partnership to meet the needs of the ageing population. As we note below, part of this challenge is ensuring that adequate resources are made available for services for older people in a context in which public funding has been withdrawn from some areas of care.

Services for older people were subject to a major policy review in 1981 (DHSS, 1981b), and since then have been through a series of changes driven largely by shifting policies in respect of public funding of care in private and voluntary sector residential and nursing homes and changing responsibilities between health and social care. These changes centred on the availability of resources through the social security budget to pay for care in these homes during the 1980s. Expenditure increased rapidly, reaching £2.5 billion a year by 1993, leading to an expansion of the private nursing home provision. It was partly in response to this that the government acted to cap spending and to make local authorities the lead agencies in arranging social care with the expectation that they would mainly act as commissioners of care from independent sector providers. The shift in policy was stimulated by a desire to move resources away from residential and nursing home provision by giving local authorities greater flexibility to develop home care and other services in line with the recommendations of the Griffiths Report on community care (see Chapter 2).

One of the consequences of these developments was that the role of the NHS in the provision of care declined significantly, focusing mainly on acute services rather than long-term or continuing care, and continuing a trend established in the 1950s (Bridgen and Lewis, 1999). The partial withdrawal of the NHS from the provision of continuing care happened by default rather than design and it represented a major shift in policy that was never debated or agreed (Audit Commission, 1997). Under the new funding arrangements, people above a certain (low) income level were required to pay for continuing care themselves instead of having access to such care in the NHS. In 1994 the Health Service Commissioner or Ombudsman upheld a complaint from the wife of a man suffering brain damage who argued that the NHS should have provided continuing care to her husband because his needs were medical. This led the DH to issue guidance to health authorities and local authorities asking them to develop local policies and eligibility criteria on continuing care and indicating that health authorities in some areas would need to increase expenditure on these services to enable the NHS to meet its obligations in the light of the Ombudsman's judgement.

The election of the Blair government resulted in the establishment of a Royal Commission to explore options for the future funding of long-term care against a background of increasing dissatisfaction with the progressive shift of responsibility from the public to the private sector and the blurred boundary between the NHS and social care. The Royal Commission reported in 1999 with the majority recommending that all nursing and personal care in care homes, and all personal care in people's own homes, should be provided free. The provision of accommodation and food would be means tested and it was estimated that the cost of making these changes would be around £1 billion initially. The minority on the Commission dissented from these proposals, arguing that they would involve the use of public funds to support better-off members of society at the expense of those most in need. Instead, the minority proposed that the existing rules on means testing should be relaxed and nursing care only should be free.

The government responded to the Royal Commission in 2000 at the same time as it published *The NHS Plan*. Many of the recommendations of the Royal Commission were accepted but not the central proposal that all care should be provided free. Rather, the government decided to go with the recommendations of the minority on the Royal Commission and make NHS nursing care free in all settings, and to maintain means testing for personal care. Additional resources were allocated to support the development of services for older people with the main emphasis being on the development of intermediate care. The establishment of the National Care Standards Commission in 2002, in response to the report of the Royal Commission, was intended to provide stronger safeguards for quality. One of the effects was to put pressure on the care homes market as providers were caught between requirements to meet new standards laid down by the National Care Standards Commission and revenues that were held down by the level of fees paid by local authorities.

Subsequently, the *National Service Framework for Older People* set out a comprehensive strategy for the provision of fair, high quality, integrated health and social care services (DH, 2001c). The framework included eight standards for the improvement of health and social care services in areas such as hospital care and health promotion. A report on progress in implementing the framework published by the DH in 2004 summarised developments in a number of areas, including improved health of older people, increased uptake of preventative services, increases in intermediate care, home care, extra care housing and support for carers, and improvements in specific services such as mental health and continence services (Philp, 2004). A review conducted by the Healthcare Commission, the Commission for Social Care Inspection and the Audit Commission acknowledged the progress that had been made but identified three areas where further action was required. These were tackling discrimination through ageist attitudes, ensuring that all the standards in the *National Service Framework* were met, and strengthening working in partnership between all the agencies providing services to older people. In response, the DH set out ten programmes of action to take forward the *National Service Framework* organised around three themes: dignity in care, joined up care and healthy ageing (Philp, 2006).

A further report from the Ombudsman published in 2003 drew attention to the failure of the NHS to meet its obligations to provide continuing care to older and disabled people (Health Services Commissioner, 2003), indicating that action taken after the Ombudsman's 1994 report on this issue had not had the desired effect (see above). The 2003 report was based on investigations into four cases and concluded that some health authorities and trusts had misinterpreted DH guidance on eligibility criteria for NHS funding, developed in response to the Coughlan judgment in the Court of Appeal in 1999. This judgment found that the NHS was responsible for meeting the costs of care of patients whose needs were primarily health or medical needs. The Ombudsman recommended that the DH should review its guidance on eligibility again and be more active in checking that local criteria followed the guidance. The decision of the Scottish Parliament to fund the costs of personal care as well as nursing care (see Chapter 7) underlined the restrictive nature of the policy developed in England and led to pressure on the government to reconsider the recommendations of the majority on the Royal Commission.

In 2004 the Ombudsman reported that DH and NHS bodies had made strenuous efforts to undertake retrospective reviews of cases where patients had been denied funding and make restitution where justified, even though the reviews had not been completed on time. The Ombudsman's report also concluded that the DH needed to lead further work to establish clear, national, minimum eligibility criteria, and develop assessment tools and training to support the criteria. In fact, shortly before the publication of the Ombudsman's report, the government announced that it would develop a national framework on eligibility for continuing care, and a consultation document on the framework was published in 2006. The framework was revised in the light of consultation and it came into effect in October 2007. Impetus was added to this work by a critical report from the House of Commons Health Committee highlighting weaknesses in the government's response to the Ombudsman's 2003 report, and arguing that artificial barriers between health and social care lay at the heart of access to continuing care funding (Health Committee, 2005). In so doing, the Committee was echoing the findings of many previous reports that had highlighted the difficulty of achieving closer integration of health and social care.

The question of how care for older people should be funded in future was the subject of a detailed review led by Derek Wanless for the King's Fund (Wanless, 2006) The Wanless social care review (not to be confused with the Wanless reviews of the long-term funding of health care, public health and progress in reforming the NHS) focused on the costs of social care for older people over the next 20 years and how these costs might be met. Using different scenarios, the review estimated that the costs of social care would rise by around 140 per cent, and that various options were available for meeting these costs. The three main options explored in the review were free personal care, as adopted in Scotland, a limited liability model in which care was means tested for three to four years and then personal care was provided without charge, and a partnership model in which people were provided with free care up to a minimum guaranteed amount with individual contributions over and above the minimum being matched by the state. The Wanless social care review led to renewed interest in issues explored by the Royal Commission a decade earlier and was one of the factors that influenced the government to set up a further review of the funding of long-term care in 2007 with the aim of preparing a Green Paper setting out options for reform. The results were expected to be published in 2009.

Children's services and maternity care

By comparison with the other services reviewed here, children's services and maternity care have only recently received sustained attention by policy-makers. The trigger for this has been twofold: first, there have been a number of high profile examples of children and families that have been failed by the NHS and social care; and second, there has been increasing recognition that a number of risk factors like obesity in children will store up problems for the future unless they are addressed with urgency. In the case of maternity care, the government has refocused attention on this area of the NHS as part of the policies discussed earlier of improving access and raising standards, including increasing the choices available to service users.

In recent years the Victoria Climbie case has come to symbolise the failure of public services to offer adequate support to children and families (Laming Report, 2003). The government responded to the report of the inquiry into the death of Victoria Climbie in Haringey by announcing the biggest reorganisation of children's services in 30 years in the Green Paper, *Every Child Matters*. The reorganisation included the appointment of an independent commissioner to protect the rights and well-being of children, the appointment of a children's director in each local authority, and the establishment of children's trusts to bring together local authority, health and some government services for children (Chief Secretary to the Treasury, 2003). One of the consequences of these changes was to separate children's services from adult social care, thereby bringing to an end the integration of social care in social services departments that resulted from the Seebohm reforms of 1971 (see Chapter 1).

Subsequently, the government published the *National Service Framework for Children, Young People and Maternity Services* (Department for Education and Skills and Department of Health, 2004) and *The Children's Plan* (Secretary of State for Children, Schools and Families, 2007). The national service framework included 11 standards for improving services for children and young people and maternity services, and the government emphasised that it would take ten years to implement the standards fully. Further guidance on maternity services was published in *Maternity Matters* in 2007 (DH, 2007e) which included commitments to increase the range of choices available to women in their use of maternity services from antenatal care, through childbirth and on to postnatal care.

A review of progress in implementing the national service framework reported that a start had been made in improving services but acknowledged that much remained to be done to translate the commitments included in the framework into action over the ten year period covered by the framework (Shribman, 2007). In recognition of this, and the need for concerted action across government to take forward the targets for child health and maternity included in the public service agreement covering the period 2008 to 2011, the Department for Children, Schools and Families and the DH set up a Child Health and Well-being Board to oversee delivery of the agreement. Many of the public health policies developed by the government have particular relevance to children in view of the increasing rates of obesity in the population and the persistence and in some cases widening of health inequalities. The need for action across government and between agencies at a local level is therefore essential in turning the commitments included in the national service framework and other documents into action. The case of Baby P in 2008, also involving child protection services in Haringey, indicated that many of the challenges in improving children's services remained to be tackled.

Health and social care integration

A theme that runs through discussions of policies for groups such as older people, people with learning disabilities, people with mental illness and children's services is the importance of closer integration of health and social care in making a reality of community care (see Glasby and Littlechild (2004) on health and social care integration for older people). A series of reports over the years have reviewed arrangements for partnership working and have made proposals for strengthening links between services. Of particular importance were the arrangements for joint planning and joint finance put in place in the 1970s. While some progress has been made in strengthening relationships, more radical proposals for change such as placing health and social care under the control of a single agency have been considered but rejected. As the DH has stated, 'Major structural change is not the answer' (DH, 1998b, p. 5), and accordingly a range of other mechanisms have been used to encourage the NHS and local government to work together.

Under the Health Act 1999, health authorities and local authorities have been placed under a duty to work in partnership. The Act provided for new flexibilities through pooled budgets, lead and joint commissioning, and integrated provision. The provisions of the Act have been incorporated in the same terms in the NHS Act 2006 and this now provides the legal framework for partnership working. One way in which integration is going forward is through the creation of care trusts, first mentioned in *The NHS Plan* in 2000. These trusts are formed when primary care trusts or NHS trusts make a joint application with local councils to commission and/or provide services in an integrated way. The first four care trusts were formed in 2002 and by 2008 ten had been established.

Alongside care trusts, the government has placed a duty on local authorities and partners in the public and voluntary sectors to cooperate in the development of local area agreements supported by joint strategic needs assessments to meet the needs of the populations they serve. Local strategic partnerships between the NHS, local authorities and other agencies have also been promoted to ensure coordinated leadership by relevant bodies in each area. These agreements and partnerships have focused on public health issues and population health improvement as well as on closer integration of funding and service delivery. Children's trusts (see above) are another mechanism for enabling the NHS and local authorities to work together. While care trusts are statutory bodies that fully integrate health and social care services for the groups they serve, children's trusts are an example of virtual integration between statutory and voluntary bodies. A review of the performance of children's trusts published by the Audit Commission (2008) found no evidence that outcomes for children and young people had improved as a result of the establishment of trusts or that value for money had improved.

In many parts of the country, intermediate care services have been developed jointly by the NHS and local authorities, often in the context of collaboration in planning for and dealing with winter pressures on the NHS. The DH has exerted strong pressure on the NHS and local authorities to avoid a repetition of the crisis that confronted the NHS in the winter of 1999/2000 and has allocated extra resources to tackle the problem of delayed transfers between hospitals and the community. This included the provision of a Delayed Discharge Grant to local authorities to enable them to increase the provision of care in the community. Under the Community Care (Delayed Discharges etc.) Act 2003, local authorities were required to pay NHS bodies for the care of people in hospital who could appropriately be looked after in the community with effect from 2004. While this policy was controversial, its introduction was associated with a significant reduction in delayed transfers, although the reduction had started before the implementation of the 2003 Act, and the impact of the requirement on local authorities to pay for care is difficult to disentangle from other policies, such as the expansion of intermediate care provision. In practice, only a minority of NHS organisations chose to impose charges on local authorities for delayed transfers, and many of those that did used the funds to pay for interventions intended to reduce delays in discharge and to support partnership working with local authorities (McCoy et al., 2007).

As a consequence of these and other developments, the nature and extent of partnership working varies between areas. If in some parts of the country there is increasingly close collaboration through the use of care trusts, children's trusts, local strategic partnerships and joint appointments, in a few cases leading to the full integration of services, in other areas much less progress has been made in developing joint approaches. This reflects the difficulties in making partnerships between different agencies work, as well as long-standing political, professional, financial and organisational differences between the NHS and local government. Evidence gathered by the Audit Commission (2005) points to an increasing use of the flexibilities available under the Health Act 1999, especially the use of pooled budgets by PCTs, while also noting the time-consuming nature of partnerships and the risks they involve for the agencies concerned. Further progress in this area depends on the outcome of the review, announced in the final report of the NHS Next Stage Review led by Lord Darzi, of how organisations that wish to go further in integrating health and social care services could be supported to do so. This is likely to build on *Putting People First*, a ministerial concordat on the future of adult social care that set out a vision of personalised care delivered in partnership and making use of joint strategic needs assessments and local area agreements (DH, 2007c).

Priority-setting

As we have seen, successive governments have developed policies for improving services in many different areas. The challenge this gives rise to is that of determining the priority to be attached to these services in a context in which the NHS budget has grown steadily but cannot meet all demands immediately. Priority-setting or rationing is not new and in the first phase of the NHS debate centred on the adequacy of the funding made available by the government and the decision to introduce charges for some services. As time went on, the lengthening of waiting lists for hospital treatment came to exemplify rationing by delay and there was also evidence that doctors rationed access to specialist services such as dialysis for the treatment of kidney failure (Halper, 1989). The latter example illustrates the more general point that NHS rationing tended to be implicit and a matter of clinical judgement rather than a process that occurred out in the open. Only in the 1970s when expenditure constraints began to bite and growth rates slowed did governments address the issue of priority-setting systematically.

The high point of priority-setting at a national level occurred in 1976 when the Labour government published a consultative document on *Priorities for Health and Personal Social Services in England* setting out quantified targets for the development of different services (DHSS, 1976b). In the following year there was a retreat from this approach with the White Paper, *The Way Forward* (DHSS, 1977b), indicating in broad terms, as illustrative projections only, the kinds of developments that might occur. This process was taken to its logical conclusion in *Care in Action* (DHSS, 1981c), the first statement on priorities produced by the Thatcher government, which gave a general account of government policies for different services and client groups, and argued that priority-setting was a matter for local decision and local action.

The reluctance of governments to take a lead in setting priorities derives from the political costs involved in taking unpopular decisions. This was illustrated by the response to the 1976 *Priorities* document and the opposition of groups representing services identified as low priorities to the approach taken by the government. In these circumstances, it is not surprising that politicians prefer to pass responsibility to health authorities or seek to mask the effects of their policies. As Klein (2006) has observed, the diffusion of blame is an enduring feature of the NHS and helps to explain why decision-makers at a local level are given the responsibility of making choices between different services. An example that illustrates this was the case of Child B, a 10-year-old girl denied funding for an experimental treatment for leukaemia by the Cambridge and Huntingdon Health Authority (Ham and Pickard, 1998). The case received extensive publicity and the senior staff of the health authority were responsible for accounting to the media and the public for their decision.

Similarly, politicians may resort to subterfuge and evasion in reconciling limited budgets and growing demands. The withdrawal of long-term care from the NHS through a series of incremental decisions (see above) is a clear illustration of this, demonstrating how care may be rationed even in the absence of public debate. Restrictions on the availability of dental services within the NHS indicate a different kind of approach, with care that was once seen as part of the core of NHS provision being withdrawn as a consequence of dissatisfaction on the part of dentists with NHS terms and conditions. In this case, the failure of successive governments to respond to the decision of dentists in some areas to no longer offer to provide services within the NHS meant that dental care de facto became a private service in these areas.

How then do NHS organisations arrive at decisions on priorities? Research evidence indicates that local decisions are shaped by inherited commitments and by bargaining between different interests. National guidance on priorities plays a major part in this process and account is also taken of the views of local people and the preferences of providers. The outcome tends to involve incremental adjustments to existing budgets rather than major changes of direction as NHS organisations spread resources around in seeking to reconcile the demands placed upon them (Ham, 1993; Klein et al., 1996). Decisions are informed by the application of techniques and evidence on cost-effectiveness, but it is the judgement of local policy-makers and their weighing of different claims that is decisive.

Put another way, priority-setting is an arena in which the politics of the NHS are played out at a local level and in Chapter 9 we explore further the dynamics of the micro politics of health care. Local responsibility for priority-setting results in variations between areas in the availability of services within the NHS. This has become known as 'rationing by postcode'. Access to care then depends on where people live and this has raised questions about the claim of the NHS to be a national service in which care is available on the basis of need. Examples include the priority attached to new drugs such as herceptin for the treatment of breast cancer, and access to services like infertility treatment. In both of these cases there are variations between areas reflecting differences between PCTs in the importance given to competing claims on the use of resources. The decision of the Blair government to establish NICE and to develop national service frameworks was an attempt to address the so-called postcode lottery.

These developments signalled the willingness of the government to take on a bigger role in priority-setting and to ensure greater equity in the provision of services. NICE guidance sets standards in four areas: the use of drugs and other technologies; the provision of certain surgical procedures; guidance on public health policies and interventions; and clinical guidelines that cover a range of topics such as care for people with depression and the care of pregnant women. Studies have shown variations in the extent to which NICE guidance is implemented in the NHS. In response, the government placed PCTs under a legal obligation to implement the technology appraisals undertaken by NICE. The assessments carried out by the Healthcare Commission involve asking PCTs to report on their performance in implementing NICE guidance. For its part, NICE has placed greater priority on implementation of its advice in the period since 2004. An inquiry carried out by the House of Commons Health Committee welcomed these initiatives but concluded that more needed to be done to reduce variations in the availability of services and drugs between areas (Health Committee, 2008b). As the Committee noted, these variations resulted from differences between NHS bodies in their ability to implement guidance and the attitudes and engagement of doctors and other clinicians.

Looking beyond NICE, while there was evidence that targets and national service frameworks contributed to the improvements in performance brought about during this period, there was also recognition that NHS organisations were suffering from target overload. Accordingly, following the 2002 election, there was a progressive move to rationalise the number of targets applied to the NHS, and to avoid introducing new targets except where there was a strong case so to do (healthcare associated infections being a good example). The more disciplined approach to the use of targets was signalled in *National Standards, Local Action* (Crisp, 2004) which provided planning guidance to the NHS for the period 2005 to 2008. This approach has been maintained in the annual operating framework for the NHS published in subsequent years.

Five key priorities were contained in the operating framework for 2008/09: improving cleanliness and reducing healthcare associated infections; improving access through achieving 18-week referral to treatment, and providing better access to GP services; keeping people well, improving overall health and reducing health inequalities; improving patient experience, staff satisfaction, and engagement; and preparing to respond to emergencies, such as an outbreak of pandemic flu. Behind these headline priorities, more specific objectives were set out, including improvements in cancer services, stroke care, maternity services and children's services. As well as these national priorities, the operating framework stated that PCTs should set local improvement plans for areas of concern identified through discussions with patients, staff and partners. Examples given in the framework included reducing mixed sex accommodation, improving services for people with learning disabilities and strengthening end of life care.

The importance of the operating framework is in making clear the main national priorities for the NHS. PCTs and other NHS bodies know they are expected to focus much of their effort and most of their resources on the implementation of these priorities, and that they will be held to account if they fail to deliver. As we discuss further in Chapter 9, this means that the government is now able to exercise more control over the implementation of core national objectives than at any time in the past. At the same time, NHS bodies retain some discretion to develop local priorities and implementation of national priorities beyond those that are seen as the most important remains uneven.

Conclusion

This chapter has shown that both Conservative and Labour governments have developed a wide range of policies designed to improve the performance of the NHS. In the past decade, it is clear that some areas of the NHS have benefited more than others from the substantial increases in expenditure that have occurred. The biggest beneficiaries have been acute hospitals which have received the lion's share of the additional resources made available in order to achieve the ambitious targets for reducing waiting lists and waiting times set by the government. The major areas of clinical priority such as cancer and heart disease have also witnessed increased investment and have used this investment to bring about measurable improvements in health and care. By comparison, services such as those for people with learning disabilities and for people with dementia have not benefited to the same degree. Primary care sits somewhere in the middle with GPs receiving large increases in pay under the new contract introduced in 2004 but services for people with long term conditions picking up the scraps of what has been left over after other priorities have been funded. Similarly, there have been improvements in care for older people and for people with mental illness, though not on the same scale as those seen in the acute services.

A theme that has recurred throughout the chapter is that of priority-setting in the NHS and the respective roles of government and NHS bodies in this process. The paradox of a national health service in which NHS bodies and doctors play a major part in resource allocation is explained by the political costs involved in explicit priority-setting at a national level, and the quest for alternative ways of diffusing blame and avoiding accountability. Recent years have seen government becoming more involved in priority-setting through NICE, national service frameworks and the use of targets for the improvement of care in high profile areas. As a consequence, the government has more influence over the decisions of NHS bodies than in the past, and the scope for local deviation from national policies has been narrowed although not eliminated. As NHS funding becomes more constrained, the willingness of politicians to maintain close involvement in priority-setting may diminish, especially if this involves taking unpopular decisions about the availability of expensive new drugs and other services. PCTs will then be back in the spotlight of public scrutiny as they grapple with the difficult choices involved in allocating fixed budgets between competing claims. We return to discuss this in Chapter 12.

Chapter 6

Policy-making in Westminster and Whitehall

The chapter begins with a definition of policy. The focus then shifts to the organisation of central government. At the core of the chapter is a description of the role of Parliament, the Prime Minister and Cabinet, ministers, civil servants, and special advisers, and relationships between government departments. This is followed by an analysis of the role of outside interests and pressure groups. The increasing part played by these groups requires that we look beyond the formal institutions of government to the role of policy networks and policy communities. The final part of the chapter assesses whether central government is best described as pluralist or corporatist in character. In exploring these issues, the chapter focuses particularly on the Blair government and the argument that power has become more centralised around the Prime Minister in the period since 1997.

What is policy?

Although many writers have attempted to define policy, there is little agreement on the meaning of the word. It is therefore tempting to follow Cunningham and argue that 'policy is rather like the elephant – you recognise it when you see it but cannot easily define it' (quoted in Smith, 1976, p. 12). Attractive as this interpretation is, it may be worth spending a little time clarifying the meaning of policy, and the different ways in which it has been used.

A useful starting point is the work of David Easton, who has argued that political activity can be distinguished by its concern with 'the authoritative allocation of values' within society (Easton, 1953, p. 136). Easton uses values in a broad sense to encompass the whole range of rewards and sanctions that those in positions of authority are able to distribute. Values are allocated by means of policies, and for Easton 'A policy ... consists of a web of decisions and actions that allocate ... values' (Easton, 1953, p. 130). A number of points can be made about this definition.

First, Easton argues that the study of policy encompasses both formal decisions and actions. He points out that a decision by itself is not an action, but merely the selection among alternatives. What happens in practice may be different from what was intended by decision-makers, and it is important to focus on the processes that follow from a decision. Put another way, we need to consider how policy is implemented as well as how it is made.

A second point about Easton's definition is that it suggests that policy may involve a web of decisions rather than one decision. There are two aspects to this. First, the actors who make decisions are rarely the same people as those responsible for implementation. A decision network, often of considerable complexity, may therefore be involved in producing action, and a web of decisions may form part of the network. The second aspect is that even at the policy-making level, policy is not usually expressed in a single decision. It tends to be defined in terms of a series of decisions which, taken together, comprise a more or less common understanding of what policy is.

Third, policies invariably change over time. Yesterday's statements of intent may not be the same as today's, either because of incremental adjustments to earlier decisions, or more unusually because of major changes of direction. Also, experience of implementing a decision may feed back into the decision-making process, thereby leading to changes in the allocation of values. This is not to say that policies are always changing, but simply that the policy process is dynamic rather than static and that we need to be aware of shifting definitions of issues.

Fourth, the corollary of the last point is the need to recognise that the study of policy has as one of its main concerns the examination of non-decisions and inaction. Although not encompassed in Easton's definition, the concept of non-decision-making has become increasingly important in recent years, and a focus on decision-making has been criticised for ignoring more routine activities leading to policy maintenance and even inertia. Indeed, it has been argued that much political activity is concerned with maintaining the status quo and resisting challenges to the existing allocation of values. Analysis of this activity is a necessary part of the examination of the dynamics of the policy process (Bachrach and Baratz, 1970).

Fifth and finally, Easton's definition raises the question of whether policy can be seen as action without decisions. Can it be said that a pattern of actions over a period of time constitutes a policy, even if these actions have not been formally sanctioned by a decision? In practice it would seem that a good deal of what happens in public agencies occurs because 'it has always been done this way', and cannot be attributed to any official pronouncement. Further, writers on policy have increasingly turned their attention to the actions of lower level actors, sometimes called street-level bureaucrats, in order to gain a better understanding of policy-making and implementation. It would seem important to balance a decisional 'top-down' perspective on policy with an action-oriented, 'bottom-up' perspective (Barrett and Fudge, 1981). Actions as well as decisions may therefore be said to be the proper focus of policy analysis.

Accordingly, in this and the subsequent chapter the main focus of attention is on the policy-making process in central government, while Chapter 8 examines the implementation of centrally determined policies and the local influences on health policy-making.

British central government

The organisation of British central government can be described simply. General elections, which must be held at least every five years, result in the election to the House of Commons of some 650 Members of Parliament (the precise number varies as constituency boundaries are redrawn). The leader of the largest single party in the Commons is asked by the monarch to form a government and the leader becomes the Prime Minister. The Prime Minister appoints from among his or her supporters around 100 people to take up ministerial appointments. The most senior of these, usually numbering around 20, comprise the Cabinet. The government is thus made up of Cabinet and non-Cabinet ministers, the majority of whom will be MPs. The remaining members of the government come from the House of Lords.

Ministers are responsible for the day-to-day running of the government's business through the departments of state. These departments include the Treasury, which is responsible for all matters to do with the economy and public spending, and the Department of Health (DH). Most of the work of the departments is in practice carried out by civil servants. Ministers are, however, individually responsible for the work done by civil servants in their name, and are held accountable by Parliament. Parliament also monitors the work of government departments through a system of select committees.

There is no written constitution in Britain and the relationship between the different institutions of government has evolved over the years. As one of the foremost students of the constitution has observed, the result is a 'curious compound of custom and precedent, law and convention, rigidity and malleability concealed beneath layers of opacity and mystery' (Hennessy, 1995, p. 7). In seeking to unravel the mystery of the unwritten constitution, much has been written about the role of the monarchy, the legislature and the executive. To summarise this literature briefly, the historical decline in the power of the monarchy and the House of Lords gave rise to the thesis that Britain had a system of 'Cabinet government'. In his book, *The English Constitution*, published in 1867, Walter Bagehot argued that the monarchy and the Lords had become 'dignified' elements in the constitution, compared with the Commons, the Cabinet and the Prime Minister which he described as the 'efficient' elements (Bagehot, 1963).

Almost 100 years later, Richard Crossman, writing an introduction to a new edition of Bagehot's book, contended that Prime Ministerial government had replaced Cabinet government. In Crossman's view, the extension of voting to all adults, the creation of mass political parties and the emergence of the civil service administering a large welfare state all contributed to the Prime Minister's power (Crossman, 1963). This interpretation was confirmed by Crossman's experience as a Cabinet minister. In addition, he noted the important part played by official committees in Whitehall, a facet of government he had not observed while in opposition; and he encountered the power of civil servants to challenge and frustrate the wishes of ministers. Students of central government have drawn on the experience of the Thatcher and Blair governments to argue that Prime Ministerial government may have become presidential or even Napoleonic (Hennessy, 2005), so powerful have recent incumbents of this office become.

One of the consequences has been to bring into question whether British central government continues to exemplify the so-called 'Westminster model' of politics, characterised by free and fair elections, Parliamentary sovereignty, control of the executive by the majority party, strong Cabinet government, a key role for government departments, ministerial responsibility for the actions of departments, and a neutral civil service. Rhodes' research (Rhodes, 1997) has invoked trends such as the privatisation and contracting out of public services, the increasing role of international organisations like the European Union, and the establishment of agencies to take on some functions of government to question the key tenets of the Westminster model. Rhodes contends that the executive is weak and not strong and that the institutions of central government have been 'hollowed out' as a consequence of privatisation and the increasing role of international organisations and agencies operating at arm's length from government. In place of the Westminster model, Rhodes proposes the 'differentiated polity model' to describe a system in which government is increasingly fragmented. In this system, networks have replaced hierarchies and institutions and organisations external to government play a bigger part in governance. The differentiated policy model, also referred to as the 'governance narrative' (Bevir and Rhodes, 2006), has, in turn, been challenged by other researchers who maintain that power is more concentrated than Rhodes suggests (Marsh et al., 2001). We explore these issues in the rest of this chapter by examining the role of different institutions and the relationship between them.

Parliament

It is important to distinguish the formal power of Parliament from its effective role. Although formally Parliament passes legislation, examines public expenditure and controls the government, effectively it carries out these functions within strictly defined limits. As long as there is a House of Commons majority to support the government, then Parliament has few significant powers within the system of central government. In Mackintosh's words, 'Parliament is one of the agencies through which the government operates and it is the place where the struggle for power continues in a restricted form between elections' (Mackintosh, 1974, p. 125).

The task of securing the government's majority in the House of Commons falls to the party whips. They ensure that MPs are present to vote, and that the government's legislative programme is passed safely. Most legislation originates from the government, and bills have to go through a number of stages before becoming law. Parliamentary debates on legislation provide an opportunity for party views to be reiterated, and occasionally the government will accept amendments put forward by opposition parties. On occasions, important legislation may be defeated or withdrawn. But the existence of a Parliamentary majority coupled with strong party discipline ensures that these occasions will be rare.

Parliament provides opportunities for individual MPs to propose legislation in the form of private members' bills. The most important method of promoting a private member's bill is through the ballot of members which takes place every session. Usually, around 20 names are drawn in the ballot, but because of the pressure on Parliamentary time only one-third to one-half of the MPs who are successful in the ballot stand a chance of having their bills debated and enacted. Even in these cases, though, the MPs concerned are dependent on the government not being opposed to the legislation they propose. The Abortion Act of 1967, promoted by the Liberal MP David Steel, is an example of a private member's bill which became law.

Individual MPs are able to use Parliament in two other main ways. First, they can put down Parliamentary questions, asking ministers about aspects of the work for which they are responsible. Some of these questions receive written replies, while others are answered orally, in which case there is an opportunity to ask a supplementary question. Second, MPs can raise adjournment debates, which are often on local or constituency issues. These debates provide a chance to air matters of concern to MPs and their constituents, and force ministers and departments to make a response. Also, although most of the Parliamentary timetable is controlled by the government, 20 days a session are available to the opposition to debate subjects of their choosing.

One of the key developments in Parliament in recent years has been the use of select committees. These are committees of MPs which investigate particular topics and publish reports on their findings. The aim of the committees is to provide MPs with a more effective means of controlling the executive, and to extract information about the government's policies. The establishment of the committees was in part a response to the perceived decline in the power of the Commons to control the government. It was the job of the Social Services Committee to monitor the work of the DHSS and it was superseded by the Health Committee when the department was divided in 1988. Recent investigations by the Health Committee have covered issues such as NHS foundation trusts and patient safety. Alongside the Health Committee, the Public Accounts Committee continues to examine the way in which government money has been spent, including spending on health services. The Public Accounts Committee has published a number of reports which have been critical of the management of the NHS, including the cost of the new contracts for general practitioners and consultants, and progress in improving quality and safety in primary care.

The actual impact of select committees on policy is largely determined by the government's willingness to accept their recommendations. Although it is expected that departments will respond to committee reports, this does not mean that the committees' findings will have an immediate influence on policy. Nevertheless, it can be suggested that committees create a more informed House of Commons, force departments to account for their actions, submit ministers to a level of questioning not possible on the floor of the House, and help to put issues on the agenda for discussion. Furthermore, at a time when the role and influence of individual MPs have come into question, the committees have given MPs useful and often satisfying work to do. They also enable outsiders to gain a better understanding of what is going on in Whitehall, and the information they extract provides ammunition for pressure groups to use in particular campaigns.

The development of the role of select committees is one of the factors that have led some writers to argue that the House of Commons is more powerful than often assumed. This is the view held by Norton (1981), who has drawn on evidence of a decline in the cohesion of political parties within Parliament and an increase in government defeats in division lobbies to suggest that the Commons can effectively scrutinise and influence government. As Norton points out, the key to government control of Parliament historically has been the existence of a single majority party with strong discipline being exercised by the whips, and any moves away from this system, such as the formation of minority or coalition governments, would further strengthen the position of those who wish to reassert the influence of the House of Commons. Norton himself summarises the role of Parliament in the following way:

> Parliament has never really been a law-making or policy-making body on any continuous basis. Its principal task in terms of proposals for public policy, as well as the conduct of government, has been one of scrutiny ... The fact that government needs Parliament to give assent to measures and its request for money means that Parliament has some leverage ... The impact of the British Parliament today, as in the past, might not be great, but it can and does have some effect on public policy. (Norton, 1997, p. 157)

Norton's views are echoed by Cowley who has argued that Parliament retains influence even if examples of it defeating governments are few and far between. As Cowley shows, even the Blair Government with its large Parliamentary majority had to negotiate with backbench MPs to secure support for its more controversial proposals, including university top-up fees and the introduction of NHS foundation trusts. As he notes, the government survived the period from 1997 to 2005 undefeated on a whipped vote in the House of Commons, but it did so 'because it was frequently willing to negotiate with its backbench critics, giving policy concessions to them, in order to stave off defeat' (Cowley, 2006, p. 44). This interpretation is supported by Norton in his more recent writings (Norton, 2005). Norton argues that there is far more to the role of Parliament than legislative scrutiny and rejecting government proposals. He contends that the decline of corporatism since the 1970s is one of the factors that has enhanced the influence of MPs, not least because pressure groups have to use a wider range of channels to promote their objectives and can no longer rely on cultivating close relationships with the executive.

The Prime Minister and Cabinet

The pre-eminence of the Prime Minister in the British system of government noted by Crossman and other commentators can be explained in a number of ways. First there is the Prime Minister's patronage. He or she has sole responsibility for appointing members of the government, and in addition has considerable discretion over the conferment of honours. Of course, the Prime Minister's power of patronage is not total, and is usually exercised with regard to the influence of other actors in the system. In appointing the Cabinet, for example, the Prime Minister will want to include people drawn from different parts of the majority party, possibly including former opponents. Nevertheless, it is ultimately the Prime Minister alone who decides, and who accepts responsibility for the appointments made.

Second, there is the Prime Minister's position as chairman of the Cabinet. This gives the Prime Minister control over the Cabinet agenda, and the power to appoint the members and chairmen of Cabinet committees. The Prime Minister may also establish informal groupings of senior ministers to act as an inner Cabinet. The inner Cabinet may serve as a sounding board for the Prime Minister, and may help to incorporate potential rivals into the centre of government decision-making. The Prime Minister will negotiate too with individual ministers in order to gain influence over specific policies. This was very much Mrs Thatcher's style of government (Hennessy, 1986) and her informal approach also characterised Tony Blair's premiership.

Third, the Prime Minister's position is strengthened by the support of the Cabinet Office. Within the Cabinet Office the Cabinet Secretary is the key person, and he or she acts as the personal adviser to the Prime Minister. The Cabinet secretariat controls the distribution of minutes and papers in the Cabinet system and enables the Prime Minister to keep a close eye on what is taking place in Cabinet committees. Fourth, since 1974, successive Prime Ministers have made use of their own Policy Unit located in 10 Downing Street. The Unit's principal purpose is to assist the Prime Minister in implementing the strategic goals of the government. The role of the Policy Unit was strengthened under Tony Blair to provide the Prime Minister with the support needed to take forward the reforming policies his government was elected to put into practice. This is discussed further below.

As well as these sources of strength, the Prime Minister's powers are underpinned by his or her position as leader of the majority party and the politician with overall responsibility for the civil service. All of these factors give the Prime Minister a more powerful role than the traditional description, *primus inter pares*, suggests. Crossman's *Diaries* (1975, 1976, 1977) indicate that there were occasions when the Cabinet did engage in collective decision-making, but these tended to be when the Prime Minister had no definite view and was prepared to let the Cabinet decide. What seems clear is that the Prime Minister is rarely defeated in Cabinet, and an alliance between the Prime Minister and the Chancellor of the Exchequer, or the Prime Minister and the Foreign Secretary, is virtually unstoppable.

Yet before consigning the Cabinet to the dignified realm of the British constitution, the limits of Prime Ministerial power should be noted. For example, during the course of 1981 proposals for cuts in public expenditure put forward by the Chancellor of the Exchequer with support from the Prime Minister were defeated by the so-called 'wets' in the Conservative Cabinet (Young, 1989). Even more dramatically, Margaret Thatcher was forced to resign as Prime Minister in 1990 when she lost the confidence of her colleagues. Her successor, John Major, faced a similar challenge to his position in 1995 and chose to resign as leader of the Conservative Party in order to fight a leadership election with his critics. In both of these examples, the challenge to serving Prime Ministers demonstrates the existence of a number of checks and balances in the British system of government, not in the form of codified rules of the kind found in the United States constitution but nonetheless effective.

The election to office of a Labour Government in 1997 marked a return to the centralisation of power around the Prime Minister and his close advisers. Tony Blair adopted a presidential style and strengthened the Cabinet Office and the Policy Unit in 10 Downing Street to ensure that adequate support was available. This included appointing trusted colleagues to senior roles, including Jonathan Powell as chief of staff and Alastair Campbell as chief press secretary and adviser to the Prime Minister. A further indication of the increasing influence of the corporate centre of government was that the number of special advisers providing support to the Prime Ministers increased from six under the Major government to 25 under the Blair government (Fawcett and Gay, 2005). Taken together, these measures meant that 'The Cabinet Office must now be considered something of a corporate headquarters overseeing government strategy' (Kavanagh and Seldon, 1999, p. 303).

During this period, the Cabinet Office was strengthened to the point where, in the view of some commentators, it had become a Prime Minister's Department (Hennessy, 2000; Riddell, 2001). Specific innovations included the establishment of a number of units within the Cabinet Office to support the Prime Minister and the government. These included the Performance and Innovation Unit and the Forward Strategy Unit, subsequently brought together in the Prime Minister's Strategy Unit; the Prime Minister's Delivery Unit; the Office of Public Services Reform; and the Social Exclusion Unit. After the 2001 general election, the Policy Unit was merged with the Prime Minister's private office to create the Policy Directorate. The significance of this change was that the special advisers who made up the majority of members of the Policy Unit were integrated with the civil servants in the private office with the aim of creating a more effective source of advice for the Prime Minister. These changes 'amounted to the biggest upgrading of the Prime Minister's resources in the history of the office' (Seldon, 2007, p. 42).

Like Margaret Thatcher before him, Blair relied heavily on bilateral meetings with ministers rather than committees, described as follows:

> Blair's preferred method of work, as in opposition, is to hold one-to-one meetings with colleagues or to convene small ad hoc groups to tackle strategic issues. He holds bimonthly stocktaking bilaterals with Secretaries of State and their top officials in his key areas of education, health and crime ... Blair and his aides are not sympathetic to the committee style of policy-making. (Kavanagh and Seldon, 1999, p. 274)

It has been argued that the Cabinet's position was further weakened by these informal working arrangements (Hennessy, 2000). Hyman has offered a first-hand account of this method of working:

> These stocktakes were gladiatorial in appearance but rather softer in reality. They would take place in the Cabinet room. The Prime Minister would sit in his normal chair, the Secretary of State would sit opposite him flanked on one side by his Minister of State and on the other by the Permanent Secretary. Assorted special advisers and officials would be present on both sides. On Tony's side of the table were normally the Cabinet Secretary, the principal private secretary, the key policy advisers ... (Hyman, 2005, p. 176)

As far as the Cabinet is concerned, it has been noted that 'Blair's Cabinet meetings are too brief (usually less than an hour) to be effective decision-making forums' (Kavanagh and Seldon, 1999, p. 273). Set against this, it is important to note one insider's observation, namely that:

> the Cabinet has the power to constrain the Prime Minister, and implicitly uses it all the time. As proposals are prepared, consideration of whether they will 'get through' Cabinet is constant; it is therefore not surprising that proposals which finally reach Cabinet tend to go through. This is not necessarily a sign of Cabinet weakness; merely that its influence has been taken into account in preparation for the meeting. (Barber, 2007, p. 311)

Here Barber is describing the rule of anticipated reactions, a term coined by Friedrich (1937) to describe the exercise of power through indirect means. Barber goes on to argue that the bilateral stocktake meetings favoured by the Prime Minister 'had been one of the great success stories of the second term' (Barber, 2007, p. 254), and yet despite this they were replaced by Cabinet committees after the 2005 general election. In practice, Tony Blair decided that Cabinet committees were less effective than stocktakes, resulting in the latter being reinstituted and working along-side Cabinet committees.

The position of the Prime Minister in British government is reinforced by the fact that on questions of government strategy or on broad economic policy departmental ministers are often reluctant to step outside their own areas of concern. Crossman bemoaned the absence of an overall strategy in the 1964–70 Labour government, and he explained it in terms of the entrenched departmentalism within Whitehall (Crossman, 1975, 1976, 1977), a theme to which we return below. The Prime Minister, unencumbered by specific departmental responsibilities, is able to take the wider view, and so can set the direction of government policy as a whole. Only when the Prime Minister's leadership poses a threat to the government and its future electoral chances is his or her dominance likely to be seriously challenged by Cabinet colleagues. The principal exception to this generalisation is the Chancellor of the Exchequer whose overview of the economy and public spending enables the occupant of this office also to see the bigger picture and from time to time to emerge as a rival to the Prime Minister.

The importance of the relationship between the Prime Minister and Chancellor was particularly apparent under the Blair Government, in which Gordon Brown as Chancellor exercised considerable influence over many aspects of policy. One of the mechanisms used by the Chancellor was the public service agreements negotiated with government departments setting out targets to be achieved with the resources agreed during spending reviews. Brown's influence under the person who was arguably the most powerful Prime Minister in the post-war era reinforces the thesis of those who caution against exaggerating the role of the Prime Minister in contemporary British politics (Kavanagh and Seldon, 1999). It also underlines the power of the Treasury in British central government (Deakin and Parry, 2000; Marsh et al., 2001). The author's own experience in central government between 2000 and 2004 confirms these analyses, in particular the way in which health policy was shaped through discussions between the Secretary of State and the DH, the Prime Minister and Cabinet Office, and the Chancellor of the Exchequer and the Treasury. To borrow a phrase from a different context, the 'iron triangle' (Heclo, 1978) that linked these institutions was the forum in which the direction of NHS reform was determined.

The influence of the Chancellor is acknowledged even by those who have emphasised the presidential nature of politics under Tony Blair: 'Brown is, in effect, overlord of the economic and domestic front. It is a bi-stellar administration with policy constellations revolving round the two stars in Downing Street' (Hennessy, 2000, p. 513). It might be added that during this period the Chancellor and the Prime Minister did not always see eye to eye on health policy and this led to disagreement and sometimes conflict on aspects of the NHS reform programme. Disagreement was particularly apparent in the wake of the 2001 general election when the Prime Minister, in association with his Secretary of State for Health, Alan Milburn, developed policies to extend patient choice and increase competition between hospitals and other providers. These policies were resisted by the Chancellor and his resistance foreshadowed much more significant differences of view on the freedoms of NHS foundation trusts, and particularly their ability to borrow money from private sources. Seldon has described how an impasse was reached over this issue and a way forward was only found with the involvement of the Cabinet Secretary (Seldon, 2007, pp. 240–47, drawing on Campbell, 2007). The way forward involved a compromise in which Brown succeeded in limiting the freedoms of NHS foundation trusts against Milburn's objections and with Blair's acquiescence.

Ministers, civil servants and special advisers

Alongside the Prime Minister and the Chancellor, ministers and civil servants in government departments exercise considerable influence, notwithstanding the increasing power of the corporate centre of government. However, the view encapsulated in the Westminster model that ministers decide policy and civil servants carry it out is no longer widely held. Ministerial memoirs and studies of government have shown that civil servants influence policy-making in various ways. Their familiarity with the Whitehall machine, coupled with access to information and a repository of knowledge developed over a period of years, creates an expertise which is not easily challenged. Often, it is the strength of the departmental view or 'official view' on an issue, rather than any ideological antipathy, which politicians have to overcome (Young and Sloman, 1982; Barber, 2007). In many cases, ministers are not well-placed to challenge this view, if only because parties in opposition devote relatively little time to developing the policies they intend to carry out when in office. In addition, ministers may not always have the skill to counter the weight of advice offered by civil servants. The debate about the relative influence of ministers and civil servants may therefore be more to do with weak ministers than conspiratorial civil servants. Ministers are not always appointed for their administrative ability or their analytical skills, and it is perhaps not surprising that they do not always carry through significant changes in policy (Hennessy, 1989). Only ministers who are particularly determined and ambitious, such as Alan Milburn, are able to make a real difference.

Another reason why ministers may be less than fully effective is the variety of different jobs they are expected to do: run their department; participate in Cabinet and Cabinet committee discussions; take care of their constituents as MPs; and take part in the work of the House of Commons. With so many competing demands on their time, it may be easier for ministers to accept the advice they are given and to rely on their departmental briefs than to attempt to exercise an independent policy-making role. It is worth noting, though, that there have been attempts to bolster the position of ministers through the appointment of special advisers. These advisers were first used on a large scale in the 1960s and they have been employed by both Labour and Conservative governments. Professor Brian Abel-Smith of the London School of Economics was used as a political adviser in the DHSS by Richard Crossman in the late 1960s, and by Barbara Castle and David Ennals in the mid-1970s. The more astute advisers are able to enhance their position by building up relationships directly with civil servants, senior and junior, rather than always working with or through ministers (Young and Sloman, 1982). The role of special advisers increased markedly under the Blair government, exemplified by the contribution made by Simon Stevens who served as an adviser to two Secretaries of State, Frank Dobson and Alan Milburn, before becoming the Prime Minister's senior health policy adviser after the 2001 general election.

The number of special advisers in government increased from 34 in 1994/95 to 83 in 2001/02. In most government departments, there are two special advisers who work alongside civil servants. One of these advisers is often involved in supporting ministers in communicating their views to the press and the public, while the other is usually engaged in the development of policy and maintaining links with the party and other important stakeholders. There is a much larger number of advisers in the Prime Minister's Office (currently around 25) reflecting the growth in importance of this office, discussed earlier. These advisers are involved in supporting the Prime Minister in work on strategy and policy, strategic communications, and government and political relations. Within departments, special advisers are increasingly active in working with ministers and civil servants in the development of policy, including the area of health policy where advisers in both 10 Downing Street and the DH have worked closely with ministers in the development of plans for the NHS. On many issues, this means that advisers may be more influential than civil servants. It also means that ministers have access to alternative sources of advice and are able to test the recommendations they receive from officials against the views of advisers and others.

The increase in the number of special advisers working in government and their higher profile has raised questions about the boundaries between ministers, civil servants and advisers (Committee on Standards in Public Life, 2002). A report by the House of Commons Public Administration Committee in 2001 concluded that special advisers had a valuable contribution to make but argued that there should be greater transparency in their method of working and a clearer framework of accountability around their activities (Public Administration Committee, 2001). In a more recent report the Committee reaffirmed that special advisers play a generally positive part in government and it underlined the variety of roles they perform, including acting as acknowledged experts, media minders and media assistants, and young policy-makers (Public Administration Committee, 2007, p. 36, drawing on evidence from Sir David Omand). Hyman has also identified a number of different types of adviser, describing them as policy wonks, spin doctors, security blankets, fixers and strategists (Hyman, 2005, pp. 251–2).

Relationships between departments

In discussing the role of the Cabinet, we noted that attempts to develop overall government strategies were frustrated by the strength of individual departments. The importance of 'departmental pluralism' (Richardson and Jordan, 1979, p. 26) is nowhere more apparent than in the budgeting process of central government, which historically centred on the PESC cycle (PESC is the acronym for the Public Expenditure Survey Committee, the committee of officials which coordinated the preparation of the government's expenditure plans). *The Castle Diaries 1974–76* provides fascinating insights into the PESC negotiations, particularly as they affected health services. During the later months of 1975 and early 1976 – a time of increasing control over public expenditure – Castle and her officials were in the position of defending the NHS budget against attempts by the Chancellor of the Exchequer and the Treasury to achieve significant reductions in planned spending levels. As Castle records in her diaries, the public expenditure White Paper 'demonstrated vividly how much more successful I have been than some of my colleagues in defending my programmes' (Castle, 1980, p. 641).

One of the aims of PESC was to develop a more corporate approach to public expenditure planning and policy-making. The Central Policy Review Staff (CPRS), the government think-tank which started work in 1971 and was disbanded in 1983, had as one of its functions the examination of issues with implications for more than one department, but its resources were small compared with those of the departments. The work of the CPRS is often cited by students of central government as an example of attempts to overcome the strength of individual departments in Whitehall. The CPRS, which worked for ministers as a whole under the supervision of the Prime Minister, carried out strategy reviews of government policy, prepared major studies on specific issues, and provided collective briefs for ministers. In a report published in 1975 the CPRS argued the case for a joint approach to social policies, stressing the importance of greater coordination between the various central government departments concerned with social policies.

From time to time government departments do publish joint guidance or joint White Papers, but most of their activity is concerned with single programmes or services, and the CPRS argued that 'a new and more coherent framework is required for the making and execution of social policies' (Central Policy Review Staff, 1975, p. 1). As at the local level, collaborative planning and policy-making is beset by such difficulties as different organisational and professional structures, a mismatch between planning systems and cycles, and competing definitions of social problems. Although the CPRS report resulted in the establishment of a coordinating committee of ministers, this had a short life and the initiative slowly fizzled out. The demise of the CPRS itself is a further indication of the difficulty of developing cross-departmental approaches within Whitehall.

Despite this, the Blair government elected in 1997 made renewed efforts to break down departmental barriers, setting up a Social Exclusion Unit in the Cabinet Office to coordinate the contribution of different departments to tackling social exclusion, and emphasising the need to develop 'joined up solutions' to complex policy problems (Bogdanor, 2005). The Social Exclusion Unit was one of several units established by the government to strengthen the capacity of the Prime Minister through the Cabinet Office to take an overview of major policy issues and their implications. In parallel, the Treasury under Gordon Brown was increasingly involved in using its position to move beyond discussions with individual departments to examine the connection between policy areas. The Treasury's efforts were focused particularly on the negotiations that took place in the comprehensive spending review (CSR).

Like PESC, the CSR centred on bilateral discussions between departments and the Treasury in which negotiations between ministers and the Chief Secretary to the Treasury followed detailed discussions between officials. This process culminated in a report to the relevant Cabinet Committee and decisions on public spending covering a three-year period for most government departments. In practice, most of the key decisions were agreed between the Prime Minister and the Chancellor. Unlike PESC, the CSR sought to link expenditure plans with performance targets in the form of public service agreements. As the CSR evolved, it came to include a number of cross-cutting reviews of policy issues that affected more than one government department (Deakin and Parry, 2000). An example was the cross-cutting review of health inequalities that reported in 2002 and that led to the development of an action plan for tackling inequalities affecting a range of services (see Chapter 10). Other topics covered by cross-cutting reviews included children at risk, the role of the voluntary sector in delivering services, and the public sector labour market.

Despite attempts to strengthen the capacity for working across departments, individual departments retain considerable power within the framework of resources negotiated during the spending review. As a study of the Prime Minister has noted:

> Compared with most departmental ministers, a Prime Minister has a tiny budget, a small staff and few formal powers. He has to work through Secretaries of State in whom statutory powers are vested. Viewed from Number Ten, Whitehall departments can look at times like a series of baronial fiefdoms, to which it can only react. Departmental ministers have large staffs, budgets, policy networks, information and expertise, and can draw up legislation in their areas of responsibility ... The strength of most departments is such that it requires enormous willpower, obstinacy, political authority and excellent briefing for the Prime Minister to prevail against them. (Kavanagh and Seldon, 1999, p. 312)

This is a salutary reminder of the continuing role of departments in the policy-making process and the interdependence of institutions and people within central government. It also helps to explain why recent Prime Ministers have sought to strengthen their own capacity for policy-making and for reviewing the performance of government departments through the changes made to the Cabinet Office described earlier. As one of those most closely involved has written:

> the federal structure of British government with departments acting as independent fiefdoms, but where the PM's head is on the line for every failure, is unsustainable. Like any chief executive, the PM needs to be in control. (Hyman, 2005, p. 75)

There is little doubt that as a consequence of the changes made since 1997 the Prime Minister is now much better placed to challenge departments and to draw on the expertise of the Policy Directorate and the Cabinet Office in so doing. The establishment of the Prime Minister's Delivery Unit after the 2001 general election has also strengthened arrangements for policy implementation in key areas of public service reform and the ability of the Prime Minister to oversee the implementation of the government's priorities (Barber, 2007).

Outside interests

So far we have discussed the process of decision-making itself and have focused on the institutions of government and the relationship between them. It is now necessary to examine inputs into the system from outside interests, in particular from pressure groups. In examining this issue, Richardson and Jordan suggest that the central policy-making machinery is divided into subsystems organised around central departments. They designate these subsystems as 'policy communities' (Richardson and Jordan, 1979, p. 44) and point to the close relationships which exist in these communities between departments and pressure groups. Indeed, the relationships may be so close that shared priorities develop between the inside and outside interests, amounting to 'clientelism' (Richardson and Jordan, 1979, p. 55). The boundaries between groups and government thereby become indistinct, with in some cases a high degree of interpenetration taking place. The increasing role of outside interests and pressure groups has given rise to the view that 'governance' rather than 'government' should be the focus of analysis in seeking to understand what happens in the core executive (Bevir and Rhodes, 2003).

The significant place occupied by pressure groups in the British political system exemplifies the growth of what Beer has called 'the collectivist theory of representation' (Beer, 1969, p. 70). This legitimises a much greater role for groups than earlier approaches such as the Westminster model. As Beer notes, as government sought to manage the economy it was led to bargain with organised groups of producers, in particular worker and employer associations. Similarly, the evolution of the welfare state provoked action by organised groups of consumers of services, such as tenants, parents and patients. The desire by governments to retain office led them to consult and bargain with these consumer groups, in an attempt to win support and votes.

Relationships between groups and governments vary, but it is the producer groups which tend to have the closest contacts and the greatest degree of influence. The extent to which some of these groups have been incorporated into the political system was illustrated by moves towards tripartism in the 1960s and 1970s, that is the three-sided talks between government, employers' organisations and trade unions which occupied a central place in the development of economic policy at that time. As Beer points out, producer groups and governments are brought together by the desire of groups to influence the authoritative allocation of values, and by the need of government departments for the information which groups are able to offer, the cooperation they provide in the implementation of policy, and the importance which group endorsement of policy brings. And as Stevens observed in her history of medical practice in England, the increasing involvement of the government in health services served to widen rather than diminish the influence of doctors through the lobbying of the British Medical Association and the medical royal colleges (Stevens, 1966, p. 366).

Consumer groups tend to have somewhat less influence, partly because their cooperation is usually not as significant for policy-makers. It is mainly information and expertise they have to offer, and consumer groups have to operate through influence rather than through the use of sanctions. Traditionally, the consumers of services have been less well-organised than the producers. However, a variety of consumer groups are active in the central policy-making system, including generalist organisations like the National Council of Voluntary Organisations, and specialist associations such as Shelter, representing homeless people, Age Concern, campaigning on behalf of older people, and MIND, concerned with mental health. Many of these organisations are consulted on a regular basis by government, and indeed public money is spent supporting their activities. These groups also participate in the extensive network of advisory bodies which assist government departments in the development of their policies. It is important to add, though, that while some groups have close connections and good relationships with government, others have to attempt to exert pressure from a distance.

Pluralism or corporatism?

The growth of pressure groups has been paralleled by work which has attempted to redefine democracy in a way which accommodates the part played by groups in the political system. Beer's (1969) analysis of the collectivist theory of representation was one of the first efforts in this direction, and Dahl's (1961) elaboration of pluralist theory was another. Pluralist theory argues that power in Western industrialised societies is widely distributed among different groups. No group is without power to influence decision-making, and equally no group is dominant. Any group can ensure that its political preferences are adopted if it is sufficiently determined. The pluralist explanation of this is that the sources of power – like money, information, expertise and so on – are distributed non-cumulatively and no one source is dominant. Essentially, then, in a pluralist political system power is fragmented and diffused, and the basic picture presented by the pluralists is of a political marketplace where a group's achievements depend on its resources and its 'decibel rating'.

The importance of pluralist theory is demonstrated by the fact that, implicitly if not always explicitly, its assumptions and arguments now dominate much writing and research on politics and government in Britain. An example is Richardson and Jordan's analysis (1979) of post-Parliamentary democracy, a study very much in the pluralist tradition. Yet, despite its influence, pluralism has come under increasing challenge in recent years from writers who have questioned whether the British political system is as open to group influence as the pluralists maintain. In particular, it has been suggested that pluralism has given way to a system of corporatism in which some groups are much stronger than others and are in a good position to influence the decisions of government agencies.

The political history of corporatism in Britain has been outlined most fully by Middlemas (1979). Middlemas argues that a process of corporate bias originated in British politics in the period 1916 to 1926 when trade unions and employer associations were brought into a close relationship with government for the first time. During this period, unions and employer associations became 'governing institutions' (Middlemas, 1979, p. 372) so closely were they incorporated into the governmental system. Middlemas's thesis finds echoes in Cawson's (1982) discussion of corporatism and welfare. Cawson argues that 'the pressure-group world is not fluid and competitive, but hierarchical, stratified and inegalitarian' (Cawson, 1982, p. 37). For Cawson, the NHS provides one of the best examples of corporatist policy-making because government intervention in the provision of health services has necessitated close cooperation between the medical profession as the key producer group and government agencies. While some writers argue that corporatism has replaced pluralism, in Cawson's analysis corporatist policy-making coexists with pluralist or competitive policy-making. In the latter, consumer groups like MIND and Age Concern bargain with government agencies but lack the leverage available to producer groups.

In making these points, the dynamic nature of policy-making and power relationships must be acknowledged. As we noted in Chapter 2, the influence of trade unions and employer associations reached a peak in the 1970s and thereafter declined, particularly in the case of trade unions, as the Thatcher government departed from the corporatist tendencies of previous administrations and reasserted the role of government itself in policy-making. There were parallel developments in the field of health policy where again the Thatcher government unsettled established relationships between the DH and organisations like the BMA and implemented reforms such as the new contract for GPs and the internal market in the face of opposition from key producer groups (Lee-Potter, 1997). Policy developments in the 1980s and 1990s therefore marked a break with the post-war consensus that had bound together the Conservative and Labour parties in many areas of public policy and reflected the commitment of the Thatcher government to tackling the sclerosis that it diagnosed had invaded the body politic. As David Owen has commented on the handling of the dispute over private practice in the NHS in the 1970s:

> we were in the last throes of the corporatist state. Leaders of the trade unions and the BMA expected to bargain directly with Ministers. It was the era of beer and sandwiches at No. 10 which ended with the Winter of Discontent in 1979 and with the defeat of the Labour Government. (Owen, 1991, p. 233)

In keeping with the Thatcher government's diagnosis, a series of reforms were introduced to the civil service involving significant reductions in the number of civil servants and the application of the new public management to the machinery of government. The process of reform did not end with the election of the Blair government in 1997. Indeed, with its commitment to the devolution of power within the United Kingdom, including the establishment of the Scottish Parliament, the Welsh Assembly and the Northern Ireland Assembly, New Labour's policies were even more radical than those of its Conservative predecessors. Not least, they raised questions about the future of the United Kingdom as a unitary state and held out the prospect of increasing divergence in the organisation of the NHS and the development of health policy. The priority attached to devolution at a time when the European Union's influence on policy-making in Britain was increasing also implied a reduction in the role of the institutions of government in Whitehall and Westminster. This was underlined by the establishment of regional development agencies in England and elected mayors in major cities like London. With power moving up to Brussels in what became seen as an embryonic federal European state, and down to the territories and regions of the United Kingdom, the pre-eminence of central government appeared to be ending, and with it the Westminster model.

Within central government, recent research into the 'core executive' (Smith, 1999) has challenged both conventional accounts of the Westminster model and interpretations in the pluralist and corporatist traditions. Smith contends that arguments over whether Britain has a system of Prime Ministerial or Cabinet government are largely irrelevant when even powerful actors are dependent on others to achieve their goals. He also emphasises the extent of fragmentation at the centre and the difficulty of coordinating the work of different actors and institutions. Smith goes further in arguing that politicians and civil servants are themselves constrained by the structure and context in which they operate, a theme to which we return in Chapter 11. The main point in his analysis of relevance to this chapter is the interdependency of the policy communities and networks in and around Whitehall and the shifting pattern of power and influence. In making these arguments, Smith is developing the work of Rhodes and the differentiated policy model, also referred to as the governance narrative, cited earlier in this chapter (Rhodes, 1997; Bevir and Rhodes, 2003, 2006). This model is based in part on the argument that the institutions of central government have been hollowed out by privatisation, the increasing role of international organisations, and the use of agencies at arm's length from government. This process has been taken forward by the devolution of power to Northern Ireland, Scotland and Wales. Rhodes also argues that the executive is fragmented and weak, and that influence is increasingly exerted in policy networks in which government departments and pressure groups are interdependent. In putting forward these arguments, Rhodes is writing in an essentially pluralist tradition.

Rhodes' approach has been challenged by Marsh et al. (2001) who draw on research into the operation of government departments to offer an alternative interpretation. At the heart of their argument is the view that the executive remains powerful, notwithstanding elements of hollowing out. Marsh and colleagues go further to note the influence of the Treasury within the executive as a whole and of ministers and civil servants in government departments – the 'fiefdoms' referred to earlier in this chapter. By contrast, in the government departments they studied, outside interests and pressure groups were comparatively weak. From this perspective, exchange relationships, policy networks and interdependencies are acknowledged to be important, but even more significant is what happens in government itself. As Marsh and colleagues comment, 'the crucial actors in the policy process remain those located within departments, i.e. ministers and civil servants' (p. 179). Equally important, they argue that pluralist interpretations of the kind advanced by Rhodes do not adequately capture the inequalities in power in government, because '[i]n general, the Prime Minister has more resources than ministers, ministers have more resources than civil servants and departments more resources than interest groups' (p. 239).

In challenging the pluralists, Marsh and colleagues are not embracing corporatism because their emphasis is on the power of government institutions rather than pressure groups. In this sense, their position is more closely aligned with that of elite theory (see Chapter 11), as indicated by the description 'asymmetric power model' attached to their approach. Their argument that central government is controlled by an elite finds echoes in Oborne's analysis of the rise of the political class and his contention that a small group of politicians, advisers, lobbyists, journalists and others dominate British politics, with members of the political class often having little if any experience outside government (Oborne, 2007). The strengthening of the Prime Minister's office under Tony Blair lends further support to those who emphasise the increasing influence exercised by actors in the core executive.

What then of the Westminster model? Dunleavy (2006) has summarised the positions taken by political scientists who have analysed the relevance of the model to contemporary British politics and the wide variety of arguments they advance. These positions range from a belief that the Westminster model still provides a good description of key political processes through to critics who deny that the model has continuing applicability. A large group of authors take an intermediate position, arguing that its applicability is either indeterminate or partial. Dunleavy himself emphasises the challenges of interpreting recent changes in the British political system, whether in the role of Parliament, the relationship between ministers and civil servants, or the long-term impact of devolution. Given this uncertainty, the Westminster model remains an important reference point among students of central government but its assumptions need to be tested and reviewed in the light of the developments described in this chapter.

Conclusion

It was stated earlier that it is possible to describe the organisation of the British political system in simple terms. As this chapter has shown, it is more difficult to locate precisely the key points of power and decision-making within the system. Although Parliament retains formal, and in a few cases effective, powers over legislation, expenditure and administration, in Bagehot's language it is more of a dignified than an efficient element of the constitution. Much more significant are government departments, the Prime Minister and Chancellor, with an increasingly important part being played by outside interests. Within departments power is shared between ministers and civil servants, the exact balance depending to a considerable extent on the strength and personality of the minister. It is naive to assume that civil servants exercise no influence, and it is equally erroneous to argue that they have absolute control. Much depends on the weight of the departmental view on issues, the quality of the advice rendered by civil servants, and the commitment of the minister to a particular course of action. Increasingly important too are special advisers, whether located in departments or in 10 Downing Street.

We have noted that the strength of individual departments is a feature of central government, and this bears out the argument of researchers who emphasise the role of political institutions in the policy process (March and Olsen, 1989). Yet departmentalism, although a barrier to the development of corporate approaches, facilitates the establishment of policy communities between departments and their client pressure groups. And it is in these policy communities that a great deal of the more routine and less controversial aspects of policy are worked out in increasingly intricate systems of governance. Our discussion of the dynamics of the policy process therefore indicates the need for caution in drawing firm conclusions about the role and influence of the institutions of government. The changes introduced by the Thatcher government and those initiated by the Blair government have affected the machinery of government and relationships with outside interests. The impact of these changes will continue to be felt as policies on devolution are implemented and as the role of the European Union increases. The emphasis in this chapter on the power of a small group of actors at the core of central government will then need to be reassessed. In the future, it seems likely that power will be dispersed more widely, although in the case of the NHS in England it remains to be seen whether the rhetoric of devolution outweighs the tendency to recentralise power in Whitehall.

What are the implications of this discussion for the student of health policy? It should be clear that the starting point for gaining an understanding of the dynamics of health policy-making is to focus on the operation of the DH. An analysis of the workings of the Department, including its relationships with outside interests and its connections with other parts of Whitehall and Westminster, would seem to offer valuable insights into how health policies are made within central government. In turn, this analysis will form the basis of a discussion of the micro politics of health policy within the NHS. As we shall see in later chapters, the role of NHS bodies in implementing national policies and the power of doctors and other health care professionals over the use of resources on a day to day basis act as important constraints on the influence of the core executive, notwithstanding the changes to the machinery of government made since 1997.

Chapter 7

Policy-making in Scotland, Wales and Northern Ireland

In this chapter, we describe the organisation, politics and policies of the NHS in Scotland, Wales and Northern Ireland. The chapter begins with a description of differences in organisation and management before devolution. This is followed by an account of the changes that came from devolution, both in NHS structures and in health policy. The challenges of comparing the performance of the NHS in the countries that make up the United Kingdom are then discussed, as is the possibility of regional devolution in England. The chapter draws extensively on policy documents from the Scottish government, the Welsh Assembly government and the Northern Ireland government as well as analyses of the impact of devolution to date (see particularly Greer, 2004; Jervis, 2007).

Differences before devolution

In its review of the funding of the NHS, the Wanless Report drew attention to differences within the United Kingdom. These differences, illustrated in Figure 7.1, include the size and age structures of the populations of England, Scotland, Wales and Northern Ireland; the health of these populations; and the availability of health service resources. Analysis has shown that NHS expenditure per capita is lowest in England and highest in Scotland, whereas health indicators tend to be best in England and worst in Scotland. With the extra resources available, the Scottish NHS buys more hospital beds and staff per capita than the English NHS and has higher rates of inpatient, outpatient and day case activity than England (Alvarez-Rosete et al., 2005). The absence of a direct relationship between health service spending and health outcomes reflects the importance of non-medical factors in influencing the health of the population, and we discuss this further in Chapter 10.

We noted in earlier chapters that the structure of the NHS in Scotland, Wales and Northern Ireland differs from that in England in certain respects. Differences in structure became even greater following the election of the Blair government. *The New NHS* White Paper in England

(Secretary of State for Health, 1997) was preceded by the publication of a White Paper in Scotland, *Designed to Care*, proposing the establishment of primary care trusts bringing together all services other than acute care (Secretary of State for Scotland, 1997). Primary care trusts were established in 1999 and they were given full responsibility for primary care and community health services, and services for people with mental illness and learning disabilities. Under the Scottish plans, local health care cooperatives were set up to involve GPs in developing the provision of services, although participation in these cooperatives was voluntary and GPs lost control of budgets as both fundholding and GP commissioning came to an end. In the new structure of the NHS in Scotland, there was a distinction between the strategic and planning roles of Health Boards and the operational management responsibility of trusts. As in England, an important objective in Scotland was the development of integrated care, and joint investment funds were intended to facilitate integration between primary care trusts and acute trusts.

Figure 7.1 *Health and health care in England, Scotland, Wales and Northern Ireland*

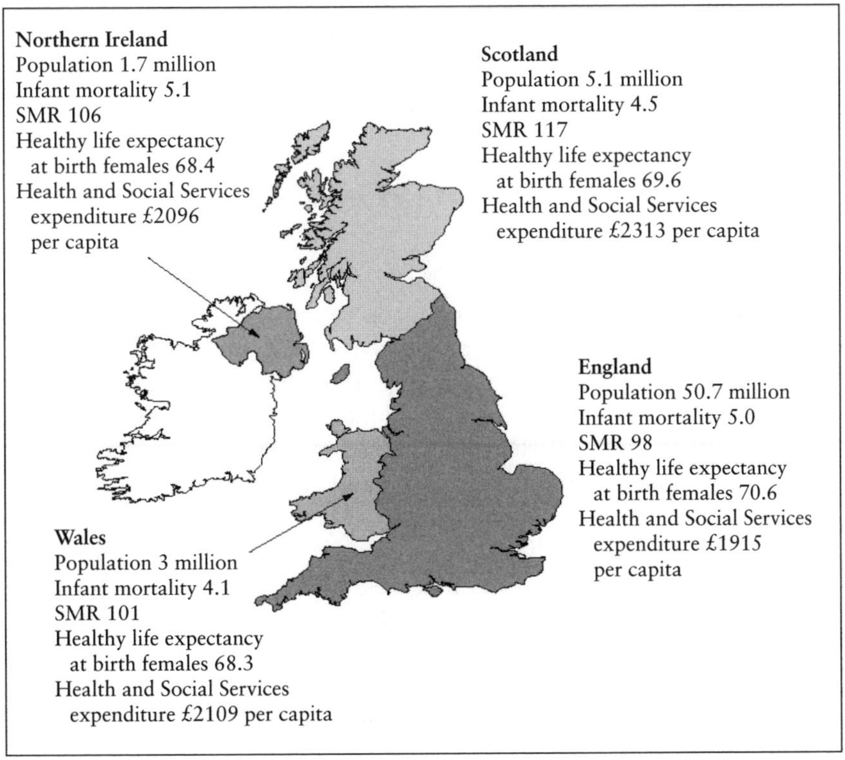

Northern Ireland
Population 1.7 million
Infant mortality 5.1
SMR 106
Healthy life expectancy
  at birth females 68.4
Health and Social Services
  expenditure £2096
  per capita

Scotland
Population 5.1 million
Infant mortality 4.5
SMR 117
Healthy life expectancy
  at birth females 69.6
Health and Social Services
  expenditure £2313 per capita

England
Population 50.7 million
Infant mortality 5.0
SMR 98
Healthy life expectancy
  at birth females 70.6
Health and Social Services
  expenditure £1915
  per capita

Wales
Population 3 million
Infant mortality 4.1
SMR 101
Healthy life expectancy
  at birth females 68.3
Health and Social Services
  expenditure £2109 per capita

Source: ONS (2008b).

The White Paper for Wales, *NHS Wales: Putting Patients First* (Secretary of State for Wales, 1998), differed from the English White Paper in proposing the establishment of local health groups instead of primary care groups. These were set up on a coterminous basis with local authorities and as subcommittees of health authorities. Initially, the White Paper indicated that local health groups would be advisory bodies but would take on greater responsibility for commissioning services over time. These groups were established in 1999 and they brought together GPs, other primary care contractors, health professionals such as nurses and other local interests. The configuration of NHS trusts in Wales was reviewed in parallel with debate on the White Paper and as a result the number of trusts was reduced from 25 to 16. There were also reductions in the number of NHS trusts in Scotland as part of the move towards acute trusts and primary care trusts.

The position in Northern Ireland was reviewed in the consultation document *Fit for the Future*, whose proposals reflected the unique features of Northern Ireland, in particular the integration of health and social care. A paper published in 1999 set out the results of consultation on *Fit for the Future* and proposed that five health and social care partnerships should take over the functions of both the health and social services boards and fundholders, and that the number of trusts should be halved. Continuing uncertainty about the political future of Northern Ireland meant that these proposals were not implemented.

Differences after devolution: 1999–2003

The governance of health services

One of the most significant changes made by the Blair government during its first term was to devolve power to Scotland, Wales and Northern Ireland. The elections that took place in May 1999 led to the creation of a 129-member Parliament in Scotland and a 60-member Assembly in Wales. While the Westminster Parliament retained power over the constitution, defence, the economy and other major areas, devolution gave the Scottish and Welsh governments control over areas such as health and social care. The Scottish Parliament has greater powers than the Welsh Assembly because of its ability to enact primary legislation and to vary the rate of income tax by up to 3 per cent but in both countries there is an opportunity to develop policies that are adapted to different needs. A similar opportunity exists in Northern Ireland where the 108-member Assembly elected in June 1998 had powers devolved to it in December 1999.

One of the immediate effects of devolution was to change the way in which the NHS is governed in Scotland, Wales and Northern Ireland. The electoral systems adopted in Scotland and Wales, involving proportional representation rather than Westminster-style first-past-the-post elections, resulted in the formation of minority or coalition governments that depended on cooperation between the political parties. Following the 1999 elections, the Labour party was the senior partner in these governments but was dependent on the support of the Liberal Democrats. A different situation prevailed in Northern Ireland where the electoral system required parties representing unionists and republicans to share power. The complex system of checks and balances adopted in Northern Ireland was designed to bring groups with a long tradition of conflict into government. Difficulties in making these arrangements work led to devolution in Northern Ireland being suspended in 2002. A period of direct rule from Westminster followed and continued until 2007.

Prior to devolution, the Secretary of State for Scotland was the political head of the NHS in Scotland, and responsibility for the NHS rested with the Scottish Office. After devolution, the Scottish Executive and the Scottish Parliament took over this role. The Scottish Executive refers both to the government of Scotland and the civil servants supporting it. The Minister for Health and Community Care in the Cabinet, now known as the Cabinet Secretary for Health and Wellbeing, supported by a chief executive and around 450 civil servants and other staff seconded from the NHS and local government, is responsible for the NHS in Scotland. The Scottish Parliament takes a close interest in the NHS and the Health and Sport Committee (originally the Health and Community Care Committee) of the Parliament is involved in scrutinising the performance of the NHS as a whole in Scotland and the affairs of health boards. As in Northern Ireland and Wales, devolution had the effect of increasing the influence of politicians vis-à-vis civil servants and managers (Woods, 2002).

A similar transition occurred in Wales where, prior to devolution, the Secretary of State for Wales was the political head of the NHS in Wales, and was supported by the Welsh Office. The Minister for Health and Social Services in the Welsh Assembly government is one of the members of the Cabinet and is responsible for the NHS in Wales. She is held to account by the Health, Wellbeing and Local Government Committee (formerly the Health and Social Services Committee) of the Assembly. The Minister for Health and Social Services is supported by the Director of NHS Wales and around 250 civil servants. In Northern Ireland, a Sinn Fein member of the Assembly became Minister for Health, Social Services and Public Safety in the first phase of devolution, and the Committee on Health, Social Services and Public Safety was established to scrutinise health and social care issues. The Department of Health, Social Services and Public Safety employs around 1000 staff and some of these staff carry out regional functions including estates and ICT.

Policy divergence

The Scottish and Welsh governments produced their own versions of *The NHS Plan* shortly after the Blair government published its intentions. In Scotland, *Our National Health* (Scottish Executive, 2000) emphasised the importance of health improvement as well as service improvement, building on the approach set out in the public health White Paper, *Towards a Healthier Scotland*, published a year earlier. Like its English counterpart, *Our National Health* identified improving services to patients by reducing waiting times and improving standards of care in clinical areas such as cancer and heart disease as high priorities. *Improving Health in Wales* (National Assembly for Wales, 2001) was similar to the NHS plan for Scotland in highlighting the importance of health improvement and reducing health inequalities. In this respect, it built on the public health White Paper, *Better Health: Better Wales*, and emphasised the need for partnership between the NHS and other organisations in improving health. As far as service improvement was concerned, *Improving Health in Wales* echoed many of the priorities set out in *The NHS Plan*, although there was less emphasis on specific targets and quantified objectives than in the English plan.

Subsequently, a review of health and social care carried out by a team advised by Derek Wanless offered a wide ranging critique of performance in Wales (Wanless, 2003a). In his foreword to the report of the review, Wanless argued that the position in Wales was worse than in the United Kingdom as a whole, as illustrated by long hospital waiting lists, significant pressures on acute hospitals, weak performance management, barriers between health and social care, and an imbalance between services provided in acute hospitals and in other settings. The report noted that the configuration of services placed an insupportable burden on hospitals and their staff, and that Wales did not get as much out of its health spending as it should. In addressing these challenges, the report recommended a reorientation towards prevention and early intervention, and a greater emphasis on individuals' and communities' acceptance of responsibility for their health. It also suggested that the Assembly should stop funding hospital deficits and should provide stronger incentives to support performance improvements. The Welsh Assembly government accepted the principal recommendations of the Wanless review and put in place a programme of work that led to the publication of a ten-year strategy for reform in 2005, *Designed for Life* (Welsh Assembly Government, 2005), discussed in more detail below.

The most important policy difference to result from devolution was the decision in Scotland to provide free personal care for older people needing long-term care. This decision followed from the report of the Royal Commission on long-term care in 1999 and its analysis of options for future funding (see Chapter 5). The central proposal of the Royal Commission that all nursing and personal care provided in care homes should be free was rejected by the Blair government in England and instead the government decided to make NHS nursing care free and to maintain means testing for personal care. The Scottish government opted to accept the Royal Commission's central proposal in full with effect from July 2002, and in so doing to commit itself to a significant increase in spending in this area of care. Partly because of the difficulties of estimating the costs of this commitment, expenditure was greater than originally planned. An independent review set up by the Scottish government calculated that the funding shortfall was around £40 million a year and recommended that the government should provide additional funds to meet the shortfall in the short term while reviewing and remodelling the costs of care in the medium term (Sutherland Report, 2008). This recommendation was accepted.

The Welsh Assembly government put pressure on Westminster to enable the same approach to be pursued in Wales but without success (Osmond, 2003). This meant that the main example of policy divergence in Wales was the decision to extend free prescriptions and eye tests, leading to the eventual phasing out of prescription charges. The introduction of free personal care in Scotland and the progressive removal of charges in Wales indicated the difference in approach of Labour politicians in these countries compared with their counterparts in England. The suspension of devolution in Northern Ireland in 2002 meant that health policy maintained its previous course.

One of the unexpected consequences of devolution was that the main source of divergence in health policy was to be found in Whitehall, particularly as the Blair government entered its second term. The willingness of the government to make greater use of the private sector as a provider of services to NHS patients, its policy of expanding the range of choices available to patients, and its active support of approaches that were similar to those used during the internal market experiment, meant that there was a widening gap in policy between different parts of the United Kingdom. To be sure, the commitment to the founding values and principles of the NHS was not affected by these developments, but the way in which these principles were applied and expressed increasingly diverged. A good example of divergence was the policy on NHS foundation trusts and the use of independent sector treatment centres that was pursued actively in England and not at all in the other three countries.

One of the constraints on the devolved governments is the way in which resources are allocated within the United Kingdom. The distribution of public expenditure is governed by the Barnett formula and this results in the allocation of blocks of expenditure to the Scottish,

Welsh and Northern Ireland governments. In view of the higher levels of public spending in these countries historically in comparison with England, the increases made available to the devolved governments under the Barnett formula were somewhat lower than those in England as the Blair government sought to move towards greater equity in resource allocation (Woods, 2004). Despite this, Scotland, Wales and Northern Ireland have benefited from the higher priority attached to the NHS by the government.

Differences in structure

Devolution also led to increasing divergence in the structure of the NHS in the United Kingdom. *Our National Health* proposed changes to the NHS in Scotland, involving the creation of unified health boards. These plans for structural change were elaborated in a further document, *Rebuilding our NHS* (Scottish Executive, 2001), and the new unified boards came into operation in 2001. In most cases, each board contained one primary care trust and one acute trust. Subsequently, *Partnership for Care* (Scottish Executive, 2003) proposed the abolition of NHS trusts and the establishment of community health partnerships in place of local health care cooperatives, and this change was implemented in 2004.

Improving Health in Wales also contained proposals for changing the structure of the NHS in Wales, involving the abolition of health authorities to enable the role of the Assembly and that of local health groups (later renamed local health boards) to be strengthened. Unlike in England, community health councils were retained in Wales. These changes took effect in 2003. In Northern Ireland, the structure inherited by the Assembly remained largely unchanged. The main exception was in respect of general practitioner fundholding which was eventually abolished in 2002 and superseded by local health and social care groups that operated as committees of the health and social services boards. These groups had limited involvement by GPs and lacked the delegated commissioning responsibilities enjoyed by fundholders. This meant that organisation of care in Northern Ireland centred on health and social services boards and health and social services trusts. Table 7.1 describes differences in the structure of the NHS in the four countries that made up the United Kingdom in 2004.

Alongside differences in structure, there was divergence in the stronger commitment to partnership working in Scotland and Wales compared with England. In reality, studies of the new systems of government indicate that the aspiration to achieve more 'joined up' government was difficult to realise in practice. Indeed, if anything devolution reinforced the separation of services because of the appointment of ministers to head each service, and the scrutiny of these services exercised by legislative committees (Jervis

Table 7.1 *Differences in the NHS in the UK in 2004*

	Central Management	Regional Structure	Health Authorities	NHS Trusts	Primary Care
England	Department of Health	Public health teams located in the government offices of the regions	28 strategic health authorities	c.280 NHS trusts	c.300 primary care trusts
Northern Ireland	The Department of Health, Social Services and Public Safety	–	4 health and social services boards	19 health and social services trusts	5 local health and social care groups
Scotland	Scottish Executive Health Department	–	15 health boards	–	c.40 community health partnerships
Wales	NHS Directorate in the Welsh Assembly Government	3 regional offices of the NHS Directorate	–	14 NHS trusts	21 local health boards and 1 unified health care board

and Plowden, 2003). Similar tendencies were at work in Northern Ireland where the structure of government and the sharing of ministerial posts between political parties, whose views were often strongly opposed, militated against integrated approaches, notwithstanding the rhetoric of policy documents. More progress was made at a local level with Scotland developing managed clinical networks to promote greater integration of care across the continuum from the community to acute hospitals, and Northern Ireland building on its history of health and social care integration. In Wales, coterminosity between local health boards and local authorities was intended to facilitate partnership working, particularly on public health issues, although progress in achieving this was patchy.

Devolution after 2004

Scotland

The pace of policy development quickened after 2004 as politicians in the devolved governments began to put their own imprint on NHS reform. In

Scotland, attention focused particularly on *Building a Health Service Fit for the Future*, a report prepared by a group chaired by David Kerr (Scottish Executive, 2005a). In a wide ranging review, the Kerr report, as it became known, drew attention to the poor health of the Scottish population and widening health inequalities. The report emphasised the need to strengthen primary care, to provide more services outside hospitals, and to achieve closer integration of primary and secondary care. The particular needs of rural communities were highlighted in the report and it was suggested that care in these communities should be provided through extended primary care, a resilient system of urgent care and rural general hospitals. In urban areas, the report advocated the development of community health centres bringing together groups of general practices and offering a wider range of services, including diagnostic facilities. In so doing, it anticipated proposals put forward by Lord Darzi for the development of polyclinics in London. As far as hospitals were concerned, the report argued that specialist services should be concentrated in fewer centres and that hospitals should collaborate in networks in order to improve quality of care while maintaining patient access.

The Scottish government responded to the Kerr report in *Delivering for Health* (Scottish Executive, 2005b) which endorsed the analysis contained in the report and set out the actions to be taken to implement its recommendations. These actions included reducing health inequalities through delivering anticipatory care for people at risk, and increasing health care provision in disadvantaged communities; enabling people with long-term conditions to live healthy lives through increased support for self-care, and identifying people at greatest risk of hospital admission and providing them with care to prevent deterioration and reduce emergency admissions; accelerating improvements in mental health services; and improving the performance of health services through further reductions in waiting times for treatment, separating planned care from unscheduled care, removing bottlenecks in diagnostic services, and concentrating specialist services in line with the recommendations of the Kerr report. To support implementation, a new Delivery Group was set up within the Scottish Executive Health Department to strengthen performance management and the monitoring of progress towards the aims contained in *Delivering for Health*. At a local level, community health partnerships have been used in every health board to help deliver the vision of care closer to home set out in *Delivering for Health*, and in some cases these partnerships involve close collaboration with local authorities.

Elections to the Scottish Parliament in 2007 resulted in significant gains for the Scottish National Party at the expense of the Labour Party. With the support of the Liberal Democrats, the Scottish Nationalists formed a minority government and its plans for the future of health and health care were published in *Better Health, Better Care* (Scottish Government, 2007). These plans built on previous policies and highlighted the importance of preventing illness, reducing health inequalities and improving the health of the Scottish people. In relation to health care, *Better Health, Better Care* also signalled a large measure of continuity with earlier policy documents, although patient safety and improving the quality of care received greater emphasis than previously. The most distinctive element of *Better Health, Better Care* was its use of the phrase 'mutual NHS' to denote the aspiration of the government to develop a partnership approach involving patients, staff and other stakeholders.

This was significant both in confirming the rejection of market based reforms of the kind adopted in England, and in laying a claim to a distinctive Scottish agenda based on cooperation and collaboration. The specifics of this agenda included recognising the rights and responsibilities of patients, strengthening arrangements for independent scrutiny of proposals for service change and reconfiguration, and consulting on the idea of there being direct elections to health boards. At the same time, arrangements for performance management were refined, with the government setting fewer and more focused targets for improvement around its key priorities.

Wales

Policy developments in Wales mirrored many of the initiatives taken in Scotland. Following the criticisms contained in the Wanless review, the Welsh Assembly government set out its vision of a world class health and social care system in *Designed for Life* (Welsh Assembly Government, 2005), focused on three main aims: promoting lifelong health, providing fast, safe and effective services, and delivering world class care. *Designed for Life* argued that hospital services needed to be delivered through regional networks to maintain quality and access, primary care resource centres should be developed to enable more services to be provided out of hospital, and telehealth and telecare should be used to support people with long-term conditions in the community.

While continuing to emphasise the importance of health improvement and reducing health inequalities, *Designed for Life* signalled that greater attention was to be given to improvements in health care than in previous policy documents, starting with targets for cutting waiting times to 26 weeks from GP referral to treatment by December 2009. The philosophy underpinning health policy in Wales, as in Scotland, was one of partnership working and collaboration as the main means of reform. At the same time, there was recognition that performance management needed to be strengthened to support implementation of the government's policies.

This was to be achieved through the establishment of a national delivery and support unit charged initially with focusing on work to support the reduction in waiting times for treatment.

A review of local public service delivery in Wales commissioned by the Welsh Assembly government reported in 2006 and concluded that 'there is a need for much more rapid and far-reaching transformation in public services than has been achieved to date' (Beecham Report, 2006, p. 55). In addressing this challenge, the review argued against structural reorganisation – even though it noted the complexity of organisational and governance arrangements – and emphasised instead the importance of engaging citizens, strengthening the delivery of policies, developing partnerships, and improving performance challenge and management. The Beecham Report argued that Wales had the potential to become an example of excellence in small country governance through a new form of engaged leadership if it was prepared to take decisive action on these issues. In making these points, the report contained loud echoes of the review of health and social care led by Derek Wanless in 2003, suggesting that the weaknesses identified by Wanless persisted and were not confined to health and social care.

Elections to the Welsh Assembly in 2007 resulted in the Labour Party losing seats to its opponents but it was still able to form a minority government with support from Plaid Cymru. An agreement between the Labour Party and Plaid Cymru was published in *One Wales: A Progressive Agenda for Wales* (Welsh Assembly Government, 2007) and this set out the new government's priorities for the future. In the case of health and social care, these priorities were to review NHS configuration, strengthen financial management, develop and improve health services, ensure access to health care, improve patient experience and support social care. The agreement emphasised the rejection of privatisation and the use of market models in health care, including the use of private finance initiative (PFI) to build new hospitals and competitive tendering for NHS cleaning contracts. The new government also made a commitment to reinstate democratic engagement at the heart of the NHS in Wales.

The appointment of a new Minister for Health and Social Services led to proposals being formulated to change the structure of the NHS, notwithstanding the recommendation of the Beecham Report that structural reorganisation of public services should be avoided. The minister's approach was stimulated in part by plans to merge NHS trusts in three parts of south Wales that had emerged from within the NHS rather than from the government. A further factor was a perception that the division of responsibilities between local health boards and NHS trusts was a legacy of the internal market reforms that had been superseded by the change of government in Westminster in 1997 and the policies pursued by the Welsh Assembly government since devolution. In a consultation document published in 2008, the minister set out plans to establish an NHS Board for Wales at a national level and to reduce the number of local health boards from 22 to 8 and the number of NHS trusts from 14 to 9.

In the event, the government went even further, deciding in the light of consultation to bring together local health boards and NHS trusts in an integrated structure similar to that adopted in Scotland. The detail of these plans was contained in a second consultation document published in December 2008. The new structure of the NHS in Wales is based on local health boards that plan, fund and provide the full range of services in most areas. The only exceptions are in Powys, where the existing local health board was unaffected by these developments and has a somewhat narrower range of responsibilities (there are no acute hospitals in Powys), and in the decision to retain the Welsh Ambulance Service Trust and the Velindre NHS Trust, an organisation providing specialist cancer services. At a national level, a National Advisory Board chaired by the minister was established, alongside a National Delivery Group chaired by the chief executive of the NHS Wales. The future of community health councils in Wales was the subject of a separate consultation.

The other significant change affecting Wales during this period was the Government of Wales Act 2006. Under the Act, the role of ministers has been separated from that of the Assembly, with the former taking on the executive powers of the government and the latter becoming the National Assembly of Wales with the function of scrutinising and monitoring the activities of the government. The Act also enables the Assembly to enact legislation in certain areas of devolved responsibility subject to agreement in Westminster and Whitehall (Jervis, 2007).

Northern Ireland

Policy developments in Northern Ireland were shaped by the suspension of devolution in 2002 and the imposition of direct rule from Westminster. In the period up to 2005, the main development affecting Northern Ireland was the Review of Public Administration that made recommendations for streamlining the administration of health and social care. The principal proposals centred on reducing the number of organisations by merging the four health and social services boards and 18 of the 19 health and social services trusts (the ambulance service trust was to retain its role) into a smaller number (either five or seven) of health and personal social services agencies, similar to the integrated structure that was developed in Scotland. Subsequently, an analysis undertaken by John Appleby on behalf of ministers provided a critique of the health and social care system in Northern Ireland comparable to that delivered by Derek Wanless in Wales (Appleby Report, 2005). The Appleby Report found that NHS productivity was lower and unit costs higher in Northern Ireland compared with England; waiting lists and waiting times for treatment were longer than in the rest of the United Kingdom; Northern Ireland had accident and emergency attendance rates that were almost a third higher than in England; and prescribing costs were nearly 30 per cent higher than in England. Other conclusions in a wide ranging review were the lack of integration between GPs and the rest of the primary care sector and weaknesses in social care, particularly relating to the provision of services in the community.

To address these issues, the Appleby Report made a series of recommendations, designed to introduce stronger incentives to reduce waiting times and tackle variations in costs and productivity. These included retaining the separation between commissioners and providers rather than adopting the recommendations of the Review of Public Administration for an integrated structure. The recommendations of the Appleby Report were welcomed by direct rule ministers who announced plans to change the organisation of health and social care. These plans involved reducing the number of health and social care trusts to five and establishing a Health and Social Services Authority covering the whole of the province. The Authority was intended to bring together the functions of the four health and social services boards and to work with local commissioning groups led by primary care, linked to the new local government structures. As in Scotland and Wales, arrangements for performance management were strengthened as the first step in addressing the problems identified in the report. The proposals in the Appleby Report to create incentives to increase hospital activity by adapting health reforms pursued in England were developed much more slowly, thereby maintaining a clear distinction between England the other three countries of the United Kingdom.

The resumption of devolution after the 2007 elections led to the appointment of a new minister drawn from the Ulster Unionist Party and a review of the plans for structural change prepared by direct rule ministers. In the event, the minister decided not to proceed with these plans in their entirety, opting instead for what he described as a local solution to local needs. The establishment of five health and social care trusts did go ahead but instead of the proposed Health and Social Services Authority the minister established a regional health and social care board and a regional agency for public health and social well-being with effect from April 2009. The regional health and social care board has taken on many of the responsibilities of the health and social services boards, leading on commissioning, performance and resource management, and is accountable to the minister. The creation of the new agency signals a strong commitment to public health and social well-being and the commissioning plans of the regional board will have to be agreed with the agency. A further change was the decision to set up a Patient and Client Council with five committees organised in the same geographical areas as the provider trusts established in 2007. These arrangements superseded the four health and social care councils that had previously represented the user's voice in the system. One of the consequences of these decisions was a commitment to streamline the role of the Department of Health, Social Services and Public Safety to bring its functions into line with the role of the new regional health and social care board and the regional agency for public health and social well-being.

Table 7.2 *Differences in the NHS in the UK in 2009*

	Central Management	Regional Structure	Health Authorities	NHS Trusts	Primary Care
England	Department of Health	Public health teams are located in the government offices of the regions	10 strategic health authorities	*c*.125 NHS trusts *c*.115 NHS foundation trusts	*c*.150 primary care trusts
Northern Ireland	The Department of Health, Social Services and Public Safety	Regional health and social care board Regional agency for public health and social well-being	–	5 health and social services trusts	5 local commissioning groups
Scotland	Scottish Executive Health Department	–	14 health boards	–	*c*.40 community health partnerships
Wales	NHS Directorate in the Welsh Assembly government; National Advisory Board, and National Delivery Group	3 regional offices of the NHS Directorate (under review)	7 health boards	Welsh Ambulance Service NHS Trust and Velindre NHS Trust	locality networks

An assessment of the performance of the health service by the Northern Ireland Audit Office (2008) reported progress in a number of areas, including improving life expectancy, reducing smoking, and reducing the rate of births to teenage mothers. At the same time, the Audit Office highlighted several challenges, such as persistent inequalities in health, the increasing prevalence of obesity and high rates of suicide. In relation to health services, the target for increasing public satisfaction with health services was achieved early, the target for reducing premature deaths from circulatory diseases had been surpassed, and most of the targets for increasing cancer survival rates had been achieved. Progress had also been made in reducing waiting times for hospital treatment. The Audit Office's report indicated that action had been taken in response to the weaknesses identified in the Appleby Report and that the population of Northern Ireland was beginning to benefit from improvements in care.

Comparing performance

Ten years after devolution, how do the health care systems of England, Northern Ireland, Scotland and Wales compare? In seeking to answer this question, the first challenge is the paucity of available data to make comparisons. This has been starkly illustrated in a recent attempt to assess the impact of devolution on health system performance, the authors bemoaning 'the difficulty, and in some cases impossibility, of obtaining valid comparable basic statistics on the NHS in the four countries' (Alvarez-Rosete et al., 2005, p. 949). Recognising this difficulty, there is evidence to suggest that England has demonstrated greater improvement on some indicators than other countries. This is most apparent on waiting times for treatment which have fallen significantly in England to the point where England's performance is close to that of Scotland. Waiting times are considerably longer in Wales and Northern Ireland. A comparison of policies in England and Wales attributed this difference to the use of targets and the approach taken to performance management in England (Hauck and Street, 2007). Data on median waiting times for selected elective procedures for 2006–07 published by the Office for National Statistics displayed in Table 7.3 show variations in performance between countries. Analysis suggests that England also achieved better performance on the response of the ambulance service to emergency calls than Scotland, Wales and Northern Ireland (Bevan and Hamblin, 2009).

Apart from waiting times, a common priority across the United Kingdom has been to improve performance in areas of clinical priority like heart disease and stroke. An analysis of cardiac services published in 2006 compared variations in the provision of these services and noted

Table 7.3 *Median waiting times* in days for elective hospital admission for selected procedures*

	2006–07			
Procedure	England	Scotland	Wales	Northern Ireland
Cataract surgery	70	69	70	101
Angiography	56	35	67	27
Bypass surgery	68	56	107	117
Endoscope of upper gastrointestinal tract	26	34	30	39
Hernia repair	99	79	118	102
Hip replacement	151	122	221	168
Knee replacement	157	126	243	196
Endoscope of bladder	31	39	50	66
Angioplasty	51	38	90	14
Tonsillectomy	113	93	195	161
Varicose surgery	127	103	217	150

* Time calculated as difference between admission date and the date the decision to admit was made
Source: ONS (2008b).

rapid progress in England driven by a major investment in frontline services and the appointment of new consultant cardiologists. Scotland, which in a previous study had been identified as providing cardiac services that were among the best in the United Kingdom, appeared not to have progressed to the same extent as England. The authors of the review noted that coronary intervention rates in Wales were 'worryingly low' and that some aspects of cardiac services in Northern Ireland were stagnating. The improved performance of England in relation to other countries was attributed to the development of the national service framework for coronary heart disease supported by additional funding. The analysis noted that differences in health policy between the four countries represented 'an intriguing experiment that may provide useful insight into the impact of different healthcare policies on activity and outcome' (Boon et al., 2006).

A separate study found that the lower priority attached to the national service framework for coronary heart disease in Wales compared with England explained the poorer performance of stroke services in Wales. Drawing on the 2006 National Sentinel Audit for Stroke, the Healthcare Commission reported that only 45 per cent of eligible hospitals in Wales had a stroke unit compared with 96 per cent of eligible hospitals in England and 92 per cent in Northern Ireland (Scotland was not included in the audit). In this audit, Northern Ireland performed better than England and Wales on six of the 12 indicators and it had the highest overall score on all 12 indicators. The Healthcare Commission noted that only 28 per cent of patients in Wales were treated in a stroke unit compared with 64 per cent in England and 73 per cent in Northern Ireland. As patients treated in stroke units have much better results than patients looked after in other settings, the Healthcare Commission concluded that Wales needed to identify systems to raise the quality of stroke care, particularly through the development of stroke units (Healthcare Commission, 2007c).

Sutherland and Coyle (2009) have assembled data on the quality of health care from different sources to present a chartbook on the performance of health services in the four countries of the United Kingdom. The results show that Scotland has the highest mortality rate from heart attacks and stroke and England the lowest. In the case of cancer, Wales had the best survival ratios after five years and Scotland the worst for all cancers, while Scotland had the highest breast cancer screening rates and England the lowest. Analysis of data from the quality and outcomes framework showed high levels of performance in all countries on indicators such as patients with heart disease receiving appropriate treatment and patients with stroke having their blood pressure and cholesterol checked. On childhood immunisation, Northern Ireland and Scotland had the highest coverage and England the lowest. In the case of people aged 65 and over, Scotland achieved the highest level of flu vaccination and Wales the lowest. As these and the other data brought together by Sutherland and Coyle suggest, there is no consistent pattern in the performance of health services in these countries.

On public health, action has been taken in all four countries to prohibit smoking in public places. Scotland led the way with legislation passed in 2005 leading to a smoking ban being introduced in March 2006. Northern Ireland and Wales followed suit in April 2007 and England in July 2007.

An assessment

In his analysis of devolution and health policy, Greer has summarised the nature of divergence and its causes in the following way:

> Each system has taken a distinct path from the 1991 baseline of Margaret Thatcher's 'internal market'. England is the most market-based ... Scotland is its near-opposite, rebuilding the unitary NHS with strong planning and service integration ... Wales diverges not only in its reluctance to work with the private sector and its strong

commitment to new public health but also in the way that commitment shapes its service organisation. Northern Ireland has changed little ... (Greer, 2003, pp. 198–9)

According to Greer (2004), the differences that have emerged following devolution reflect the role of policy advocates in each country. In Scotland the influence of medical elites and the emphasis on professionalism help to explain that country's preference for planning and integration and the priority attached to public health. Lacking the Scottish tradition of professionalism, Wales was more open to influence by other interests and this enabled local government and the trade unions to shape health policy, with its emphasis on public health and localism. In Northern Ireland, managers and civil servants occupied the vacuum left by politicians but the consequence was limited impact on public policy. England by contrast experienced rapid change as policy advocates favouring market solutions gained the ascendancy and public health advocates exerted limited influence.

Despite these differences, the degree of divergence after a decade was limited, with Wales and Northern Ireland both refocusing their attention on health care as data emerged about their poor performance on issues such as waiting times for treatment in relation to England and Scotland, at the same time as policy-makers in England recognised the need to give higher priority to public health and health inequalities. The size of England in relation to the other countries that make up the United Kingdom means that it continues to exercise a significant influence on health policy in the devolved governments on some issues, especially where there is evidence that England has made more progress in improving performance than is the case elsewhere. As Jervis (2007) has observed, while differences between the four countries are real, they are primarily about means rather than ends, and about the sequence in which issues should be tackled rather than the issues themselves.

Alongside the limited degree of divergence in health policy, reflecting underlying tendencies to policy maintenance discussed elsewhere in this book, there was a sense in some quarters that devolution had produced more negative than positive consequences. As an early study of the impact of health policy and devolution observed:

Some claim that the freedoms given to the devolved legislatures, and the greater responsiveness of the devolved executives, have produced both processes and outcomes which are actually worse than before devolution. The quality of debate in the legislatures has been described to us as unimpressive, while ministers' closeness to the public and to the arena in which decisions have to be implemented appears often to have had the effect of delaying necessary decisions, or of inhibiting the choice of potentially unpopular options. The cumulative effects of this militate against strategic thinking. (Jervis and Plowden, 2003, p. 54)

A more positive assessment was offered by Hazell who noted both the smooth introduction of devolution and the promising early results:

Devolution has made a difference, in broadly the ways it was intended to. It has brought government closer to the people of Scotland, Wales and Northern Ireland; it has enabled the devolved governments to introduce policies more closely tailored to the needs of the local people; and it has introduced a new kind of politics to the United Kingdom. (Hazell, 2003, p. 285)

The most recent verdict by Jervis (2007) of the impact of devolution on health concluded that it was harder to sum up the consequences of devolution in 2007 than it had been in 2003 because of changes in the parties in power in the devolved governments alongside pressures for convergence from the European Union (EU) and elsewhere.

Regional government in England

The devolution of power to Scotland, Wales and Northern Ireland raises the issue of regional devolution in England and its potential impact on the NHS. Government offices of the regions have existed since 1994 and they bring together in one organisation the activities of a number of government departments. Since 2002 the DH's regional public health teams have been located in the government offices and they work with colleagues in areas such as education and skills and transport in developing public health strategies and services in their regions. In parallel, regional development agencies were set up in 1999 and their main role is to coordinate regional economic regeneration and development and promote business efficiency and employment. In the case of London, the establishment of the Greater London Authority in 2000, including an elected mayor, indicated the government's interest in devolving power within England. The mayor has a duty to safeguard and promote Londoners' health and has worked closely with NHS bodies, particularly on public health issues.

Following a White Paper, *Your Region, Your Choice*, published in 2002, legislation was passed in 2003 to create powers to enable elected regional assemblies to be established where public support is expressed for them in a referendum. This opened up a debate that was resolved at the time of the inception of the NHS when the views of Aneurin Bevan that the NHS should be established as a national service under separate administrative agencies carried the day against Herbert Morrison's argument that local government control was the preferred option (see Chapter 1). At the time, Bevan acknowledged that putting the NHS under elected authorities was an option for the future, and the constitutional radicalism of the Blair government appeared to make this a real possibility. In the event, the only referendum on regional government was held in the north-east in 2004 and it resulted in decisive rejection of proposals to establish an elected regional assembly (Jervis, 2007). Plans for other referenda were then abandoned.

The European Union

Health policy in Britain has been affected by the actions of the EU in a number of areas. In the past, the impact of the EU on health policy has resulted either from actions to encourage the free movement of people, goods, services and capital, or through public health initiatives, rather than policies directed at health services. Examples of the former include the working time directive, under which the time worked by doctors in training has been reduced considerably to enable the United Kingdom to comply with EU law, and regulations designed to enable health care professionals who are trained in one country to work in other EU countries. Examples of the latter include action on major public health priorities such as the control of tobacco advertising and sponsorship and initiatives on drug misuse and infectious diseases.

Health care is a responsibility of member states rather than the EU, although recent decisions of the European Court of Justice have lent support to patients who have received treatment in EU countries other than their own (Mossialos and Palm, 2003). These decisions require national governments to fund hospital treatment in other EU countries if patients would suffer an undue delay in receiving treatment in their own countries. In 2008 the European Commission published a proposal for a directive on patients' rights in cross-border health care aimed at clarifying the position in relation to patients receiving care in other EU countries, and at the time of writing it is not clear if this will be adopted by member states. Questions have also been raised as to whether EU competition law applies to health care services at a time when health care reforms have included the introduction of market principles in some countries. This law was invoked in the BetterCare judgment in 2002 in which a private company supplying nursing and residential care in Northern Ireland successfully challenged the price it was paid for providing care to the NHS (Pollock and Price, 2003). The European Court of Justice has ruled that health care providers and insurers are subject to single market rules if they compete in the health care market as organisations similar to companies competing in other markets (Lear and Mossialos, 2008). The precise implication of this ruling is unclear, not least because health services were excluded from the services directive in 2006 that would have applied market principles to health services as a whole.

As these examples show, the impact of the EU on health policy in Britain is increasing. This will act as a brake on policy divergence within the United Kingdom, even though there is no prospect of systems of health financing and provision being harmonised across the EU.

Conclusion

The developments described in this chapter underline the argument that a family of health services now exists in the United Kingdom, rather than a single national health service (Jervis and Plowden, 2003). In the first decade of devolution, there has been increasing divergence in NHS structures and the political processes impacting on health policy, with increased scrutiny by politicians in the devolved governments and greater accountability on the part of civil servants and managers. There have also been examples of policy divergence, through the Scottish approach to personal care for older people, the Welsh policy on user charges, and the English strategy of promoting greater plurality of provision and increased patient choice. Policy divergence may well increase in the future, particularly if there is greater diversity in the parties that make up the governments in the four countries of the United Kingdom.

At the time of writing, policy-makers seem more interested in pursuing their distinctive agendas than learning from the differences that have emerged. The natural experiments in the governance of health that have been stimulated by devolution have tended to reinforce national insularity rather than cross-systems comparisons. Yet with the public and the professions not constrained by national borders, and with information about differences in health and the performance of health systems increasingly available and transparent, the apparent lack of interest shown by politicians in what is happening outside their own jurisdictions may not be sufficient to stem the exchange of policy ideas. An early sign of this was the response of the Welsh Assembly government to the Wanless Report on Wales, including the decision to allow patients in Wales who had been waiting 18 months for an operation the choice of having their treatment at a different hospital. Echoing as it did the policies pursued in England to reduce waiting times and improve responsiveness to patients, this decision was an indication that initiatives developed in one country did not have to be rejected in others simply because they were not invented there.

A further counterweight to national insularity is the EU. In a number of areas the EU is having an impact on health policy, including the working time of staff and waiting times for patients. Although the jurisdiction of the EU in relation to health services is an uncertain and contested question, it seems likely that policy divergence within the United Kingdom will be constrained in some areas by policy developments in Europe. The one safe prediction is that the sources of policy innovation and development will extend well beyond established centres of power as systems of government and governance multiply and fragment. In this pluralistic environment, the new governments of Scotland, Wales and Northern Ireland will coexist with the Westminster government and the institutions of the EU. Health policy in the constituent parts of Britain will be forged out of the interplay of these different systems.

Chapter 8

Policy-making in the Department of Health

The aim of this chapter is to examine the policy-making process in the Department of Health (DH). The chapter begins by describing the organisation of the Department and the way in which this has evolved. This leads into a discussion of the health policy community and the influence of different organisations and interests in policy-making. The chapter concludes by reviewing attempts to strengthen the Department's capacity for policy analysis. Throughout the chapter the influence of different actors is explored in an attempt to illuminate the debate between advocates of the Westminster model, commentators who highlight the increasing power of the core executive and those who advance the governance narrative as alternative ways of seeking to understand the dynamics of policy-making in central government. The experience of the Blair and Brown governments is drawn on to understand the resilience of established institutions and the increasing role played by new actors, such as special advisers.

The Department of Health

The backstory

Originally established as the Ministry of Health in 1919, the work of the DH has evolved as a result of changes to the machinery of government and the structure of the NHS. The Ministry was merged with the Ministry of Social Security to form the Department of Health and Social Security in 1968. Twenty years later the Department was divided by Margaret Thatcher when it was perceived to be too large for any Cabinet minister to run effectively. Reforms to the civil service in the 1980s resulted in a reduction in the number of civil servants and the establishment of the NHS Executive (formerly the NHS Management Executive and Management Board) within the Department to oversee the implementation of policy and the performance of the NHS.

From the 1990s onwards the Department was reorganised on a number of occasions as ministers and civil servants sought to improve its capability for policy-making and overseeing the implementation of policies in the

NHS and other agencies. One of the consequences was that the NHS Executive lost its separate identity in 2001. The most recent development has been the Capability Review of the Department of Health undertaken by the Cabinet Office (2007) which identified weaknesses in the strategy and leadership capabilities of the Department. The appointment of a new Permanent Secretary and NHS Chief Executive provided a platform for action on these and other issues as the top leadership attempted to address concerns highlighted in the Capability Review.

The current organisation

The Secretary of State for Health sits at the head of the Department and is a member of the Cabinet. He or she is supported by a number of ministers and in 2009 there were two Ministers of State and three Parliamentary Under Secretaries of State, one of whom sits in the House of Lords. The responsibilities of these ministers reflect the full range of the Department's responsibilities and encompass public health and social care as well as the NHS. The Secretary of State chairs the National Stakeholder Forum whose members include people drawn from professional organisations, patients' groups and NHS management. The Forum meets three or four times a year and it enables the Secretary of State to discuss current issues of concern with stakeholder interests.

On a day-to-day basis, the work of the Department is carried out by civil servants. In 2009 there were around 2200 civil servants working in the Department, excluding those employed in executive agencies, and its running costs were £214 million. The most senior of these civil servants are the Permanent Secretary, the NHS Chief Executive and the Chief Medical Officer. The Permanent Secretary leads the Department as a whole, the NHS Chief Executive leads the NHS and is chief adviser to the Secretary of State on NHS matters, and the Chief Medical Officer leads on public health matters. The Department's staff are based in London and Leeds, and in addition the public health teams are based in each of the government offices of the regions. Two executive agencies support the work of the Department. These are the Medicines and Healthcare Products Regulatory Agency and the NHS Purchasing and Supply Agency.

The overall aim of the Department is 'to improve the health and well-being of the people of England' (DH, 2008a). In pursuing this aim, it has four main roles:

- setting the direction for the NHS, adult social care and public health
- supporting and mobilising the health and social care system to deliver improvements for patients and the public

- leading on the integration of health and well-being into wider government policy
- supporting ministers in accounting to the public and Parliament for health and social care.

In undertaking these roles, the Department works with ministers in developing policy, securing resources through the spending review negotiations, promoting legislation through Parliament, and ensuring accountability for the use of resources and the performance of the health and social care systems. In parallel, the Department works with the NHS, social care and other partners on policy implementation and the delivery of improvements in care. The staffing of the Department reflects the complexity of its functions, comprising career civil servants, NHS managers and clinicians, and people from the private and voluntary sectors.

A Departmental Management Board supports ministers in developing strategy for the health and social care system and overseeing its implementation. The Board's members include the Permanent Secretary, the Chief Executive of the NHS and the Chief Medical Officer. The NHS Management Board is chaired by the NHS Chief Executive and its members include the directors general concerned with NHS matters and chief executives of strategic health authorities. The Corporate Management Board is chaired by the Permanent Secretary and is responsible for the internal running of the NHS. The organisation of directorates within the Department under the Chief Medical Officer, Permanent Secretary and NHS Chief Executive is illustrated in Figure 8.1.

One feature of continuing importance in the DH is the strong professional contribution to policy-making. The Department has six chief professional officers who are leaders in their professions and who advise ministers, other government departments and the Prime Minister. These are the Chief Medical Officer, the Chief Nursing Officer, the Chief Dental Officer, the Chief Health Professions Officer, the Chief Pharmaceutical Officer and the Chief Scientific Officer. Civil servants from these and other professional backgrounds work alongside generalist administrators and their work has increasingly been integrated into the Department rather than being organised through separate professional hierarchies. At the same time as divisions between generalist administrators and civil servants from professional backgrounds have become less significant, the appointment of NHS managers to senior roles, including to the post of NHS Chief Executive, has opened up new tensions. One of the many reviews of the Department's functions that took place during this period noted that 'the NHS Executive faces in two directions' and added:

Figure 8.1 *The structure of the DH, 2008*

Chief Medical Officer	Permanent Secretary	NHS Chief Executive
Research & Development	Finance & Operations	Chief Nursing Officer's Directorate
Health & Improvement Protection	Policy & Strategy	NHS Medical Directorate
9 Regional Public Health Groups/ Directors of Public Health	Social Care, Local Government & Care Partnerships	Commissioning & System Management
The Medicines & Healthcare Products Regulatory Agency	Communications	Workforce
	Equality & Human Rights	Commercial
		NHS Finance, Performance & Operations
		Chief Information Officer
		NHS Purchasing & Supply Agency

As the top management of the NHS, the Executive must be 'of' the NHS, culturally close to it and credible if it is to lead and influence. That is why a distinct identity is so important. At the same time, the Executive is unequivocally a part of government, responsible for implementing the Government's policies for the NHS, holding health authorities to account on behalf of Ministers, and supporting and advising Ministers on health service matters. (Banks Review, 1994, p. 11)

The Janus-like character of the Department was dissected in a study of the two cultures of mandarins and managers (Day and Klein, 1997), while a recent analysis has argued that the Department has become 'NHS-dominated, with a strong managerial ethos and very little civil service representation at the top' (Greer and Jarman, 2007, p. 31). The Cabinet Office's Capability Review drew attention to the difficulties created by the appointment of people from outside the career civil service, commenting:

The high proportion of staff drawn from the NHS and other non-civil service backgrounds combined with a number of restructuring exercises have contributed to a sense that the Department lacks its own culture distinct from that of the NHS or a set of behavioural values that are common to all DH staff and which drive a positive culture.

This ... exacerbates the lack of a sense of the Department as a corporate entity. (Cabinet Office, 2007, p. 18).

The Review added that 'The Department too often operates as a collection of silos' (p. 19) and it argued that there was an urgent need to develop a more corporate approach. This indicates that the challenge of coordinating the Department's many responsibilities, not least providing leadership for the NHS and supporting ministers in developing policy, remains unresolved.

While much of this comment relates to the Department's role in relation to the NHS, it is important to emphasise that its responsibilities also encompass public health and adult social care. It has often been difficult to ensure that there is effective coordination of these responsibilities, although recent changes to the structure of the Department have sought to promote closer integration. In reality, successive governments have seen the NHS as the highest priority and this has meant that neither public health nor adult social care have received the same attention. The coexistence of staff involved in NHS, public health and adult social care work adds to the complexity of the Department and reinforces the centrifugal tendencies that we now go on to discuss.

The policy community

In Chapter 6 we introduced Richardson and Jordan's idea of the policy community to denote the extent to which policies are increasingly developed in consultation between government departments and the organisations concerned with their work. Consultation may take place through a variety of channels: through standing advisory committees or groups; through ad hoc enquiries or working groups set up to advise on particular issues; and through the more or less regular pattern of negotiation and discussion in which the Department engages with outside interests like the British Medical Association (BMA). In Richardson and Jordan's terms it may be misleading to use the word 'outside' to describe these interests. Their analysis emphasises the high degree of interpenetration which exists between pressure groups and government, and they point to the similarities which develop between departments and their client groups (Richardson and Jordan, 1979). Recognition of the involvement of pressure groups in policy communities is one of the factors behind the argument that governance has become more important than government in contemporary British politics.

Valuable as this analysis is, it is necessary to recognise that not all groups are equally well integrated into the national health policy community. Consumer groups, for example, are relatively weak and Brown, commenting on this in the 1970s, has noted that 'the machinery on the health and welfare side of the DHSS tends to be dominated by those who provide services rather than those for whom the services are intended' (Brown, 1975, p. 193). Thus, although the health policy-making system appears to be pluralistic in that a wide range of interests is involved in the policy process, in practice this system may be skewed in favour of the well-organised groups who have a key role in the provision of health services. Producer groups are well able to promote and defend their interests, and this puts the Department in the position of appeasing these groups and resolving conflicts whenever they occur. As we argued in Chapter 6, corporatism may be a more accurate description than pluralism of a policy-making system in which producer groups are dominant.

One of the consequences of producer group dominance is that policy-making tends to be incremental, characterised by what Lindblom (1965) has termed 'partisan mutual adjustments'. Bargaining between the Department and pressure groups often results in small changes in the status quo, and this tends to be to the advantage of established interests. A great deal of the activity of the Department is not in fact concerned with policy-making as such. Rather, it is aimed at the continuation of existing services and policies and the maintenance of good relationships with key interests. Policy-making is a comparatively rare occurrence because:

> public resources for dealing with issues are relatively scarce. They are scarce in many terms – money and manpower obviously since public finance and public servants are finite quantities, but scarce also in terms of legislative time, media coverage, political will, public concern ... Political systems can only cope with a limited number of issues at once and these are always subject to displacement by new emerging issues of greater appeal and force. (Solesbury, 1976, p. 382)

Solesbury argues that issues must pass three tests if they are to survive the policy-making process. They have to command attention, claim legitimacy and invoke action. It helps issues to command attention if they have particularity. Part of the reason why long-stay hospitals commanded attention is that they were associated with specific institutions, such as Ely Hospital, which came to symbolise the problems in this area of the NHS (see Chapter 5). Crises and scandals of this kind are often important in forcing an issue on to the agenda. Issues also need to become generalised. This helps them to claim legitimacy and attract the attention of existing political forces. Thus, a particular interest in Ely Hospital came to be generalised into a wider concern with social justice and humanitarian values, thereby bringing it within the dominant political culture and drawing the interest of established political groupings. An issue which has commanded attention and acquired legitimacy has passed two tests, but it must also invoke action. At this stage, issues run the risk of suppression, transformation into other issues, and token or partial responses.

Also relevant here is the notion of symbolic policy-making, a term developed by Edelman (1971) to refer to action intended to demonstrate that something is being done about a problem, rather than action which is a real attempt to tackle the problem. While there are undoubtedly difficulties in identifying the intentions and motives of policy-makers, in a number of areas it would appear that policies have significant symbolic elements. For instance, successive attempts to give greater priority to groups such as the mentally ill, people with learning disabilities and older people have not been accompanied by the allocation of significant amounts of additional resources, nor have ways been found of achieving a major shift towards these groups within existing budgets. In cases such as this, policies may act primarily as a way of maintaining political support and stability. Support is maintained in that the messages contained in policy statements may satisfy key political groups, thereby forestalling demands for more fundamental reforms. It is in this sense that words may succeed and policies fail (Edelman, 1977).

To return to Solesbury's discussion, what is valuable in his analysis is the examination of the hurdles which issues have to jump before they invoke action, the changing nature of issues, and the importance of subjective definitions in issue emergence. As Solesbury notes, in the policy process issues are:

> moving forward on many fronts, sometimes concerned with legitimacy, sometimes with attention, the issue itself changing its definition as it goes forward, linking with other issues, splitting from yet others, sometimes becoming totally transformed into a new issue altogether. The agenda metaphor provides the best indication of the nature of the process. (Solesbury, 1976, p. 396)

The agenda metaphor is developed at much greater length by Kingdon (1995) who contends that agendas are forged through the interaction of problems, politics and participants. In some cases, issues emerge on to the agenda because conditions are defined as problems. In other cases, changes in the political environment help shape the agenda. In yet other cases, participants may be important either in raising the salience of an issue or in framing the alternatives. These different streams come together into a 'policy primeval soup' (p. 200). The outcome is affected by the activities of policy entrepreneurs and by the opportunities offered by policy windows. There is a much greater chance of policy development occurring when problems, politics and participants are linked together, although this is not essential. Kingdon's framework allows for both random responses and predictable patterns of development, his key point being the complexity and messiness of the policy process and the lack of any simple explanations.

Pressure groups

There are many sources of inputs into the health policy-making process, several of which have already been mentioned. First, there are the inputs which come from pressure groups. As we noted in Chapter 6, the collectivist theory of representation legitimates a much greater role for groups than earlier theories of representation, and increasing state involvement in managing the economy and in the welfare state has led governments to negotiate and consult with pressure groups. A distinction has already been made between producer groups, which are often in a strong position to bargain for what they want, and consumer groups, which are relatively weak. There are also groups that exist to pursue a particular cause, an example being Action on Smoking and Health (ASH) which campaigns for control of smoking and limitations on advertising by tobacco companies. ASH has backing from a key producer group, the Royal College of Physicians (RCP), demonstrating the difficulty of making clear distinctions in the pressure group world surrounding the Department (Popham, 1981).

Both the BMA and the medical Royal Colleges expect to be consulted over the development of policy and Eckstein (1960) has shown how often it is negotiation rather than consultation which characterises the relationship between these groups and the government. Occasionally relationships become strained, as in the dispute over pay beds in the 1970s, the NHS reforms in the 1980s and more recently the development of polyclinics, but on many issues there is a partnership between the medical profession and the Department, equivalent to those that exist in the educational and agricultural policy communities between the relevant departments and their client groups. Under the Blair government, the appointment of a number of senior doctors to work in the Department as national clinical directors or 'tsars' provided further evidence of the insider status of the medical profession.

The position of consumer groups within the health policy community is not as strong (Ham, 1977). Consumer groups are heavily dependent on the advice, information and expertise they have to offer, and cannot threaten sanctions in the same way as producer groups. Because their cooperation is usually not vital to the implementation of policy, consumer

groups are dependent on the quality of their arguments and the willingness of ministers and civil servants to listen to what they have to say. In
most cases, too, they have to supplement the pressure they exert on the
Department by operating through Parliament and mass media. Recent
research has described the resources available to consumer groups and
the activities they undertake, including their links with civil servants and
ministers. This research concluded that while consumer groups have some
influence over health policy, medical and commercial interests remain
dominant on many issues (Baggott et al., 2004).

The pressure exerted by producer and consumer groups may be
welcomed by ministers as it may help them in their negotiations with
Cabinet colleagues. This explains why some groups receive financial
support from government. In her diaries, Barbara Castle indicates that in
her time as Secretary of State she encouraged the National Association of
Health Authorities 'to become a pressure group for the NHS' (Castle,
1980, p. 459). She also notes that during the dispute with the medical
profession over pay beds, ministers stimulated trade union activity to
persuade the BMA to accept limitations on private practice within the
NHS. Similarly, civil servants with responsibility for policy for particular
client groups, such as the mentally ill, may welcome pressure from organisations like MIND as it may strengthen their hand in the competition for
resources and priority within the Department. It is important to remember,
then, that demands may not always arise autonomously in the community,
and that pressure may sometimes be encouraged by policy-makers.

Pressure groups make demands on a wide range of issues. These
demands may require a change in legislation, a decision by a civil servant,
or intervention by ministers. Occasionally, they may involve the Prime
Minister, the Cabinet and other government departments. The effectiveness of groups in pressing their demands will depend on a variety of
factors: the information they possess, their contacts with policy-makers,
their expertise and the sanctions they have at their disposal. In responding
to groups, policy-makers will weigh their own preferences against those
of the groups. They will also be alert to the need to secure the compliance
of key interests, and to the electoral consequences of their decisions. The
exact process of decision-making is difficult to define because, as Solesbury notes, it is at this stage that 'one passes into the relatively closed
world of the executive departments of state, and to a lesser extent interdepartmental and Cabinet committees, where the consideration given to
issues and possible responses by politicians and officials is largely shielded
from the public gaze' (Solesbury, 1976, p. 392).

Despite the difficulties of penetrating the intricacies of decision-making
within central government, it can be suggested that the national health
policy community is itself fragmented into a series of sub-communities

concerned with specific aspects of policy. These sub-communities are organised around issues such as policies for older people, primary care, health inequalities and so on. Different parts of the DH have different characteristics, and in one sense the Department itself can be seen to be made up of pressure groups for particular functions, services and client groups. Outside pressure groups are drawn towards those parts of the Department which have responsibility for the policies which the groups are interested in, and sub-communities are formed from the relationships which develop between these groups and civil servants. In an attempt to analyse these relationships, one study of policies for older people suggested that these policies were worked out in an 'iron triangle' rather than an 'issue network' (Haywood and Hunter, 1982, drawing on Heclo, 1978). The key participants were Departmental officials, leading medical and nursing professionals, and two key producer groups – the Royal College of Nursing and the British Geriatrics Society. Although the consultative process was later widened to encompass a range of other groups, the crucial decisions at an early stage were arrived at by this small set of interests. However, Haywood and Hunter warn that on other issues, such as pay beds and health service organisation, issue networks may be a more appropriate metaphor.

Parliament and the mass media

Not all the demands made by pressure groups will invoke action and groups which are unsuccessful in their attempt to influence civil servants and ministers will often turn their attention to Parliament and the mass media. Here, then, are two further sources of inputs into the health policy-making system, and not just as vehicles for pressure group demands, but as originators of demands themselves. The mass media have played a particularly active role in publicising the low standards of care that exist in the so-called 'Cinderella' services. Ever since the appearance of newspaper reports of cruelty to patients in the mid-1960s, the media have been prominent in the campaign to improve conditions for groups such as the mentally ill and people with learning disabilities. Television programmes on Rampton Special Hospital and on hospital services for disabled people have maintained public attention on this area of the NHS to the extent that journalists and television producers have taken on the appearance of pressure groups for underprivileged sections of the community. Other issues on which the media has adopted a campaigning stance include the standards of care for older people and the funding of this care, and the ability of patients to pay for drugs not available on the NHS while receiving the rest of their care free.

The role of Parliament was discussed in Chapter 6. It will be recalled that Parliamentary inputs to health policy-making take the form of MPs' questions, issues raised during debates, private members' bills and reports from select committees. Some indication of the volume of Parliamentary business is given by the fact that in 2005–06 there were almost 15,000 written Parliamentary questions (more than twice the number received by any other department) and nearly 100,000 letters were received. The accountability to Parliament of the Secretary of State for Health requires a considerable amount of detailed information about health services to be fed up to the Department by NHS bodies. This acts as a centralising influence within the NHS.

Equally, demands raised in Parliament may have an influence on health policy-making and on the local operation of health services. An obvious example would be legislation resulting from a private member's bill, such as the Abortion Act. On other occasions, government-sponsored legislation may be amended in the course of its passage through Parliament. An example was the legislation that established NHS foundation trusts on which the government accepted a series of changes as a result of debate on the Health and Social Care Bill in the House of Commons and the House of Lords. These changes included the creation of a board structure for the independent regulator of NHS foundation trusts instead of a single office holder, and a requirement that trusts should ensure that their membership was representative of those eligible to become members.

Increasingly, too, the House of Commons Health Committee and the Public Accounts Committee have provided an informed contribution to the policy-making process. The Health Committee has produced a variety of reports on health service issues. Recent inquiries have included the National Institute for Health and Clinical Excellence, NHS foundation trusts and Monitor and the NHS Next Stage Review. The MPs on the Committee are supported by a small group of full-time staff and specialist advisers appointed for particular inquiries. Select committees tend to have greatest impact when they present unanimous reports and in this respect the choice of topics for investigation is important. In its work, the Health Committee has chosen to examine issues which in the main are non-controversial in party political terms and this has helped the Committee to present a united front. The work of select committees rarely leads directly to changes in policy but they have strengthened Parliamentary scrutiny of government departments and over a period of time their reports may influence the work of these departments. As a study of the former Social Services Committee noted of the Committee's investigations into the expenditure plans of the DHSS, 'their cumulative effect has been to make the Department improve its own procedures for reviewing and coordinating its policies, as well as preparing and presenting expenditure plans' (Nixon and Nixon, 1983, p. 352).

The Public Accounts Committee scrutinises government spending as a whole and in recent years has examined a number of different aspects of the NHS, including the private finance initiative, NHS Direct, the new contracts for general practitioners and consultants, and the national programme for information technology, Connecting for Health. Nairne has referred to the Public Accounts Committee as 'the premier committee of Parliament' (Nairne, 1983, p. 254) and has described the pressures placed by the Committee on the Permanent Secretary in his capacity as Accounting Officer. This has been confirmed by Stowe, another former Permanent Secretary, who has described his relationship with the Committee as:

> a powerful reinforcement of the Permanent Secretary's authority and an even more powerful incentive for him or her to take very seriously his obligation to ensure that publicly financed programmes of expenditure are managed with integrity and efficiency. (Stowe, 1989, p. 57)

As Stowe notes, the power of the Committee derives in large part from the support it receives from the Comptroller and Auditor General and the National Audit Office. Staff of the National Audit Office have continuous access to the Department's files and the reports they produce provide the basis for investigations by the Committee. Stowe has observed that the relationship between the Department and the National Audit Office 'is anything but cosy: a mutual admiration society it is not. Some of the most fractious dogfights in my experience occurred in this quarter' (*ibid.*). Certainly, ministers and civil servants have faced some rigorous questioning from the MPs on the Committee and the Committee has had a demonstrable impact on some issues. In recent times, the NHS Chief Executive has appeared before select committees much more frequently than the Permanent Secretary because the work of the committees has focused mainly on NHS issues.

NHS bodies

NHS bodies (the collective term for health authorities and trusts) represent a fourth source of inputs into the Department's policy-making system. Indeed, these bodies do not simply carry out nationally determined policies, but have important policy-making responsibilities in their own right. In many cases, policies are developed jointly by civil servants and NHS managers, an example being the performance indicators for the NHS published in 1983 which were the result of work done by staff from the Department and the Northern RHA. There are many other examples of policy proposals developed jointly by the centre and the periphery. The Department is dependent on NHS bodies for information about the local development of services and for actually providing the services, while these bodies are dependent on the Department for the resources required to carry out their functions. This mutual dependence helps to explain why national policies are often shaped and influenced by NHS bodies.

The establishment of the NHS Management Board and its successors, the NHS Management Executive and the NHS Executive, within the Department served to strengthen the links between the centre and the NHS. Senior health service managers played an important part in the work of both bodies. This was first evident in the appointment of Duncan Nichol, a regional general manager, as Chief Executive of the NHS in 1988 followed by Alan Langlands in 1994 and Nigel Crisp in 2000. Following Crisp's departure in 2006, another senior manager, Ian Carruthers, became acting chief executive on an interim basis before David Nicholson's substantive appointment. Other NHS staff have been appointed as directors general or have been seconded to work in the Department, and a number of civil servants have spent time in the NHS.

Ministers as well as civil servants draw on advice from within the NHS in developing their policies. For much of the history of the NHS, this found expression in regular meetings between the Secretary of State and health authority chairmen. Norman Fowler, Secretary of State in the mid-1980s, explained that regional chairmen 'operate as a health cabinet as far as I am concerned' (Social Services Committee, 1984, p. 165). Virginia Bottomley, Secretary of State from 1992 to 1995, also valued the contribution of regional chairmen, commenting that 'the people I had a lot of time for were the regional chairmen' (quoted in Ham, 2000, p. 47). Meetings with regional chairmen were two-way affairs in which ministers explained their thinking and priorities and regional chairmen reported on developments within the NHS. These meetings continued under the Blair government but over time more emphasis was put on relationships between senior civil servants and strategic health authority chief executives and directors. These relationships were formalised under Nigel Crisp in the establishment of the Top Team comprising senior civil servants, health authority chief executives and the national clinical directors or tsars. The Top Team met on a regular basis to review NHS performance and to be briefed on national policy issues and priorities.

A further source of advice is the NHS Confederation. This has gone through a number of guises and it exists to represent the views of NHS bodies to government. Membership of the NHS Confederation comprises a high proportion of health authorities and trusts and the staff and officers of the Confederation meet regularly with ministers and civil servants to discuss issues in health policy and the NHS. As we noted earlier, Barbara Castle encouraged the forerunner of the NHS Confederation to be a pressure group for the NHS and it publishes a number of reports on current developments and lobbies to ensure actively that the opinions of NHS bodies are heard. Alongside the Confederation, the views of primary care groups are articulated by organisations like the NHS Alliance and the National Association of Primary Care and these organisations and their predecessors have been particularly vocal on behalf of GPs and other staff working in primary care.

The consultative machinery

A fifth input to policy-making comes from the consultative machinery attached to the Department. An important part of this machinery in the past were the standing advisory groups, such as those on medical issues and on nursing and midwifery, that met regularly to give advice on health policy. The work of these committees was brought to an end by the government in 2005 because various other channels for obtaining medical and nursing advice had been developed. These channels are often specific to the policy issues of concern to the government and they may involve doctors, nurses and others being asked for their views on an ad hoc basis as required. In this way, government is able to draw on a wider range of expertise and individuals than is possible through the use of standing groups with fixed memberships. As examples, the consultations that took place before the preparation of *The NHS Plan* in 2000 and the White Paper, *Our Health, Our Care, Our Say,* in 2006 involved seeking views from many hundreds of individuals, comprising health care professionals, managers, patients and the public.

Royal commissions and inquiries provide a further means of seeking the views of stakeholders. Examples of royal commissions include the Royal Commission on the NHS that reported in 1979 (see Chapter 1) and the Royal Commission on Long-Term Care that reported in 1999 (see Chapter 5). Examples of inquiries include investigations into inequalities in health in 1980, NHS management in 1983, community care in 1988, and paediatric heart surgery at the Bristol Royal Infirmary in 2001. The reports that emanate from royal commissions and inquiries provide an almost continuous flow of demands into the Department. As with other inputs into the political system, demands coming from these sources have to compete for the time and attention of policy-makers. Some may be rejected out of hand, others may be subjected to further discussions, while others may be adopted immediately.

As well as advice provided by royal commissions and inquiries, there are the regular rounds of formal consultation with NHS bodies and pressure groups which have already been referred to. Formal consultation typically occurs when a consultative document on a particular issue is published. The extent to which these documents are really open to influence varies: in many cases there may be little scope for groups to influence what is decided, but on some occasions a well-organised group can have a significant impact. Whether groups are able to exercise influence may depend on the stage during the consultative process that they become involved. Haywood and Hunter (1982) point out that formal consultation is often preceded by informal consultation on draft documents. In some cases informal consultation may itself be foreshadowed by discussions among a small number of key participants, as in the iron triangle which develops policies for older people. As a rule of thumb, the earlier a group becomes involved, the more likely it is to influence what is decided.

Ministers and civil servants

Sixth, and most important, there are demands which come from ministers and civil servants within the Department. A new Secretary of State is likely to have a number of issues he or she wants to pursue while in office. Many will have been developed in Opposition, and may have been included in an election manifesto. Both Banting (1979) and Kingdon (1995) suggest that politicians are particularly important in making certain issues salient, and in defining the agenda for discussion.

In the case of health policy, Webster has noted on the basis of his historical analysis of the NHS many examples of politicians influencing the agenda (Webster, 1996). Examples cited by Webster include Kenneth Robinson's involvement with the Charter for the Family Doctor Service in the 1960s, Richard Crossman's emphasis on improving conditions in long-stay hospitals, and Keith Joseph's reorganisation of the NHS in the 1970s. Another area in which politicians made a difference was private health care which for many years was not a salient issue. Only in 1974, when Barbara Castle attempted to reduce the number of pay beds in NHS hospitals and limit the growth of private hospitals, did the issue become prominent. Private medicine remained a salient issue when the Conservative government elected in 1979 reversed Castle's policy and sought to encourage the growth of the private health care sector. As we note below, the influence of politicians was especially strong after the election of the Blair government at a time of significant increases in spending and continuous NHS reform.

Having made this point, it should also be noted that ministers have to work with and through civil servants to take forward policy. In the case of pay beds referred to above, Barbara Castle notes in her diary that the Permanent Secretary at the time, Sir Philip Rogers, had submitted a paper stating that DHSS officials 'feel they would be failing in their duty if they did not let me know how opposed they all were to the phasing of private practice out of NHS hospitals' (Castle, 1980, p. 170). Castle's account is confirmed by the memoirs of one of her junior ministers at the time:

> In the summer of 1974 Sir Philip Rogers came to see Barbara Castle and myself to discuss privately our controversial manifesto commitment to phase pay beds out of NHS hospitals. Sir Philip deployed a strong case against our taking any action. He warned us that the mood of the medical profession was very brittle and said that the considered judgement of himself, the Chief Medical Officer and all the top officials was that, in the best interests of the NHS, we should avoid a confrontation with the doctors on this issue. Rather movingly, he insisted that if the Secretary of State, having heard him out, came to a different conclusion then that was the last that she would hear of it and everyone in the Department would carry out her policy faithfully and to the best of their abilities.

> Sir Philip kept his promise and from then on defended our decisions and refused to let the British Medical Association get away with the attempt to present officials as not being fully behind our policy. It was a fine example of the best of the civil service tradition of serving governments irrespective of party. (Owen, 1991, p. 232)

Of course, civil servants are not a homogeneous group, and Castle herself notes that 'the department is split into two different worlds: the conventional, change-nothing world of the top Establishment; the challenging irreverent world of the press office and some of the younger officials' (Castle, 1980, p. 209). Of particular interest in this context is the role of doctors in government (Sheard and Donaldson, 2006, provide an historical account of the development of the Chief Medical Officer role). As we noted at the beginning of the chapter, there is strong medical involvement in decision-making in the Department, and a former Chief Medical Officer, Sir George Godber, has observed that 'the doctor in Government has to be facing two ways: he is a Civil Servant and his Minister must be able to rely on his complete loyalty: but he is also a member of his profession, which must be able to trust him too' (Godber, 1981, p. 2). These dual loyalties create the possibility that conflicts may arise in which professional ties will emerge the stronger. Godber notes that such a possibility arose during Crossman's tenure as Secretary of

State but did not reach the point where the Chief Medical Officer would have resigned. On another occasion Godber states that 'The Permanent Secretary and I once declined to accept our Civil Service increases so long as the doctors' incomes were frozen' (Godber, 1981, p. 3).

Clearly, then, civil servants have their own loyalties and views, and these views have an influence on policy-making. Further evidence of this point comes from Pater's study of the creation of the NHS. Pater argues that the credit for the establishment of the NHS should be widely shared, but he contends:

> There is no doubt, however, that the main credit for the emergence of a viable and, indeed, successful service must rest with two ... officers of the ministry: Sir William Jameson, chief medical officer from 1940 to 1950, and Sir John Hawton, deputy secretary from 1947 to 1951 and permanent secretary thereafter until his retirement through ill-health in 1960. (Pater, 1981, p. 178)

Another example of a policy where internal factors were important is the Hospital Plan of 1962. This was prepared by hospital boards and committees under the guidance of the Ministry of Health. Although outside interests were pressing for increased spending on hospital build-ings, the origins of the Plan owed a great deal to the minister at the time, Enoch Powell, his Permanent Secretary, Sir Bruce Fraser, and the Deputy Chief Medical Officer, Sir George Godber. These three men effectively transformed a vague idea about the need for an expanded building programme into a detailed plan. The coincidence of interests between the minister and senior civil servants helped to account for the promotion of this development in policy. In this and other cases, policy evolved through a partnership between civil servants and ministers (Allen, 1979).

A recent study of the Secretaries of State who held office between 1988 and 1997 drew on interviews with the ministers concerned to note the importance of the views and experience of ministers themselves and their reliance on civil service advice and support. The latter included the advice provided by the civil servants working in the Secretary of State's private office and not just the most senior officials. Secretaries of State for Health were influenced too by pressure groups and outside interests. Of particu-lar importance were producer groups like the BMA whose role in the implementation of policy acted as a constraint on the radicalism of politi-cians. As the study concluded:

> it is the influence of individuals working within established structures that shapes health policy. The interdependency of these individuals and their interaction with key organisations leads to bargaining and

negotiation out of which policy evolves. Politicians are important in shaping the agenda and in working with civil servants to identify and choose between policy options. Outside organisations and interests are involved in this process to a greater or lesser degree, with some like the BMA particularly well placed to influence the direction of policy. Periods of relative stability and continuity are interrupted by periods of innovation and change, most obviously when politicians external to policy communities seek to question the established consensus. (Ham, 2000, p. 72)

Among civil servants, economists and analysts have had increasing influence in recent years. A former chief economic adviser in the Department of Health, Clive Smee, has noted that the number of economists and operational researchers in the Department increased from zero to well over 50 between 1970 and 2002. Over this period, he contends that the contribution of analysts to policy-making was evident in a number of areas, including the use of cost-effectiveness data to support decisions, the development of performance management and performance indicators, and the examination of alternative funding options. In much of this work, economists within the DH collaborated with economists in universities and other organisations to strengthen the role of analysis in policy-making. As a consequence, 'health care policy-making has generally become more evidence based and rigorous' (Smee, 2005, p. 192). Echoing Jeremy Hurst, one of his longstanding colleagues in the Department, Smee emphasises that the role of economists and other analysts was mainly to provide advice and support to the generalist administrators who led on policy development. The influence of the chief economic adviser has been attested to by former Secretaries of State for Health (Ham, 2000).

Special advisers and the core executive

Special advisers did not figure prominently in the recollections of Secretaries of State when they were asked about the influences on policy-making in the 1990s. As we noted in Chapter 6, the number of advisers and their influence grew under the Blair government, both in 10 Downing Street and the Department of Health. The involvement of special advisers in health policy is not new, as the use of Brian Abel-Smith by the Labour government in the 1970s illustrates. Nevertheless, advisers played a significant part in the development of health policy after 1997, working closely with ministers in the development of major policy documents. One of the most influential of these advisers was Simon Stevens who worked with Frank Dobson and then Alan Milburn in the Department of Health before moving to work as a senior health policy adviser in 10 Downing Street. Other influential special advisers during this period were Darren Murphy, Paul Corrigan and Julian Le Grand.

The rise of special advisers under the Blair government was paralleled by the close interest shown by the Prime Minister himself in health policy and NHS reform. Whereas the Secretaries of State who held office between 1988 and 1997 attested to the influence of the Prime Minister only at times of major reviews, such as the one that led to *Working for Patients* and the internal market reforms, in the decade after the election of a Labour government Tony Blair was personally and closely involved in many aspects of health policy. This was evident in his announcement of major increases in NHS funding on a television programme in 2000, and subsequently in the work that went into *The NHS Plan, Delivering the NHS Plan* and *The NHS Improvement Plan*. At all stages, the Prime Minister played a significant part in working up the policies that appeared in these documents and in overseeing their implementation.

During this period, health policy formulation involved close collaboration between the Department of Health and 10 Downing Street, with the Treasury also having an important influence on some issues (see Chapter 6). This included inviting outside experts to lead major reviews. Examples included the review of the long-term funding needs of the NHS led by Derek Wanless at the invitation of the Chancellor of the Exchequer, and the Health Strategy Review undertaken by Adair Turner at the invitation of the Prime Minister. Both reviews had a real impact on health policy, and illustrated an increasing tendency to outsource policy analysis work to acknowledged experts rather than to conduct the work within government or use more traditional mechanisms like royal commissions.

The influence of the Prime Minister on health policy in the past decade, and the involvement of health ministers and special advisers, runs counter to the argument of those who contend that governance has superseded government in contemporary British politics. The reality is that actors within government remain the main initiators of policy and their decisions are influenced to a greater or lesser degree by other participants in the networks that make up the health policy community. As one study has noted:

> the health policy-making process, particularly in relation to the NHS, seems to have been less affected than other areas of public policy by the appearance of new actors, the move to new institutional arenas and the transformation of relationships than the 'from-government-to governance' thesis would predict (Alvarez-Rosete and Mays, 2008).

An examination of the processes of policy-making and the various inputs into those processes creates, rightly, the impression of a complex policy system in which those responsible for making policy are subject to numerous competing demands. Although change is possible, it is difficult to achieve because of the operation of demand regulation mechanisms which limit the number of issues on the agenda at any one time. And even in relation to these issues, incremental changes to the status quo are more probable than major shifts in direction. This has been clearly demonstrated in a study of government policy on smoking, where it has been argued that decisions were:

> the outcome of a process in which groups have played a major role ... For many years tobacco interests had no difficulty in keeping the subject off the political agenda; their power took a non-decision-making form. Forerunners of ASH, such as the National Society of Non-Smokers, encountered indifferent or hostile attitudes from Government ... It took the prestige and evidence of elite medical groups, such as the BMA and the RCP, to break the agenda barrier. Even then Government response was cautious because possible adverse electoral consequences were feared by some Ministers if too rigorous a policy of discouragement was pursued. (Popham, 1981, p. 345)

Inertia in policy-making is reinforced by the existence of stable relationships in the health policy community. The power of the medical profession in these relationships derives in no small part from the need of government for the support of doctors and their representatives in the implementation of policy. Comparative analysis of policy networks in the United Kingdom and the United States has shown (Smith, 1993) that health policy in Britain involves a relatively stable and cohesive policy community and this tends to result in incremental change. To be sure, stability and incrementalism may be challenged when politicians like Margaret Thatcher and Tony Blair seek to promote fundamental reforms to the NHS, but the evidence suggests that these periods are relatively unusual and short-lived.

Industrial and commercial interests

The example of smoking draws attention to the role of industrial and commercial interests in the health policy community. At least three sets of interests need to be considered. First, there are those interests involved in the provision of private sector health care services. Private sector interests include both the provident associations such as BUPA and private for-profit providers from the United Kingdom and other countries. While some of these interests are mainly concerned with health insurance, others are engaged in the provision of hospital, community and primary care services. The reforms pursued by the Blair government encouraged the entry of new providers into the market as policies to increase patient choice and develop competition between providers gathered pace. In developing these policies, ministers and civil servants consulted extensively with both the NHS and private sector interests, the latter being invited on a regular basis to advise the government on the role they could play in the emerging market and the policy changes needed to facilitate their entry. This included participating in meetings at 10 Downing Street as well as the Department of Health. The establishment of the Commercial Directorate in the Department in 2003 signified the increasing importance of the private sector at this time.

A second set of interests consists of those companies supplying goods, equipment and services to the NHS. These include firms seeking to obtain contracts for the provision of services such as catering and laundry; the manufacturers of medical equipment and supplies; and the drugs industry. The last of these is particularly significant in view of the fact that the drugs bill makes up over 10 per cent of total NHS expenditure. Although the industry contributes significantly to employment and exports there has been concern at the level of profits earned. Regulation occurs through the Pharmaceutical Price Regulation Scheme, a voluntary scheme in which the government attempts to control prices and profits in the industry. Despite this, the House of Commons Public Accounts Committee has criticised the Department for not doing more to limit profits, and in response to the Committee's criticism action was taken to introduce tighter controls.

A third set of interests is represented by companies producing goods which may be harmful to health. The tobacco, alcohol and food-processing industries are included in this category. The influence of the food industry has been examined by Cannon (1984) in an analysis of the response to a report on nutritional guidelines for health produced by the National Advisory Committee on Nutrition Education. The report, which recommended reduced consumption of sugar, salt and fat, and increased intake of dietary fibre, was opposed by the food industry. Cannon demonstrates how government is divided between ministers principally concerned with issues of public health and ministers concerned with economic and employment issues. Changes in eating habits which pose a threat to jobs and profits in the food industry are likely to be resisted not only by the industry but also by politicians and civil servants involved in spheres such as trade, industry and agriculture. Only in recent years, in the face of increasing recognition of the challenges posed by obesity and overweight in the population, have public health concerns about eating habits and diet been taken seriously, leading to the development of a cross-government strategy in 2008.

Similar issues arise in the case of tobacco. In a thorough analysis, Taylor (1984) has investigated why governments have historically done so little to regulate the tobacco industry in the face of overwhelming medical evidence about the harmful effects of cigarette smoking. As Taylor points out, the tobacco industry is composed of a relatively small number of large and wealthy multinational companies whose power derives not so much from their activity as pressure groups – although this may be important – as from their position in the economy. The industry is significant as an employer and as a source of tax revenues, and while ministers may want to control the industry on health grounds, ministers in the Treasury are inclined to oppose regulations on economic grounds. As Taylor comments:

> In principle, as guardians of the public health, governments ought to be the tobacco industry's fierce opponents, but in practice they are often its firm ally. Cigarettes provide governments with one of their biggest and most reliable sources of revenue; they create tens of thousands of jobs in hard economic times; they present a healthy surplus on the balance of payments; they help development in Third World Countries where tobacco is grown. In purely economic terms, the political benefits of cigarettes far outweigh their social cost. (Taylor, 1984, p. xix)

For this reason, government action to warn the public of the dangers of cigarette smoking was based for many years on seeking the voluntary cooperation of the tobacco industry and only in 2007 did legislation come into effect in England to ban smoking in public places.

The development of alcohol policy exhibits many of the same features. As Baggott (1986) has shown, successive governments have been slow to develop policies to control the misuse of alcohol. He attributes this to the power of commercial interests, the relatively weak and diffuse nature of the groups pressing for reforms, the hostility of voters and public opinion, and opposition by government departments who stand to benefit from a strong alcohol industry. As with food and tobacco, government policies to combat the adverse consequences of alcohol have been strengthened recently in the face of mounting evidence of the long-term effects on the public health.

The examples of food, tobacco and alcohol lend support to Lindblom's (1977) thesis about the power of business corporations in contemporary politics, and it is this power which helps to account for the predominance of policy maintenance and incremental changes. These examples also illustrate the importance of what Moran (1999) refers to as 'production politics' in the health care state, by which he means the process of negotiation and bargaining between commercial interests involved in health and health care and government.

The role of ideas

The policy process is not, however, entirely a matter of responding to political demands. An increasingly important part of the process is the attempt to examine a wider range of options, and to subject existing policies to a more thorough analysis. There are two aspects to this. First, there is the contribution which academics and researchers make to policy-making. As Banting (1979) points out echoing the work of Heclo (1974), policy-making is both an intellectual activity and a political process. Thus, as well as examining the impact of pressure groups, politicians and other key actors, it is necessary to look at the role of ideas and information in shaping policy. One of the areas of health policy where ideas have had an influence is the organisation of the NHS. The administrative structure introduced in 1974, for example, derived from theories of management and organisational behaviour developed by organisational sociologists at Brunel University and management consultants at McKinsey.

A second area where ideas had an impact was in the thinking behind the Black Report on inequalities and health. The Report was the outcome of the deliberations of an expert working group whose most influential member was Peter Townsend, then Professor of Sociology at Essex University. Townsend's previous work on the nature and causes of poverty and deprivation clearly contributed much to the analysis and recommendations of the Black Report. What is interesting is that Townsend's work is very much in the LSE social administration tradition which Banting found to have had a strong influence in other areas of social policy (Banting, 1979). It is apparent, though, that this tradition, of which Brian Abel-Smith, a special adviser to a number of Secretaries of State, was also a part, has had a greater impact on Labour governments than Conservative governments. Special advisers are often a channel through which ideas find their way into the policy process as studies of the history of the NHS have noted (Webster 1996).

A third example of ideas contributing to policy formulation was the influence of the American economist, Alain Enthoven, during the Ministerial Review of the NHS. In 1985 Enthoven published a monograph entitled *Reflections on the Management of the NHS* (Enthoven, 1985) in which he proposed the establishment of an internal market in health care.

These ideas were picked up and developed during the Ministerial Review and had an appreciable influence on the White Paper, *Working for Patients*. The government's debt to Enthoven was acknowledged by the Secretary of State at the time of the Review, Kenneth Clarke. In an interview about the NHS reforms, Clarke referred to Enthoven's advocacy of internal markets, arguing 'I liked it because it tried to inject into a state owned system some of the qualities of competition, choice, and measurement of quality that you get in a well run private enterprise' (Roberts, 1990, p. 1385).

Think tanks and independent research units are a further source of policy ideas. Among the think tanks, the Institute for Public Policy Research, the Social Market Foundation, Demos, Civitas and Reform, among others, have contributed a stream of ideas on the reform of the NHS through their reports and seminars. The health policy community also includes a number of independent research units, some based in universities and others in foundations like the King's Fund, the Nuffield Trust and the Health Foundation. These units adopt various working styles ranging from seeking to influence policy by developing good relationships with government and maintaining a low profile, to publishing reports and seeking press coverage to ensure high visibility for their ideas. The study of Secretaries of State cited earlier found that the contribution made by think tanks, independent research units and respected academic commentators did have some influence on policy-making, even though it was not the most significant input from the perspective of those interviewed (Ham, 2000).

Academics and researchers apart, there have been a number of attempts within the Department to develop a more 'rational' approach to policy-making. In varying degrees, these mechanisms have sought to introduce a greater measure of analysis into the policy process, and in the final part of this chapter we review the recent experience of policy analysis in the Department.

Changes in the Department

Policy analysis

In 1970 the Conservative government published a White Paper setting out proposals for increasing the policy analysis capabilities of central government. Among the innovations to follow from the White Paper were the Central Policy Review Staff, established to provide advice on government policies independent of that offered by existing departments, and Programme Analysis and Review, involving an in-depth study of specific topics within departments. Both innovations affected central government as a whole. At around the same time, and reflecting the spirit of the White Paper, a number of specific developments were taking place in the DHSS designed to improve the Department's capacity for reviewing its policies and priorities. These included the introduction of programme budgeting, and the creation of a planning system for the Department.

Within central government as a whole, the spirit of the 1970 White Paper gave way to a particular concern to increase management efficiency and cut down on bureaucracy after the election of the Thatcher government in 1979. Programme Analysis and Review and the Central Policy Review Staff were terminated, to be replaced by Rayner Scrutinies, reductions in manpower, and an initiative on financial management (Cmnd 9058, 1983). In the DHSS, the planning system was wound down – a victim, like its NHS counterpart, of exaggerated expectations. The programme budget, split into separate programmes for hospital and community health services and personal social services, continued to be used, but more as a tool for monitoring past trends in expenditure than as a mechanism for projecting future growth rates. Alongside the emphasis on efficiency, there was a continuing concern to improve the Department's capacity for strategic policy-making stimulated in part by the reports of the House of Commons Social Services Committee (Social Services Committee, 1980). In response to these reports, the Department set up a number of new committees and groups to undertake policy analysis. One of these groups was the Policy Strategy Unit which was similar to the Central Policy Review Staff, except that it worked only within the DHSS. In the end, the Unit met the same fate as the CPRS, being superseded in 1984.

Back to management

As the 1980s progressed, the concern to strengthen the Department's capacity for managing the NHS gained momentum. The most visible manifestation of this was the establishment of the NHS Management Board following the Griffiths Report of 1983. Victor Paige was appointed as the Board's first chairman but almost immediately difficulties emerged. In the words of the then Permanent Secretary, Sir Kenneth Stowe, 'it was nearly a disaster' (Stowe, 1989, p. 52). One of the reasons for this was the limit imposed on the Board's activities by politicians. As Paige has written:

> because of Ministers' accountability to Parliament, the high political pressures and sensitivity associated with virtually every central management decision within present policies, then the reality is that ministers take all the important decisions, political, strategic and managerial. (Paige, 1987, p. 7)

This meant that it was impossible to devolve executive authority to the Board. Unable to operate within political constraints, Paige resigned in 1986. Reflecting on what happened, Stowe has maintained that government will never be able to operate like a commercial business. He stated that:

[i]nevitably tensions will arise between, on the one hand, ministers (and those officials supporting them) who must always be accountable to Parliament, and on the other, officials (irrespective of their nomenclature) who have been charged by those same ministers with the task of achieving an efficient delivery of services within prescribed policies and predetermined resources. (Stowe, 1989, p. 54)

In an attempt to tackle these tensions more effectively, membership of the Board was changed after Paige's resignation, with the Minister of State for Health taking the chair, and Len Peach (from IBM) being appointed as chief executive. This was superseded in 1988 when the NHS Management Executive (ME) was created. The NHS ME was chaired by a chief executive drawn from the NHS and it operated under the strategic direction of the Department's Policy Board. Although it remained firmly within the Department and accountable to the Policy Board, the ME began to take on the appearance of an agency at arm's length from political control and able to operate semi-autonomously. This impression was reinforced by the relocation of the ME to offices in Leeds in 1992. The functions and manpower review which reported in 1993 examined the possibility of the ME becoming an executive agency but ministers concluded that this option should not be pursued because of the intense public and political interest in the NHS and the need to ensure effective accountability in a service spending over £30 billion a year at that time.

Implementation of the Banks Review (1994) of the Department resulted in a further shift in the balance of work and power to the NHS Executive as it came to be known. The decision to place responsibility for policy in the hands of the NHS Executive meant that the wider Department focused mainly on public health and social care. As a consequence of the Banks Review, the recommendations of the Griffiths Report were finally implemented over a decade after its publication, although it should be emphasised that the Permanent Secretary remained the head of the Department and retained oversight of all its responsibilities. This was reflected in the wording of the Statement of Responsibilities and Accountabilities prepared after the Banks Review which noted that the Permanent Secretary had the task of 'advising the Secretary of State on the discharge of all the duties of his or her office' while the Chief Executive of the NHS

Executive was 'the Secretary of State's principal policy adviser on all matters relating to the NHS' (DH, 1997, paras 1.7 and 1.8).

The tensions in this arrangement came to a head in 2000 when a decision was made to create a single post of Permanent Secretary and NHS Chief Executive. This decision resulted from the increasingly marginal role played by the Permanent Secretary in circumstances in which ministers were mainly focused on improving the performance of the NHS. The desire of the Secretary of State, Alan Milburn, to have a clear chain of command from his office through the Department and into the NHS was a key factor in the merger of these roles. The combined post was filled by Nigel Crisp who had pursued a career as an NHS manager before becoming a regional director of the NHS Executive. In the jockeying for power between the mandarins and managers, to borrow the language of Day and Klein (1997), managers therefore emerged as the more powerful, and this reflected the increasing emphasis within the civil service under the Blair government on management expertise and the delivery of government targets. The creation of the post of Permanent Secretary and NHS Chief Executive was followed by the reintegration of the NHS Executive into the Department in 2001 as part of an effort to achieve more effective coordination of the full range of the Department's responsibilities. This included an attempt to achieve better links between those parts of the Department dealing with the NHS, public health and social care.

Court politics in the Department

Yet before concluding that Nigel Crisp's appointment represented a triumph for managerialism in the Department, it is important to recognise the role of other actors at this time. As we noted in Chapter 6, Alan Milburn himself was particularly determined and ambitious and he worked extremely closely with his special advisers, including Simon Stevens, Darren Murphy and latterly Paul Corrigan. Milburn was personally involved in all major health policy issues between his appointment in October 1999 and his resignation in June 2003. During this period, senior NHS managers may have occupied most of the top jobs in the Department, but their scope for independent action was constrained by a Secretary of State with clear views of his own who had the explicit endorsement of the Prime Minister and the benefit of ideas supplied by special advisers who could claim a great deal of expertise in their own right. This was exemplified in the work done on *The NHS Plan* which involved gathering the views of a large number of stakeholders in the initial stages, developing and refining these views within the Department with the contribution of senior civil servants, leading in the final stages to an intensive process of drafting led by Milburn and involving a very small group of advisers and officials, both in the Department and in 10 Downing Street.

In adopting this approach, Milburn was mimicking the informal style of policy-making and the reliance on special advisers that Tony Blair developed in Downing Street during his time as Prime Minister. The phrase 'court politics' (Fawcett and Rhodes, 2007) has been coined to describe this style. In the Department of Health, court politics meant that the formal organisational chart often bore little relationship to the day-to-day realities of policy-making. Ministers of the day preferred to work through advisers and civil servants whose advice they had come to trust and respect, whatever their position in the hierarchy, and this resulted in considerable fluidity in the people who shaped policy-making. The Secretary of State's private office served as the lynchpin in these arrangements with some members of the private office themselves having an influential role in policy-making even though they were not the most senior civil servants in the Department. The role of the private office in supporting the Secretary of State, organising and attending meetings, ensuring the timely submission of papers and reports, and acting as the conduit to 10 Downing Street, the Treasury and other parts of Whitehall is not widely understood outside government and yet it is at the heart of how the DH works. The placing of the special advisers' office alongside that of the Secretary of State and the private office symbolised the nature of the core decision-making process in the Department at this time.

To close the circle, the end of the 1990s also witnessed a renewed interest within the Department in policy analysis and strategy. This was indicated by the establishment of a Strategy Unit in 2000 (led by the author) to report directly to the Secretary of State. The Strategy Unit worked closely with special advisers, and its work programme included much of the analysis that lay behind *The NHS Plan, Delivering the NHS Plan*, and *The NHS Improvement Plan*. In addition, members of the Strategy Unit worked with the rest of the Department on a range of issues, often with the aim of offering the Secretary of State alternative policy options to consider. The location of the Strategy Unit alongside special advisers and the Secretary of State, rather than as part of the Departmental hierarchy, was intended to introduce some grit into the oyster and occasionally it led to tensions. However, for the most part, senior civil servants came to see the value of working with the Strategy Unit, not least as a way of ensuring that their ideas were put to ministers. Although not formally able to manage the work of civil servants, special advisers played a major part in shaping the activities of the Strategy Unit, either alone or in combination with the Secretary of State, and in ensuring that the outputs of the Unit met the needs of the Secretary of State. During this time members of the Strategy Unit were often more closely involved in the development of policy than other members of the ministerial team or indeed the Department's most senior civil servants.

The Strategy Unit was the creation of Alan Milburn and its role evolved after his resignation in 2003. Subsequently, a Strategy Directorate was established as part of the changes to the Department introduced in 2004, and the role of the Strategy Unit in reporting directly to the Secretary of State came to an end. The establishment of the Strategy Directorate reflected wider reforms to the civil service in which the size of departments was reduced and their strategic capability increased. These changes stemmed from an initiative led by the Prime Minister and Cabinet Secretary and were an attempt to achieve a better balance between management expertise and strategic capability in central government. Notwithstanding these developments, the Cabinet Office's Capability Review highlighted weaknesses in the Department's strategy and leadership capabilities, while also drawing attention to its strengths in planning and performance management. This assessment was consistent with the analysis of Greer and Jarman (2007) to the effect that the Department had become a 'Department for Delivery' because of its focus on the NHS and the appointment of a large number of NHS managers to senior positions. The corollary was that the Department's role in policy-making and setting clear and consistent strategies was underdeveloped, at least in part because of the reduced role of career civil servants in the upper echelons of the Department.

A similar conclusion had been reached by Patricia Hewitt, who was appointed as Secretary of State for Health following the 2005 general election. Hewitt commissioned a review of the organisation of the Department from the management consultants, McKinsey, and following the review Nigel Crisp retired from his post as Permanent Secretary and NHS Chief Executive. This post was subsequently divided with Hugh Taylor, a career mandarin, being appointed as Permanent Secretary and David Nicholson, a strategic health authority chief executive, becoming NHS Chief Executive in 2006, thereby reversing Alan Milburn's decision in 2000 to combine these roles. Steps were also taken to streamline the functioning of the Department leading to the adoption of the structure described in Figure 8.1. One of the aims of these changes was to strengthen the Department's capabilities in the area of strategy and policy-making to address the concerns identified by Hewitt following her appointment and echoed in the Cabinet Office Capability Review. The new structure was also an attempt to achieve greater integration in the work of the Department (a recurring theme in many of the reviews of the Department that have been undertaken over the years) and to balance the strong emphasis on delivery and performance review that had been put in place to support implementation of *The NHS Plan* with a new focus on commissioning. A further objective was to raise the profile of social care in the Department.

The involvement of McKinsey in the review of the Department draws attention to one other important feature of the policy-making process. This is the increasing use of management consultants to advise the government and to prepare options for ministers. While the use of management consultants is not new, companies like McKinsey have been closely involved in a number of key health policy issues in the period since 2003, including the development of the regulatory regime for NHS foundation trusts, the review of regulation of health and social care undertaken in 2005, and the development of world class commissioning in 2008. The outsourcing of policy analysis and policy advice to management consultants provides a further challenge to the conventions of the Westminster model.

Conclusion

As this chapter has illustrated, the Department of Health is not a monolith. The existence of a variety of professions, divisions and groups gives rise to a high degree of pluralism within the Department and this is complicated by the interplay with outside interests. The landscape of the Department is continuously being reshaped in response to changing needs and fashions and the struggle for power between different interests. In the 1980s and 1990s the main distinction was between those responsible for policy and those overseeing the NHS and the implementation of policy. This was eventually resolved when the NHS Executive took charge of both functions after the Banks Review. The role and influence of the NHS Executive within the Department was progressively extended and it came to occupy a pivotal position between ministers and the wider Department on the one hand and the NHS on the other. The reintegration of the NHS Executive into the Department strengthened the position of managers at a time when management expertise was highly valued in the civil service.

The health policy community that surrounds the Department contains a large number of organisations and interests. Pressure groups are drawn towards those parts of the Department that deal with issues of concern to them and sub-communities emerge around these issues. In these policy communities, producer groups have greater influence than consumer groups and are often involved in negotiation with ministers and civil servants rather than consultation. Other inputs to the policy process come from Parliament and the mass media, NHS bodies, royal commissions and inquiries, industrial and commercial interests, and academics and researchers. Ministers and civil servants themselves are particularly important in policy formulation, as are special advisers. Both the Prime Minister and the Chancellor of the Exchequer have also become more closely involved in health policy formulation in the past decade.

One of the consequences of the diversity of interests in the policy community is that policy maintenance is more common than policy initiation. This is reinforced by stability within the health policy community and the need on the part of government for the support of the medical profession and its representatives in the implementation of policy. Only occasionally, as in the major reforms to the NHS initiated by the Thatcher and Blair governments, have actors in the core executive been able to initiate policies that unsettle established relationships. There have been a number of attempts to strengthen the Department's policy analysis and strategic functions. Nevertheless, bargaining, negotiation and accommodation between different interests are the principal forces that shape the development of policy. Also important is the way in which policy is adapted and amended as it is implemented, and it is to a consideration of policy implementation that we now turn.

Chapter 9

Implementing Health Policy

The aim of this chapter is to examine the implementation of health policy and the micro politics of the NHS. The chapter begins with a description of the organisation of the NHS and the role of NHS bodies such as health authorities and trusts. This leads into a discussion of the relationship between the Department of Health and the NHS and of policy-making within the NHS. The influence of the medical profession is reviewed and the chapter concludes by summarising the various factors relevant to an understanding of health policy implementation. During the lifetime of the NHS, the pendulum has swung back and forth between the Department and the NHS, and current moves to strengthen the grip of the centre over implementation need to be seen in this historical context. It is an open question as to whether the commitment made in the final report of the NHS Next Stage Review to promote further improvement in the performance of the NHS from the bottom up, and led by clinicians, can be realised in practice. While the chapter focuses mainly on the NHS in England, the changing balance of power between the centre and the periphery and the influence of doctors over implementation are also important features of health policy implementation in Northern Ireland, Scotland and Wales.

The organisation of the NHS

The Secretary of State for Health has overall responsibility for health and health services, and he or she discharges this responsibility through a range of NHS bodies at the regional and local level. Although nominally a *national* health service, the NHS varies both between the four countries of the United Kingdom (see Chapter 7) and within each of these countries. In the case of England, the variations that exist reflect different histories and the discretion available to NHS bodies, acting as the agents of the Secretary of State, to adapt the policies that are promulgated by central government to suit local needs. The past decade has witnessed a sustained attempt by the Blair and Brown governments to exert greater control over the NHS from Westminster and especially Whitehall, alongside policies ostensibly designed to shift the balance of power to a local level. The most important of these policies has been the creation of NHS foundation trusts as public benefit corporations no longer in a hierarchical relationship with the Secretary of State for Health. The simultaneous pursuit of centralisation and decentralisation cautions against simple interpretations of the balance of power between central government and NHS bodies.

The organisation of the NHS can be contrasted with that of adult social care, which is also the responsibility of the Secretary of State for Health in England. Social care comes under the control of local authorities rather than NHS bodies and they have traditionally enjoyed considerable autonomy from central government. Local elections give local authorities an independent power base, while the existence of council tax as a source of revenue provides the means by which authorities can determine spending levels within the overall framework set by ministers. As in the case of the NHS, central government involvement in local affairs has increased in recent years, but local authorities retain some freedom to decide on the range and mixture of services to be provided in their areas. The fundamental difference between the NHS and adult social care relates to accountability which in the NHS is primarily upwards to the Secretary of State while in social care it is mainly outwards to the communities being served. Despite this difference, there are variations in how services are commissioned and provided in both the NHS and social care, reflecting the ability of elected local authorities and appointed NHS bodies to flex national policies to local circumstances. What this indicates is that the legitimacy that derives from elections and the flexibility offered by revenue raising powers are not the only factors that explain deviations from the policies developed by central government.

The regional tier and strategic health authorities

The need for a regional agency in the NHS has been recognised ever since the establishment of the Service in 1948. In the first phase of the NHS, regional hospital boards played a crucial role in turning a disparate collection of hospitals into a planned and coordinated service. In 1974 their functions were extended and their name changed to regional health authorities. After 1992 regional health authorities coexisted with regional outposts of the NHS Management Executive, set up to oversee the performance of NHS trusts. The functions of regional health authorities and regional outposts were combined when regional offices of the NHS Executive were established in 1996. Regional directors were accountable directly to the Chief Executive of the NHS Executive and sat alongside him as members of the NHS Executive Board. The effect was to strengthen the grip of the centre over local management by moving towards the single chain of command for the NHS proposed in *Working for Patients*.

Subsequently, regional offices were abolished and replaced by four new regional directorates of health and social care in the DH. This change in the regional tier was part of the programme of reforms to the structure of the NHS announced in *Shifting the Balance of Power in the NHS* in 2001 (DH, 2001a). As well as announcing the abolition of regional offices, *Shifting the Balance of Power* included proposals to reduce the number of health authorities. In the event, 28 strategic health authorities (SHAs) were established in April 2002 in place of the previous 95 health authorities, and one of their core functions was to manage the performance of NHS trusts and primary care trusts. Changes to the organisation of the DH introduced in 2003 led to the abolition of regional directorates of health and social care and meant that SHAs became, in effect, the regional tier of the NHS. In parallel, regional public health groups, based in the nine government offices of the regions, were responsible for taking forward the wider public health agenda.

To bring the story up to date, the fifth restructuring of the regional tier in 14 years took place in 2006 when the number of SHAs was further reduced from 28 to 10 as part of the reforms that followed from *Commissioning a Patient-Led NHS*, described in Chapter 3. SHAs act on behalf of the Secretary of State in providing leadership on health and health care issues and in overseeing the implementation of national policies in their areas. This includes managing the performance of primary care trusts (PCTs) and NHS trusts, leading in the development of clinical and public health networks, and managing the health care system. Each SHA has a board of directors comprising a non-executive chair and usually five non-executive directors, appointed by the NHS Appointments Commission, together with a chief executive, finance director and other executive directors. The current structure of the NHS in England is illustrated in Figure 3.3 (p. 68).

The DH assesses the performance of SHAs in relation to the objectives set out in the annual operating framework for the NHS in England. Health authority chief executives meet regularly with the NHS Chief Executive to review progress towards these objectives and there are numerous formal and informal links between senior staff of SHAs and their counterparts in the Department that focus on performance management and the implementation of national policies. Under the Blair government, performance management was considerably strengthened, and this has resulted in much closer alignment between national policies and local action in key priority areas like the targets for reducing waiting times and healthcare associated infections. However, beyond these key priority areas, there is no certainty that national policies will be implemented locally. The existence of SHAs made up of appointed chairs and non-executives as well as senior managers creates the possibility that national policies will be modified during the course of implementation as the members of authorities put their own interpretation on these policies and adapt them in the light of local knowledge and circumstances. Not only this, but also health authorities themselves are not always in a position to carry through the intentions of ministers even when they agree with the direction that has been set as they have to work through primary care trusts and NHS trusts. The discretion exercised by GPs, hospital specialists and other frontline staff within the NHS is another important factor that affects the implementation of national policies.

There are difficulties in achieving local compliance with national policies in the field of public health as well as health care. This was demonstrated in a study of the impact of *The Health of the Nation* during the 1990s. This study found a significant gap between the objectives of the national health strategy and its implementation (DH, 1998a). As the study noted, one of the reasons for this was the large number of policies and priorities being pursued by the government at the time. In a situation of priority overload and initiative conflict, some policies did not receive attention and management effort was directed to other areas. Specifically, *The Health of the Nation* was seen as a low priority by the DH and NHS bodies and the signal this sent out meant that neither regional offices nor health authorities saw it as a priority issue. It was therefore not surprising that the strategy failed to make a major impact, indicating that the ability of those at the centre of the NHS to influence decisions at a local level depended at least in part on the commitment put behind national initiatives. The more directive approach to performance management adopted by the Blair government was in part a response to the failure to achieve effective implementation of policies like *The Health of the Nation*.

NHS trusts and NHS foundation trusts

NHS trusts were first established in 1991 under the changes set out in the White Paper, *Working for Patients*. Each trust is run by a board of directors comprising a chair and normally five non-executive directors appointed by the NHS Appointments Commission, together with a chief executive, finance director, medical director and other executive directors. Like SHAs, NHS trusts work as corporate bodies and are collectively responsible for their actions. In 2009, there were around 125 NHS trusts in England.

The main function of NHS trusts is to manage the services for which they are responsible. The configuration of services controlled by NHS trusts varies with some trusts running acute hospitals, others managing mental health services, and yet others combining some of these responsibilities. There are also trusts responsible for ambulance services. The income of trusts derives from the service agreements negotiated with PCTs and other commissioners and they are expected to deliver care to the specifications contained within those agreements. They also have a duty to put and keep in place arrangements for monitoring and improving the quality of care. This duty is a core element in the drive to improve standards and to promote clinical governance within the NHS. The performance of NHS trusts in achieving appropriate standards of care is regulated by the Care Quality Commission.

NHS trusts were set up as self-governing organisations and the intention was that within the framework of the NHS they should have considerable freedom to run their own affairs. To this end, *Working for Patients* included plans to enable trusts to borrow money, hire and fire staff on their own terms, and take decisions without having to seek permission up the management line. In practice, the freedoms of NHS trusts were constrained by Treasury rules and by the reluctance of the Major government to follow through the logic of its reform programme (Ham, 2003a). NHS trusts were further constrained by the changes introduced by the Blair government during its first term and the emphasis placed by the government on partnership working in the NHS rather than organisational independence. The decision to make NHS trusts accountable to health authorities and to give SHAs responsibility for the performance management of trusts was consistent with these changes. In overseeing the performance of NHS trusts, SHAs intervene when necessary to ensure that trusts are achieving the government's targets for the NHS, and they also support trusts to become NHS foundation trusts.

Ministers developed their ideas on NHS foundation trusts in 2002 in part because of difficulties they experienced in seeking to manage the NHS directly from Whitehall, and in part because of a desire to place more emphasis on patient choice and provider competition in the health reform programme (see Chapter 3). NHS foundation trusts are public benefit corporations with members drawn from the communities they serve. Members elect a board of governors which also includes stakeholder representatives from primary care trusts, local authorities, universities and other organisations. The board of governors appoints the chair and non-executive directors of the board of directors, and they in turn appoint the chief executive and the other executive directors. The board of directors is accountable to the board of governors for the performance of the organisation, rather than to the SHA and the Secretary of State. These governance arrangements are intended to establish stronger connections between NHS organisations and local communities and to mark a decisive break from the nationalised industry model on which the NHS was based when it was established in 1948 (see Chapter 12).

NHS foundation trusts have a number of freedoms not available to NHS trusts. These freedoms include the ability to retain operating surpluses and to borrow money from the public and private sectors. NHS foundation trusts can also establish private companies and joint ventures and are able to vary staff pay from nationally determined terms and conditions. However, like NHS trusts they are expected to provide services in accordance with the specifications set out in the service agreements negotiated with PCTs, and they are regulated by the Care Quality Commission. A further constraint on the freedom of NHS foundation trusts is a requirement that they comply with the terms of their authorisation which is determined by Monitor, the independent regulator of NHS foundation trusts. Monitor takes a close interest in the performance of NHS foundation trusts, particularly in delivering national priorities, and intervenes in those NHS foundation trusts whose performance gives cause for concern. The government expects all NHS trusts to become NHS foundation trusts when they have shown that they are capable of running their services as public benefit corporations. The first NHS foundation trusts were established in 2004 and by the beginning of 2009 their numbers had increased to 115. These included organisations running mental health services as well as those responsible for acute hospitals.

Primary care trusts

Primary care trusts (PCTs) were formed in 2002 and they took over functions previously undertaken by health authorities (for example the commissioning of services) and NHS trusts (for example managing community health services in many parts of the country). PCTs currently have three main functions. These are to improve the health of the community, develop primary and community health services, and commission secondary care services. Each PCT is run by a board comprising a lay chair and non-executive directors and a minority of executive directors, including the chief executive, the finance director and the director of public health. The NHS Appointments Commission is responsible for appointing the chair and non-executives and they in turn appoint the chief executive and work with him or her to appoint the other executive directors. The PCT works with the professional executive committee, made up of a majority of professional members such as GPs and nurses, in discharging its responsibilities. Following changes to the organisation of the NHS introduced in 2006, there are currently 152 PCTs in England.

The performance of PCTs is managed by SHAs and centres on progress in implementing their strategic and operational plans for improving health and health services. These plans derive from guidance on priorities issued by the DH in the annual operating framework for the NHS. SHAs are responsible for signing off these plans and for reviewing their implementation. PCTs are expected to focus their activity on ensuring the delivery of national policies and priorities and SHAs intervene in cases where there is evidence that performance is departing from agreed trajectories. PCTs use the service agreements they negotiate with NHS trusts, NHS foundation trusts, their own provider arms and independent sector providers to take forward these policies, and they work in partnership with local authorities and other agencies in seeking to implement national and local priorities for public health and health improvement. The performance of PCTs in achieving appropriate standards of care is regulated by the Care Quality Commission as part of the annual health check (see Chapter 10). A key challenge faced by PCTs is to engage GPs and other primary care clinicians in bringing about improvements in health and health services. The involvement of clinicians in managing budgets and services came later to primary care than to hospitals, and many GPs value their independence and are reluctant to become involved beyond their own practices in the development of services.

Priority has also been attached to assisting PCTs to become more effective commissioners through the world class commissioning programme of support and development and to the closer involvement of GPs in commissioning via practice based commissioning. World class commissioning came on to the policy agenda in 2006 in response to evidence that PCTs were struggling to carry out their commissioning responsibilities effectively and in recognition that the health reform programme had given more attention to the development of providers than commissioners in the initial stages. At the same time, ministers and civil servants have sent out a signal that PCTs should divest themselves of responsibility for providing services directly in a rerun of the ill fated policy put forward in *Commissioning a Patient-led NHS* in 2005 (see Chapter 3). The role of PCTs in improving the health of their communities has also been emphasised, in particular through working collaboratively with local authorities and other agencies in local strategic partnerships and by undertaking joint strategic health needs assessments.

Care trusts have been established where a PCT and local authority wish to achieve closer integration of the services for which they are responsible. There are currently ten care trusts in England and they have been established mainly in relation to mental health services and services for older people. The boards of care trusts include local authority councillors in recognition of their role in commissioning and providing health and social care services.

Arm's-length bodies

A number of services are organised and delivered through arm's-length bodies in England. There are three main types of arm's-length body: executive agencies, non-departmental public bodies, and special health authorities.

There are two executive agencies that relate to the DH: the Medicines and Healthcare Products Regulatory Agency and the NHS Purchasing and Supply Agency. Non-departmental public bodies include the Health Protection Agency and the Human Fertilisation and Embryology Authority. Special health authorities have been set up in a number of areas and they include the National Institute for Health and Clinical Excellence (NICE) and the National Patient Safety Agency. Each authority is run by a board whose chair and non-executive directors were appointed by the Secretary of State until this function was taken over by the NHS Appointments Commission, which is itself a special health authority. The Commission not only makes appointments to NHS boards but also ensures that there is a system of annual appraisals in place and that training and development is provided for board members.

The existence of arm's length bodies symbolises both the 'hollowing out' of the state referred to in Chapter 6 and the growth of audit and inspection arrangements discussed in Chapter 10. They can also be seen as further evidence of a shift from a managed to a regulated health care system. In response to concerns about the increasing role of these bodies, the DH set up a review of their number and functions and this reported in 2004. As a result of the review, the government decided to implement a reduction of almost 50 per cent in the number of arm's length bodies. This was expected to deliver savings of 25 per cent in the number of people employed in them and savings estimated at approximately £0.5 billion in annual operating costs.

The role of the DH

It is apparent, then, that a large number of NHS bodies are involved in the commissioning and provision of health services in England. The intentions of the DH have to be filtered through SHAs, NHS trusts and NHS foundation trusts, PCTs and care trusts, and arm's length bodies of different types before they have an impact on service provision. NHS bodies are the Secretary of State's agents, but the agency role does not involve merely implementing instructions received from above. These bodies are semi-autonomous organisations who themselves engage in policy-making, and as such exercise some influence over the implementation of central policies. The fact that NHS bodies are governed by appointed boards comprising executive and non-executive directors increases the possibility that government intentions will be adapted in the process of implementation, particularly in the case of NHS foundation trusts that were established in order to strengthen accountability to local communities rather than to reinforce central control of the NHS.

Having stressed the point that NHS bodies are not simply a means of translating central policy into local action, it is important to remember that the NHS in England is a national service for which the Secretary of State is accountable to Parliament. The basis of Parliamentary accountability lies in the voting by Parliament of funds for the NHS, and the statutory responsibility of the Secretary of State for the way in which these funds are spent. The existence of Parliamentary accountability is a centralising influence, and requires that the Secretary of State is kept informed of local developments. As we noted in earlier chapters, MPs are able to ask questions and raise issues in debates about the operation of the NHS, and the Secretary of State is expected to be in a position to respond to these questions. Also, the investigations carried out in the NHS by the Public Accounts Committee and the Health Committee require that ministers and civil servants have available relevant facts about the local organisation of health services. NHS bodies therefore have to provide the DH with detailed information about specific aspects of service provision, as well as routine statistical returns, to enable the Secretary of State to answer MPs' enquiries.

The influence of the DH is most apparent in the case of the budget for the NHS and its allocation. These matters are determined centrally and there are no significant independent sources of revenue available within the NHS. Also NHS bodies have a statutory duty to keep within their budgets and this acts as an overriding constraint on their freedom of manoeuvre. The DH gives guidance on the use of resources in a number of forms. First, government circulars were traditionally used to set out national policy which NHS bodies are expected to follow. Some of these circulars were prescriptive and identified procedures that had to be implemented, but much of the guidance issued in this form was advisory, allowing scope for local interpretation. Circulars were often discussed in draft form with NHS staff and this enabled local influence to be brought to bear on national guidance. In theory, this increased the likelihood of local compliance, although research indicated that circulars were of doubtful effectiveness as a means of central control (Ham, 1981). Circulars continued to be used on a regular basis until 2001 when 26 health service circulars were issued by the DH but they have since been superseded by other forms of guidance.

Second, the DH publishes White Papers and consultative documents (also known as Green Papers) proposing developments in specific areas of service provision. This form of guidance is often used to make a major statement of government policy and to set out options for change. Consultative documents usually prepare the ground for White Papers, and enable NHS bodies and other interests to influence the more definitive statements incorporated in White Papers. White Papers set out general directions in which the government wishes policy to develop, and may represent a departure from previous intentions. They may also prepare the ground for legislation. Examples include the White Papers *Working for Patients* and *The New NHS* which contained the proposals of the Thatcher government and the Blair government respectively for the reform of the NHS. A different example was the White Paper on the future of care outside hospitals, *Our Health, Our Care, Our Say*, published in 2006.

Third, the DH issues regular guidance on priorities for service development. This process started in 1976 with the consultative document on *Priorities for Health and Personal Social Services in England* (DHSS, 1976b), and was followed by publication of *The Way Forward* in 1977 (DHSS, 1977b) and *Care in Action* in 1981 (DHSS, 1981c). The aim of these documents was to inform NHS bodies of priorities for the development of health and personal social services. National guidance on priorities has varied in the degree to which it has prescribed what should be done, the advisory nature of *Care in Action* in 1981 – 'We want to give you as much freedom as possible to decide how to pursue these policies and priorities in your own localities. Local initiatives, local decisions, and local responsibility are what we want to encourage' – giving way to a much more prescriptive approach in the period since 1997. At some points, prescription has been connected with the earmarking of NHS resources for defined purposes, although earmarking has fallen out of favour in recent years.

The operating framework for the NHS for 2008/09, issued in 2007, set out health and service priorities for 2008/09 as the first year in a three-year planning round (DH, 2007d). The operating framework was based on the public service agreement negotiated between the DH and the Treasury. Five key priorities were contained in the framework: improving cleanliness and reducing healthcare associated infections; improving access through achieving 18-week referral to treatment, and providing better access to GP services; keeping people well, improving overall health and reducing health inequalities; improving patient experience, staff satisfaction and engagement; and preparing to respond to emergencies, such as an outbreak of pandemic flu. Behind these headline priorities, more specific objectives were set out, including improvements in cancer services, stroke care, maternity services and children's services. As well as these national priorities, the operating framework stated that PCTs should set local improvement plans for areas of concern identified through discussions with patients, staff and partners. Examples given in the framework included reducing mixed sex accommodation, improving services for people with learning disabilities and strengthening end of life care. The operating framework for 2009/10, issued in December 2008, reiterated this guidance in the context of the final report of the NHS Next Stage Review, *High Quality Care for All*.

DH guidance on priorities is part of the more general attempt by central government to influence local patterns of service provision. The NHS Planning System, introduced in the 1970s (DHSS, 1975b), was intended to reveal cases where health authorities were deviating from national policies, and in the early 1980s it was superseded by the accountability review process. This process involved a scrutiny of regional plans and performance leading to annual review meetings. The purpose of the meetings was to review the long-term plans, objectives, efficiency and effectiveness of the region, and to provide a means of holding the RHA to account. Following the regional review, the RHA held a series of review meetings with each of its health authorities. The procedure was similar to that followed at regional reviews and an action plan was agreed at the end of the meeting. The review process was described by the Griffiths Inquiry into NHS Management as 'a good, recent development which provides a powerful management tool' (Griffiths Report, 1983, p. 12).

The system of accountability reviews has developed and been adapted in line with the changing structure of the NHS. In a detailed account of the history of performance management in the NHS, Smee has observed that although the accountability review process appeared to be a command and control system, 'it has more accurately been described as management by exhortation' (Smee, 2005, p. 104). A more active approach to performance management was adopted after 1997, involving a 'switch in the centre's role in relation to the NHS, from requiring a loose accountability to explicitly driving performance improvement and behavioural change through every conceivable instrument' (*ibid*. p. 113). Comparing the approach taken under the Blair government with that of the 1980s, Smee identifies five new ingredients:

- clearly defined targets
- publicly disclosed data on provider performance
- the use of incentives for purchasers, providers and clinicians
- strong support for the dissemination of best practice, and
- independent monitoring and inspection.

The increasing scrutiny of the Department's own performance by the Treasury through public service agreements and the Prime Minister's Delivery Unit has reinforced the Department's management of NHS performance. Current arrangements are founded on the annual operating framework and this provides the basis on which PCTs and SHAs develop plans for implementing national priorities in their areas. The Department receives information each week on progress in delivering these priorities and implementation is discussed at monthly meetings between SHA directors of performance and their counterparts in the DH. Every quarter the NHS Chief Executive meets with each SHA chair and chief executive to review performance, and he is also able to discuss performance with SHA chief executives collectively at the NHS Management Board (see Chapter 8). In turn, SHAs adapt these performance management arrangements in their regions to ensure that PCTs are on track in implementing national priorities and are taking appropriate action where they are at risk of missing key objectives.

In areas of major significance to the government, such as the target of achieving a maximum 18 week wait from referral to treatment by the end of 2008 and of treating 98 per cent of patients in A&E within four hours, this means that there is much closer alignment between local performance and the goals set out by ministers than has traditionally been the case. NHS bodies know that their performance is being actively managed and that they are expected to ensure delivery of national priorities in their organisations. However, beyond the national 'must dos' there may be a gap between policy intent and what happens on the ground. This is well illustrated by an analysis of variations in NHS spending priorities which showed wide differences in the expenditure on different disease areas that were unrelated to different needs (King's Fund, 2006; Appleby and Gregory, 2008). Again this reflects the discretion available to NHS bodies as well as the difficulty facing central government in achieving consistency across a wide range of policies and service areas in an organisation as large and complex as the NHS. Also, as the King's Fund's analysis commented, 'it is important to note that PCT spending is not wholly determined by PCTs themselves. The ... data used here will in large part reflect the myriad individual clinical decisions that health care professionals take every day – decisions over which PCTs exercise little control' (King's Fund, 2006, p. 4).

The other instrument of control, and potentially the most significant of all, is the Secretary of State's power of direction. This power enables the Secretary of State to direct NHS bodies to comply with his or her wishes in relation to any aspect of their work under the NHS Acts 1977 and 2006. Details of how this power is used are available on the DH website (http://www.dh.gov.uk/en/Publicationsandstatistics/Legislation/

Directionsfromthesecretaryofstate/index.htm). In addition, the Secretary of State is able to suspend SHAs, NHS trusts and PCTs. In practice, these powers are used sparingly. As Brown explained in the 1970s, they are used:

> only when a Minister decides to use them – in other words when he feels that the political or administrative need to wield the big stick outweighs the political and administrative cost that will be incurred. The more drastic powers are about as usable in practice as nuclear weapons. None can be used as an instrument of day-to-day control. (Brown, 1979, pp. 10–11)

There is some overstatement here, as the suspension of the Lambeth, Southwark and Lewisham AHA in 1979 and its replacement by a team of commissioners appointed by the Secretary of State indicates. Twenty years later the Secretary of State removed the non-executive directors of the Guild Community Health Care NHS trust in Lancashire because of concerns about the management of the trust. Nevertheless, Brown's underlying point is valid, and the reason why these powers are used so rarely is that only very occasionally do they need to be invoked. The DH is able to maintain oversight of the NHS through the other instruments already described, and through bargaining and negotiation rather than sanctions. This includes persuading chairs and non-executive directors of NHS bodies to resign should this be necessary, rather than using legal powers to remove them from office. Recent examples include the resignation of the chair and non-executive directors of the University Hospital of North Staffordshire NHS trust in 2005 in the wake of significant financial problems, and the resignation of the chair of the Maidstone and Tunbridge Wells NHS trust in 2007 following concerns about health-care associated infections.

The way in which performance failures have been handled in the past has been ad hoc, with interventions by the DH or SHAs acting on its behalf being determined on a case by case basis. This can be contrasted with the approach taken by Monitor in relation to NHS foundation trusts which is based on an explicit compliance regime. Monitor applied this regime for the first time in 2004 in the case of the Bradford NHS Teaching Hospitals foundation trust. Monitor's intervention led to the resignation of the chair and subsequently the departure of the chief executive following concerns about financial performance and the leadership of the trust. Drawing in part on the experience of Monitor, the DH published proposals in 2008 for clarifying and strengthening the NHS performance regime in relation to PCTs and NHS trusts (DH, 2008b). These proposals set out a 'rules based' approach which involved the suspension or removal of board members in the case of so-called challenged organisations that are deemed to be unsustainable. The Health Bill announced in the Queen's Speech in 2008 included powers to implement these proposals.

In cases where there are concerns about the quality of care provided, the Secretary of State is able to ask the Care Quality Commission to conduct an investigation, and indeed the Commission itself can initiate an investigation if it feels a serious problem exists in an NHS body. Recent examples of investigations carried out by the Commission's predecessor, the Healthcare Commission, included cardiothoracic surgical services at the Oxford Radcliffe Hospitals NHS trust, outbreaks of *Clostridium difficile* at Maidstone and Tunbridge Wells NHS trust, and services for people with learning disabilities at Cornwall Partnership NHS trust. In cases where a full investigation is not needed, the Commission undertakes interventions to find out more about the problem concerned and to advise on action that needs to be taken.

The balance of power between the centre and the periphery in the NHS has been viewed in various ways. Enoch Powell, Minister of Health from 1960 to 1963, argued that the centre had almost total control (Powell, 1966). Richard Crossman, Secretary of State from 1968 to 1970, maintained that the centre was weak and the periphery strong (Crossman, 1972); and Barbara Castle, Secretary of State from 1974 to 1976, likened Regional Health Authorities to:

> a fifth wheel on the coach. They neither speak as elected representatives nor do they have the expertise of their own officials. And their attitude to the Secretary of State and department is necessarily pretty subservient – they want to keep their jobs! (Castle, 1980, p. 315)

The subservience noted by Castle was not much in evidence in a report on the workings of the DHSS prepared by three Regional Health Authority chairmen in 1976 (Regional Chairmen's Enquiry, 1976). The report was highly critical of the DHSS, and argued that more powers should be delegated to health authorities. One point made in the regional chairmen's enquiry was that there should be a greater interchange of staff between the NHS and the DHSS as a way of improving understanding and communication. This has happened on an increasing scale, with a number of civil servants undertaking secondments in the NHS, and a number of health service managers and other staff being seconded into the Department. The process was taken a stage further in 1988 with the appointment of a regional general manager, Duncan Nichol, as Chief Executive of the NHS Management Executive. Nichol's successors have all come from the NHS even though there have been suggestions that managers with a private sector background should be appointed to this role. Other senior civil service roles have also been filled by NHS managers to the point where a recent analysis concluded that the DH had become NHS dominated (Greer and Jarman, 2007). The NHS Chief Executive uses regular meetings with SHA chief executives as a key mechanism for explaining national policies and receiving feedback on the impact of these policies in practice. It is through these regular interchanges and other contacts that the DH works with the NHS in the development and implementation of health policy.

It is apparent from this discussion that neither the DH nor NHS bodies in England can act independently of one another. The reason for this is that underlying the relationship between the different tiers of management in the NHS is the dependence of one tier on the other for resources of various kinds: finance, manpower, information and so on. As a result of this dependence, a process of exchange develops through which policies are implemented (Rhodes, 1979). An alternative way of viewing the interaction between management tiers is not as a system of exchange, but rather as a negotiating process in which policy is evolved as it is implemented (Barrett and Fudge, 1981). Whichever conceptualisation is adopted, a key factor in the implementation of health policy is the link between members of the same profession at different levels. Of particular importance is the position of the medical profession, and we now turn to an examination of its influence on the implementation of health policy.

Professional influences on policy implementation

The medical profession is involved in the management of the NHS at all levels. In the DH, doctors are represented at the very top of the Department through the Chief Medical Officer and the NHS Medical Director. Also, under the Blair government, a number of NHS doctors have been appointed as national clinical directors or tsars within the Department to lead the development of services in areas of major clinical priority such as cancer and coronary heart disease. At the regional level, directors of public health are responsible for taking forward the public health strategy, and they do so by working both through the NHS and other government departments and agencies. Within the NHS, the boards of SHAs and trusts include at least one senior manager from a medical background. Their contributions are supplemented by advice received from medical advisory committees and from individual clinicians whose views will often carry considerable weight in the policy-making process. The establishment of PCTs exemplifies the influence of doctors in the new NHS with GPs strongly represented on the professional executive committees of trusts and therefore in a position to exert considerable influence over policy-making.

As well as having access to the DH, SHAs and trusts, the medical profession is in an influential position because of the role of doctors as the direct providers of services. In the case of GPs, this is reflected in their status as independent contractors within the NHS. Family doctors have for a long time resisted political or managerial interference in their work and have preferred to contract with the NHS to provide a service to patients rather than to be employed by health authorities. As independent contractors, GPs have been able to deliver care in the way they consider appropriate and only since the late 1980s have governments sought to monitor standards in general practice and give NHS bodies more influence over primary care. This has included the option of employing GPs on a salaried basis, enabling PCTs to negotiate local personal medical services contracts with practices, using funds to improve premises and staffing levels and employing professional advisers to review prescribing patterns.

There have also been moves to encourage GPs to take part in clinical audit and to develop clinical governance in PCTs. Studies have shown that clinical governance has involved local professional leaders exercising influence over their peers in a form of 'soft' governance of primary care provision rather than managers seeking to impose hierarchical control (Sheaff et al., 2003). Other research has confirmed the important role of PCT prescribing advisers in influencing the decisions of GPs and nurses working in primary care, while also emphasising that most decisions are more strongly shaped by the experience of these staff and their tacit knowledge than by evidence based guidelines (Gabbay and le May, 2004). The creation of PCTs and the establishment of professional executive committees whose members include doctors, nurses and other clinicians have been important in enabling some GPs to play a bigger part in the management of services and in breaking down professional isolation. While GPs retain a good deal of freedom to organise their work and determine how services should be provided, the effect of these developments has been to strengthen arrangements for accountability. Despite this, only a minority of GPs have been appointed to leadership roles and engaging all GPs in the work of PCTs remains a work in progress. Also, PCTs have relied on carrots to improve the performance of primary care services and have been hesitant about using sticks to tackle poor clinical performance (Smith and Goodwin, 2006).

Hospital doctors are salaried employees of the NHS, but again their actions cannot be directly controlled by managers and NHS trusts. The reason for this, as the DHSS has explained, is that:

> At the inception of the NHS, the Government made clear that its intention was to provide a framework within which the health professions could provide treatment and care for patients according to their own

independent professional judgement of the patient's needs. This independence has continued to be a central feature of the organisation and management of health services. Thus hospital consultants have clinical autonomy and are fully responsible for the treatment they prescribe for their patients. They are required to act within broad limits of acceptable medical practice and within policy for the use of resources, but they are not held accountable to NHS authorities for their clinical judgements. (Normansfield Report, 1978, pp. 424–5)

Consequently, hospital doctors determine what is best for their patients, including the place and length of treatment, and the kinds of investigation to be carried out. Medicine is one of the clearest examples of an occupation that has achieved the status of a profession, and a key feature of professions is the autonomy of their members to determine the content of their work. A central issue in the implementation of health policy is therefore how to persuade doctors to organise their work in a way that is consistent with central and local policies. Because doctors have a major influence on the use of resources in the NHS, it is ultimately their behaviour that determines patterns of resource allocation and service development. And because they have considerable clinical autonomy, there is no guarantee that policies will be carried out.

Nevertheless, attempts are made to influence medical practices, as in the consultative document on *Priorities* (DHSS, 1976b), which contained a bibliography of reports concerned with alternative ways of providing services. As the consultative document noted, 'decisions on clinical practice concerning individual patients are and must continue to be the responsibility of the clinicians concerned. But it is hoped that this document would encourage further scrutiny by the profession of the resources used by different treatment regimes' (DHSS, 1976b, p. 28). This attempt to influence professional behaviour suggested that more attention might be given to the important part played by doctors in determining the use of resources. In fact, the successors to the consultative document on *Priorities* placed less emphasis on this issue, and *Care in Action*, published in 1981, stressed instead the scope for improving the efficiency of non-medical services (DHSS, 1981c). This has begun to change as resources have become constrained and attention has focused on the efficiency with which these resources are used. Particular attention has been paid to the involvement of doctors in management.

In the past, the main vehicle for achieving greater medical participation in management was the so-called 'cogwheel' system whose name derived from three reports on the organisation of medical work in hospitals which were published between 1967 and 1974 with a cogwheel design on their covers (see Ministry of Health, 1967). The Griffiths Report into

NHS management in 1983 suggested that the cogwheel system should be used as basis for developing management budgeting in which doctors and other clinicians would be involved in managing budgets and services. In 1986, management budgeting was superseded by the resource management initiative, involving the appointment of doctors as clinical directors to run services with support from a nurse manager and a business manager. Government policy throughout the 1990s continued to support moves to involve doctors in management in both hospitals and general practice. By the end of that decade, the principles of resource management had become widely established throughout the NHS, albeit with continuing variation in the detailed arrangements that were adopted.

In parallel, successive governments promoted the use of clinical audit in the hospital and community health services. Until 1998 this was done on a voluntary basis with resources being earmarked by the DH to provide the support needed to introduce audit arrangements and to encourage doctors and other health care professionals to participate. Participation in clinical audit became compulsory following a series of cases that identified failures in clinical performance within the NHS (Kennedy Report, 2001). The action taken by the Blair government to improve the quality of care, including the establishment of NICE and the Commission for Health Improvement and the introduction of clinical governance, heralded the beginnings of a new era in medical accountability. Not least, these initiatives sent out a clear signal that self-regulation was no longer seen as sufficient to safeguard standards and patients. The adoption of these policies was possible because of the accumulation of evidence that existing arrangements for ensuring quality were inadequate and this created a policy window (Kingdon, 1995) for politicians to push through changes that had previously been ruled off the agenda because of anticipated opposition from the medical profession.

Policy-making in NHS bodies

From the point of view of the DH and NHS bodies, clinical freedom may appear to be entirely negative, an obstacle to the implementation of national policies. However, the definition of policy adopted in Chapter 6, emphasising the idea that policy involves actions and decisions, drew attention to what might be called a bottom-up as well as a top-down perspective on policy. From a bottom-up perspective, the local autonomy of both NHS bodies and the medical profession is a positive feature in that it permits the development of policies that are appropriate to local circumstances, or at least local preferences. Indeed, local autonomy may lead to innovations that might not occur in a highly centralised system. In the final part of the chapter we therefore examine the local sources of policy change and development, and the micro politics of the NHS.

We have argued that, subject to broad guidance on policy from the DH, NHS bodies have some freedom to determine what policies to pursue in their areas. However, it is important to recognise that NHS bodies, like the DH, are not wholly or even mainly concerned with making new policies or initiating developments. As studies of policy-making in health bodies have shown, policy maintenance is more prevalent than policy-making, and any changes that do occur are likely to involve marginal adjustments to the status quo. The reason for this is that within the NHS various interests are competing for scarce resources, and in the absence of any one dominant group, bargaining between these interests tends to result in incremental change. A further consideration is that health policy development exhibits 'path dependency' (Wilsford, 1994) with previous decisions constraining future options. As the author has argued in a study of policy-making in the NHS between 1948 and 1974:

> In policy systems where there are many different interests and where power is not concentrated in any individual or group, it is easier to prevent change than to achieve it. Successful policy promotion in such systems is dependent on the winning of a coalition of support by an active individual or 'interest'. (Ham, 1981, p. 153)

With this in mind, what interests contribute to health policy-making at the local level? Hunter, in a study of resource allocation in two Scottish health boards in the 1970s, suggests that decisions were influenced by a policy triad, comprising health board members, managers, and professional and lay advisory bodies (Hunter, 1980). Hunter argues that the influence of health board members on resource allocation was minimal. Also, while managers appeared to be in control of the business of their authorities, they were constrained by inherited commitments, established patterns of service provision, and the power of the medical profession. Hunter expresses the point in the following way:

> allocations ... did not always reflect directly the wishes and wants of doctors; nor did they arise from some conspiracy on the part of the medical profession to win for itself the biggest share of available resources, so depriving other groups in need of them. The process was altogether more subtle ... in their present established position as leaders of the health care team and as the primary decision-makers, doctors' decisions to treat patients commit resources ... and impose additional pressures on administrators charged with allocating resources. (Hunter, 1980, p. 195)

The author's own work on policy-making in the Leeds Regional Hospital Board (RHB) came to similar conclusions. Through a variety of channels, medical interests were able to influence what was decided, and overall 'the distribution of power was weighted heavily in favour of the professional monopolists' (Ham, 1981, p. 198). The terminology used here is derived from the work of Alford, who argues that health politics are characterised by three sets of structural interests: professional monopolists, who are the dominant interests; corporate rationalisers, who are the challenging interests; and the community population, who are repressed interests (Alford, 1975a). Applying these concepts to the Leeds RHB suggested that 'the history of hospital planning between 1948 and 1974 can be seen as the history of corporate rationalisers, represented by regional board planners, trying to challenge the established interests of the medical profession, with the community hardly in earshot' (Ham, 1981, p. 75). A key point to appreciate is that because the medical profession is in an established position, small changes do not seriously threaten professional dominance.

Further light is shed on local health policy-making by a study of two health authorities carried out between 1981 and 1985 (Ham, 1986). In the case of issues which were initiated at a national level, the study showed that the most influential interests were DHSS ministers supported by RHA chairs. In the case of issues that were initiated at a local level, no one group or interest emerged as most influential. The medical profession was actively involved and undoubtedly exerted influence but this was mediated by the views of DHA managers and chairs. This did not mean to say that managers had replaced doctors as the dominant interest in the NHS, even though the Griffiths Report undoubtedly served to strengthen the position of managers. In neither of the two DHAs was the prevailing value system seriously questioned and doctors were therefore able to maintain their influence. There was also no evidence that community interests had moved out of their repressed position.

As Hunter found in his Scottish study, the power of the medical profession was manifested not so much through formal bids for development considered by health authorities, as through the continual process of innovation that pre-empted resources for development. This was well illustrated by the way in which growth money was taken up by creeping development resulting from doctors deciding to use particular drugs and introduce new methods of treatment with significant implications for supplies and equipment. Put another way, the influence of doctors was exercised through decisionless decisions (Bachrach and Baratz, 1970). The clinical freedom of doctors to do the best for their patients, and the consequent power of clinicians over resource allocation, was thus an important factor limiting the role of health authorities. This was reinforced by the influence of the medical profession at other levels, as in the requirements imposed by the medical royal colleges on the training and staffing of hospitals. These requirements define the parameters within which policies are formulated at a local level and constrain NHS bodies in the planning of specialist services by forcing compliance with professionally determined standards.

Studies of policy-making in NHS bodies in the 1990s have sought to analyse whether established relationships have been altered by the reforms initiated by the Thatcher government. These studies point to some evidence of change with the members of NHS boards appearing to have increased their influence in certain cases and the balance of power within the medical profession shifting away from hospital doctors towards GPs. In parallel, hospital doctors who took on management responsibilities as a consequence of resource management became more prominent and there was evidence of managers gaining some influence in relation to the medical profession (Ferlie et al., 1996). Researchers who in an earlier study had found strategic change taking place in some areas but not others (Pettigrew et al., 1992), concluded in their later analysis that there was evidence of transformational changes in the NHS, while adding that many of these changes were not well-embedded (Ferlie et al., 1996). Notwithstanding this, the same analysis contended that the dominance of the medical profession remained largely intact.

This was confirmed by McDonald in her study of decision-making in a health authority in relation to coronary heart disease services which emphasised in particular the influence of hospital consultants and GPs and the limited power of health authorities. As she commented:

> HAs charged with assessing need and commissioning care to meet that need have little control over the supply and demand of care. Their staff engage in the production of policy documents, but the extent to which these impact on patients is questionable. They disseminate guidelines, but have no control over the prescribing practices of local GPs. They contract for additional elective activity at the margins, but often this is dictated by the length of waiting lists and they have no choice in the matter. They have little or no control over demand for services, particularly in the context of emergency care. (McDonald, 2002, pp. 164–5)

These comments are reinforced by the analysis undertaken by the Kennedy Inquiry. In a comprehensive review of the events leading up to the failures in paediatric heart surgery that occurred at Bristol, the

Inquiry found that there were neither external nor internal mechanisms in place to monitor the quality of care provided by hospital consultants. The chair and non-executive directors of the NHS trust were not closely involved in overseeing the services provided and the chief executive, himself a doctor, delegated a large measure of responsibility to individual consultants and clinical directors. The culture of the hospital emphasised the importance of clinical autonomy and did not encourage scrutiny of clinical standards and performance by managers or external bodies like health authorities. Clinical audit was not an effective mechanism for monitoring and reviewing standards, and as a consequence problems in the provision of children's heart surgery persisted (Kennedy Report, 2001).

Evidence from primary care underlines the continuing influence of doctors over decision-making and the persistence of medical autonomy. Within PCTs in England the main governing and performance management bodies are the board of executive and non-executive members and the professional executive committee (PEC). The key individuals in these bodies are the PCT chair, the chief executive and the PEC chair who is usually a GP. These individuals function as the three at the top (Smith and Goodwin, 2006, p. 85) of PCTs and work with their colleagues to implement national policies and influence the provision of primary care services. Within PCTs, ministers have promoted practice based commissioning as a means of engaging GPs and other frontline staff in decisions on the use of resources. Notwithstanding these developments, many GPs play little part in the management of services beyond their own practices, and PCTs have few levers to change how care is delivered to patients other than through persuasion and the use of the soft governance techniques referred to earlier.

The conclusion this suggests is that while the decline of corporatism may have weakened the influence of the medical profession in negotiations over *national* policy, the power of doctors within the NHS remains significant. In Alford's terms, the challenge of corporate rationalisers, especially that of politicians and managers, has not eroded medical dominance at the micro level. Furthermore, the exclusion of the medical profession from national policy developments like *Working for Patients* was followed by the reincorporation of doctors into policy-making when the influence of the profession in policy implementation led to a realisation that it was better to involve doctors and their representatives throughout the policy process (Ham, 2000). The reincorporation of the medical profession continued under the Blair government through the appointment of senior doctors as national clinical directors or tsars in the Department of Health, and the establishment of PCTs in which GPs exert influence over the use of NHS resources.

The NHS today

Yet before concluding that the power of doctors remains intact, it is important to return to the swinging pendulum between the centre and the periphery that has been present since the inception of the NHS. Studies of policy-making in NHS bodies under the Blair government highlight the increasing influence of national policies, reflecting the strengthening of performance management of the NHS discussed above and the increasing role of government targets in local decision-making (Greener and Powell, 2003; Deeming, 2004; Pickard et al., 2006). In these circumstances, managers find themselves acting as agents of the government in the implementation of national policies, to the point where one study described them as 'little more than conduits for the policies of the centre' (Blackler, 2006, p. 5). Another study reached similar conclusions, reporting that managers 'felt they have been relegated to a peripheral role by the performance measurement regime' (Greener, 2005, p. 104). In his analysis, Smith has emphasised that the use of targets and the ranking of the performance of NHS bodies through the use of performance indicators (see Chapter 10) created a culture in which 'The jobs of senior executives of poorly performing organizations came under severe threat, and the performance indicators (especially the key targets) became a prime focus of managerial attention' (Smith, 2008, p. 71).

Propper and colleagues use even more graphic language to describe how the implementation of policies to improve patient access to care by reducing waiting times resulted from 'targets and terror' (Propper et al., 2007). None of these studies found that the interests of patients and the public played a major part in local policy-making, but rather describe a 'general picture of slow, modest, patchy and superficial progress in engaging users in service management' (Pickard et al., 2006, p. 380). The limited influence of patients and the public resulted in part from continuing changes in the arrangements for representing the public's voice in local policy-making, following the abolition of community health councils in 2003 and their replacement in rapid succession by patient and public involvement forums, overview and scrutiny committees, the patient advice and liaison service, the independent complaints advocacy service, and local involvement networks.

To return to Smee's assessment, the evidence from recent research suggests that management by exhortation in the 1980s had become command and control in the 2000s with much of the time of NHS bodies and their senior managers directed at the implementation of national policies. And while it was managers who were on the receiving end of these policies, implementation often involved negotiation with medical staff on changing clinical practices to enable the targets to be met. An obvious example was cutting waiting times for treatment which depended critically on paying hospital doctors to undertake additional work or asking senior doctors to play a bigger part in the provision of care in accident and emergency departments than had traditionally been the case. Politicians used managers to take forward their policies and priorities within the NHS, and where necessary to negotiate with doctors in the delivery of new ways of working. The challenge for NHS bodies in this context was to satisfy the centre and the regulators that they were implementing these policies while not alienating doctors and other clinical staff through heavy-handed attempts to control clinical practice. This prompted renewed interest in finding ways of engaging more doctors in leadership roles to persuade their peers to comply with the centralist turn in health policy. In some NHS foundation trusts, service line management (in many ways a new name for what had been called resource management in the 1980s) was adopted as a means of persuading medical poachers to become gamekeepers and to take more responsibility for the performance of NHS bodies in the emerging NHS market.

To make this point is to acknowledge a tension in the direction of the health reform programme as the first decade of the twenty-first century drew to a close. On the one hand, government policies appeared designed to strengthen the grip of the centre over the NHS, while on the other hand the extension of patient choice, payment by results and competition between providers signalled a commitment to use market mechanisms to improve performance from the bottom up as part of a 'self-improving system' (the phrase is Patricia Hewitt's – see Chapter 3). The emphasis on change being driven bottom up and being led by doctors and other frontline staff was at the heart of the final report of the NHS Next Stage Review, *High Quality Care for All*, and it was reiterated in the Department of Health's operating framework for 2009/10:

> The NHS Next Stage Review process accelerated the shift from top-down targets to more devolved ownership so that services are increasingly developed by frontline staff around the needs of empowered local populations. (DH, 2008d, p. 7)

This tension found concrete expression in proposals for developing the NHS performance regime published by the DH in 2008. The proposals focused particularly on options for dealing with challenged NHS organisations, including explicit recognition that 'the NHS is an integrated system rather than a true market, and it may therefore not always be within the gift of an organisation, acting alone, to effect recovery' (DH, 2008e, p. 11). As in the 1990s, this sent out a clear indication that the NHS was a managed market in which elements of competition were combined with planning and intervention (see Chapter 2). The establishment of a Cooperation and Competition Panel to oversee the working of the NHS market appeared to signal that ministers remained committed to using choice and financial incentives to achieve improvements in performance, although at the time of writing the extent to which the continuing emphasis on central controls and system management will attenuate these incentives remains to be seen. There is also uncertainty about whether ministers and civil servants are serious in their expressed commitment to ensure that the next stage of NHS reform is led locally by frontline staff.

Conclusion

Policy-making in NHS bodies involves a range of interests each seeking to influence what is decided. In assessing the strength of these agencies and interests, the powerful position occupied by the medical profession is again apparent. Although governments have taken action to make doctors more accountable, as in the changes to the regulation of the medical profession introduced by the Blair government, the time taken to make clinical audit compulsory and to introduce a greater measure of independent scrutiny into the assessment of quality and standards speaks volumes about the ability of the profession to delay or resist policies that threaten clinical autonomy. While it is difficult to overemphasise the strength of medical interests, it should be noted that in some areas of service provision other interests may also be important. For example, policies for mentally ill people and people with learning disabilities may be more open to lay and community influences than policies for other client groups. It is, of course, particularly in these areas that the medical contribution is at its weakest. Again, for similar reasons innovations in community health services and prevention may arise among consumer groups and may develop through non-medical interests. Increasingly, too, managers and chairs are playing a bigger part in policy-making.

Granted these qualifications, the general conclusion of this discussion is that nationally determined health policies are mediated by a range of interests at the local level, among which the medical profession is the most significant. Managers have become more influential since the Griffiths Report of 1983 and they are used by ministers to implement national policies, but managers cannot direct the work of doctors and for the most part have to negotiate changes in working practices rather than impose them. The picture that emerges, then, is of a wide range of interactions between the centre and periphery, through which each attempts to influence the other. While the existence of Parliamentary accountability (and its equivalent in Northern Ireland, Scotland and Wales) gives the appearance of centralisation in the NHS, the reality is more complex. Recognising that the stance taken by the centre tends to change over time, it can be said that the DH is able to exercise control over total health service spending and its distribution, but has less control over the uses to which funds are put. Circulars, consultative documents and White Papers, and guidelines on priorities are the main instruments the Department uses to attempt to influence the decisions of NHS bodies, but the advisory nature of these documents, and often their ambiguity, leaves some scope for local interpretation of national policy.

The accountability review process was a significant innovation in the 1980s and led to greater central involvement and in some cases central control over policy-making. The review process has been considerably reinforced by the strengthening of performance management and the oversight of the NHS exercised by the Department. The use of targets and the ranking of NHS bodies according to their performance enable the DH to drive forward national policies in key areas, like the reduction of waiting times, in a way that was simply not possible before 1997, although its influence in other areas is more limited. This has resulted in much closer alignment between national policies and local action in some policy areas. The major uncertainty is whether ministers will continue to rely on central direction to achieve further improvements in NHS performance or whether they will make a reality of their rhetoric by devolving power to NHS bodies in England and create a self-improving system in which change is brought about through the choices of patients and the ability of managers, doctors and other staff to compete effectively in the emerging but still embryonic NHS market.

Chapter 10

Auditing and Evaluating Health Policy and the NHS

The aim of this chapter is to examine how health policy is audited and evaluated and the way in which the results of audit feed back into policy-making. The chapter begins by tracing the evolution of interest in audit and evaluation, in particular the use of performance indicators and performance ratings. This leads into discussion of the audit explosion and the rise of the regulators, including the National Audit Office, the Audit Commission and the Care Quality Commission. This is followed by a review of changes to the regulation of the medical profession following the Kennedy Report and the Shipman Inquiry. The evaluations carried out by independent organisations and government itself are considered next, before the chapter moves on to assess the performance of the NHS. This is done in relation to health improvement and access to health care. The chapter makes use of evidence from various sources to draw up a balance sheet of the achievements of the NHS in relation to its original objectives.

The context

Auditing the implementation of policy and evaluating impact and outcome are continuing activities. Both the Department of Health and NHS bodies in England play a part in audit and evaluation, and their work is supplemented by ad hoc inquiries and investigations and reviews undertaken by Parliamentary committees and bodies like the Audit Commission and the Care Quality Commission. Similar arrangements are in place in Northern Ireland, Scotland and Wales. Increasingly, too, researchers are contributing to this process through studies commissioned both by government and independent foundations. A wide variety of audit arrangements is currently in place but this has not always been the case. Historically, the capacity for audit and evaluation was not well developed, and the current emphasis placed on audit and performance management needs to be located in its historical context.

As far as the DH is concerned, for many years the Department lacked the means to undertake a sustained review and analysis of health policies. Brown has noted that part of the reason for this was that 'until 1956 the Ministry had no statistician, no economists and no research staff or management experts apart from a small group of work study officers' (Brown, 1979, p. 12). Although there were moves to make greater use of statistical information and economic analysis during the 1960s, the most significant changes did not occur until the reorganisation of the DHSS in 1972 and the parallel development of the Department's policy analysis capability. A number of innovations resulted from these developments, including the use of programme budgeting to analyse expenditure on health and personal social services, and the publication of studies of policies on the acute hospital sector (DHSS, 1981e), community care (DHSS, 1981a and 1981d), and the respective role of the general acute and geriatric sectors in the care of elderly hospital patients (DHSS, 1981f). The DHSS also published a review of the performance of the NHS over the decade to 1981 (DHSS, 1983). These were all indications that the Department's auditing role was being given greater priority.

Yet it remains the case that audit and evaluation are difficult tasks to perform within the NHS. This was noted in a memorandum submitted by the DHSS to the House of Commons Expenditure Committee in 1972 on services for older people. The Department argued that general aims could be formulated for services, such as 'to enable the elderly to maintain their independence and self-respect', but measuring the extent to which these aims were achieved was problematic (Expenditure Committee, 1972, p. 3). Nevertheless, the Department noted that:

> this is not to say that the problems are wholly insoluble. It may, for instance, be possible in time to devise means of measuring the condition of individuals against agreed scales of, for example, mobility or social participation and correlating changes in different areas over time with the pattern of services provided; or to establish indicators of the health and social wellbeing of the elderly in particular communities or areas and to undertake similar correlations ... But it will take many years to develop and test agreed measures, to establish a methodology for applying and interpreting them and to collect the necessary information. (Expenditure Committee, 1972, p. 4)

Many of these points apply to other areas of the NHS. The objectives of service provision are often stated only in general terms, and they may not be entirely consistent with one another. Devising measures in order to assess whether objectives have been met is beset with difficulties, and as a result many of the indicators used concern either inputs into health care, for example expenditure and staffing levels, or activity levels, such as the number of beds occupied or patients treated. Outcome indicators, for example on mortality or morbidity rates, have come to prominence only recently, and this has made it difficult to judge whether policy is having an impact on the health of the population. Measures of clinical outcome, such as death rates following surgery and the quality of life of patients following treatment, have been slow to develop, although this is beginning to change with the emphasis given to patient reported outcome measures or PROMs.

Performance indicators and performance ratings

In the 1960s and 1970s, the area of service provision in which performance indicators were applied most consistently was that of hospital services for the mentally ill and people with learning disabilities. Following pioneering work by John Yates, a series of reports published by the DHSS identified those hospitals falling within the lowest tenth of all hospitals for these patients for certain grades of staff and services (see for example DHSS, 1972). Thereafter, the reports measured progress made in achieving minimum standards of staffing and patients' amenities (see for example DHSS, 1974). Subsequently, considerable effort went into the production of a set of performance indicators covering clinical activity, finance, manpower and estate management functions. Notwithstanding these developments, the Griffiths Report commented in 1983:

> The NHS ... still lacks any real continuous evaluation of its performance ... Rarely are precise management objectives set; there is little measurement of health output; clinical evaluation of particular practices is by no means common and economic evaluation of these practices extremely rare. Nor can the NHS display a ready assessment of the effectiveness with which it is meeting the needs and expectations of the people it serves. (Griffiths Report, 1983, p. 19)

Performance indicators formed one part of a series of initiatives promulgated by the DHSS in the search for greater efficiency in the NHS in the 1980s (see Chapter 2). The indicators published in 1983 were seen as experimental and a joint NHS/DHSS group was established to advise on future developments. They were later renamed health service indicators and greater emphasis was placed on their publication in a user-friendly form. The importance attached to the indicators by ministers was indicated in a speech made by the Secretary of State to accompany publication of the 1986/7 indicators. The Secretary of State highlighted the fact that there were:

> considerable variations in performance between districts. For example, some districts treat only 25 patients a year in each surgical bed whilst others manage 53. Even when adjusted to take into account differences between the patients treated, some districts are still treating 14 per cent fewer patients than would be expected, whilst others are treating 27 per cent more.
>
> Similarly there are districts with an average length of stay 13 per cent longer than expected, whilst others manage a length of stay almost 22 per cent less than expected.
>
> And if we turn to costs we again find large variations. Costs within any one group of similar districts can vary by as much as 50 per cent. Even when adjusted for different types of patients, some districts are 15 per cent more costly than expected, others 15 per cent less. In other words, £1 spent on health care in one place might buy £1.15 worth of product, whereas somewhere else it might buy only 85 pence worth.
>
> So despite the Health Service's unquestionable achievements in boosting efficiency, I am convinced there is room for yet more improvements in performance. (Moore, 1988)

Moore's refrain has been echoed by his successors over the years.

Smee (2005) has noted that the introduction of the internal market in 1991 acted as a spur to the development of performance indicators. The most significant initiative at this time was publication of performance tables illustrating how providers were performing on the standards contained in the *Patient's Charter*. In his assessment, Smith (2005) argues that despite the *Patient's Charter* and the performance tables it spawned, during the internal market performance indicators received a low profile from the DH and NHS bodies in England, with more effort focused on writing and monitoring the contracts that purchasers were required to negotiate with providers. It took the election of the Blair government in 1997 to breathe new life into performance indicators and initially this found expression in the development of the NHS performance assessment framework (PAF) covering six domains, displayed in Table 10.1 (Secretary of State for Health, 1998b). A key component of the Blair government's approach was a commitment to go beyond the indicators of access and convenience contained in the *Patient's Charter* to assess clinical performance and the outcome of treatment. This approach took

Table 10.1 *NHS performance assessment framework domains, 1998*

1. Health improvement
2. Fair access
3. Effective delivery of appropriate health care
4. Efficiency
5. Patient/carer experience
6. Health outcomes of NHS care

forward work that had been started by the Major government and was given added impetus by evidence of failures of clinical performance within the NHS that came to light after the 1997 general election, such as the inquiry into paediatric heart surgery at the Bristol Royal Infirmary (Kennedy Report, 2001).

Subsequently, performance indicators for health authorities and NHS trusts were published and effort focused on the development of a system of performance ratings (also referred to as star ratings) for NHS trusts and primary care trusts. Performance ratings for NHS trusts providing acute hospital services were first published in 2001 and in later years they were followed by ratings for specialist trusts, ambulance trusts, mental health trusts and primary care trusts. The initial ratings were based mainly on the performance of trusts as measured by their success in achieving key government targets, especially access to care, rather than the full set of indicators used in the performance assessment framework. These measures resulted in trusts being placed in one of four categories: three stars were awarded to trusts with the highest levels of performance; two stars were awarded to trusts performing well overall; one star was awarded to trusts where there was some cause for concern; and trusts with the poorest levels of performance were awarded a zero star.

The operation of the performance rating system can be illustrated by the approach taken to NHS acute trusts in England in 2002. The performance of these trusts was assessed in relation to the following key targets: no patients waiting more than 18 months for inpatient treatment, fewer patients waiting more than 15 months for inpatient treatment, no patients waiting more than 26 weeks for outpatient treatment, fewer patients waiting on trolleys for more than 12 hours, less than 1 per cent of operations cancelled on the day, no patients with suspected cancer waiting more than two weeks to be seen in hospital, improvement to the working lives of staff, hospital cleanliness, and a satisfactory financial position. The broader range of indicators used to assess the performance of acute trusts covered clinical issues, such as deaths within 30 days of surgery and emergency readmissions following discharge; patient issues, such as waiting times and patient survey results; and issues concerned with capacity and capability, such as staff satisfaction and the sickness and absence rate for staff. On this basis, 45 acute trusts were awarded three stars, 77 received two stars, 34 received one star and 10 were awarded a zero star. The same four categories of performance were used for other trusts, although the targets and indicators against which performance was assessed were modified to reflect the services delivered by these trusts.

Performance ratings were given extensive publicity and were intended in part as a guide for the public on the performance of their local health services. The ratings were also used by the DH to reward NHS trusts that were performing well and to intervene in trusts that were performing poorly. In the case of trusts awarded three stars, extra resources were made available, and these trusts were also given additional management freedoms. With the advent of NHS foundation trusts, only NHS trusts that achieved three stars were initially eligible to apply to become NHS foundation trusts. Trusts that received zero stars were expected to produce a plan to demonstrate how they intended to improve performance and if these plans were not satisfactory then the DH required a new chief executive to be appointed. In a few cases this entailed the so-called 'franchising' of management, with the chief executives of high performing NHS trusts being appointed to help poorly performing trusts to improve. As time went on, franchising was extended to allow private sector companies the opportunity to take on the management of zero star trusts. Zero star trusts also received support from the Modernisation Agency and the DH to help them recover and improve their ratings.

Responsibility for performance ratings was transferred from the DH to the Commission for Health Improvement in 2002 and the Commission published its first assessment of performance in 2003. This work was carried forward by its successors, the Healthcare Commission and the Care Quality Commission, and a major change to the ratings was made by the Healthcare Commission in 2006. The new system, known as the annual health check, was made up of two parts: quality of services and use of resources. The previous star ratings were replaced with a four point scale: excellent, good, fair and weak. The basis of the system was compliance with 24 core standards developed by the DH and each trust was asked to assess and declare its performance against these standards. Trusts were also assessed on their performance in achieving government targets. The Healthcare Commission then visited selected trusts where there was evidence that standards might not have been achieved based on views from local stakeholders, information from other regulators and data from patient and staff surveys. The results were made available on a dedicated website to enable patients and the public to see how their local trust rated.

The third annual health check published by the Healthcare Commission in October 2008 provided an opportunity to review progress over time. Of the 391 trusts whose performance was rated, 42 received excellent ratings both for their quality of services and use of resources. Thirty eight of these trusts were NHS foundation trusts and the Healthcare Commission noted that NHS foundation trusts continued to outperform NHS trusts. Overall, the biggest improvements in performance were found in acute and specialist trusts with much less progress reported in PCTs. Mental health trusts also performed well, although the assessment process for these trusts was less demanding than for other types of trust. The Healthcare Commission noted that improvements had occurred in most areas of England, adding that the NHS in London faced significant challenges in improving its performance. An evaluation of the annual health check process funded by the Healthcare Commission reported that on balance NHS bodies recognised that it had helped them to improve their performance, even though a great deal of work was involved in undertaking the assessment and there was duplication with other regulators (Healthcare Commission, 2008a). Independent research has confirmed that the rating system has improved reported performance on key targets (Bevan and Hood, 2006).

In commenting on the development of the ratings, Smith has noted that 'the measures used in the first set of performance ratings show a preoccupation with waiting times, with only a tangential reference to clinical quality' (Smith, 2002, p. 110). This was despite the government's stated aim of attaching higher priority to clinical quality. Given that performance ratings had a greater impact on NHS bodies than the PAF, in terms of the allocation of funds and the implications for chief executives, this meant that the focus on access and convenience that had been so much a feature of health policy in the 1990s was maintained under the Blair government. In so far as clinical performance and quality did receive somewhat greater attention, this was mainly through the introduction of clinical governance and the work done to develop measures of clinical outcome in areas such as cardiac surgery. Also, the experience of patients was given higher priority through the work on patient surveys instituted by the Blair government. Publication of the results of these surveys added to the interest in NHS performance generated by performance ratings. As a consequence, work on performance indicators and performance ratings moved decisively out of the committee room and into the public domain.

Looking back over the development of performance indicators since the 1980s, Smee (2005) has highlighted four main trends. These are the broadening of the performance domains and the development of performance frameworks; a move from indicators to raise questions about performance to measures backed by rewards and sanctions; a

switch of interest from the performance of purchasers to the performance of providers; and the hiving off of monitoring to an independent
agency. These trends are consistent with the development of performance management in the NHS discussed in Chapter 9. For his part, Smith
(2005) contends that the NHS has been an innovator in seeking to
disseminate performance data, and that the performance ratings regime
developed in the past decade has had a tangible impact on improvements in NHS performance, particularly in relation to waiting times for
treatment. Against this, he also notes some unintended and adverse
effects of targets and performance ratings, including distorted behaviour, ineffective responses and fraud. A similar conclusion has been
reached by other researchers who have studied the impact of targets and
performance management in the English NHS (Bevan and Hood, 2006;
Bevan and Hamblin, 2009). It was partly in recognition of negative
consequences of ratings that the final report of the NHS Next Stage
Review led by Lord Darzi placed the emphasis on change being led
locally by clinicians and asserted that no new national targets were
contained in the report.

The audit explosion and the rise of the regulators

Alongside work done in the DH and the NHS to assess and improve
performance, a number of other organisations are involved in audit
activity. The National Audit Office (NAO) is the longest established of
these organisations and it is involved in assessing on behalf of Parliament the use of public funds, including value for money in the NHS in
England. The reports of the NAO cover a wide range of issues and in
recent times these have included the prescribing costs in primary care,
pay modernisation, improving services and support for people with
dementia and improving quality and safety in primary care. These
reports are often used as a basis for enquiries by the Public Accounts
Committee (PAC) which calls ministers and civil servants to give
evidence and to be questioned on their stewardship of public funds (see
Chapter 8). In a number of areas, the NAO has had a clear influence on
health policy, as in its work on stroke care and on dementia discussed in
Chapter 5.

The work of the NAO and the PAC is complemented by that of the
Audit Commission whose remit was extended to the NHS in 1990. The
Audit Commission has a role in both financial audit and performance
audit or national studies of major policy issues. Recent national studies
carried out by the Audit Commission have included the impact of policy
on the delivery of health improvement programmes and services, the

implementation of practice based commissioning, and the impact of payment by results. An analysis of the work of the Audit Commission noted that the Commission's national studies 'have directed a powerful searchlight on the activities of the service' (Day and Klein, 2001). Whereas the NAO supports Parliament in auditing the use of NHS funds, the Audit Commission's work is directed towards improving performance in the NHS, although this distinction has become less clear-cut in recent years, as illustrated by work undertaken jointly by the NAO and the Audit Commission on issues like tackling childhood obesity and financial management in the NHS. Also, as an independent body, the Audit Commission contributes to public debates and understanding of the performance of public services, including the NHS. Recognising the difficulties in distinguishing the impact of the Audit Commission from that of other influences on NHS performance, the evidence suggests that managers in the NHS do perceive its work to be influential, especially when local auditors carry credibility (Day and Klein, 2001). At a national level, the Audit Commission has played an increasing part in assessing the overall performance of the NHS, as indicated by its analyses of progress in implementing health reform programmes (see Audit Commission and Healthcare Commission, 2008a).

The role of the Audit Commission has changed as a result of the establishment of the Commission for Health Improvement (CHI) and its successors, the Healthcare Commission and the Care Quality Commission. The Healthcare Commission came into existence in 2004 and it brought together functions previously undertaken by the Commission for Health Improvement, the Mental Health Act Commission, and the National Care Standards Commission. The national reviews carried out by the Healthcare Commission into the performance of maternity services and the provision of care to people with diabetes and heart failure covered aspects of health care that previously would have fallen within the remit of the Audit Commission, and in some areas the two organisations joined forces, as in a study of the government's public health policies (Audit Commission and Healthcare Commission, 2008b). As well as carrying out these studies, the Healthcare Commission performed a number of other functions. These included carrying out the annual health check of the performance of NHS organisations (see above), conducting independent reviews of patients' complaints, undertaking inspections of NHS organisations, for example for compliance with the government's hygiene code, and establishing inquiries into organisations where there are grounds for serious concern about the quality of care they are providing. The Healthcare Commission also arranged for annual surveys to be carried out into patient and staff views and it presented a report to Parliament every year on the state of health care.

Following a review of arrangements for health and social care regulation, the government decided to legislate to merge the Healthcare Commission with the Commission for Social Care Inspection into an integrated regulator known as the Care Quality Commission. This came into being in April 2009. One of the consequences was a requirement that health and social care providers, including NHS providers and independent sector providers, should register with the new regulator in order to provide services. The requirement to register was linked with the ability of the Care Quality Commission to use enforcement powers to ensure compliance with registration requirements. It was expected that an early priority for the new regulator would be healthcare associated infections and specifically action to ensure that the progress made in reducing rates of MRSA and *Clostridium difficile* would be accelerated. Alongside these new powers, the Care Quality Commission took on functions previously undertaken by its predecessors, including the annual health check.

Monitor, the independent regulator of NHS foundation trusts in England, was unaffected by the reform of regulation. As we noted in the previous chapter, Monitor adopted an explicit rules based compliance regime in regulating the performance of NHS foundation trusts, and this included direct intervention in organisations where there were concerns about financial performance and the quality of care provided. The Health Committee commended Monitor's approach in its report on NHS foundation trusts (Health Committee, 2008c), and proposals put forward by the DH for developing the NHS performance regime in 2008 drew directly on Monitor's experience. Monitor's role seems certain to increase as the number of NHS foundation trusts increases in future. Having made this point, it should be noted that the transition from a hierarchical to a regulated system has not always been easy. On some issues Monitor has found itself in conflict with ministers and civil servants in the DH as the latter sought to reassert their control over the whole health care system rather than follow through the logic of the reforms and allow Monitor to use its powers to ensure the implementation of national priorities. This suggests that the age-old debate as to whether the NHS is best viewed as a firm or an industry (Smee, 2005) has life left in it yet.

Another national institution involved in auditing the performance of the NHS is the Health Services Commissioner or Ombudsman. The Ombudsman is particularly involved in investigating complaints and publishes an annual report identifying trends and issues arising in his or her work as well as reports into selected investigations. The Ombudsman has also published reports on issues of wider significance. An example of the latter which was particularly influential in shaping policy was the report published in 1994 into the failure of the NHS in Leeds to fund the continuing care of a patient. More recently, the Ombudsman

produced a report on the funding of long-term care of older and disabled people that highlighted the failures of the NHS to adopt the correct
policies and procedures in relation to charging people for the use of
long-term care (Health Services Commissioner, 2003). In the case of
both reports, the DH acted to issue revised guidance requiring health
authorities and local authorities to review local policies and services to
ensure that statutory obligations were being fulfilled. As we noted in
Chapter 5, this eventually resulted in the introduction of a national
framework for continuing care to address the concerns identified by the
Ombudsman and the slow progress made by the NHS and local authorities in establishing compliant policies.

As these comments indicate, there has been a considerable expansion
of audit activity both within the NHS and by statutory bodies and related
organisations. This reflects the 'audit explosion' (Power, 1994) across
government as a whole in the 1980s and 1990s, and the particular concern
in the case of health services to strengthen existing forms of regulation,
including the regulation of medical work (Allsop and Mulcahy, 1996).
Reviewing the history of regulation in the NHS, Walshe has argued that
the election of the Blair government was a watershed:

> The real growth in healthcare regulation in the UK has occurred since
> 1997. The present Labour government has moved away from relying
> on the market as a primary mechanism for managing and improving
> performance in the NHS for both ideological and pragmatic reasons,
> but has been unwilling to rely on the traditional bureaucratic mecha-
> nisms for controlling the NHS through the line of accountability from
> the Department of Health downwards to NHS trusts and primary care
> trusts. Instead it has turned increasingly to regulation. (Walshe, 2003,
> p. 113)

Under the Blair government, the growth of regulation was part of the
attempt to develop a third way in health policy, and initially, as Walshe has
noted, this was presented as being different from traditional bureaucratic
mechanisms and the internal market of the 1990s (see Chapter 3). As time
went on, and the government reinvented the internal market in a much
more radical form, tighter and more focused regulation was developed
alongside competition and choice. Not only this, but also, as we have
noted in earlier chapters, ministers used targets and performance management to support implementation of their key priorities. In common with
other parts of the public sector (Hood et al., 1999), the NHS was subject
to a number of different approaches to performance improvement in what
at times appeared to be a complex and contradictory high-octane fusion of
managerial, market and regulatory mechanisms.

The extension of audit into the quality of medical care marks a further stage in the development of audit within the NHS, building on self-regulation and peer review by clinicians and introducing new mechanisms for promoting high standards of care. As the Kennedy Report noted, in the 1980s and early 1990s neither external organisations nor NHS bodies saw it as their role to review clinical standards, and it was left to hospital consultants to ensure that the care provided to patients was of the appropriate quality. The failure of some doctors in Bristol to audit and review their practices meant that children undergoing heart surgery died unnecessarily. The Kennedy Report concluded that more effective safeguards were needed for patients and it endorsed steps already taken by the Blair government to improve the quality of care, such as the establishment of CHI and the introduction of clinical governance. In addition, the report made a series of recommendations for improving performance, including the regulation of health care professionals to ensure that they maintained their professional competence, and the validation of NHS trusts to ensure that they met generic standards. The report also endorsed the government's proposal to set up a National Patient Safety Agency (NPSA), and this came into existence in 2001. The role of the Agency is to run a mandatory reporting system for logging all failures, mistakes and errors and to introduce an approach for dealing with errors and learning the lessons.

In its response to the Kennedy Report, the government accepted both the analysis of why things had gone wrong at Bristol and many of the recommendations for reform. This included setting up the Council for Healthcare Regulatory Excellence in 2003 to ensure consistency and good practice in health care regulation. Beyond these proposals, the government placed particular emphasis on the need to make better use of information to audit and improve performance, and it underlined the role of the National Clinical Assessment Authority, set up in 2001 to provide a fast response to concerns about doctors' performance. In support of these initiatives, plans were announced to publish over time data on the clinical performance of consultants, and to undertake national audits of each of the clinical priority areas of *The NHS Plan*. An important step in this direction was the publication by the Healthcare Commission of survival rates after heart surgery in association with the Society for Cardiothoracic Surgeons in 2006.

One of the effects of the Kennedy Report was to accelerate moves to strengthen the role of the General Medical Council (GMC) by streamlining its membership and speeding up its procedures. As we noted in Chapter 1, the GMC was set up in the nineteenth century, and it represents a good example of state sanctioned self-regulation. Concerns about the role and functioning of the GMC began to emerge in the 1970s and 1980s and some limited reforms were made following the Merrison

Inquiry (Stacey, 1992). Criticisms of the GMC centred on the dominance of doctors in its membership and proceedings, its cumbersome and lengthy procedures for disciplining doctors, and the limited protection offered to patients. Donald Irvine, a past president of the GMC, has traced the history of attempts to reform the GMC in the past decade, and the changes that resulted (Irvine, 2003). These changes were precipitated by events at Bristol and elsewhere, events that made it difficult for doctors who were opposed to reform to win the argument. As a consequence, the number of members of the GMC was reduced to 35, and new systems for appraising doctors and revalidation were introduced. The aim of these changes was to strengthen self-regulation and to restore public and professional confidence in the GMC.

Further changes to the role of the GMC were set out in the White Paper, *Trust, Assurance and Safety – the Regulation of Health Professionals in the 21st Century* (Secretary of State for Health, 2007b). These changes were proposed by the Chief Medical Officer in response to the concerns raised by the Kennedy Report and by other high profile cases, such as that of Harold Shipman, the GP responsible for murdering over 200 of his patients. In what amounted to the most radical review of professional regulation in the history of the NHS, the White Paper included proposals to make the GMC more independent of the medical profession through changes to its membership. These changes involved a further reduction in the number of members of the GMC, from 35 to 24, and the appointment of 50 per cent of the membership from the general public (previously lay members had been in a minority). The new Council met for the first time in January 2009. In addition, the government announced plans to strengthen revalidation of all health professions. In the case of doctors, these plans involved a requirement to renew the licence to practice every five years and specialist recertification for all doctors including GPs.

Other changes included clarifying the role of local and national bodies in addressing concerns about performance, entailing separating responsibility for investigation and prosecution from that of adjudication in cases involving doctors. The latter proposal followed from Dame Janet Smith's report into the murders committed by Harold Shipman. Specifically, a new adjudicator was proposed to decide whether individual health professionals should remain in practice, with Responsible Officers being appointed to oversee the conduct and performance of doctors at a local level. The burden of proof during disciplinary hearings was also changed from the criminal standard to a civil standard. These and other reforms were opposed by the BMA as an attack on self-regulation but they were carried into law in the Health and Social Care Act 2008. Whereas in the previous decade, government and the medical profession had circled around each other exploring various options for the reform of medical regulation without making significant progress (Salter, 2007), the Act marked a fundamental break with the past.

Evaluation by independent organisations and government

The audit explosion of recent years has not been confined to the establishment of new organisations to regulate and inspect health services and the work of external inquiries. There has also been increasing involvement by independent organisations and by government itself. The work of independent organisations is exemplified by the research carried out by the King's Fund, a charity involved in health policy analysis whose studies have included a review of the impact of the reforms pursued by the Blair government and the additional expenditure committed by the government (Wanless et al., 2007). Of increasing importance too have been the publications of Dr Foster, an organisation that uses NHS data to produce consumer guides to the quality of health services. The topics covered by these guides include hospitals, maternity services and cancer services. The most comprehensive independent evaluation of government policy was the Nuffield Trust's analyses of the Blair government's quality agenda (Leatherman and Sutherland, 2003; Leatherman and Sutherland, 2008). This analysis reported progress towards the objectives set by the government while also noting a number of weaknesses and risks for the future.

Partly in response to the growth of external audit and scrutiny, government has strengthened its own capacity for monitoring and review. Within government, this takes the form of regular reviews between the Treasury and the DH on progress towards the public service agreement targets (see Chapter 3), and between the Prime Minister's Delivery Unit and the DH on progress in delivering the priorities set out in *The NHS Plan*. These reviews involve detailed assessments of NHS performance and may lead to action to strengthen implementation in areas where there is a risk that targets will not be achieved (Barber, 2007). For its part, the DH has published a series of reports on the implementation of the national service frameworks (see, for example, Secretary of State for Health, 2008d), and it has offered a number of assessments of overall progress towards *The NHS Plan* targets. Although, by definition, these reports and assessments are less independent than those conducted by bodies such as the Healthcare Commission and the Audit Commission, they are further evidence of the importance attached to audit and delivery, to use a phrase in currency in the second term of the Blair government.

Alongside the expansion of audit, there has also been an increasing interest in the evaluation of health policy. Of particular importance in this context has been the establishment of the NHS research and development programme and the DH's policy research programme, both of which have provided funding and support not only for the evaluation of clinical interventions, but also for studies of the implementation and impact of health policy in England. Examples of policy evaluations commissioned by the DH include studies of the introduction of total purchasing within the NHS (Mays et al., 1998), the implementation of *The Health of the Nation* (DH, 1998a), the introduction of primary care groups and trusts (Regen et al., 2001; Wilkin et al., 2002), the implementation of health action zones (Bauld and Judge, 2002), and the impact of quality improvement programmes (Joss and Kogan, 1995; McNulty and Ferlie, 2002; Ham et al., 2003). DH funding also supported evaluations into the impact of the new contract for GPs introduced in 2004, the health reform programme in England, and the impact of policies to improve the quality of care for people with long term conditions, such as the Expert Patient Programme and the introduction of community matrons.

After a period at the beginning of the 1990s when ministers were reluctant to evaluate health policy, many major initiatives are now launched in association with independent assessments funded by government. In parallel, there are examples of evaluations conducted by researchers with the support of research councils and independent foundations. Because of its size and resources, England has a greater capacity to undertake evaluations than Northern Ireland, Scotland and Wales. Also, there are more independent organisations actively involved in scrutinising health policy in England than in these countries. Despite this, there is no certainty that the results of evaluations will be acted upon, and it is sometimes the case that initiatives ostensibly launched as trials to be assessed before being implemented nationally are often taken forward before the findings of evaluations are known. Nevertheless, there is some evidence to suggest that the contribution of ideas and research to policy-making, one of the themes addressed in Chapter 8, is increasing as a result of the emphasis placed on evaluation.

Audit and evaluation are important in providing feedback on the impact of health policy and in so doing may influence policy-making. As we have emphasised throughout this book, the policy process is complex and is subject to a range of political and other influences. Those involved in audit and evaluation, whether within the NHS or outside, are only one set of actors in this process. In Kingdon's terms, the influence of audit and evaluation depends on the coming together of problems, politics and participants at a time when there are opportunities to influence policy (Kingdon, 1995). The results of audit and evaluation contribute to the development of policy by identifying problems that demand attention, and linking these problems with participants in a position to influence the outcome. A good example would be the reform of medical regulation, discussed above, which was directly influenced by the inquiries into paediatric heart surgery in Bristol and the case of Harold Shipman.

Against this background, we now turn to an examination of the performance of the NHS. This is a large topic and it is one that may be approached in a number of ways. For the purposes of this chapter, and given the space available, the focus is on health improvement and access to health care. In Chapter 12 we examine the performance of the NHS in the context of the experience of other countries.

Health improvement

The health of the population has improved steadily not just in the lifetime of the NHS but over the past 175 years. This is demonstrated by a major review of trends in mortality in Britain undertaken by the Office for National Statistics (Charlton and Murphy, 1997). In the period from 1841 to 1991, the expectation of life increased at all ages and was particularly pronounced in the younger age groups. A boy born in 1841 could expect to live until 41 years and a girl until 43 years; by 1991 the comparable figures were 73 years for boys and 79 years for girls. More recent data show that expectation of life at birth increased to almost 77 years for boys and over 81 years for girls in the United Kingdom by 2005.

Another way of examining improvements in health is to look at trends in death rates by age. These trends illustrate declining death rates at all ages with the decline initially being greatest in the younger age groups. Charlton's analysis has shown that improvements in survival in the nineteenth century were in fact confined to children and young adults (Charlton, 1997). These improvements extended to other age groups in the twentieth century, although life expectancy for people aged 75 and over only increased from around 1950. Analysis shows that by 2000, 83 per cent of deaths in England and Wales occurred at age 65 and over compared with less than 25 per cent a century earlier (Griffiths and Brock, 2003). Between 1984 and 1994 the greatest improvement in health occurred among adults aged 15–19 and 45–64, and the least improvement among adults aged 20–44 (Dunnell, 1997). Data also demonstrate a substantial decline, since 1993, in deaths that are considered amenable to medical intervention, mainly because of falling premature deaths from heart disease, stroke and cancer (Wheller et al., 2007). This decline helps to explain the increasing numbers of older people in the population.

In the case of infants, there was a marked acceleration in the decline of infant deaths after the Second World War. For boys born in England and

Wales in 1950, 96.6 per cent survived to the age of one compared with 99.1 per cent of those born in 1990. For girls the figures were 97.4 per cent in 1950 and 99.3 per cent in 1990 (Botting, 1995). Infant mortality rates have continued to fall since then and reached 5 deaths per 1000 births in the United Kingdom in 2005. Data from the national birth cohort studies illustrate trends in health in the second half of the twentieth century and show improvements in childhood health as measured by growth in height and survival of low weight at birth (Ferri et al., 2003). More recently, there has been an increase in the prevalence of obesity among children as well as adults, raising concerns that improvements in health may not continue.

Long-term improvements in health have been associated with changes in the causes of death. As we noted in Chapter 1, public health measures taken in the nineteenth century played a major part in tackling infectious diseases which at that time accounted for one death in every three. In place of infectious diseases there have been marked increases in mortality from cancers, heart attacks and stroke, although death rates from many of these causes have started to fall recently. At the end of the twentieth century, heart disease and stroke accounted for around 30 per cent of deaths in England and Wales, and cancers accounted for around 25 per cent of deaths. There is evidence that the decline in premature mortality has been accompanied by an increase in morbidity as measured by patient consultations with GPs and self-reported illness (Dunnell, 1997). Data from the General Household Survey show that the prevalence of self-reported long-standing illness increased from 21 per cent in 1972 to 33 per cent in 2006 and the prevalence of limiting long-standing conditions increased from 15 per cent to 19 per cent over the same period (ONS, 2006).

The increase in self-reported morbidity may reflect rising expectations on the part of patients as well as increased survival time following initial diagnosis. In relation to the latter, if medical science has contributed to the decline in premature mortality, then it has done so at least in part by turning fatal conditions into treatable (or at least containable) illnesses. Examples include cancer and heart disease where medical advances have resulted in a range of effective interventions, encompassing surgery, drugs and radiotherapy, enabling many people with these conditions to be treated with increasing likelihood that death will be postponed and quality of life improved. There is also evidence of an increase in the prevalence of chronic diseases, sometimes referred to as long term conditions, like diabetes and arthritis. Many of these conditions are not life threatening, but nor can they be cured. The changing pattern of health identified in the national birth cohort studies, including rising levels of obesity and depression, help to explain why chronic conditions have become more important (Ferri et al., 2003). With more people surviving into older age, the challenge facing the NHS is increasingly how to prevent and treat these conditions, particularly when many people have more than one illness.

A major uncertainty in this regard is whether the improvements in life expectancy that have occurred have resulted in people living longer in good health or poor health. Research carried out in the 1990s suggested that the number of years of healthy life had increased but not at the same rate as overall increases in life expectancy (Bebbington and Darton, 1996; Kelly and Baker, 2000). A similar conclusion was reached by the Wanless (2006) social care review undertaken by the King's Fund. This work appeared to indicate that people were living more years in poor health or with a limiting long-standing illness. Analysis of more recent trends paints a different picture, showing evidence of an increase in the number of years of disability free life expectancy between 2000/02 and 2004/06 (Smith et al., 2008). These trends lend support to the compression of morbidity thesis advanced by Fries (1980) which suggested that the time people spent in poor health would become shorter as a consequence of medical advances and other developments. Despite this, it is likely that the increasing numbers of older people in the population, linked to the rising prevalence of dementia and other conditions, will put pressure on health and social care budgets, even under optimistic scenarios (Wanless, 2006)

To make these points is to put into perspective the contribution of the NHS to health improvement. The gains in health made in the past 60 years may have been associated with the introduction of health services available free at the point of use to patients, but this is not the same as demonstrating that they have been caused by the NHS. Just as in the nineteenth century when public health legislation and the provision of pure water supplies and better housing were instrumental in the fight against infectious diseases, so too in the twentieth century factors outside the NHS exert an important influence on the health of the population. As Ferri and colleagues note in commenting on long-term trends in childhood health:

> The improvements are likely to be the outcome of a combination of improvements in education, housing and nutrition, and in the reduction of poverty, as well as the result of improved preventive care and the treatment of disease. (Ferri et al., 2003, p. 305)

The existence of inequalities in health between social groups underlines the importance of non-medical influences on health. The extent of health inequalities was documented in the 1980 Black Report and the findings of this report have been updated and confirmed by later analyses.

Social class inequalities have traditionally been analysed using the classification of occupations employed by the Registrar General. This divided occupations into five main groupings varying from social class I, which contains professional occupations such as accountants and doctors, to social class V, which contains unskilled manual occupations like labourers and office cleaners. An analysis of death rates revealed evidence of social class differences in all age groups (Dreyer and Bunting, 1997). Class differences in morbidity have been reported in the General Household Survey in relation to self-reported long-standing illness (Bunting, 1997) and in the Health Survey for England in relation to the prevalence of disability (Bajekal and Prescott, 2003). The national birth cohort studies have also demonstrated socio-economic inequalities in health and have emphasised the origins of inequalities in childhood (Ferri et al., 2003).

Of particular concern in recent times has been the long-term trend in class differences in health. Analysis shows that the gap in mortality between professional and unskilled manual men increased almost two-and-a-half times between 1930–32 and 1991–93 (DH, 2003a). Data also indicate a widening in inequality between the 1970s and 1990s in the adult population, and a narrowing of differences among infants (Dreyer and Whitehead, 1997). In the case of life expectancy at birth and at age 65, inequalities widened between the 1970s and the 1990s as illustrated in Figure 10.1. A boy born into social class I in 1997–99 could expect to live to age 79 whereas a boy born into social class V could expect to live to age 71. For girls, the comparable figures were 83 years for social class I

Figure 10.1 *Changes in life expectancy at birth by social class between 1972–76 and 1997–99 in England and Wales*

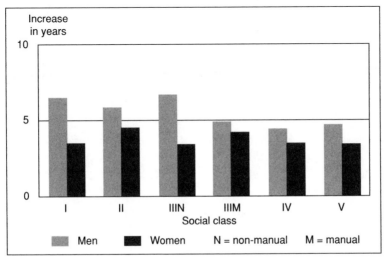

and 77 years for social class V. There are also class differences in self-reported illness and disability. Figure 10.2 illustrates these differences in relation to reported disability for men and women.

The argument of the Black Report was that 'differences in the material conditions of life' (Black Report, 1980, p. 357) were mainly responsible for health inequalities, although the Report acknowledged that the causes were complex and multiple. The implication that followed was that steps to reduce inequalities needed to focus on tackling these material conditions. This entailed action in a range of areas of public policy, including, in the view of the Black Report, increases in child benefit, the introduction of a childcare allowance, improvements to housing conditions, and free school meals for children. These proposals were rejected by the Thatcher government which disputed both the explanation of health inequalities offered in the Black Report, and the proposal that additional public expenditure was required to address these inequalities. This meant that the issues raised in the Report were largely ignored in central government despite evidence that inequalities in the 1980s not only persisted but also increased (Whitehead, 1987).

It took the election of the Blair government in 1997 to refocus attention on health inequalities. The Acheson Report (1998) was commissioned by the government to update the findings of the Black Report and particularly to advise on priorities for policy development. In so doing, the Acheson Report emphasised the importance of measures to

Figure 10.2 *Prevalence and severity of disability (age-standardised), by social class*

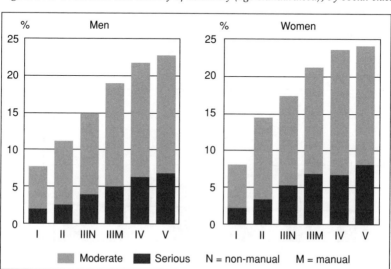

Source: Bajekal and Prescott (2003).

reduce poverty, improve education, increase work opportunities, and strengthen access to housing. It also noted that action in the NHS should be concentrated on the prevention of ill-health and premature mortality. In this area, the proposals of the Acheson Report included ensuring equitable access to effective health care and the development of partnerships between the NHS and other agencies. Like the Black Report, the Acheson Report stressed the need to improve the health of families and children, drawing on the findings of the national birth cohort studies (Ferri et al., 2003) and the emphasis placed by those studies on the origins of inequalities in childhood. Other research has confirmed the importance of early life influences on health while also noting that for some medical conditions deprivation during adulthood appeared to be a more significant factor (Davey Smith et al., 2001). The Acheson Report also examined inequalities between the genders and those affecting minority ethnic groups.

The Blair government accepted the Acheson Report and argued that a wide range of policies were in place to tackle inequalities. The agenda for action set out by the government encompassed raising living standards and tackling low income, initiatives relating to education and early years, and measures within the NHS to help people in the poorest health. Subsequently, national targets were set for reducing health inequalities, and a cross-cutting review was set up to assess progress and agree the priorities for future action. The cross-cutting review was important in bringing together ministers and officials from across government departments and from local government to make recommendations for further work to tackle inequalities. In a wide-ranging analysis, the report of the review emphasised the need to break the cycle of health inequalities through education, parental employment, tackling smoking in pregnancy, and reducing teenage births. The report also reiterated the importance of tackling the major killers such as heart disease and cancer, and it identified smoking as 'the single most significant causal factor for the socio-economic differences in the incidence of cancer and heart disease' (Cross-Cutting Review, 2002).

The report noted too the importance of nutrition and physical activity. In the case of public services, it argued that access to services, including the NHS, by disadvantaged groups needed to be improved, and it highlighted the role of area-based initiatives in strengthening communities. These initiatives included the government's Neighbourhood Renewal strategy. Finally, the need for targeted interventions for specific groups such as rough sleepers and prisoners was emphasised. The report of the cross-cutting review was followed by publication of a programme of action to be taken forward across government (DH, 2003a). An analysis of European experiences of tackling inequalities in health compared the approach taken in different countries and concluded that 'the UK, after a period of lagging behind other European countries, now is ahead of continental Europe in development and implementation of policies to reduce socio-economic inequalities in health' (Mackenbach and Bakker, 2003).

To bring the story up to date, a major review of progress in implementing the programme of action that reported in 2008 found that while life expectancy and infant mortality were continuing to improve, the overall health gap remained (DH, 2008f). Similarly, there had been progress in the 12 cross-government headline indicators set out in the programme of action, covering issues such as teenage pregnancy, road accident casualties and fruit and vegetable consumption, but in most cases this was not associated with a reduction in inequalities. This suggested that there would be major challenges in reaching the targets set by the government for reducing inequalities in infant mortality and inequalities between areas with the worst health and deprivation indicators and the population as a whole by 10 per cent by 2010. As in previous reviews, the report argued that the NHS had a major contribution to make by action on smoking cessation and the prevention of heart disease and stroke, alongside action on the wider determinants of health such as reducing child poverty, improving educational attainment and tackling worklessness and inactivity. The review argued that lack of progress in reducing health inequalities was not surprising in view of the short period of time that the programme had been in place, and it identified a number of lessons to guide future action. These included ensuring that there was local action and leadership on this issue, developing more effective partnerships between NHS bodies, local authorities and other agencies, and spreading good practice from those parts of the country where progress was being made to other areas. In its response to the review, the DH acknowledged that achievement of the 2010 targets would be difficult and it announced a redoubling of efforts in support of the programme of action, including further support through the National Support Team for Health Inequalities and other interventions (DH, 2008g).

What does the evidence about improvements in health and the persistence of inequalities tell us about the performance of the NHS? It would be simplistic to give credit to the NHS for all the improvements in health that have occurred since the Second World War, in the same way that it would be wrong to blame the NHS for the persistence and widening of health inequalities. Recognising that the role of medicine in improving the population's health has been more significant in the twentieth century than the nineteenth century, it can be suggested that by making available medical advances to the population the NHS has contributed to the long-term trends we identified at the beginning of this section. The main gains have occurred from the prevention of ill-health, for example through vaccination, and also through the extension of life made available by new forms of treatment for cancer and heart disease. The contribution of improved treatments has been analysed in a study of changing patterns of heart disease, demonstrating a strong association between improved outcomes and the use of treatments like clot-busting drugs and cardiac surgery (Tunstall-Pedoe et al., 2000). The use of cholesterol-lowering drugs such as statins has also been important and has been supported by the new contract for GPs introduced in 2004 that provided financial incentives for practices to identify patients at risk and provide treatment in line with evidence based guidelines. A further contribution has been in relation to the quality of life where medical advances have contributed to the relief of pain and suffering, for example through surgery for joint replacements.

By comparing trends in mortality from avoidable causes and other causes between 1950 and 1994, Charlton and colleagues suggest that the application of medical advances has had a beneficial effect. This is illustrated in Table 10.2 which shows that the decline in mortality from conditions where effective treatments are available is around twice that for other conditions (Charlton et al., 1997). It has been argued that medical care will have a much bigger influence in health improvement in the future, both in increasing life expectancy and improving quality of life (Bunker, 2001), especially in view of evidence that the benefits of spending in areas such as treatment of heart attacks exceed the costs (Cutler and McClellan, 2001). Evidence to support this can be found in a recent analysis of trends in avoidable mortality in England and Wales between 1993 and 2005. This found much bigger reductions in mortality amenable to medical intervention than mortality from other causes. The authors of this study concluded that 'Medical interventions are likely to have contributed positively to reductions in avoidable mortality, as are public health initiatives, though perhaps to a lesser extent' (Wheller et al., 2007, p. 10). It follows that ensuring that the population has access to cost effective care will be an increasingly important objective of health policy, and we now turn to an examination of the record of the NHS in relation to access.

Table 10.2 *Comparison of mortality rates per million population in England and Wales in 1950 and 1994*

Cause of death	1950	1994	Percentage fall
Eight 'avoidable' causes (all ages)*	513	102	80
All other	12,451	7669	38

Note: * Tuberculosis, hypertensive disease, cerebrovascular disease, chronic rheumatic heart disease, appendicitis, cholelithiasis and cholecystitis, cervical cancer, Hodgkin's disease.

Source: Charlton et al. (1997).

Access to health care

The Bill that established the NHS stated:

> All the Service or any part of it, is to be available to everyone in England and Wales. The Bill imposes no limitations on availability – e.g. limitations based on financial means, age, sex, employment or vocation, area of residence, or insurance qualification. (Ministry of Health, 1946, p. 3)

Over 50 years later, the NHS can claim considerable success in meeting this objective. Notwithstanding the introduction of charges for some services, the Royal Commission on the NHS argued in 1979 that 'one of the most significant achievements of the NHS has been to free people from fear of being unable to afford treatment for acute or chronic illness' (Royal Commission on the NHS, 1979, pp. 10–11). For a generation brought up on a health service largely free at the point of use, it is easy to overlook this achievement. Yet at a time when some other developed countries, such as the United States, have still to ensure access to health care for all citizens, it is salutary to remember that the United Kingdom takes this for granted and the population does not live in fear of bankruptcy in the event of contracting serious medical conditions. More positively, international comparisons indicate that funding health services through general taxation, as in the United Kingdom, is more equitable than other methods (van Doorslaer et al., 1993; Wagstaff et al., 1999). Despite this achievement, there remains a variety of inequities in health and health care. Four aspects are important, including regional disparities; social class differences; the quality of care provided to groups such as older people, people with learning disabilities and the mentally ill; and access to hospital treatment.

Looking first at regional disparities, data for the English regions (defined here as regions covered by strategic health authorities) illustrate differences in health, health services provision and resource allocation. For example, in 2005 the infant mortality rate in England stood at 5, and within England the rate varied from 3.9 in South East Coast to 6.1 in Yorkshire and Humber. In the same year the perinatal mortality rate for England was 8, and within England the rate varied from 6.4 in the East to 9.9 in the West Midlands. There were similar variations in the standardised mortality ratio, ranging from 90 in the South West to 111 in the North East, compared with 98 for England and 100 for the United Kingdom in 2005. These differences between regions mask even bigger variations in health within regions. Variations in the provision of services also exist. These illustrate that in 2005/06 the number of available beds per 1000 population varied from 4.4 in the North East to 2.9 in the South East. These variations are related to differences in the allocation of NHS resources to the English regions.

These differences have been recognised since the early 1970s. An internal DHSS review led to the introduction of a new method of allocating revenue in 1971–72, and in 1975 the Resource Allocation Working Party (RAWP) was established to produce a formula:

> To reduce progressively, and as far as is feasible, the disparities between the different parts of the country in terms of opportunity for access to health care for people at equal risk; taking into account measures of health needs, and social and environmental factors which may affect the need for health care. (DHSS, 1975c)

The RAWP report recommended a formula based on the size of each region's population, weighted for age, sex and morbidity, with standardised mortality ratios being used as a proxy for morbidity (DHSS, 1976a). Using this weighted capitation approach, the Working Party found that some regions had allocations around 10 per cent below their target share of resources, and others had allocations more than 10 per cent above. In accepting the recommendations put forward, the Secretary of State recognised that they would have to be implemented in stages, and the result was a progressive reduction in inequities in resource allocation. The slow pace of implementation was, however, a source of frustration to health authorities below their weighted capitation target and was one of the reasons the Acheson Report recommended that there should be more rapid movement towards target allocations.

The principles of the RAWP approach have been maintained even though the details of its application have changed, sometimes quite significantly, in the light of research into the indicators that best reflect variations in need and alterations to the structure of the NHS. The Advisory Committee on Resource Allocation oversees the development of the formula and in the light of its recommendations in 2008 ministers decided to place more weight on factors such as age and chronic diseases and less on health inequalities. This had a significant impact on some areas with PCTs in parts of London finding themselves considerably above their target allocation and PCTs in other areas finding themselves well below. As in the past, the DH decided to work towards the new targets over time to avoid creating too much instability in areas that were overfunded according to the revised formula.

Alongside regional differences there are social class differences in access to health care. The significance of these was recognised by Titmuss writing in 1968:

> We have learnt from 15 years' experience of the Health Service that the higher income groups know how to make better use of the Service; they tend to receive more specialist attention; occupy more of the beds

in better equipped and staffed hospitals; receive more elective surgery; have better maternity care; and are more likely to get psychiatric help and psychotherapy than low income groups – particularly the unskilled. (Titmuss, 1968, p. 196)

Support for Titmuss's analysis came from Alderson's examination of a number of mainly preventative services. This found underuse of services in relation to need, and Alderson commented:

The data presented are compatible with the hypothesis that there is a group in the community who are aware of the provisions of the health service and who obtain a higher proportion of the resources of the health service than would be expected by chance and a much higher proportion in relation to their needs when compared with others in the community. (Alderson, 1970, p. 52)

One of the explanations of variations in the utilisation of services by social class is that these services may not be equally available in different parts of the country. It is this observation that lies behind the inverse care law formulated by Julian Tudor-Hart which states that 'the availability of good medical care tends to vary inversely with the need of the population served' (Tudor-Hart, 1971, p. 412). Tudor-Hart's thesis is that areas of social deprivation containing high proportions of people from the lower social groups tend to have access to less good health services even though their need for these services is greater than that of higher social groups. This argument is reinforced by the work of Le Grand who combined data on the utilisation of services and need to demonstrate that higher social groups benefited more from the NHS than lower social groups (Le Grand, 1978). In other words, Le Grand contended that in terms of utilisation the NHS was pro-rich.

Later evidence has been reviewed and summarised by Propper (1998). Her analysis of data on utilisation and need reported much less systematic variation in the use of services in relation to need than was evident from Le Grand's study. On the other hand, research into the provision of specific interventions does demonstrate variation. For example, the use of GP services was related to social class, with people in the lower social groups making greater use of these services than those in higher social groups. In this area, at least, it appeared that the NHS was pro-poor. There is a more mixed picture in relation to hospital services, with evidence of services being provided in proportion to deprivation in some areas but not in others. On the basis of its review of the evidence, the Acheson Report commented, 'For many ... NHS hospital treatments, there is little evidence of systematic inequities in access between deprivation groups' (Acheson Report, 1998, p. 113). The most recent review of the evidence notes that 'the picture overall is a confusing one' (Dixon et al., 2003, p. 18), at least in part because of variations in the quality of research, and it concludes that on balance there are inequities in utilisation in key areas of health service provision. These inequities were found in relation to preventative services and hospital services, including cardiac surgery and elective surgical procedures such as hip replacements, hernias and treatment of gallstones. An analysis of the use of services by older people also reported inequities in relation to the use of GP services, outpatient services and dental care, although not inpatient services (Allin et al., 2006).

A third area in which inequities in access are evident is in relation to the care available to groups such as older people, people with learning disabilities and the mentally ill. We noted in Chapter 1 that concerns about the quality of care provided to these groups was one of the factors behind the reorganisation of the NHS in 1974. The issue was brought to prominence in 1967 when a pressure group known as Aid for the Elderly in Government Institutions published a book called *Sans Everything – A Case to Answer*, containing allegations of ill-treatment to elderly patients in psychiatric and geriatric care (Robb, 1967). The Minister of Health asked regional hospital boards to set up independent enquiries and the general conclusion of the enquiries was that the allegations were unfounded.

A rather different picture emerged from the report of the committee of enquiry set up to investigate conditions at Ely Hospital, a hospital for people with learning disabilities in Cardiff. The committee found that many of the allegations of ill-treatment of patients were true, and that there were serious deficiencies at Ely. A number of recommendations were made for improving standards at Ely and at long-stay hospitals generally, including the establishment of a system of inspection to ensure that the local managers of services were aware of what was required (Ely Report, 1969). The Secretary of State at the time of Ely, Richard Crossman, used the report to give greater priority to long-stay services. The Hospital Advisory Service was set up to provide the system of inspection recommended by the committee of enquiry, although it was presented as a means of giving advice rather than an inspectorate. In addition, Crossman earmarked funds to be spent specifically on hospitals for people with learning disabilities. The momentum generated by Crossman was maintained through the publication of a series of further reports into conditions at long-stay hospitals, and by the policies set out in the consultative document on *Priorities* in 1976. These actions were an attempt to allocate a greater share of resources to an area of the NHS which it was recognised had fallen behind required standards (Martin, 1984).

Progress towards achieving the kinds of priorities set out in 1976 has been slow and uneven. Part of the difficulty of achieving national priorities is that NHS bodies may not share the objectives of the DH. The claims of other groups, particularly in the acute hospital sector, may be pressed strongly at the local level, and may push service development in a different direction from that desired by central government. As we noted in Chapter 9, the implementation of national priorities can therefore be problematic. This continues to be the case today, 40 years after the Ely Report, as evidenced by the investigations carried out by the Healthcare Commission into the failure to provide appropriate standards of care to people with learning disabilities in areas such as Cornwall and Sutton and Merton. Undoubtedly one of the reasons for this is that, despite the priority given by the DH, these services are relatively weak in the struggle for scarce resources that occurs in the NHS. Put another way, the micro politics of the NHS may run counter to the macro politics leading to a gap between intention and action. The decision to move responsibility for learning disabilities from the NHS to local authorities may help to bridge this gap, but it still leaves open the challenge of how to increase investment in services for older people and people with mental health problems.

A fourth area in which access to care has emerged as an issue is the time patients spend waiting for hospital treatment, including differences between NHS and private patients. Waiting lists for surgery have existed ever since the establishment of the NHS and reducing waiting lists and waiting times has been a high priority for policy-makers and NHS managers in the past decade. In examining this issue, it is important to recognise that even when waiting lists and waiting times were much longer than they are today, half of patients were admitted within six weeks, and over two-thirds within three months. Analysis has shown that five specialties account for around three-quarters of patients waiting, and at various times initiatives within the NHS have succeeded in cutting both waiting lists and waiting times, in some cases significantly. Although there are differences between areas in the experience of patients waiting for treatment, from an equity perspective a more important consideration is the ability of some patients to access treatment through the private sector rather than having to wait for an NHS operation.

As Yates (1987, 1995) has shown, there is in fact a perverse incentive for hospital specialists in that their income from private practice is in part dependent on the existence of NHS waiting lists and the willingness of some people to pay for treatment to avoid waiting. This derives from the bargain struck between Bevan and the medical profession at the inception of the NHS after which Bevan famously claimed to have stuffed the mouths of specialists with gold to entice them into the NHS (see Chapter

1). The effects are still felt today with private practice coexisting with NHS work, and patients who are able to pay for treatment receiving this treatment in a matter of days as opposed to weeks. Only under the Labour government in the 1970s did this issue become a matter of political controversy, and even then attention focused more on the existence of private beds in NHS hospitals than the employment contract of specialists. One of the effects of the reforms to the NHS initiated by the Thatcher government was an expansion of private provision by NHS trusts and this meant that paradoxically the NHS became a major provider of acute services to private patients. The consequence was to make even more stark the inequities in access that arise from the persistence of private practice within the NHS.

Reducing waiting lists has been a high priority for both Conservative and Labour governments. The Blair government that came to power in 1997 promised to reduce the number of people on inpatient waiting lists by 100,000 and it achieved this objective by allocating extra resources for this purpose and exerting pressure through the management line. The focus of attention shifted from waiting lists to waiting times on publication of *The NHS Plan*. The targets set out in the plan included a maximum waiting time of six months for inpatient admission and 13 weeks for an outpatient appointment by the end of 2005. Progress towards these targets enabled an even more challenging target to be set in *The NHS Improvement Plan*, namely that no patient should wait longer than 18 weeks from GP referral to treatment by the end of 2008. The focus on access to services also encompassed appointments with GPs and the time spent in hospital accident and emergency departments. More ambitious waiting time targets were set for high priority services such as cancer and heart disease, reflecting the importance attached to these clinical conditions.

One of the reasons that waiting for treatment has been singled out as a priority is a concern that an increasing number of people may choose to 'go private' if they are unable to receive treatment in the NHS in a reasonable time, and that this may undermine support for the NHS as a universal service. Another reason is evidence that waiting is a major concern for the public and the aspect of NHS provision of which they are most critical. At a time when taxes have risen to fund the additional investment made in the NHS, the government has been particularly concerned to show that increases in expenditure are producing better results in areas of service provision that are of importance to the public. To this end, the NHS Modernisation Agency focused much of its effort on supporting the NHS to achieve the waiting time targets. In so doing, it placed particular emphasis on assisting NHS staff to work more smartly by redesigning services to make them more efficient and more convenient for patients.

This included a series of 'Action on' programmes targeted at specialties like orthopaedics and ENT where access presented particular challenges.

One of the first redesign programmes led by the Agency (and its predecessor, the National Patients' Access Team) was an initiative to offer patients the opportunity of booking the time of their hospital appointments as a way of reducing uncertainty and increasing convenience. Following the piloting of this programme, the government decided to extend booking throughout the NHS. The policy on waiting and booking was developed further in 2002 with the establishment of pilot programmes to extend the range of choices available to patients. The first two pilots focused on patients waiting longer than six months for heart surgery and patients in London waiting longer than six months in a number of specialties. Subsequently, the government announced that all patients waiting longer than six months for elective surgery would be offered the choice of an alternative provider from the summer of 2004, and in 2006 the policy was extended to enable patients to exercise a choice of four or more providers at the point of GP referral. From April 2008, patients have been able to choose services from any hospital provider in England that meets NHS standards and costs. The policy on access and choice was supported by a drive to increase the proportion of operations carried out as day cases and to increase the capacity for elective surgery. The latter included making greater use of spare capacity in private hospitals and commissioning a number of new independent sector treatment centres specialising in elective work (see Chapter 4). A small number of NHS patients also travelled overseas for treatment as part of a pilot undertaken in 2002. The NHS Choices website was developed by the government to provide information to patients about the services available in order to support informed choice.

In practice, the policies that made the biggest difference to waiting times were the targets set by the government for bringing waiting times down and the allocation of additional funds to enable more treatments to be undertaken. Coupled with the use of performance management to ensure effective implementation of targets, and an unforgiving approach to failure to deliver, these policies had the desired effect, resulting in major improvements in access throughout the 2000s, as illustrated in Figure 10.3. The focus on improving access, and the use of 'targets and terror' (Propper et al., 2007), had two adverse consequences. The first was to encourage some NHS managers to report inaccurate information on waiting times in their hospitals. The extent to which this happened was examined by the National Audit Office and the Audit Commission and both organisations found evidence of the mismanagement and misreporting of waiting list data at a small number of NHS trusts. The second adverse effect, to return to our

Figure 10.3 *Trends in inpatient and outpatient waiting times in England*

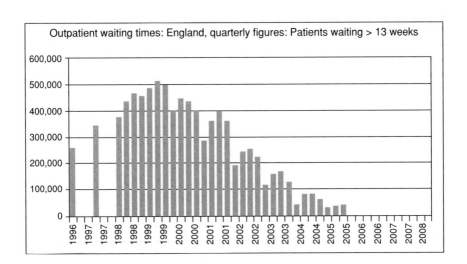

earlier discussion, was that the overriding priority attached to cutting waiting times meant that resources were not available for other purposes, such as improving services for older people and people with mental illness and learning disabilities. To be sure, the additional funding made available to the NHS by the Blair government meant that these other services were able to develop, but they did not benefit to the same extent as acute hospital services.

Viewed in the longer perspective, the improvements in access that occurred under the Blair and Brown governments were the most important gain to occur during a period of unprecedented investment and reform. This was acknowledged by the Healthcare Commission which described the progress made as 'dramatic' and 'particularly significant' (Healthcare Commission, 2008b). Against this, both ministers and managers were slow to recognise the increasing prevalence of healthcare associated infections, and only in 2004 was concerted action taken to address this challenge. As in the case of waiting time reductions, this involved a combination of targets, intervention and support, and by 2008 there was evidence of falling rates of MRSA and *Clostridium difficile*. The lesson here was not only the ability of the DH to use its authority to drive improvements in NHS performance, but also the ability to rise to the challenge of doing so across a number of priority areas at the same time. Recognition of the limits of central control lay behind the emphasis placed on stimulating change from the bottom up and not just the top down in Lord Darzi's report, *High Quality Care for All*, not least to avoid the demoralising and demotivating effects of 'targets and terror' as a long-term change strategy. As the NHS approached the end of the first decade of the twenty-first century, the policy rhetoric shifted to engaging staff and developing clinical leaders to promote change as part of the commitment to developing a 'self-improving' system, to use Patricia Hewitt's phrase.

Conclusion

In this chapter we have traced the evolution of audit and evaluation of health policy and the NHS. A wide range of arrangements are currently involved in the audit of health service performance in contrast to the early phases of the NHS when these functions were underdeveloped. We have seen how the results of audit feed back into policy-making, an example being the report by the Health Services Commissioner which led to changes of policy in relation to continuing care. We have also noted that for audit to influence policy-making, ministers and civil servants must be predisposed to act on the results. In this respect, the rejection of the recommendations of the Black Report by a Conservative government stands in contrast to the willingness of a Labour government to change the principles of NHS resource allocation in the light of evidence about continuing inequalities in the distribution of the budget between regions.

Data on the performance of the NHS demonstrate improvements in health and health care since its inception. Nevertheless, there are a number of inequities in access to services affecting different geographical areas, social classes and care groups. Of particular importance in the recent history of the NHS have been waiting lists and waiting times for treatment. The ability of some people to avoid NHS queues by paying to go private is one of the most obvious inequities in the United Kingdom health care system, and the priority given to improving access and increasing patient choice is an attempt to address this. Successive governments have sought to reduce waiting lists and waiting times and the available data indicate significant progress in this regard.

The wider question raised by this chapter is whether the audit explosion and the growth of regulation signal a fundamental change to the management of the NHS. At the time of writing, audit and regulation have been overlaid on a system that retains many of the traditional characteristics of hierarchical control and performance management that were discussed in the previous chapter. Not only this, but also many of the features of the discarded internal market have reappeared in a new guise. The result is a complex mix of performance management, regulation and competition. The establishment of the Healthcare Commission and the policy of shifting the balance of power within the NHS, together with the entry of new providers and the introduction of a system of paying providers by results, seems to herald the emergence of a regulated system in which less reliance is placed on performance management. As we discuss in the final chapter, it may be that regulation through the Care Quality Commission and Monitor will become more significant in the future.

Chapter 11

Power in Health Services

Our examination of the auditing and evaluation of health policy and the NHS in Chapter 10 revealed various inequalities in health and health services. Explaining the distribution of benefits within health services requires us to ask: who controls those services and who influences the allocation of resources? A number of macro theoretical approaches have been developed in an attempt to answer these questions. These approaches range from pluralist theories that focus on the role of pressure groups through structuralist approaches that analyse the interests that systematically gain or lose from the organisation of health services to Marxist theories that emphasise class divisions within society.

Alongside these macro theoretical approaches, health policy analysts have made use of a number of middle range theories of the dynamics of policy-making in seeking to understand the distribution of power in health services. These middle range theories include those that emphasise the path dependent nature of policy-making, work that focuses on agenda setting, and approaches that highlight the role of institutions in explaining policy outcomes. We have drawn on these theories at various points to illuminate the complexities of health policy in Britain. The core argument of this chapter is that the explanatory power of these middle range theories needs to be located within the perspective offered by macro theoretical approaches. This includes linking different levels of analysis and exploring how health care institutions may themselves shape the structure and functions of the state.

Pluralist theories

The essence of the pluralist democratic theory of power is that the resources which contribute to power are widely distributed among different groups. As we noted in Chapter 6, pluralists argue that no one group is dominant, and each is able to exercise some influence (see for example Dahl, 1961). Power is in fact shared between official groups in governmental agencies and outside interests exerting pressure on these agencies. This helps to ensure there is no consistent bias in the allocation of values, although pluralists would recognise that groups vary in their ability to exercise power. Developments in health services and health policy are explained in terms of the interplay between pressure groups. Since there is no dominant interest, pluralists analyse the distribution of power in relation to particular issues, studying who wins and who loses through often detailed examination of the preferences of different interests and the extent to which decisions match up with expressed preferences. The question of who has power is an empirical question for the pluralists, to be answered by means of case studies of particular policy areas. A range of factors may be important, including party manifestos, key individuals, official reports and the activities of pressure groups, but their relative influence must be studied in specific cases.

Examples of studies of the NHS which have their roots in the pluralist democratic tradition are Willcocks' (1967) examination of the creation of the NHS and Eckstein's (1960) analysis of the operation of the BMA. Each author analyses the way in which decisions are reached in a system of pressure group politics, and each is able to show how the outcomes were the result of compromise between the various interests involved. Professional interests vie with consumer interests, and civil servants with politicians, but alliances change, leading to the fragmentation of power which pluralists observe. The strength of pluralist theory is the richness of detail provided about decision-making and the high degree of sophistication which has often been achieved in the analysis of individual, group and organisational influences on policy processes.

However, pluralism does not provide a completely adequate theory of power. For example, in earlier chapters we noted the key position occupied by the medical profession in the organisation of health services, and our discussion of how policies are made and implemented in the NHS suggests certain inadequacies in the pluralist position. In particular, the strength of producer groups and the relative weakness of consumer groups cast doubt on the pluralists' argument that any group can make itself heard effectively at some stage in the decision-making process, and that no group is dominant (Ham, 1977). Accordingly, attention needs to be paid to the work of Alford, who has maintained that it is important to analyse the nature of structural interests within health services.

Structuralist approaches

Alford argues that structural interests are those interests which gain or lose from the form of organisation of health services (Alford, 1975a). There are three sets of structural interests: dominant, challenging and repressed. Dominant interests are the professional monopolists; challenging interests are the corporate rationalisers; and repressed interests are the community population. Dominant interests are served by existing social, economic and political institutions, and therefore only need to be active when their interests are challenged. Alford argues that the medical profession is dominant in health services, but the profession may be challenged by corporate rationalisers such as health planners and administrators. Again, patient and consumer groups representing the community population may seek to move out of their repressed position by organising to articulate their interests. These struggles between structural interests are not the same as the competition for power between pressure groups. Pressure group competition may well take place within structural interests, as between, for example, different groups of doctors. These conflicts are important, but they leave unchallenged the principle of professional monopoly and dominance. Pressure group politics coexist with struggles between structural interests, and may explain how particular issues are resolved. Structural interests are, however, more significant in influencing the overall distribution of benefits, and in shaping the main contours of power relationships.

The value of Alford's framework has been demonstrated in a study of policy-making in the NHS (Ham, 1981), and the inequalities in power he highlights indicate a position close to elitist interpretations of the power structure. In the health sector, professional control of knowledge, recruitment and training, as well as claims to professional autonomy over the content of work, provide the basis of the medical profession's power. Its organisation through powerful pressure groups in continuous contact with governmental agencies, coupled with involvement at all stages in the system of administration, enhance this power. Structuralist approaches recognise the existence of pressure group politics but contend that studies which remain at the level of groups are incomplete.

Marxist theories

A different approach is offered by Marxists who argue that medical care in societies like Britain must be seen as part of the capitalist mode of production (Doyal, with Pennell, 1979). Within capitalism, Marxists contend that there is an important division between the owners of the means of production and those who have to sell their wage labour. It is the capitalist mode of production which gives rise to class relations of production, and Marxists go on to argue that the economically dominant class is also politically dominant. The state therefore acts in the long-term interests of the dominant class, and performs a number of functions.

In O'Connor's terms, the state assists in the process of capital accumulation, and also performs the function of legitimation (O'Connor, 1973).

State expenditures are directed towards these ends, and are made up of social capital and social expenses. State expenditures on health services comprise partly social capital, in so far as health services involve the reproduction of a healthy labour force, and partly they comprise social expenses, in so far as health services help to maintain non-working groups and promote social harmony. State involvement in the provision of health services stems from two sources: action by the dominant class to reduce the costs of labour power and to prevent social unrest; and action by the subordinate class to win concessions. However, Marxists argue that there may develop a fiscal crisis for the state when the demand for expenditure on health services outstrips the ability of the state to fund that expenditure. At this point a restructuring of public expenditure may occur to the disadvantage of state health services. Marxists would interpret this as an attack on the interests of the subordinate class, even though health services are seen as a form of social control (Gough, 1979).

Within this theoretical perspective, inequalities in service provision between client groups are explained in terms of the lack of productivity of the mentally ill, people with learning disabilities and older people. It is suggested that because these groups cannot make a significant contribution to the development of the economy, they will receive a lower quality service than productive groups. Similarly, social class inequalities in health are interpreted by Marxists as evidence of the continuing influence of economic factors on health and the persistence of class divisions within society. The distribution of benefits within health services is therefore explained by reference to class conflict.

At a macro level of analysis a number of authors have used Marxist theory to explain developments in health policy. Yet a convincing theory of power must also be able to explain the processes of policy-making and implementation described in Chapters 8 and 9. Marxist approaches are much weaker at this level of analysis, and Marxist studies of particular decisions, issues or health care organisations are little developed. In contrast, pluralist theories, with their focus on the role of pressure groups and bargaining and negotiation within policy communities, offer a range of insights into the dynamics of health policy-making, while structuralist theories provide a way of explaining differences in influence between pressure groups. This suggests that what is required is an approach which builds on the strength of each of the theoretical positions discussed here.

The key issue, then, is to develop 'mediating frameworks to connect macro-theory with specific policy issues' (Dunleavy, 1981, p. 4). One approach to this is through the examination of dominant value systems in particular policy areas and their influence on policy. More specifically, by analysing the operation of professional ideologies in health services, it may be possible to establish links between the way issues are defined and resources allocated, the nature of structural interests and the distribution of power, and macro theories of the state (Ham, 1980). The difficulties of doing this are considerable, but a start can be made by exploring the role of the medical profession and the way in which the profession's view of health has come to occupy a dominant position.

Concepts of health

There are many different concepts of health. Margaret Stacey has identified three dimensions along which these concepts vary: individual or collective; functional fitness or welfare; preventative or curative (Stacey, 1977). Stacey notes that in Western societies the individualistic concept of health tends to dominate, and it is usually associated with ideas of functional fitness and curative approaches. This concept seeks the causes of illness within the biological systems of individuals, and it attempts to provide a specific cure for illness in order to make individuals fit for work. Alongside the individualistic concept of health, Stacey notes the existence of a collective concept which emphasises the importance of prevention. The collective concept seeks the causes of illnesses within the environmental, economic and social systems in which people live, and attempts to prevent illness arising by tackling the unhealthy aspects of those systems. Stacey also notes the existence of a welfare concept of health, emphasising the importance of relieving pain and providing care.

While these concepts coexist, it is the individualistic, functional fitness, curative approach which is the most influential. This approach has been characterised as the medical model of health, a model in which doctors have a central role and hospitals play a major part. It has been suggested that the model has two components: a disease component, which holds that illness results from pathological processes in the biochemical functions of the body; and an engineering component, which sees the body as a machine to be repaired by technical means (Illsley, 1977). The medical model emphasises specific, individual causes of illness and searches for specific individual cures for these illnesses. Acceptance of the medical model is important, first, in justifying the pre-eminent position of the medical profession in health matters, and second, in helping to explain the pattern of investment in health services. Within the NHS, the bulk of resources is allocated to personally oriented, general and acute hospital services. Much less importance has been attached to collective, preventative and welfare approaches to health.

Using a historical perspective, Fox (1986) has shown how the medical model replaced the collective concept of health in the early decades of the twentieth century. As a consequence, the focus of health policy shifted from public health measures and the relief of poverty to the organisation of medical services. Fox uses the phrase 'hierarchical regionalism' to describe the principles on which health policy evolved. These principles include the view that the causes of illness and disease are discovered in medical schools. For most of the twentieth century, a key aim of policy has been to ensure that the results of medical science are made available to the population through hierarchies of services organised on a regional basis. In these hierarchies, specialist hospital services play a major part.

Alternative approaches, such as those emphasising the social and environmental influences on health, have received less attention. However, this may be changing as the medical model comes under increasing challenge. The challenge to medical dominance in the health field has been spearheaded by writers such as McKeown, who have questioned the significance of the medical contribution in bringing about improvements in health. McKeown's work has demonstrated that improved nutrition, purer water supplies, behavioural changes limiting family size and leading to the better spacing of births, and improved methods of sewage disposal, have been mainly responsible for the advances in health which have occurred in the past 200 years. These factors contributed to the decline in infectious diseases, and assisted in reducing death rates and increasing life expectancy. In contrast, medical science had very little impact until the introduction of vaccines and certain drugs in the twentieth century. Yet McKeown argues that even these interventions came at a time when overall death rates were already in decline as a result of earlier environmental and behavioural changes. On the basis of his analysis, McKeown contends that:

> medical science and services are misdirected, and society's investment in health is not well used, because they rest on an erroneous assumption about the basis of human health. It is assumed that the body can be regarded as a machine whose protection from disease and its effects depends primarily on internal intervention. The approach has led to indifference to the external influences and personal behaviour which are the predominant determinants of health. (McKeown, 1976, p. xiv)

McKeown's work has had a major influence in the development of the health field concept articulated by Lalonde (1974). This concept analyses illness and disease in terms of four elements: human biology, the environment, lifestyle and health care organisation. Human biology includes aspects of health, such as ageing, which are developed within the body as a result of the basic biology of man. The environment comprises matters relating to health external to the body, over which the individual has little or no control. Lifestyle refers to the decisions by individuals which affect health and over which they have control. And health care organisation consists of the arrangements made to provide organised health services to individuals. Like McKeown, Lalonde suggests that while most efforts to improve health have centred on medical interventions through health care organisation, it is the other three elements which are more important in identifying the causes of sickness and death. In particular, Lalonde points to the need for people to adopt healthy lifestyles in order to prevent illness arising.

This is very much in line with the policy on public health adopted by the government in the 1970s. As we noted in Chapter 4, the DHSS used the work of people like McKeown to argue that greater emphasis should be given to prevention, and that individuals should look after themselves by giving up smoking, adopting an appropriate diet, taking exercise and so on. This individualistic approach to prevention does not seriously threaten the medical model, and it has been criticised for 'blaming the victim'. A growing body of research indicates that life-style may be less significant than the environment (defined as the social, economic and cultural factors that have a bearing on health) in influencing illness and disease and that a collective approach to health is needed if progress is to be made in tackling contemporary health problems. This was the argument of the Black Report and other studies have drawn attention to the industrial and environmental causes of cancer (Doyal and Epstein, 1983), the impact of unemployment on health (Brenner, 1979), and to the various ways in which the processes of production, distribution and consumption contribute to illness and disease (Draper et al., 1977). These studies constitute a significant challenge to the medical model, not least because they imply a reduced role for doctors, and they have begun to influence health policy. In particular, as we noted in Chapter 10, policies to tackle health inequalities adopted since 1997 have included actions directed at the broader determinants of health. It must be added, though, that medicine has remained remarkably resilient in the face of criticism, and continues to provide the dominant explanation of health problems in contemporary Western societies.

What are the implications of this analysis for the earlier discussion of power in health care systems? What we hope to have shown is that the medical model, as the dominant (though not the only) value system in the health field, exercises a key influence on the definition of issues and the allocation of resources. The question this raises is whose interests are served by the medical model? Stacey (1977) has reminded us that concepts do not stand alone, they must be understood in terms of the power of different groups. Let us then return to the examination of theories of power for help in explaining the dominance of the medical model.

Power, interests and ideology

In the pluralist framework, concepts of health and the role of medicine are not seen as having special significance. The medical profession is viewed as one interest among many, albeit in most studies a key interest; and concepts of health are implicitly assumed to have emerged out of the underlying consensus on which pluralist theories are based. Within this consensus, prevailing concepts of health are no more than a reflection of the shifting balance of power between interests. The fact that they have remained the same over time is seen by pluralists as an indication of the large measure of agreement between these interests on the meaning of health and the manner in which services should be provided. The question that needs to be asked about this interpretation is whether the consensus which pluralists observe is genuine or false. In other words, is the consensus the result of spontaneous agreement among different groups in the population, or does it derive from manipulation by dominant groups?

This question is not easily resolved. Pluralists would argue that people's expressed preferences are the only reliable guide to their interests, and the fact that these preferences demonstrate strong support for the medical profession is in itself sufficient to show that the consensus on values is genuine. In contrast, critics of pluralism would argue that people's real interests may differ from their expressed preferences, in which case the possibility of a false consensus being manipulated by dominant groups cannot be ruled out. The problem with this approach is how to establish the existence of real interests which are different from expressed preferences (Saunders, 1979). One line of analysis in the health field would be to develop McKeown's work, which, as we have noted, has suggested that society's investment in health is not well-used because it is based on the medical model. What this indicates is that people's real interests might be better served by an alternative pattern of investment. That is, improved health might result from a reorientation away from personally oriented, hospital-based health care towards a system in which more emphasis was given to the social causes of illness and disease. If this could be demonstrated, then a rather different explanation of the interests served by dominant concepts of health would be needed.

Such an explanation is provided by structuralists. For structuralists, dominant concepts of health serve the interests of the medical profession because they legitimate the profession's claim to control in health services. In other words, prevailing concepts of health are explained by the position of the medical profession as a dominant structural interest and its success in getting individualistic definitions of illness and disease accepted. The dominance of medicine is in turn explained historically in terms of the success of physicians, surgeons and apothecaries in winning state approval for their position, and in turning their occupations into professions having exclusive control over their area of work (Wilding, 1982; Stacey, 1992). Medical dominance does not imply a conspiracy against subordinate groups. Rather, it reflects the power of doctors, their control of key resources such as expertise and knowledge, and their ability to achieve acceptance for their own concept of health. This concept of health makes sense to groups in the population other than doctors, but as we have shown, it is not the only concept, and it is not necessarily the concept which best serves the interests of the population.

Like structuralists, Marxists would challenge the pluralists' position that consensus is genuine, but would see dominant concepts of health not as an indication of the power of the medical profession, but as evidence of the control exercised by the dominant class. In particular, Marxists argue that the individual, disease-based model of curative medicine helps to maintain the position of dominant groups by masking the real causes of illness which lie within the social and economic system of capitalism. As Navarro has put it:

> the social utility of medicine is measured primarily in the arena of legitimation. Medicine is indeed socially useful to the degree that the majority of people believe and accept the proposition that what are actually politically caused conditions can be individually solved by medical intervention. From the point of view of the capitalist system, this is the actual utility of medicine – it contributes to the legitimation of capitalism. (Navarro, 1976, p. 208)

For Marxists, the medical model is a key linking concept explaining not only how issues are defined and benefits distributed in the policy process, but also highlighting underlying class divisions within society. The conclusion to be drawn from the Marxist analysis is that the prevailing concept of health serves class interests, that power is weighted heavily in favour of those interests, and that doctors, although seemingly in a powerful position, merely administer the health care system on behalf of dominant groups.

It thus emerges that Marxists and structuralists see different interests being served by dominant concepts of health. Structuralists argue that the medical profession has power in its own right, not simply power deriving from its utility to dominant groups. In contrast, Marxists argue that medical power results from class power. The Marxist position is well summarised by Navarro, who criticises writers such as Alford for:

> their failure to recognise that those elites (for example medicine) are in reality segments of a dominant class and that, when they are consid-

ered in a systemic and not just a sectorial fashion, they are found to possess a high degree of cohesion and solidarity, with common interests and common purposes for transcending their specific differences and disagreements. (Navarro, 1976, pp. 189–90)

The question which needs to be raised about this argument is whether all conflicts are 'in reality' class conflicts, and if so how disagreements between the state and the medical profession can be explained. A key theme of this book has been the challenge to medical dominance in the NHS since the 1980s as politicians have questioned the autonomy of doctors and have pursued policies which have been strongly opposed by the BMA and other interest groups. In the final section of this chapter we analyse the significance of these developments and what they tell us about power in health services.

Theories and practice

The underlying determinism of Marxist approaches has increasingly been challenged by writers who have pointed to developments in policy and practice which cannot adequately be explained by these approaches. Saunders, for example, has argued that state expenditure on health services may be dysfunctional rather than automatically serving the interests of dominant groups (Saunders, 1981). The fiscal crisis of the state that began in the 1970s has illustrated the importance of Saunders' criticism, and has indicated that while expenditure on areas of collective consumption like the NHS may benefit professional interests, it may be against the interests of dominant groups, whose main purpose is to maintain capital accumulation. A similar point is made by Cawson (1982) who argues that the growth of public expenditure has been fuelled by the bargaining processes between the state and producer groups. Cawson explains this in terms of the development of a corporate sector in the British political system in which producer groups like the BMA are intimately involved both in the making of policy and its implementation. Cawson predicts that expenditure cuts will be resisted by producer groups and that governments faced with a fiscal crisis will seek to reduce the burden of public expenditure by privatising services.

Although this has happened in some policy areas, a comparative study of welfare reform in the USA and the United Kingdom (Pierson, 1994) has highlighted the political difficulties in cutting back public services, including health care, and has shown how governments used a variety of indirect strategies to bring about change rather than risk confrontation and electoral unpopularity. These strategies were pursued in part because of the strength of existing bureaucratic and professional institutions and their ability to resist change. Health policy in Britain in the 1980s and 1990s exemplifies this and demonstrates that the response to the fiscal crisis that developed at that time was mediated by the influence of pressure groups and other interests. While there was some growth in the contribution of the private health sector in this period, privatisation of NHS services was limited to non-clinical areas such as catering, cleaning and laundry services which were opened up to competitive tendering, and increases in charges for prescriptions, dental care and ophthalmic services. The indirect strategies pursued were of greater significance and included the use of private finance to pay for new capital projects, the unannounced transfer of long-term care from the NHS to social services and to private funders and providers, and the use of private hospitals for the treatment of some NHS patients. These policies all stemmed from a concern to control public expenditure at a time when changes in the economy and in political alignments undermined the post-war consensus on the expansion of the welfare state and led to the examination of more radical alternatives. From this perspective, many of the most important effects of health reform result from policy drift rather than bold initiatives taken by governments in what has been described as 'change without reform' (Hacker, 2004, p. 693).

Further evidence of the limits to state-led reform can be found in the policies of the Thatcher government which considered but rejected moving away from tax funding of the NHS to private funding both because of the political costs associated with such a move and evidence that alternative methods of funding appeared to offer little benefit. In other words, the fiscal crisis that prompted a review of policy did not lead automatically to the response predicted by some analysts. Rather, the eventual outcome represented a compromise between the ideological instincts of politicians in power and their assessment of what was feasible and desirable. It was this that led the Thatcher government to focus on ways of increasing efficiency and of curtailing professional power. In so doing, the government had to overcome the objections of the BMA and related organisations and it had to persuade civil servants in the Department of Health to support policies that unsettled established routines in the health policy community. To this extent, corporatist relationships in the health sector made it more difficult for a reforming government of the centre-right to pursue those policies that it instinctively favoured. The reforms that were adopted did have some impact on the NHS and relationships between different interests, but the path dependent nature of health policy meant that government policies were adapted in the course of implementation and were less radical in their effects than politicians expected or hoped (Wilsford, 1994; Bevan and Robinson, 2005).

In relation to health services, the reforms initiated since the Griffiths Report can be seen as an attempt to strengthen the hand of managers in their challenge to medical dominance. The appointment of general managers, and the call for doctors to be more closely involved in management, were both designed to introduce greater control over the activities of the medical profession and to influence the behaviour of consultants in their position as the key influencers of resources in the NHS. What is more, the recommendation in the Griffiths Report that arrangements for public consultation on decisions should be streamlined was interpreted by some observers as an attempt to maintain community interests in their repressed position. As Day and Klein noted at the time, one of the implications was that conflict between managers and professionals was more likely to occur, particularly if clinical freedom was questioned and challenged (Day and Klein, 1983). Coincidentally, publication of the Griffiths Report occurred within days of a claim that clinical freedom had died, 'crushed between the rising costs of new forms of investigation and treatment and the financial limits inevitable in an economy that cannot expand indefinitely' (Hampton, 1983, p. 1238). While this obituary appeared premature, the medical profession was not slow to recognise the threat posed by Griffiths and to argue that doctors should take on the general management role whenever possible.

In practice, the appointment of doctors as general managers was the exception rather than the rule, and the introduction of general management did lead to a more active management style in which managers were increasingly involved in questioning medical priorities (Flynn, 1991). The extent to which this resulted in a shift in the frontier of control between managers and doctors is disputed with the balance of evidence maintaining that change was limited. To quote Harrison, who has made an extensive study of general management:

> the basic sources of (in Alford's terms) the doctors' structural monopoly remain unchanged. It is still general practitioners who provide the selection for consultants to work on. It is still consultants who decide which, and how many patients to see, and how to diagnose and treat them ... The prime determinant of the pattern of the health services is still, just as before Griffiths, what doctors choose to do. (Harrison, 1988, p. 123)

The Griffiths reforms were taken a stage further by *Working for Patients*. The White Paper built on the introduction of general management and sought to reinforce measures already taken to increase the accountability of the medical profession. As a consequence, general managers took part in the appointment of hospital consultants, negotiated job plans with each consultant, and participated in deciding which consultants should receive distinction awards. In parallel, new disciplinary procedures were introduced for hospital doctors, the resource management initiative was extended throughout the NHS, and clinical audit received higher priority.

The separation of purchaser and provider responsibilities and the introduction of contracts posed a further challenge to medical dominance. The establishment of health authorities and GP fundholders as purchasers created a countervailing power to established interests in NHS trusts, and over time this had an impact on priority-setting and resource allocation. To some degree, the effect was to shift influence within the medical profession, for example between hospital doctors and GPs, and to some degree it enhanced the role of managers in relation to doctors. These reforms also created new hybrid roles in which doctors, particularly GPs, adopted some of the characteristics of corporate rationalisers by assuming responsibility for budgets as fundholders and by taking on management roles within primary care trusts (North, 1995; North and Peckham, 2001). Again, though, the impact of these changes should not be exaggerated. Just as with the introduction of general management, the effect on roles and relationships within the NHS was complex as patterns of pluralistic bargaining among doctors mediated the implementation of these changes and defeated attempts to explain their impact from any single perspective. Put another way, while the relative position of structural interests changed only at the margins, there were shifts *within* each set of interests which had an influence on policy-making, and a blurring of the categories identified by Alford in his analysis. Because of this, it is difficult to sustain Wilsford's contention that:

> Mrs Thatcher used the strong structural levers of the British political system and the NHS to fundamentally transform health care delivery in the United Kingdom, doing so against fairly well mobilised providers. (Wilsford, 1995, p. 603)

The policies pursued by the Blair government elected in 1997 have also sought to make doctors more accountable for their performance. These policies build on both general management and the separation of purchaser and provider responsibilities and focus particularly on the introduction of new forms of regulation to raise standards within the NHS. Specifically, doctors are required to take part in clinical audit and to work within the guidelines set at a national level by the National Institute for Health and Clinical Excellence. The work of the Care Quality Commission provides a means of independent examination of performance, and the publication of comparative data on clinical outcomes marks the beginning of an attempt to open up variations in standards to public scrutiny. The genesis of these policies lies in part in examples of failures of clinical performance within the NHS, but it is also the latest manifestation of a long-term trend to enhance professional accountability. In examining this trend, Moran (1999) notes that the relationship between government and professionals has traditionally been characterised by state sanctioned self-regulation, and he describes this as 'pre-democratic'. Reforms to the way in which professionals are governed have resulted from social and cultural changes, including the emergence of a more demanding and less deferential public. As a consequence:

> closely integrated oligarchies dominated by professional and corporate interests, operating with a substantial degree of independence from the core institutions of the state, are being replaced: by looser, more open, more unstable networks; by networks in which professional and corporate elites still exercise great power but in a more contested environment than hitherto; and by an institutional setting in which the core institutions of the state exercise much tighter surveillance and control than hitherto. (Moran, 1999, p. 178)

As this observation makes clear, the private government of standards by the medical profession has come under challenge with the state acting in response to changing social attitudes to strengthen accountability. Despite this, it would be wrong to argue that state power has replaced medical power. As Salter (2007) has shown, government and the medical profession circled around each other on the reform of medical regulation, and only at the end of a lengthy process of consultation and debate were significant changes introduced (see Chapter 10). In Alford's terms, dominant structural interests retain considerable power with corporatist patterns of policy-making coexisting with the more open pluralist arrangements described by Moran. Klein puts the point rather differently, arguing that the medical profession has lost much of its traditional influence in the policy-making process, but it remains powerful because of the role of doctors in implementation (Klein, 2006, p. 263).

In the process, the state's role in health policy-making has increased, but it would be too simple to see relationships between actors in zero-sum terms. Health policy in Britain has been characterised by more active government, increased lobbying by groups representing patients and the public, and a medical profession that has retained a position of considerable power and influence in the face of unprecedented questioning. Also important has been the enhanced role taken on by managers, often acting as agents of government, and expected to challenge doctors in implementing government policies. As we noted in Chapter 9, the challenge for managers in these circumstances was to lead the implementation of government policies without alienating the medical profession, and again this reinforced attempts to involve doctors themselves more effectively in management. The global financial crisis that emerged in 2007 brought into sharp relief the dynamics of power within the NHS, and held out the prospect that the corporate rationalisers, represented by politicians and managers, would once again be put in the position of challenging the professional monopolists to use resources more efficiently at a time when NHS funding was more constrained than at any time in its history.

While this chapter has emphasised the need to locate changes in health services in their wider social, economic and political context, there are occasions when health care institutions may themselves shape the structure and functions of the state. At a time when health services consume a large and often growing share of national income in most developed countries, the actions of policy-makers and the organisations in which they operate are increasingly influenced by the dynamics of health services. Under the Blair government, this was exemplified by the close involvement of the Prime Minister and the Chancellor of the Exchequer in health policy and the commitment made by the government to unprecedented increases in NHS funding. This commitment had a significant impact on other spending programmes by pre-empting resources that might have been used in alternative ways, and led to changes in the machinery of government as the Treasury and No. 10 Downing Street set up new forms of scrutiny, like public service agreements and the Prime Minister's Delivery Unit, to review how resources were being used (see Chapter 6). Debate about creating greater independence for the NHS by distancing politicians from its day-to-day management is a further indication of the impact of health care institutions on the structure of the state. This debate arose in 2007 and attracted interest from both think tanks and politicians as a potential solution to the problem of the NHS being dominated by a target driven culture (see Chapter 12). Understanding the *reciprocal* relationship between health services and the state is therefore an increasingly important area of analysis for students of health policy.

Conclusion

At first sight, pluralist theories offer a convincing explanation of the distribution of power within health services. After all, the NHS comprises a large number of different groups competing for resources, and most decisions result from bargaining between these groups. Furthermore, health policies tend to involve small adjustments to what has gone before, and a variety of interests are often involved in policy-making. This is in part the picture which has emerged from the discussion of health policy-making and implementation in earlier chapters, and it fits the description of political activity put forward in the pluralist model.

Marxist theories challenge the assumptions behind pluralism and provide an alternative explanation. Instead of focusing on immediate conflicts between pressure groups, Marxists seek to relate health care systems to the economic systems within which they are located. By analysing the underlying processes at work, Marxists argue that health services are shaped by dominant groups, whose interests are served by prevailing concepts of health and illness. Health services help to legitimate capitalism and to promote capital accumulation. Pluralists are unable to perceive this because they concentrate on surface struggles and neglect deeper class conflicts. Furthermore, pluralists take dominant concepts of health for granted, and do not question seriously the beneficial impact of medicine or the possibility that conflict may be limited to a narrow range of issues through ideological domination.

In contrast to both approaches, Alford's theory of structural interests looks beyond the surface politics of pressure group conflicts and finds not class struggle but professional dominance. This approach recognises that the world of everyday politics may well approximate to pluralist theories, but it goes further to identify wide discrepancies in power in relation to dominant, challenging and repressed structural interests. Alternative concepts of health are acknowledged to exist, and prevailing concepts reflect the ability of dominant groups to get their definitions accepted. Within this framework, it is possible to encompass both the strengths of pluralist theory, recognising the diversity and variety of pressure group behaviour, and some of the insights of the Marxist analysis, acknowledging that what appears to be going on may obscure underlying conflicts between key interests.

It is suggested, then, that future work might usefully build on this framework and seek to further explicate the 'problematic and contingent' (Alford, 1975b, p. 153) nature of relationships between individual and group action on particular issues of health policy, the role of structural interests, and the characteristics of the state. Our earlier analysis of professional ideologies in the health care system provided some hints on how this might be done, and further empirical studies are required. Above all, it is the interaction of the different levels of analysis which is in need of further investigation. Sophisticated studies of specific policy issues need to be related to the action and inaction of structural interests and the changing role and functions of the state (nationally and internationally) if a complete understanding of the complexities of health policy is to be obtained. This includes testing the explanatory power of different middle range theories of the policy-making process, recognising that a number of different approaches are likely to be helpful in accounting for the formulation and implementation of health policies (Klein, 1995, 2006; Greener, 2002).

Harrison's analysis of the introduction of general management into the NHS (Harrison, 1994) has illustrated how a variety of theoretical perspectives can help to explain particular initiatives, thereby paving the way for other studies. As we argued at the beginning of the book, individuals and groups may have an impact on policy, but under conditions not of their own choosing. This has been demonstrated by Smith (1999) in his analysis of power within government, and Smith's contention that actors are central but are constrained by context and structure reinforces these arguments. Articulating the relationship between action and structure is therefore of the utmost importance, and the discussion in this chapter has pointed to some directions in which work might proceed. This includes exploring the way in which actors influence structure as well as vice versa.

Chapter 12

Looking Back and Looking Ahead

In this chapter, we look back at the achievements of the NHS and look ahead to the challenges it faces in the future. The chapter begins by asking, how good is the NHS? A variety of data sources are used including information that compares the performance of the NHS with that of health care systems in other countries. This includes comparing population health outcomes as an indicator of the effectiveness of public health policies. The chapter then moves on to review information about patient and public attitudes. This leads into discussion of options for the future in relation to the organisation and management of services and the funding of health care. In this section, the role of hierarchies, markets and networks is considered, as is the contribution of private health care provision. The future funding of health care is also discussed in a context in which demand seems certain to increase as a result of demographic changes, rising public expectations and medical advances. This presents challenges in relation to priority-setting or rationing and the prospects for the NHS are considered against the backdrop of experience in other health care systems. The chapter concludes by turning to political futures and the policy options that have been advanced by the main political parties for the further reform of the NHS.

How good is the NHS?

The sixtieth anniversary of the founding of the NHS in July 2008 provided an occasion for commentators to take stock of the achievements of the NHS in relation to its objectives (as examples see the series of articles by Delamothe (2008) and the collection of papers edited by Timmins (2008a)). One of the areas in which the NHS performs well in comparison with some other countries is in having removed or reduced the costs of medical care for patients. Survey data show that far fewer people in the United Kingdom report that they did not visit a doctor, take out a prescription or undertake a test or treatment because of cost than in Australia, Canada, Germany, New Zealand and the United States (Schoen et al., 2005). This has been interpreted as 'an indication that service provision is equitable across different income groups' (Leatherman and Sutherland, 2008, p. 238) in the

United Kingdom, notwithstanding the evidence summarised in Chapter 10. In taking away the fear of how to meet the costs of medical care during sickness, the NHS has succeeded in creating the sense of serenity that Aneurin Bevan aspired to at its inception. This has not been lost on overseas observers, especially those from the United States, who continue to draw attention to the achievement of the United Kingdom in providing the whole population with access to more or less comprehensive services that are largely free at the point of use, thereby avoiding the inequities which are so much a feature of health care across the Atlantic.

The annual international health policy surveys carried out by the Commonwealth Fund provide evidence on other aspects of performance such as the experience of patients with complex health care needs, the experience of sicker adults, and the experience of primary care physicians. In a report published in 2007, the Commonwealth Fund brought together the results from different surveys to compare the performance of six countries on a number of dimensions, namely quality of care, access, efficiency, equity, healthy lives and health expenditures (Davis et al., 2007). The results showed that the United States ranked last among this group of countries and the United Kingdom ranked first (see Figure 12.1). The areas of performance in which the United Kingdom did least well were access, defined as waiting for an appointment, and patient-centred care (see below). It is notable that in this survey the United Kingdom had moved into first position from third place in 2006 and in 2004. One interpretation of these findings is that the programme of investment and reform pursued by the Blair and Brown governments was having an effect. This is confirmed by the findings of the British Social Attitudes' Survey, discussed later in this chapter.

The findings of the Commonwealth Fund's surveys can be contrasted with the assessment of health system performance undertaken by the World Health Organization (WHO) in 2000. The WHO sought to rank countries along a number of dimensions including the health of the population, responsiveness to the population, and fairness of financial contribution. On this basis, the United Kingdom was ranked 18 out of 191 countries, lower than France which came out first but higher than Sweden, Germany and Denmark (WHO, 2000). The United Kingdom scored particularly well on fairness of financial contribution, a finding that is consistent with other research on equity of health financing (Wagstaff et al., 1999) and with the Commonwealth Fund's surveys reported above. By comparison, the United Kingdom scored less well on responsiveness to the population. In interpreting these results, it should be noted that the WHO's methods and data for assessing performance have been heavily criticised (Musgrove, 2003), and they should therefore be used with caution. It should also be noted that the WHO used data from the 1990s that do not reflect improvements to the NHS that have occurred since then.

Figure 12.1 *The Commonwealth Fund's ranking of health system performance, 2007*

	Australia	Canada	Germany	New Zealand	United Kingdom	United States
Overall Ranking (2007)	3.5	5	2	3.5	1	6
Quality Care	4	6	2.5	2.5	1	5
Right Care	5	6	3	4	2	1
Safe Care	4	5	1	3	2	6
Coordinated Care	3	6	4	2	1	5
Patient-Centered Care	3	6	2	1	4	5
Access	3	5	1	2	4	6
Efficiency	4	5	3	2	1	6
Equity	2	5	4	3	1	6
Healthy Lives	1	3	2	4.5	4.5	6
Health Expenditures per Capita, 2004	$2,876*	$3,165	$3,005*	$2,083	$2,546	$6,102

Note: Rankings range from 1 (highest) to 6 (lowest)

* 2003 data

Source: Calculated by the Commonwealth Fund based on the Commonwealth Fund 2004 International Health Policy Survey, the Commonwealth Fund 2005 International Health Policy Survey of Sicker Adults, the 2006 Commonwealth Fund International Health Policy Survey of Primary Care Physicians, and the Commonwealth Fund Commission on a High Performance Health System National Scorecard.

International comparisons have only recently started to examine the quality of care provided in different systems. Work in this area has been led by the Commonwealth Fund and the Organisation for Economic Cooperation and Development (OECD) and has focused on developing a list of indicators of quality and ensuring comparability of data. Studies that have compared the performance of the NHS with that of other countries, such as those commissioned by the Nuffield Trust (Leatherman and Sutherland, 2008), have made increasing use of these indicators. Typical indicators include survival rates of people diagnosed with cancer, screening rates, hospital mortality rates within 30 days of admission for stroke and heart attack, treatment of people with diabetes and flu vaccination rates (Armseto et al., 2007). The results show that individual countries tend to perform better on some indicators than others with little evidence of any country doing consistently well (Hussey et al., 2004). Data on quality comparisons are of value in showing a number of areas in which the United Kingdom can improve its performance relative to other countries, including cancer survival rates and MRSA rates.

Linked to this work, there has also been analysis of outcomes in relation to a number of age-related diseases (OECD, 2003). This analysis
confirmed that the United Kingdom had lower survival rates following
breast cancer than the other countries included in the study and it also
showed that outcomes following heart attacks and stroke were relatively
poor. On the other hand, a review of the quality of care in Germany, the
United States and the United Kingdom conducted by McKinsey reported
that the UK performed well in the case of people with diabetes. This was
attributed to the greater use of patient self-management with more effective identification and treatment of people with severe diabetes (McKinsey Global Institute, 1996). These studies pre-date the new contract for
GPs which provided financial incentives to raise the standard of chronic
disease management in primary care and it is likely that performance in
this area of the NHS has continued to improve. Some evidence to support
this is found in a survey conducted in 2008 in a group of eight countries
showing that the quality of chronic care provided in the United Kingdom
compared well with experiences reported elsewhere with only the Netherlands appearing to perform better (Schoen et al., 2009).

Another way of examining the performance of the NHS is by comparing the health of the population with that of other countries. An analysis
carried out for the Wanless review of public health used routinely available data to compare England with Australia, Denmark, Canada, Finland,
France, Germany, the Netherlands and Sweden (Wanless, 2003b). The
analysis showed that, among this group of countries, life expectancy at
birth in England was lower for women than in any of the other countries
except Denmark. For men, the position was more favourable, with
England having better life expectancy at birth than Denmark, Finland
and Germany. In the case of another widely used measure of population
health, potential years of life lost before age 70, for men the United
Kingdom performed less well than Sweden, the Netherlands and Canada,
and for women less well than all countries except Denmark. The same
analysis showed that compared to other countries, England has relatively
high rates of death from respiratory diseases, circulatory disease, and, in
women, cancer. More positively, the rate of decline in premature deaths
(under the age of 65) from cancers and circulatory diseases in the United
Kingdom has been rapid since the 1990s. Despite this, an analysis of
trends in deaths amenable to medical intervention in 19 countries showed
that the United Kingdom ranked 16th in 2002/03 (Nolte and McKee,
2008), only a marginal improvement on its position in 1997/98, although
the rate of improvement was faster in the United Kingdom than in other
countries (Leatherman and Sutherland, 2008, p. 109).

Surveys carried out by the Picker Institute have provided insights
into patient experience in a number of countries. One study focused on

hospital patients and covered the United States, Germany, Sweden and Switzerland, as well as the United Kingdom, between 1998 and 2000. There were similarities between countries in the types of problems reported by patients, with continuity of care and transition being the most frequently reported. Other problems concerned information, emotional support, respect for patients' preferences, and involvement of family and friends. Overall, the highest satisfaction ratings were reported by patients in Switzerland and the lowest by patients in the United Kingdom (Coulter and Cleary, 2001). A more recent comparative survey of patient experience examined issues concerning communication, information, involvement and choice in eight countries (Coulter and Magee, 2003). Conducted during 2002, the survey found that patients in the United Kingdom were generally positive about their experiences. For example, the United Kingdom performed better than all other countries when patients were asked whether doctors gave them time to ask questions, listened to patients and gave clear explanations. The United Kingdom also ranked first when patients were asked whether doctors involved them as much as they wanted in decisions about their care. On the other hand, the United Kingdom performed much less well in relation to choice, ranking equal sixth on this aspect of patient experience.

Building on this work, Coulter (2006) has analysed data from the Commonwealth Fund's international health policy surveys carried out in 2004 and 2005 to compare the United Kingdom with the other countries included in the surveys (these were Australia, Canada, New Zealand and the United States in 2004, together with Germany in 2005). In some areas, the United Kingdom performed well, for example in relation to having access to alternative sources of information and advice such as NHS Direct and receiving reminders to participate in organised screening programmes. However, in most areas the results for the United Kingdom were worse than those for the other countries. Examples included providing patients undergoing surgery with information about the surgeon who carried out the operation and a choice of surgeons; offering patients opportunistic advice about weight, diet, exercise or stress reduction; involving patients in treatment decisions and informing them of the side effects of drugs; and patients having a treatment plan and support for self-management. Reviewing these findings, Coulter noted:

> None of the countries in the study excels in promoting patient engagement, but British patients receive less support from health professionals for engagement with their health care than those elsewhere. (Coulter, 2006, p. 5)

The other recent source of data is the Eurobarometer survey under-taken by the European Commission in 2007 to explore public attitudes to the health care systems in the 27 European Union countries (European Commission, 2007). In this survey, the United Kingdom performed better than the European Union average in public attitudes to the quality of hospital care, availability of and access to hospitals, and the affordability of hospital care. A different picture emerged in the case of dental care where the United Kingdom was below the European Union average in public attitudes to the quality of dental care and the availability of and access to dental care, although above the average for the affordability of dental care (suggesting that the increasing use of private financing to pay for dental services is not confined to the United Kingdom and indeed may be more significant in most other European Union countries). As far as medical and surgical specialists were concerned, there was a mixed picture with the United Kingdom below the European Union average in public attitudes to the quality of specialists, very close to the average in relation to availability of and access to specialists, and above average for the affordability of specialists. Finally, for GPs, the United Kingdom was above the European Union in the public's assessment of the quality, just below the average in relation to availability and access, and well above average on affordability.

These findings can be set alongside trends in patient experience and public attitudes within the NHS. A review of the findings from 26 national patient surveys carried out in England found significant progress between 2002 and 2007 in improving access to both primary and secondary care. Patients reported a high degree of trust and confidence in health care professionals and felt they were treated with dignity and respect. Overall, patient satisfaction with all types of NHS care was high and there were particular improvements for some priority groups, for example patients with cancer and heart disease, and also mental health care where patient experience had improved significantly from a low base. Alongside these positive findings, the review highlighted areas where several important challenges remained. These included access to out-of-hours GP advice, support for self-care, patient access to medical records, standards of hospital cleanliness and infection control, hospital food, and noise levels and privacy in hospitals. One of the main findings was that paternalistic approaches to patients persisted, with patients not engaged sufficiently in their own care and not involved in decisions as much as they would wish (Richards and Coulter, 2007).

A review of findings from the British Social Attitudes' Survey between 1983 and 2007 showed longer term trends in public attitudes towards different aspects of the NHS. Satisfaction levels fell from 55 per cent in 1983 to 36 per cent in 1989 and 36 per cent in 1997 before increasing to

51 per cent in 2007. The period since 2001 has witnessed the longest overall period of increases since the survey began, leading to the observation that:

> It is hard to resist the conclusion that massively increased NHS spending over the last seven years, enabling the NHS to increase its staffing considerably and, through concerted effort, reduce waiting times to their lowest since the inception of the NHS, must have played a significant part in boosting satisfaction with the NHS overall by nine percentage points since the turn of the century (and by 17 points since 1997). (Appleby and Phillips, 2009)

In relation to individual services, the survey found consistently high levels of satisfaction with GP services, lower levels of satisfaction with dentistry, increasing satisfaction with outpatient services and declining satisfaction with inpatient services. In the case of these and other services, reported satisfaction was higher among respondents with recent contact with services than among those without such contact. Satisfaction levels also increased with the age of respondents.

Another perspective on the performance of the NHS in the recent past is provided by the State of Healthcare reports produced by the Healthcare Commission. The fifth and final of these reports provided the Commission with an opportunity to assess progress in NHS performance during its existence. Overall, the Commission offered a positive judgement, commenting:

> Our assessments show that the NHS as a whole is getting better at using and managing its resources, and that it is performing better against the wide range of national targets it has to deliver and the core standards it has to meet. (Healthcare Commission, 2008b, p.6)

The Commission drew particular attention to the reductions in waiting times that had occurred and to falling death rates from cancer and heart disease, while also noting that patient safety was receiving increasing attention. Less positively, it identified a number of areas of concern, including persistent inequalities in health and risks to health created by obesity, excessive alcohol consumption and sexually transmitted infections. The Commission also drew attention to the variable quality of care, including poor standards of care for people with learning disabilities, a mixed picture in services for children and concerns about dignity and respect in the care of older people.

Piecing together these fragments of data paints a picture of an NHS which is showing clear signs of improvement both in relation to its own past performance and the performance of other health care systems. While health ministers are quick to draw attention to the Commonwealth Fund's recent assessment in support of their argument that government policies are producing results and delivering improvements in health and care for patients, the verdicts of the Healthcare Commission, the Nuffield Trust, the Picker Institute, the Eurobarometer Survey and the British Social Attitudes' Survey offer a more nuanced version of the state of the NHS today. After 60 years, the NHS retains its traditional strengths as a universal, more or less comprehensive and largely free at the point of use system, and is increasingly able to provide care that is accessible and responsive to patients. Within this system, the health of the population continues to improve and there is evidence of progress towards the higher standards of health enjoyed in some other developed countries. The main weaknesses of the NHS relate to the quality of care provided, where the United Kingdom does not do as well as other countries on some indicators, and on aspects of patient experience, including the failure to engage patients in their own care. The NHS also has room for improvement in relation to public health both in tackling health inequalities and in addressing risk factors for the future.

In interpreting these findings, it is worth remembering the argument of the original Wanless review of the long-term funding needs of the NHS to the effect that health outcomes were related to health care resources and that the cumulative underfunding of the NHS relative to the European Union average amounted to £267 billion over the period 1972 to 1998. The increases in the NHS budget that have occurred in recent years have enabled the NHS to catch up with the European Union average but they do not *make up* for this long-term underfunding. It is therefore perhaps not surprising that the United Kingdom still has some way to go before it achieves the same level of performance as countries like France, Germany, the Netherlands and Sweden that have not shared its history of neglect. Not only this, but also some of these other countries face significant challenges of their own, including deficits in health care budgets in France and concerns about performance in Germany. The reality is that improving the performance of the health care system is an almost universal preoccupation and the strengths and weaknesses of the NHS need to be seen in this light.

The aspect of the NHS that is arguably most admired by other countries is primary care. The existence of GPs as the first point of contact and as the gatekeepers between patients and specialists is often cited as one of the factors that contribute to the achievements of the NHS. The key research in this area is the work of Starfield who compared 11 systems in the 1980s. Starfield demonstrated that primary care in the United Kingdom was both more prominent than in other countries and accounted for the ability of the United Kingdom to deliver comprehensive services for a comparatively low level of expenditure (Starfield, 1992). As we have noted, survey evidence indicates that the services of GPs are rated highly by patients and more positively than hospital services. Patient registration with GPs together with continuity of care over time and the ability of primary care teams to offer a wide range of services are some of the most important strengths of general practice in the United Kingdom. Primary care has a critical role to play in meeting the needs of people with chronic diseases now and in the future, and in this regard the NHS is much better placed than the United States where primary care is in a state of crisis from which it may not recover.

The organisation and management of the NHS

On its establishment in 1948, the NHS was a creature of its time. The post-war Labour government took control of a number of sectors of the economy and used the nationalised industry model for this purpose. As we noted in Chapter 1, various options were considered for the organisation and management of the NHS, including giving local authorities control over hospitals, but these were rejected in favour of the model that was eventually adopted. In recent years there have been recurrent debates about whether this model remains fit for purpose at a time when nationalised industries in other sectors have long since disappeared and when the difficulties of running an organisation as large and complex as the NHS from Whitehall and Westminster have become increasingly apparent. These debates have found expression in Gordon Brown's argument that the NHS should aspire to be the best *health insurance* system in the world, with the implication that it need not take responsibility for owning and running the full range of health services. Government policies that have explicitly encouraged the emergence of a more mixed economy of health care provision alongside organisational innovations such as NHS foundation trusts and social enterprises have started the process of reforming the organisation and management of the NHS. It should be emphasised that these policies have found favour almost entirely in England and have gained no traction in the rest of the United Kingdom.

The development of independent sector treatment centres (ISTCs) has been at the heart of moves to create a mixed economy of health care provision. As we have seen in earlier chapters, politicians have promoted the use of treatment centres as a way of reducing waiting lists and waiting times, in particular by separating services for patients admitted to hospitals as emergencies from services for patients receiving planned care. When the ISTC programme was announced, ministers claimed that up to

15 per cent of planned NHS procedures would be carried out in ISTCs, but in practice its overall contribution has been no more than half of this (DH, 2006c, p. 11) and on some estimates less than 5 per cent of the total (Timmins, 2008b). This is partly because of delays in procuring new capacity and partly because the additional capacity that has been procured has not always been fully used by NHS patients. As we noted in Chapter 3, on becoming Prime Minister Gordon Brown decided to scale back the ISTC programme on the grounds that some of the additional capacity included in the programme was not needed. This meant that not all of the planned procurement in the second wave went ahead. During this period, the NHS made significant progress in reducing waiting lists and waiting times but the role of ISTCs in improving access was limited. Paradoxically, ISTCs had a much bigger impact on existing private health care providers than on the NHS, leading to a series of mergers and acquisitions as new entrants to the market challenged the position of these providers.

ISTCs operate under five-year contracts agreed with the government and there is uncertainty about what will happen at the end of these contracts. Patients may choose to use private hospitals for their NHS treatment where these hospitals provide care at NHS prices and to the standards set by the Care Quality Commission but whether they will do so in sufficient numbers to ensure that ISTCs are financially viable when their guaranteed central funding comes to an end remains to be seen. One possibility is that ISTCs will start competing for private patients and in so doing may stimulate a growing market for private care (Timmins, 2007). Even in the unlikely event that all ISTCs continue to provide care to NHS patients, their combined impact will remain limited and the vast majority of care will still be delivered by NHS providers. Evidence indicates that NHS spending on ISTCs and other privately provided care increased rapidly after 1997 and yet even so PCT expenditure on care commissioned from the independent sector amounted to less than 5 per cent of all care commissioned by PCTs in 2007/08 (National Audit Office and Audit Commission, 2008).

Controversy has also accompanied the introduction of NHS foundation trusts as public benefit corporations, no longer in a line management relationship with the Secretary of State for Health. By the beginning of 2009, over half of the NHS trusts eligible to become NHS foundation trusts had done so and it was expected that the remaining half would be approved as NHS foundation trusts by the end of 2010. NHS foundation trusts have a number of freedoms not available to NHS trusts and we noted in Chapter 10 that their performance in the annual health check undertaken by the former Healthcare Commission was better than that of NHS trusts. A review conducted by the Health Committee (2008c) noted that the superior performance of NHS foundation trusts might have resulted from a continuation of long-term trends rather than the freedoms they enjoyed, as the process of selecting NHS foundation trusts meant that only those organisations achieving a high level of performance were granted NHS foundation trust status. In the view of the Health Committee, NHS foundation trusts had some proven strengths and concerns about their potential adverse effects had not been realised. On the other hand, there was little evidence that NHS foundation trusts had fulfilled their potential, for example in relation to innovation and public involvement, even though witnesses who gave evidence to the Committee reported that NHS foundation trusts benefited from being able to make quick decisions and from their financial freedoms. The Committee argued that research was needed to assess the performance of NHS foundation trusts in order to enable a balanced judgement to be made.

The other policy that has had an impact on the organisation and management of the NHS is the encouragement given to social enterprises and third sector providers. Organisations of this kind have always played some part in the provision of services to NHS patients but in recent years they have been actively encouraged to compete for contracts alongside NHS providers and private sector for-profit providers, including ISTCs. The Department of Health (DH) has supported the emergence of social enterprises in a number of areas, and it is anticipated that their contribution will increase in future, particularly in the provision of community health services that in the past have been mainly provided by PCTs. An indication of the shape of things to come is Central Surrey Health, an organisation established in 2006 when NHS staff who had previously been employed by a PCT to provide community nursing and other services decided to establish a new organisation that they own and run. Other examples of social enterprises in health care are SCA Healthcare, an industrial and provident society based in Southampton that provides a range of community services, and Principia Partners in Health, a coalition of GP practices, community professionals, a community pharmacy and local people in Nottingham.

To complete the picture, the provision of primary care is changing as government policies have sought to improve access to GP services and increase capacity in under-doctored areas. Primary care has always differed from other aspects of NHS provision in that most GPs are independent contractors rather than salaried employees, and they provide care to patients under the terms of contracts negotiated with government or PCTs. Under the Equitable Access to Primary Care procurement, launched in 2007, the DH has required every PCT to invite bids for the provision of a GP-led health centre, and it has provided additional funds for the establishment of over 100 new practices in areas of greatest need.

Existing practices have competed for these contracts with GP-led companies and for-profit corporate providers, with a number of social enterprises also involved. At the time of writing, the evidence indicates that GP-led bidders have achieved the greatest measure of success with corporate providers securing only a tiny proportion of the contracts that have been awarded (Ellins et al., 2008). As in the case of planned care and the encouragement given to ISTCs, this suggests that moves to increase plurality of provision and to shift away from the dominant model of publicly owned and run hospital and community health services working alongside GP practices are progressing slowly.

This evidence casts serious doubts on the claim that 'The NHS is being dismantled and privatised. Very soon every part of it will have been "unbundled" and commodified ... The disaster that is unfolding is overwhelming in its complexity and its magnitude. Even rail privatisation looks modest alongside it' (Pollock, 2004, pp. 214–5). The reality, as we have seen, is much more mundane. The role of private sector providers in delivering care to NHS patients has increased but the limited scale of private sector involvement belies claims of widespread privatisation and dismantling. To return to the starting point of this chapter, if Aneurin Bevan were still alive today he would find the NHS looking different but much more recognisable than any of the other sectors that were nationalised by the reforming post-war Labour government of which he was a key member, even though both Conservative and Labour governments since the 1980s have at various times adopted what appeared to be radical policies. Although these policies have made some difference, their impact has been much more marginal than often claimed as the inertia of established arrangements has moderated the reformist ambitions of politicians.

Hierarchies, markets and networks

The shift away from the 1948 nationalised industry model is closely linked to discussion of the mechanisms that should be used to improve the performance of the NHS. Drawing on the literature on organisational analysis, Le Grand (2002) notes that in stylised terms there are three main approaches available. Hierarchies use managerial command-and-control mechanisms to allocate resources; markets allocate resources through competitive processes; and networks rely on social relationships that involve trust and cooperation. Although the NHS has often been described as a command-and-control system, Le Grand argues that for much of its history it was characterised by professional networks operating in the context of self-regulation combined with weak central controls. Markets came to prominence in the 1990s under Margaret Thatcher and John

Major but were used alongside hierarchies and networks in an attempt to improve efficiency and responsiveness. The development of ISTCs and the establishment of NHS foundation trusts were associated with the promotion of market based reforms under Tony Blair and Gordon Brown.

The importance of hierarchical controls has never been greater than in the period after the election of the Blair government in 1997. The establishment of the National Institute for Health and Clinical Excellence (NICE), the promulgation of national service frameworks, the setting of national targets, and the strengthening of performance management led to a command-and-control approach that was much more directive than anything that had been attempted before. In parallel, the government took steps to create arrangements for inspection and regulation, particularly through the establishment of the Commission for Health Improvement and the National Care Standards Commission, and their successors the Healthcare Commission and Care Quality Commission. Subsequently, following publication of *Delivering the NHS Plan*, elements of competition were added to the policy mix through the emphasis placed on patient choice, money following patients under payment by results, and plurality of provision through the establishment of NHS foundation trusts and the use of ISTCs.

What will be the impact of this policy mix in the longer term? Drawing on the experience of the internal market in the 1990s, Le Grand (2002) notes the problems that may arise when different organisational models are combined. As the author has argued elsewhere (Ham, 1997a), the internal market was in reality a politically managed market in which competitive incentives were severely weakened by the controls exercised by government. For their part, the Blair and Brown governments have retained hierarchical controls alongside the greater use of regulation and inspection and the reintroduction of competition. In other words, rather than regulation replacing hierarchies and markets, as some commentators have suggested (Walshe, 2003), elements of all three have been used, and the professional networks that have been so much in evidence since the inception of the NHS continue to be important. Experience in other sectors in the 1980s and the 1990s (Hood et al., 1999) suggests that the risk in such an approach is that the NHS may suffer from a surfeit of different models.

These developments lend support to the argument that health care reform, even where it embraces a stronger role for competition, also tends to increase the role of the state (Freeman, 2000). In this context, Tuohy's analysis of the dynamics of change in the health care arena in the United States, the United Kingdom and Canada offers some pointers to possible developments (Tuohy, 1999). Tuohy argues that health care in the United Kingdom is an example of a hierarchical, state system with elements of collegial processes. The market-oriented reforms of the 1990s had a limited impact because their effects were attenuated by hierarchical controls and professional relationships and networks. By extension, it can be suggested that the reforms implemented by the Blair and Brown governments will similarly be modified in the course of implementation by the strength of existing institutional arrangements and by past patterns of behaviour. In line with the analysis advanced by path dependency theories of policy development, the outcome is likely to be incremental adjustment rather than a radical break with the past, a conclusion that is consistent with our assessment above of the marginal impact of policies such as ISTCs and NHS foundation trusts.

Continuing reliance on hierarchical controls is reinforced by the disappointing effects of markets as a tool of health care reform. In a series of publications, Le Grand has made the case for markets by reference to the motivations of the providers of public services (Le Grand, 2003, 2007). Specifically, he argues that providers exhibit both knightly and knavish behaviours and that public service reform cannot rely on the assumption that providers are essentially altruistic individuals who are committed to delivering high-quality services to users. Rather, Le Grand contends that quasi markets are needed to counteract the risk of self-interested behaviour by providers, the bias towards the middle classes that arises when reforms depend on users exercising voice, and the disempowerment that results from overreliance on hierarchical controls. In the case of health care, he argues that quasi market reforms have to be carefully designed if their potential is to be realised. This includes ensuring that there is real competition between providers and informed choice by patients. Recognising the political difficulties in dealing with providers that do not compete successfully, Le Grand proposes that an agency independent of government should be set up to deal with these providers and to distance politicians from unpopular decisions.

In making these points, Le Grand is underlining the practical challenges of converting the general argument for markets into detailed policy interventions. These challenges include not only arrangements for dealing with market exit and entry but also how to ensure that the commissioners of health care can negotiate on equal terms with providers, and options for organising providers within the market. The need for there to be effective commissioners within the NHS has long been recognised and as we noted in earlier chapters it is being taken forward by the DH through the world class commissioning programme. In practice, it will take time for this programme to provide PCTs and practices with the skills they need to perform effectively within the emerging NHS market. Indeed, as a review of international evidence has shown, in no health care system is health care commissioning, as understood in the NHS, done consistently well (Ham, 2008b). For this reason, it remains an open question as to whether the neglect of commissioning in the early stages of the health reform programme in England can be rectified in time for the quasi market to function effectively.

In relation to the organisation of providers, there is some evidence that points to the superior performance of integrated delivery systems in the United States health care market as exemplified by the experience of the Veterans' Health Administration (Jha et al., 2003) and by organisations such as Kaiser Permanente (Enthoven and Tollen, 2004). This evidence lends support to the case for there to be competition and choice between integrated systems rather than between a multitude of hospitals and other providers operating in a highly fragmented manner. Analysts of the performance of health services in the United States, such as Porter and Teisberg (2006), have acknowledged the strengths of integrated delivery systems, even though they argue for more radical reform to address what they describe as 'the wrong kind of competition' in that country. Similarly, Christensen and colleagues (2009) argue that integrated systems hold out the best hope for overcoming the weaknesses of the health care market in the United States. The advocates of markets as a tool of public service reform in the United Kingdom have yet to work through the implications of these kinds of challenges, and yet they are of fundamental importance in converting the case for markets into arrangements that will work on the ground. The failure to take the argument for competition beyond generalities and into specifics is likely to continue to hamper efforts to reform public services like the NHS.

A practical example that illustrates this point is the establishment of the NHS Cooperation and Competition Panel only in 2008, fully six years after the plans to reintroduce a quasi market were first announced in *Delivering the NHS Plan*. The Panel's role is to oversee the functioning of the market and to advise where disputes arise. Part of its rationale is to ensure a level playing field between independent sector providers and those from the NHS and to avoid the commissioners of care discriminating against new entrants. The delay in setting up the Panel was reminiscent of the time it took in the 1990s to publish guidance on market management and regulation (see Chapter 2) during the Conservatives' internal market reforms. This underlined that policy-makers were again making it up as they went along as well as providing evidence of policy amnesia, the flip side of policy learning.

The role of politicians

As many of these comments suggest, central to the debate about the future organisation and management of the NHS is the role of politicians. This is illustrated by the use of targets and hierarchical controls to improve NHS performance. To exaggerate only a little, the relationship between politicians and targets can be compared to the relationship between an addict and the drugs of his or her choice. Politicians know that too many targets should be avoided, but the 'high' they receive when targets work creates a dependency from which it is difficult to break free and only serves to reinforce behaviour which risks becoming destructive and ultimately self-defeating. In recognition of this, a debate has begun to emerge about creating greater independence for the NHS by removing politicians from close involvement in the day-to-day management of services. At the heart of this debate is the argument that ministers should set the strategic direction for the NHS and leave civil servants and experienced managers with responsibility for implementing their policies.

While not a new debate, the case for independence has recently attracted a number of serious contributions, and has received support from Conservative politicians as we discuss below. In his review, Edwards has outlined seven potential models for what he describes as an independent NHS Authority ranging from a modernised NHS Executive within the DH, through an NHS Corporation that fully manages the NHS to the NHS as a public insurance company (Edwards, 2007). All of these options face the challenge of how to reconcile greater detachment on the part of politicians with the need for accountability for the use of over £100 billion of public resources that are voted by Parliament and the unhappy experience in other sectors, like the prison service, where attempts to distance politicians from operational matters have proved difficult to implement successfully. Experience shows the challenges of separating responsibility for strategic direction from execution and implementation, and in a service as visible and valued as the NHS there will always be a tendency for politicians to want to micromanage the delivery of their policies and respond to media criticisms.

An alternative to NHS independence would be to shift the locus of accountability from central government to local government. In essence, this would entail adapting the arrangement used in the Nordic countries under which local authorities have a major role in both the funding and provision of health care. Again, this is not a new debate and it contains echoes of the discussions that took place at the inception of the NHS when Morrison sought unsuccessfully to ensure that local authorities retained control over the hospital service. In the case of the NHS today, one line of argument is that the commissioning of health care should be transferred to local government with councils having powers to raise some of the costs of care through the council tax or other sources of revenue (Glasby et al., 2006). If this were to happen it might increase rather than reduce the involvement of politicians in the running of the

NHS, and it is also likely to accentuate variations in the availability of services in different parts of the country. Other options such as having elections to the boards of NHS bodies would offer an alternative way of enhancing local accountability without transferring control of the NHS in its entirety to local authorities. A proposal along these lines has been put forward in Scotland and it would emulate the arrangement that exists in New Zealand where district health boards comprise some members appointed by the health minister and others elected by local people.

The future demand for health care

International comparisons show that a higher proportion of total health expenditure derives from public sources in the United Kingdom than in almost all OECD countries. According to the latest figures, 87 per cent of total health expenditure in the United Kingdom was classified as public expenditure in 2006 compared with the OECD average of 73 per cent. The proportion of total health expenditure attributable to public sources has risen during the past decade as a consequence of government policies that have led to an unprecedented increase in the NHS budget. A big question for the future is whether this will continue to be the case or whether private expenditure will increase at a faster rate than public expenditure, in this way bringing the United Kingdom closer to the position found in other parts of the OECD. In addressing this question, the pressures to increase health expenditure should be noted. These pressures include the ageing population and the rising prevalence of chronic diseases within the population; advances in medicine in the form of new drugs, surgical and medical interventions that offer increased possibilities for diagnosis and treatment; and rising public expectations (see Table 12.1).

Notwithstanding the increases in NHS spending that have occurred in the past decade and tangible improvements in performance in a number of areas of concern to patients, there is widespread acceptance of the need for further increases in the future, albeit at a lower level, to consolidate the gains that have been made and to address new priorities. This was recognised in the Wanless review of the long-term funding needs of health care that argued for a period of high rates of spending increases designed to enable the United Kingdom to catch up with other countries, to be followed by a number of years in which NHS spending would increase at a slower rate to ensure that it kept up with these countries (see Chapter 4). The period of high rates of spending increases came to an end in 2008 and the comprehensive spending review undertaken by the government resulted in planned increases in the NHS budget of around 4 per cent each year in real terms between 2008 and 2011. These planned increases were

Table 12.1 *Drivers of demand*

The ageing population
Increases in life expectancy and declining fertility rates will combine to alter the balance between older and younger people. The ageing of the population will increase the demand for health care while the growth of single-person and lone-parent households may reduce the capacity of families to share responsibility for care. Reductions in the size of the working population and an increase in the dependency ratio (that is the ratio of people aged under 16 and over 65 as a proportion of the working age population) will put pressure on policy-makers in raising sufficient funds via tax to meet rising demands. As the Wanless Report on long-term funding noted in its analysis, over the next 20 years demographic trends are likely to have a significant impact on future levels of demand and expenditure for health care. The conclusion of the Wanless Report is supported by an analysis by the OECD suggesting that expenditure on health care is likely to increase even if disability levels among older people decline (Jacobzone et al., 2000).

Medical advances
Medical advances tend to increase health care costs as well as improve health. This was one of the factors that led the Wanless Report on long-term funding to argue for a sustained increase in funding to enable the NHS to catch up with other countries and then to keep up with them in delivering responsive and high quality services. Looking to the future, advances in genetics are likely to result in greater understanding of the causes of illness and eventually to the development of new forms of diagnosis and treatment. Similarly, new drugs will open up further possibilities for treatment of the major medical conditions such as cancer, heart disease and mental illness. Developments in pharmacogenomics will bring together understanding of genetics with pharmaceutical advances to enable drugs to be used more effectively, for example by tailoring their use to the genetic make-up of patients. The use of herceptin in the treatment of breast cancer is an example. Alongside these developments, developments in stem cell research may enable treatments to be developed for Parkinson's and Alzheimer's diseases, spinal cord injury, and to enable new organs to be grown for use in transplantation.

Rising public expectations
The emergence of a younger generation with higher expectations of public services has been a major influence on the policies adopted under the Blair and Brown governments. These policies have been designed to improve access, choice and responsiveness in order to secure the continuing commitment of people in their twenties and thirties to a universal, tax funded NHS. Meeting the needs of younger people will continue to be an important driver within the NHS, as will responding to the needs of retiring baby boomers. This generation, born in the aftermath of the Second World War and entering retirement with greater assets and more generous pensions than their predecessors, will put pressure on health services to deliver a higher standard of care than has traditionally been the case. The evidence summarised earlier on public and patient attitudes showed that the NHS has some way to go before it fully engages patients in their care and provides services in a way that respects the dignity of service users, especially older people. Addressing these issues requires changes in attitude and culture as well as increased funding.

a little lower than those recommended in the Wanless review and were in any case soon brought into question by the downturn in the British economy that followed from the credit crunch and the turmoil in the world's financial markets. Although the government promised to honour its commitment to implement the outcome of the comprehensive spending review in the period up to 2011, it was clear that the NHS budget would fall for a number of years after 2011. The government's pre-budget report at the end of 2008 also signalled that the NHS would be expected to find greater efficiencies than previously thought in order to contribute to the much more demanding financial targets required by the economic downturn and the huge sums of public funding provided to support commercial banks that had run into difficulty. The existence of a budgetary surplus of £1.7 billion in 2007–08 indicated that the NHS was well placed to deal with much tighter financial prospects in the short term, even if the position after 2011 looked to be much more challenging (National Audit Office and Audit Commission, 2008).

A number of organisations have analysed the prospects for NHS funding and the balance of public and private spending on health care. In its contribution, the King's Fund emphasised the difficulty of determining how much spending would be needed in future, and it argued that the evidence base on the benefits of additional spending needed to be strengthened, for example by extending the role of NICE to examine new areas of treatment and policy initiatives (Appleby and Harrison, 2006). Three main options for future NHS spending were identified by the King's Fund, namely:

- carry on spending at current rates and postpone the inevitable decision to contain spending
- carry on spending at current rates and improve efficiency and productivity
- align NHS spending growth to general, long-term growth in the economy as a whole.

The third of these options was seen to be the medium to long-term goal, while recognising the difficulties that would arise in meeting increased demands with constrained resources. This included being explicit about the degree of inequality in access to health care that would be acceptable as more affluent groups in society supplemented the care provided through the NHS with privately funded services.

A review commissioned by BUPA from NERA Economic Consulting and Frontier Economics also drew attention to the financial pressures likely to be faced by the NHS after 2008 (Bramley-Harker and Booer, 2006). This review used a whole system model of the NHS to simulate the behaviour of the NHS in the period to 2015 and the likely activity levels and resource requirements. On the basis of the assumptions made in the Wanless review and the likelihood that NHS spending would grow by around 3.5 per cent per annum between 2008 and 2015, it was estimated that a funding shortfall of around 10 per cent would exist at the end of that period. This would have seriously detrimental consequences unless ways could be found of filling the funding gap. Three possible options were set out in the review:

- increase the level of public funding going into the NHS through tax increases or the redistribution of public spending
- increase the NHS's resources by improving productivity, raising income through other sources or reducing the services it provides
- adopt more radical approaches to generate additional income such as greater use of co-payments or developing entirely new funding streams.

BUPA's review favoured the third option and specifically recommended further work to explore the role of co-payments, the use of incentives to encourage employers to offer private medical insurance, and the use of supplementary funding to enable individuals to top up their NHS entitlements to access additional services and different care settings. In so doing, it echoed the Wanless review of long-term funding which also urged the government to consider a greater role for co-payments in future (see Chapter 4).

In its analysis, the centre-left Institute for Public Policy Research (IPPR) also identified a likely shortfall in NHS spending and it concluded that private funding was unlikely to fill the gap, even though it had a valuable role in supplementing the contribution made by public expenditure on health care (Farrington-Douglas and Coelho, 2008). Echoing previous reports on health care funding, the IPPR argued that collective financing would remain the most efficient way of financing health care, and that a debate was needed on the merits of hypothecation or social insurance compared with general taxation as the main way of paying for health care. In this respect, the IPPR was in agreement with the review commissioned by BUPA which also concluded that public funding should be the main way of paying for health care.

Other reviews have been more positive about the potential role for increased private spending on health care. Examples include a report written by the former Labour Cabinet Minister, Charles Clarke, advocating a bigger role for user charges in public services, including the NHS (Clarke, 2008), and a pamphlet prepared by Doctors for Reform arguing for a greater role for top-up payments in health care (Charlson et al., 2007). The latter document emphasised in particular the need to allow patients the opportunity to choose to top up the care funded by the NHS at a time when public expectations were rising and patients expected choice, diversity and instant access in other areas of their lives. In this context, it is worth noting the recommendations of a report by the Health Committee that reviewed the role of user charges in the NHS and called for greater clarity and consistency in the use of charges in future (Health Committee, 2006a).

These issues came to a head during 2008 in relation to the funding of cancer drugs that had not been approved for use in the NHS by NICE. A number of terminally ill patients were told that they were not entitled to free care in the NHS if they chose to pay for these drugs out of their own pockets. In the face of mounting media interest in the plight of these patients and concern that the government was being too rigid in the application of this policy, ministers asked the national clinical director for cancer, Mike Richards, to review the issues and make recommendations. In his report, Richards noted that views on this issue were polarised and centred on the tension between the principle of equity, that access to services should be based on need and not ability to pay, and the principle of autonomy, that individuals should be free to spend their money as they choose. Richards argued that patients should not lose their entitlement to NHS care because they purchased drugs privately, adding that where this happened the two elements of care should be provided separately.

In order to minimise the number of patients who wanted to pay for additional drugs, he recommended improvements to NICE's decision-making processes to speed up the appraisal of new drugs, and proposed that PCTs should collaborate with each other in deciding on priorities for funding while also being more transparent in their decision-making. The other principal recommendation in the Richards review was that NICE should review the value attached to end-of-life treatments to ensure that these treatments were available within the NHS when appropriate (Richards, 2008). These proposals were accepted in full by ministers and draft guidance on their implementation was issued for consultation. As the Richards review was proceeding, the government was also considering options for the future funding of long-term care, and a Green Paper setting out options for the future was expected to be published in 2009 (see Chapter 5).

Increasing efficiency in the NHS

In the debate about the future funding of health care, a recurring theme is the scope for using existing budgets more efficiently as well as how to increase the size of the budget. A series of reports over the years has highlighted opportunities for productivity improvements, not least through reducing variations in performance within the NHS. This is illustrated by the quotation from a speech by a former Secretary of State, John Moore, in Chapter 10 of this book, giving examples of variations in the use of hospital beds and lengths of stay in hospitals in the 1980s. In more recent times, the Health Strategy Review undertaken by Adair Turner at the request of Tony Blair in 2001/02 focused on what it described as 'core medical processes' such as the prescribing of drugs by GPs and the use of day surgery in hospitals in identifying ways in which resources could be used more efficiently (Turner, 2002). For its part, the DH carried out a financial sustainability review as part of the work that went into the 2007 comprehensive spending review and found potential savings of over £6 billion through reforming pay and the workforce, improving procurement, and reducing variations in clinical practice (Ham, 2007a). Further evidence in the same vein has been summarised by the NHS Institute for Innovation and Improvement which has listed a number of opportunities for releasing resources, including £975 million through length of stay reductions and £510 million through pre-operative bed day reductions.

The main question to be asked about this evidence is whether the right levers and incentives are in place under the NHS reform programme to release resources by tackling these and other variations in performance. In concept, the incentives contained in payment by results should help to increase efficiency within hospitals by reducing lengths of stay and encouraging the substitution of day surgery for inpatient treatment where appropriate. This is because the fixed prices hospitals receive under payment by results enable them to benefit when they are able to cut their costs without compromising the quality of care provided. If government decides to squeeze the NHS by limiting the uplift in the prices paid under payment by results, then it might be expected that this would accelerate the search for productivity improvements by stimulating providers to find ways of cutting their costs. Similarly, practice based commissioning offers incentives for GPs to manage demand and examine more closely their use of local hospital services in so far as practices perceive that they will benefit from any savings made by using the resources released to develop a wider range of care in their own surgeries. This includes exploring the scope for improving prescribing practices by using cheaper generic drugs in place of branded alternatives where appropriate.

Realising these potential gains hinges in large part on the clinical teams delivering care to patients seeing the connection between the changes in practice needed to address variations in performance and the consequences for their own work. In hospitals, the development of service line management in which the staff working in different clinical departments are provided with information on the income they attract and the costs they incur through their work is a step in this direction (see Chapter 9). Service line management provides a foundation on which to develop clinical departments into business units or profit centres, thereby rewarding staff in these departments where they contribute to improvements in performance within the hospital. Likewise, practice based commissioning enables primary care teams to see that there are benefits for the work they undertake and the patients they serve when their decisions help to release resources for use on priority services. The difficulty with both service line management and particularly practice based commissioning is engaging a sufficient number of clinical teams to make a significant difference to the delivery of care. Studies have shown that involving doctors and other clinical staff in the management of services and budgets is a work in progress, with many teams more focused on the delivery of care to patients than other commitments.

With the prospects for NHS funding much tighter than for some time, accelerating this work and linking clinical decisions with financial and management responsibility, as the Griffiths Report argued in 1983, remains a high priority. This conclusion is underlined by the review undertaken by Adair Turner for the Prime Minister in 2001–02 which found that efficiency improvements had a much bigger impact on the future funding requirements of the NHS than progress in giving higher priority to prevention and public health (Turner, 2002), notwithstanding the assessment of the Wanless review of the long-term funding needs of the NHS discussed in Chapter 3.

Priority-setting or rationing

The debate on 'top-up' payments for NHS care was in part a debate about the balance between public and private expenditure on health care and in part a debate about priority-setting decisions within the NHS. Operating within a fixed budget and committed to providing comprehensive services to the whole population, the NHS cannot escape the need to set priorities for the use of resources and in extreme cases ration the funding of expensive and experimental treatments. Other health care systems face the same challenge and various studies have described the approach taken to rationing in different countries (Klein et al., 1996; Ham, 1997b; Ham and Robert, 2003). In some systems, such as the state of Oregon, explicit rationing has involved defining a list of services to be funded. In others, policy-makers have shied away from excluding services from public funding and have focused instead on trying to ensure that resources are allocated to treatments that offer demonstrable benefit to patients. This is the approach adopted in New Zealand where the committee set up to define the core services to be funded in that country's health care system declined to undertake this task and instead made recommendations on the services that should receive priority in the budget-setting process. In addition, the committee organised a series of consensus conferences on particular treatments or conditions, it developed guidelines for the provision of services, and it worked with clinicians to agree criteria to determine priority for access to elective surgical procedures.

A number of countries have approached rationing by seeking to define the values that should inform priority-setting. Norway was one of the first countries to go down this route and its example finds echoes in the reports of priority-setting committees in the Netherlands and Sweden. For example, the Swedish Parliamentary Priorities Commission proposed an ethical platform for rationing based on three values: human dignity, equity or solidarity, and efficiency. In the Commission's view, human dignity, or respect for the rights of individuals, was of overriding importance, and meant that discrimination based on age, birth weight, lifestyle and similar considerations would not normally be allowed. Furthermore, the equity principle was intended to ensure that the needs of vulnerable groups and people with disabilities received priority. Only after dignity and equity had been taken into account did the Commission feel it was appropriate to consider the efficiency of different treatments. These national approaches to rationing have emerged in response to the increasing pressures confronting health care systems and the reluctance of clinicians to continue taking responsibility for the consequences of rationing decisions. As Moran has noted, the dynamics of governing consumption in health care have involved a shift over time from doctors rationing care implicitly to greater explicitness in decision-making. The challenge this has thrown up is that:

> choices have to be made in a world where the control systems exercised by the old medical oligarchies have been weakened, and where it is increasingly difficult to manipulate the consuming citizen by either cultural or institutional mystification. (Moran, 1999, p. 188)

It would be wrong to infer from this that politicians have replaced doctors as the main agents of rationing. International experience indicates the difficulties that arise in explicit, national approaches, and the resilience of blame diffusion strategies (Ham and Coulter, 2001). For example, policy-makers in the Netherlands faced criticism where explicit rationing meant excluding some services from funding, and this led to a retreat from rationing through exclusions. Instead, greater emphasis was given to rationing by guidelines, with professional networks playing a major part in the development and promulgation of guidelines. In the process, the onus has been placed on decision-makers at the sub-national level to work with professional networks in the implementation of guidelines and in priority-setting. This was also the approach adopted in the NHS in the 1990s when health authorities were at the forefront of rationing. Cases like that of Child B, a 10-year-old girl with leukaemia who was denied funding for an experimental treatment by the Cambridge and Hunting-don Health Authority, came to symbolise the dilemmas facing health authorities in balancing the needs of individuals against those of communities (Ham and Pickard, 1998).

In this context, the decision of the Blair government to adopt a more explicit approach to rationing at the national level through NICE and national service frameworks could be seen as swimming against the tide of international developments in so far as other countries are retreating from such an approach. What is distinctive about NICE, however, is the creation of an agency at arm's length from government to take a lead on rationing. The existence of such an agency has provided policy-makers with some distance from decisions that risked attracting criticism and unpopularity. Also, the introduction of NICE at a time when the NHS budget was growing at historically unprecedented levels, meant that it was possible to absorb the effects of its decisions, even though most of those decisions added to the pressures on the NHS. The unanswered question was what would happen when the increase in resources come to an end? Assuming that there is a commitment to maintain the NHS as a universal service, and that the political costs of exclusions remain too high, then a limited list of options is on offer.

In keeping with the experience of social policy reform in the 1980s and 1990s (Pierson, 1994), it seems likely that rationing will occur in part through the back door, following the examples of dentistry and long-term care described elsewhere in this book, rather than by government defining the scope of the benefits package more narrowly following a process of open debate and discussion. Also, traditional devices such as rationing by delay, dilution and diversion will continue to be used. If this assessment is accurate, then the danger is that such an approach may undermine trust in government. This could occur if the public perceive that the scope of the NHS is being limited through a series of incremental and largely invis-ible decisions that cumulatively have a significant impact on the services they assumed would be available to them. Here is a further illustration of the impact that health services may have on government and one that in the longer term could have profound implications for the political system as a whole.

An alternative interpretation is that the existence of NICE and the development of greater explicitness in rationing will help to expose areas of underfunding and generate pressure for sustained increases in NHS funding beyond those already announced. Support for this view comes from experience in systems like Oregon, Israel and New Zealand where explicit rationing did have this effect. The issue then is the willingness of governments and electorates to provide through the tax system the volume of resources needed to fund medical advances deemed to be effective. This suggests that some difficult choices lie ahead, not just within the NHS but in government as a whole in debates about relative spending priorities and the level of taxes needed to pay for these priorities. These choices have become much more challenging following the credit crunch and the turmoil in the world's financial markets with significant sums of public money in the United Kingdom being used to support commercial banks that have got into difficulty. Resources that in other circumstances might have been used to increase spending in the NHS and other public services are no longer available for this purpose.

One way of squaring the circle is for government to set the national framework for rationing and to continue to rely on PCTs to make judgements about relative priorities at the local level. One of the difficulties in this strategy is the decision in 2003 to treat NICE guidance as effectively mandatory for the NHS, thereby reducing the discretion available to PCTs to arrive at such judgements. The prospect is therefore of increasing tension between the DH and PCTs as the Department seeks to achieve greater consistency in the provision of services and PCTs attempt to juggle competing (and increasingly non-discretionary) priorities within the constraints of fixed budgets. This suggests that the dynamics built into governing consumption will be worked out through the organisational politics of the NHS, in particular the relationship between the centre and the periphery.

The question then is how will PCTs respond to the challenge of rationing and the inevitable tensions created by rising public awareness and expectations, the emphasis placed by government on reducing variations in provision, and the reluctance of doctors to mask the effects of resource constraints through implicit decision-making? This is precisely the issue raised in the Richards review of top-up payments in the NHS and the argument in the review that PCTs need to strengthen their decision-making processes is a timely reminder that those responsible for rationing decisions within the NHS need to put in place mechanisms that will allow them to demonstrate 'accountability for reasonableness' in their decisions. The phrase is that of Daniels and Sabin (1997), and its application to the NHS is discussed in Ham and Pickard (1998) and Ham and McIver (2000). As this book was being finalised, the DH issued guidance to PCTs on developing their decision-making processes, proposing criteria remarkably similar to those included in the accountability for reasonableness

approach. Whether transparent and accountable decision-making processes by PCTs will be sufficient to meet the concerns of an increasingly
demanding public supported by industrial and commercial interests skilled
in lobbying for funding and support for the medical advances they offer is
one of the biggest uncertainties for the future.

Political futures

Throughout this book we have emphasised the way in which health policy
is shaped by bargaining and negotiation between structural interests,
governmental and non-governmental institutions operating at different
levels, pressure groups representing producers, consumers, and other interests, and the myriad actors with a stake in the NHS and the wider economy
of health and care. In this final section we consider alternative futures
viewed from the perspective of the main political parties in Westminster. In
doing so, it is important to emphasise that debates between the parties on
the future of the NHS occupy a narrow terrain. There is a large measure of
agreement between the Conservatives, Labour and the Liberal Democrats
on the funding and delivery of health care, with none of the parties proposing to move away from the founding principles of the NHS in pursuit of a
radically different model. In the case of the two main parties in Westminster, the adoption by the Labour Party under Tony Blair of policies to
promote choice and competition and to develop a mixed economy of health
care goes a long way to explaining the extent of the common ground on the
future of the NHS. New Labour has pursued reforms in a number of public
services that in the past would have more naturally been associated with
the Conservative Party, leaving limited scope for the latter to carve out a
distinctive policy agenda. At the time of writing, Conservative health policy
differs from that of the Labour Party in three main respects.

First, the Conservatives have been critical of Labour for the excessive
use of targets to improve NHS performance, arguing:

> Labour is letting down the NHS. Their bureaucratic approach, running
> our health services through perpetual political interference and the
> imposition of top-down targets, is failing patients and undermining
> hard-working doctors and nurses ... This target-driven approach
> diverts precious time and money from genuine clinical priorities, and
> is driven by political imperatives rather than patients' needs. It is one
> of the reasons why Britain's health outcomes – for example, five-year
> cancer survival rates – remain poor compared with those of other
> European countries. (Conservative Party, 2008, pp. 5–6)

In place of targets, the Conservatives propose to focus on improving outcomes rather than care processes. Seven areas for improving outcomes have been identified, including five-year cancer survival rates that exceed the European Union averages by 2015, premature mortality from stroke and heart disease below the European Union average by 2015, and year-on-year improvements in patient reported outcomes for patients living with long term conditions. By publishing data on outcomes and other measures of performance, the Conservatives argue that patients and health care professionals will have the information they need to drive up standards of care. The implication is that targets such as the maximum wait of four hours in A & E departments would no longer be applied. Whether in practice a future Conservative government would be able to hold this line remains to be seen.

Second, closely linked to the use of outcomes rather than targets, the Conservatives have argued that they would place much greater emphasis than Labour on empowering frontline staff to bring about improvements in performance. In part, this will be achieved by abolishing the targets that some frontline staff argue distort their work by focusing effort on meeting the government's objectives rather than patients' needs, and in part it will be achieved by placing the emphasis on doctors, nurses and other staff leading change within the NHS. This includes giving primary care organisations responsibility for the majority of the NHS budget, and extending the freedoms of NHS foundation trusts. Specifically in relation to commissioning, the Conservatives have argued that this should be clinician-led and that practice based commissioning needs to be strengthened to enable GPs to hold real budgets with all GPs being expected to take part. On NHS foundation trusts, the Conservatives are committed to strengthening the role of Monitor to enable it to become an economic regulator, with control over the payment by results tariff and responsibility for promoting competition.

Third, the Conservatives have supported calls for greater independence for the NHS, discussed earlier in this chapter, and have indicated that if elected they will create an independent NHS board made up of executive and non-executive members to oversee the management of the NHS. This will enable the DH to become a public health department with the task of leading action across government on population health improvement with resources for public health being ring-fenced. The Secretary of State for Health would agree objectives with the NHS board based on improvements in health outcomes consistent with the level of resources available to the NHS. To strengthen the voice of patients, a new national body called HealthWatch will be established with statutory rights to be consulted over the care patients should receive and over decisions on how NHS care is provided. The Conservatives have proposed enshrining core NHS principles in legislation, mirroring the Brown government's plans to incorporate *The NHS Constitution* in the Health Bill as announced in the 2008 Queen's Speech.

The Liberal Democrats' health policy is based on four key principles. The first is fairness and includes delivering high quality services to all, irrespective of income. To this end, a number of proposals have been formulated, including a care guarantee for older people entitling them to a personal care payment based on need and not ability to pay, and setting out entitlements for people needing care and carers; appointing a Secretary of State for Public Health in place of the Secretary of State for Health to make public health a priority across all government departments; ensuring closer integration of the work of local authorities and PCTs on public health initiatives; and enshrining NICE's independence in law to avoid the risk of political interference. The second principle is empowering patients to improve quality of care. This includes piloting a network of patient advocates to provide information, guidance and support to patients; expanding the use of direct payments and individual budgets in social care and extending them into areas of health care; and expanding and developing expert patient initiatives.

The third principle is local democratic accountability and devolved decision-making. Here the Liberal Democrats have proposed replacing centrally appointed boards of PCTs with directly elected Local Health Boards with the option of the commissioning role being passed to local authorities if this was supported in a referendum; establishing a regional body made up of representation from Local Health Boards to take responsibility for planning tertiary services; and encouraging the development of public benefit organisations to enable voluntary organisations and social enterprises to play a bigger part in service delivery. The fourth and final principle is the efficient use of public resources in delivering high quality services. This includes promoting integration of health and social care, creating an independent NHS Funding and Advisory Commission to allocate resources using a needs-based funding formula, and placing a statutory duty on Local Health Boards to demonstrate value for money.

As these summaries of the policies of the Conservatives and Liberal Democrats indicate, debates on the future of the NHS are likely to focus more on means rather than ends. With the main political parties in Westminster competing to demonstrate the strength of their commitment to the values and principles on which the NHS is based and to enshrine these commitments in statutes and constitutions of various kinds, the main choice facing the electorate is whether this commitment should be pursued through devolution of authority to an independent NHS board in the case of the Conservatives or elected Local Health Boards in the case of the Liberal Democrats, or indeed whether the Labour Party should be entrusted with a fourth term of office to continue the programme of reform initiated under Tony Blair and Gordon Brown. In relation to Labour's policies for the future, the approach set out in the final report of the NHS Next Stage Review of change being driven locally and led by clinicians echoes many of the proposals put forward by the Conservatives and the Liberal Democrats, reinforcing the sense that the areas of common ground between the political parties are more important than the differences. The unanswered question is whether Labour and its main rivals are serious in their stated commitment to devolution or whether in the harsh reality of government, and faced with evidence about performance concerns in the NHS, the default position of hierarchical controls and targets will prevail.

The other question raised by the plans put forward by the political parties is whether public health really will receive greater attention in future. As we noted in Chapter 4, the policy rhetoric on public health has outstripped the reality for many years and it has proved difficult to increase the share of resources allocated to prevention in the face of continuing pressures to expand diagnostic and treatment services in the NHS. Although the evidence for a reorientation towards public health is compelling, it remains uncertain whether institutional innovations of the kind advanced by the Conservatives and Liberal Democrats will be sufficient to address the weakness of public health advocates in the continuing struggle for scarce resources. With the public appearing to value improvements in the performance of the NHS more than progress on public health, it would be a brave Secretary of State who would stand idly by if the gains made in the NHS in recent years are reversed.

Conclusion

In this chapter we have seen that the performance of the NHS in the past decade has improved considerably. Viewed in the international context, it can be said that the NHS has retained its traditional strengths as a universal, more or less comprehensive and largely free at the point of use system, and is increasingly able to provide care that is accessible and responsive to patients. The health of the population continues to improve and there is evidence of progress towards the higher standards of health enjoyed in some other developed countries. The main weaknesses of the NHS relate to the quality of care and aspects of patient experience. There is also room for improvement on public health.

The organisation of the NHS has been reformed as part of the quest for improvements in performance. Significant innovations include ISTCs, NHS foundation trusts and social enterprises as part of a move towards a mixed economy of care. Claims that the NHS is being privatised and dismantled are not sustained by the available evidence with the value of care commissioned from these providers comprising a small proportion of total expenditure. Many of the improvements in NHS performance have resulted from the use of hierarchical controls together with increased spending. Regulation and competition have been used alongside hierarchical controls and there is a risk that the NHS may suffer from a surfeit of different models. The quasi market reforms that were reintroduced in 2002 have had a limited impact to date, in part because advocates of markets have yet to convert the general argument for choice and competition into detailed policy interventions.

The emphasis on hierarchical controls has given rise to a debate about the role of politicians in the NHS, including proposals that politicians should not be involved in the day-to-day management of services. Various options have been put forward for NHS independence, although it is not clear how these can be reconciled with the accountability for expenditure of over £100 billion a year and experience in other public services demonstrating the difficulty of separating responsibility for strategic direction from execution and implementation. A key issue of continuing concern to politicians and the public is the future funding of health care in the case of the ageing population, medical advances and rising expectations. In the short term, the NHS appears to be well placed to deal with much tighter financial prospects, even if the position after 2011 is much more challenging. The balance between public and private funding of health care is again in the spotlight and the Richards review of top-up payments for cancer drugs suggests that private funding may play a bigger part in future. The outcome of the government's review of the funding of long-term care will hold some important pointers to the future.

Whatever the outcome of the review, priority-setting or rationing is likely to become more difficult within the NHS. The Blair and Brown governments have shown a greater willingness to develop a more explicit approach to rationing at the national level through NICE and national service frameworks. As resources become more constrained, tougher choices will arise, and PCTs will have the unenviable task of balancing national requirements against local needs while also balancing their budgets. This will require PCTs to strengthen their decision-making processes to be able to demonstrate accountability for reasonableness to those affected by their decisions.

The policies put forward by the main political parties show that there is much common ground between politicians of different persuasions on the future of the NHS. Insofar as there are differences, these relate more to means than ends. The Conservatives have placed the emphasis on empowering frontline staff to bring about improvements in care through refocusing attention on outcomes rather than care processes. The Conservatives' policies include support for greater independence for the NHS. For their part, the Liberal Democrats advocate local democratic accountability and devolved decision-making. This includes support for directly elected local health boards and even local government taking responsibility for commissioning health care where this is supported locally. The policies pursued by the Brown government since the completion of the NHS Next Stage Review also emphasise that change needs to be driven locally and led by clinicians, underlining the similarities between the main parties in Westminster.

Chapter 13

Reflections on the Reform of the NHS: 11 Lessons for Policy-makers

In this final chapter, I move beyond the analysis of the literature and evidence accumulated by myself and others to offer some personal reflections on the experience of NHS reform in the hope this will be of value to both students of health policy and those involved in policy-making. These reflections are brought together in eleven lessons for health policy-makers. The lessons focus mainly on the process of reform and the role of politicians, civil servants, managers and frontline staff in this process. The chapter is written in a deliberately pithy manner as I plan to return to these lessons at greater length in future work.

Taking stock

If the United Kingdom has become a laboratory for public service reform in the past decade, then the experiment that has been taking place in the NHS has been especially bold, to use a word favoured by Tony Blair. The ingredients of reform have been many and varied, encompassing targets and performance management, regulation and inspection and choice and competition, as well as a host of institutional innovations such as NICE and the NHS Modernisation Agency. The aims of NHS reform have been equally diverse, ranging from improvements in health outcomes through a concern to raise the standards of care and increase the focus on patient safety to the main objective of cutting waiting times and providing patients with quicker access to care. At this stage in the progress of the NHS experiment, recognising that it is still underway and the eventual outcome hard to predict, what can be said about the lessons learnt?

1. Policy-making in Opposition is often weak

When I make presentations about the NHS reforms to managers and clinicians, one of the first questions I am asked is, did the Blair government have a master plan for the NHS when it was elected that foresaw the migration from targets and performance management, through regulation and inspection to choice and competition? As should now be clear to readers of this book, the government had no such plan, and the evolution of NHS reform in the period since 1997 can be seen as a further example of policy-making on the hoof (a previous example being the evolution of the internal market in the 1990s), or in the language of policy analysts, an exercise in policy learning. A major reason for this, as we emphasised in Chapter 3, is that on its election the Blair government had a clearer idea of what it was against than what it was for in the NHS. The first six months of the new government were taken up working through its own policies for the NHS and *The New NHS* White Paper was the product. My first lesson is therefore the weakness of policy-making in Opposition and the failure of political parties to invest time and effort in working through their thinking to enable them to put their ideas into place when elected into government.

2. Politicians are inexperienced in leading large scale change

A second lesson is the inexperience of the current political class outside politics. The significance of this is that when MPs become ministers they bring little if any track record with them of management and leadership in other sectors. When one of these politicians becomes executive chairman of Britain plc and another becomes executive chairman of the most complex health care system in the world, they take on responsibilities of a quite different order to those they have previously exercised (even turning around a failing Labour Party does not get close). Of course, they are able to call on advice from civil servants, special advisers and many others, but few of these individuals have experience of exercising leadership in an organisation that comes anywhere near the size and complexity of the NHS. Even the most senior NHS managers who become civil servants have held chief executive roles in hospitals and health authorities operating on a much smaller scale. In view of this, it is hardly surprising that new ministers charged with oversight of the NHS struggle to understand the potential and the limits of the powers at their disposal and take a number of false turns along the way. In this respect, they are no different from other newly appointed leaders, except that the possibilities they have to do good or ill are much greater.

Tony Blair's preferred method of compensating for the inexperience of his ministers was to use people from business and other backgrounds as advisers. David Simon from BP and John Birt from the BBC were employed in this way by 10 Downing Street, while the work done by Derek Wanless and Adair Turner on the NHS for the Chancellor and the Prime Minister arose from the same motivation. Gordon Brown has gone much further by bringing into government people from outside politics with deep knowledge of different sectors. Examples include Shriti Vadera who became a business minister having worked in investment banking and then the Treasury; Digby Jones, the former director general of the Confederation of British Industry, who was appointed as a trade minister; Mervyn Davies, the former chairman of Standard Chartered who became a trade minister; and in the case of the NHS, Ara Darzi, a surgeon who had advised Alan Milburn and who was appointed as Health Minister in 2007. All of these individuals were ennobled to allow them to enter government. The appointment of people from outside politics as ministers gave rise to the argument that Gordon Brown was creating a government of all the talents (or 'goats' to use the acronym favoured by journalists). The larger question this raises is whether appointing experts to ministerial roles with seats in the House of Lords or as unpaid advisers to the government can be squared with the requirement for accountability in a modern political system?

3. It takes time to deliver change

A third lesson is that it takes time for the results of reform to become evident. In the case of the NHS, it can be argued that the Blair government only became serious in its intentions when Alan Milburn was appointed as Secretary of State for Health in October 1999 and the Prime Minister made his commitment in January 2000 to bring spending up to the European Union average. It was at that time that the government started to strengthen its approach to targets and performance management ('targets and terror' characterised Milburn's era much more than Dobson's) and that *The NHS Plan* set out a road map for the next ten years. Yet within 18 months of the Prime Minister's announcement on spending, and 12 months of publication of *The NHS Plan*, the government had decided to place much greater emphasis on choice and competition in the next stage of reform in the wake of the 2001 general election. A major reason was frustration at the slow pace of change in the NHS and the time it was taking for the increased investment that was occurring to produce results.

With the benefit of hindsight, it is clear that targets and performance management, together with increased investment, have made the biggest contribution to the improvements in the NHS that have occurred under the Blair and Brown governments. However, this was not apparent in the summer of 2001, and the understandable impatience of ministers to prove to the public that their policies were having an effect led them to overlay choice and competition on to targets and performance management. To complicate matters, publication of the Kennedy Report in 2001 served to strengthen the emphasis placed on regulation and inspection just at the time when policy on choice and competition was being worked up. The main ingredients of the complex policy mix discussed throughout this book were in this way brought together even if their respective contributions to the objectives being pursued remained uncertain and contested. The point to emphasise here is that confronted with evidence of limited progress in achieving their aims, ministers reacted by changing course rather than maintaining faith in the direction that had been set in 2000.

4. Things may get worse before they get better

A fourth lessons is that turning around an organisation as large and complex as the NHS may involve a deterioration in performance before the effects of increased spending and reform are felt. This first became clear in the autumn of 2001 when the then chief operating officer of the NHS had the unenviable task of explaining to the Secretary of State for Health the latest statistics on NHS performance. Not only did these statistics show that the extra spending allocated to the NHS had not delivered commensurate improvements in activity, but also in some areas of care there was evidence that things were getting worse. Arguments that the NHS needed time to translate the government's commitment to increased spending and root and branch reform into tangible benefits for patients after many years of neglect and a long history of underspending carried little weight with ambitious ministers whose horizons were shaped by the prospect of a general election in which the NHS promised to be the most important issue influencing the voting decisions of the public.

The experience of the NHS at that time lends support to the argument that large scale change programmes are often characterised by the so-called 'J-curve' in which there is a dip in performance before the positive effects of reform are felt. Related to this, Rosabeth Moss Kanter (1984), the eminent business researcher and consultant, has observed that everything can look like a failure in the middle of organisation transformations. Many involved in the changes that occurred in the NHS in recent years can testify to the accuracy of Kanter's observation. The implication is that experienced leaders (and as we have noted most politicians do not fit this description) know this and have the courage and stamina to see through their plans in the face of negative reports. Again, the challenge is how to do so when the natural inclination of government ministers is to favour bold strokes rather than to make a commitment to the long and often painful march of reforming public services in which the default setting of 'business as usual' is often stronger than the drive to innovate and improve.

5. Improvement is rarely linear

Linked to this, a fifth lesson is that where improvement does occur, it is rarely linear. The best examples are the emergence of concerns about healthcare associated infections in 2004 and financial deficits in many NHS organisations in 2005–06, just at the time when evidence had started to accumulate that on many key indicators the NHS was making real progress towards the objectives set by government. With waiting times for treatment falling rapidly, and measurable improvements taking place in areas of major clinical priority like cancer and heart disease, the government could begin to claim with some justification that its policies were taking effect. A different example from the public health field is the rising awareness of the risks posed by increased prevalence of overweight and obesity in the population alongside evidence of success in reducing premature deaths from heart disease and cancer.

The implication for those leading major change programmes is the need to focus both on established priorities and to be constantly alert to the likelihood that new challenges will emerge. This requires well-developed intelligence systems that connect those responsible for steering reform at a national level with managers and clinicians delivering services on the ground to provide feedback on major operational issues as they arise. It also demands a capability for strategic policy-making in government focused on scanning the horizon for new threats and opportunities. While the DH had elements of each of these at the time under review, the increasing focus on the delivery of the NHS reform programme, especially following the establishment of the Prime Minister's Delivery Unit in 2001, and the appointment to the top ranks of the Department of senior NHS managers, to the point where it had become seen as the Department for Delivery (see Chapter 8), meant that strategy issues progressively received less attention, particularly after Alan Milburn's resignation.

6. Changes in leadership may impede progress

A sixth lesson is that changes among the guiding coalition that is leading reform almost invariably impede progress. Looking back, the period from 1999 to 2004 was unusual in that a small group of individuals at the core of government exerted a powerful and consistent influence on the direction of reform. At the very heart of this group were the Prime Minister, the Secretary of State for Health and their special advisers. Close to the heart, but not part of it, were the Chancellor of the Exchequer and senior civil servants and advisers in 10 Downing Street, the Cabinet Office and the DH. These civil servants included members of the Prime Minister's Delivery Unit and Strategy Unit, influential individuals such as Derek

Wanless and Adair Turner, and a small group of people at the top of the DH. The importance of these individuals, and especially those at the heart, was that they worked from a common script on the reform of the NHS and functioned tirelessly and relentlessly to ensure that it was carried into action. The group began to unravel when Alan Milburn resigned unexpectedly in June 2003, to be replaced by John Reid, and it suffered a major loss of momentum in 2004 following the departure of Simon Stevens as senior health policy adviser to the Prime Minister.

The appointment of a new Secretary of State in 2003, and again following the 2005 election when Patricia Hewitt took on this role, did not mean that the process of NHS reform stopped, but it did have the effect of creating a hiatus while those who were appointed took stock of their inheritance. This was particularly apparent after Patricia Hewitt's appointment, with the new Secretary of State and her team taking six months to review the direction of reform and putting their own imprint on policy. In theory, the continuity provided by the senior civil service should have enabled momentum to be maintained, but in practice the influence exerted by ministers and special advisers outweighed the contribution of officials and meant that further progress in taking forward the health reform programme was delayed, although not derailed. While it might have been expected that the core executive, and especially the Prime Minister and his advisers, would exert pressure to avoid this happening, changes in key personnel in 10 Downing Street at around this time meant that this pressure was comparatively weak.

7. NHS reform requires a combination of approaches

A seventh lesson is that in the messy reality of public service reform, a combination of approaches is always likely to be necessary. The question then becomes, what is known about their application in practice? The evidence reviewed in this book has shown that targets and performance management have clearly made a significant impact on the reform of the NHS. Regulation and inspection, after a slow start, are also contributing, as seen in the improvements in performance achieved in the annual health check. The quasi market has yet to make a tangible difference in the view of most independent observers (Audit Commission and Healthcare Commission, 2008a), although it may be too early to reach a considered judgement given that this element in the health reform programme is still in the process of implementation. As with targets and performance management, more time may be needed for the effects of the quasi market to be felt in full.

It is also clear that each of these approaches has weaknesses as well as strengths. In the case of targets and performance management, the main weaknesses are the disempowerment of frontline staff, the stifling of innovation and the risk of gaming. In the case of regulation and inspection, there is the risk, and in some cases the reality, of overload on the organisations providing care to patients. And in the case of the quasi market, the principal drawback relates to the need to use competition with discrimination in the NHS, recognising that collaboration and partnership working also have a role (see below). A further significant challenge in applying market principles to the NHS, as discussed in Chapter 12, is that of designing detailed policy interventions that address weaknesses that arose in the internal market and that have become evident in the reintroduction of competition under the Blair and Brown governments. Equally important, if not more so, is the willingness of politicians to follow through the logic of the market and allow unsuccessful providers to fail, even if this creates unpopularity with the public (Ham, 2007b).

8. Regulation and inspection are likely to become increasingly important

For these reasons, an eighth lesson is that regulation and inspection may come to play an increasingly important part in future if politicians are serious in their stated commitments to reduce reliance on targets and performance management and continue to struggle to make the quasi market work. With the prospect that almost all NHS trusts will have become NHS foundation trusts in 2010, the government's influence over the NHS will be exerted primarily through PCTs as commissioners. NHS foundation trusts, removed from a hierarchical relationship with the DH, will be regulated by Monitor and the Care Quality Commission, and these two bodies will in many respects provide the drive for improved performance that was previously exercised by the DH through SHAs, especially at a time when the commissioning of services by PCTs remains a work in progress. Much therefore hinges on the performance of the regulators and their ability to use the powers at their disposal to work with NHS providers and their counterparts in the independent sector to take the NHS to the next stage of development.

9. Levers and incentives are needed to support collaboration alongside competition

A ninth lesson is that the diverse and complex nature of the care and services provided in the NHS means that different approaches to reform need to be matched to different services. Under the Blair government, policies on choice and competition were developed primarily in support of the government's main aim of reducing waiting times for treatment. With ministers concerned to increase hospital activity in order to improve access to care, it made eminent sense to offer patients the opportunity to go to the hospital of their choice and to use the payment by results reforms to ensure that money followed patients' choices (see Chapter 3). It is much less clear that these policies will help support improvements in other priority areas, such as improving the quality of care for people with chronic diseases and improving the health of the population (Ham, 2008c). Indeed, it could be argued that the fragmentation that has resulted from the use of ISTCs and the development of NHS foundation trusts concerned to improve their own performance without necessarily having regard to the wider health care system of which they are a part will make it more difficult to achieve objectives that require a more collaborative and partnership based approach.

This can be illustrated by the example of patients requiring urgent and unplanned care where a strong case can been made for the development of care networks that link together the services delivered in hospitals, the ambulance service, the GP out of hours service, NHS Direct and other settings. Indeed, as noted in Chapter 5, in many areas of care, including cancer, cardiac and stroke services, the argument for developing networks is more powerful than the argument for increasing choice and competition. Despite this, the levers and incentives to support networks and increased collaboration between providers are much weaker than those used to promote choice and competition. This creates a major challenge in view of the fact that most of the care provided in NHS hospitals is in fact unplanned care that results from patients being admitted as emergencies rather than from the waiting list. To express the point in more colloquial language, there is a clear risk of the planned care tail wagging the NHS dog, and future policy needs to address this as a matter of urgency. Various documents, including *Our Health, Our Care, Our Say* (Secretary of State for Health, 2006) have recognised this but policy-makers have been slow to put in place the levers and incentives needed to support collaboration.

10. Frontline staff, especially doctors, need to be fully engaged in reform

Whatever combination of approaches to reform is used, a tenth lesson is that there is a need to find ways of engaging frontline staff in the process of reform and improvement. While I was working in the DH as director of the strategy unit, I wrote a paper for *The Lancet* in which I reflected on the limited impact of big bang health care reforms in different countries (Ham, 2003b). At the heart of my argument was the contention that reforms based on ideas like public/private partnerships, managed competition and managed care had not lived up to expectations because they had failed to make a significant difference to the day-to-day decisions of frontline staff. As I wrote, 'the ability of managers, politicians, and others to influence decision-making is more constrained and contingent than in other organisations. Thus, ways have to be found of generating change bottom-up, not just top-down, especially by engaging professionals in the reform process' (p. 1978). These ideas gained some traction when Patricia Hewitt became Secretary of State for Health and began emphasising the need to develop a 'self-improving NHS' (see Chapter 3), but they really came to the fore in the NHS Next Stage Review undertaken by Lord Darzi and the argument in *High Quality Care for All* (Secretary of State for Health, 2008a) that reform should to be driven locally and led by clinicians.

The importance of engaging frontline staff in reform stems from the nature of health care organisations as professional bureaucracies, to borrow the phrase of organisational theorist Henry Mintzberg (1983). The point about professional bureaucracies is that they have an inverted power structure in which people at the bottom generally have greater influence over decision-making than those who are nominally in control at the top. In these disconnected hierarchies, organisational leaders have to negotiate rather than impose new policies and practices. Failure to recognise this and to carry professionals along with change almost invariably results in partial implementation of reform efforts. Bringing about change in health care organisations typically entails slow and painstaking work in which reformers, whether politicians or managers, need to engage clinicians and opinion formers in persuading their colleagues to do things differently.

In the long march of organisational transformation, leaders drawn from professional backgrounds have an important part to play in bringing about change. For this reason the emphasis placed recently by the government on the greater involvement of doctors, nurses and other clinicians in leadership roles is a step in the right direction. As this is taken forward, it must be recognised that clinical leaders need to work in partnership with experienced managers. Research evidence (Rundall et al., 1998) as well as the experience of organisations like Kaiser Permanente and Mayo Clinic demonstrates that those organisations that are clinically led *and* administratively managed have achieved most success in working towards higher levels of performance. This evidence reinforces the need for the NHS to strengthen both clinical and managerial leadership rather than emphasising one at the expense of the other.

11. The NHS needs to build capability for change and improvement

The eleventh and final lesson is the need to build capability for change and improvement throughout the NHS. This lesson stems from evidence that the NHS lacks many of the skills that are needed to make change happen (Bevan et al., 2008). It follows that devolution to the front line will lead to improvement being slow and uneven unless priority is given to equipping staff with the project management and service redesign skills that are needed to take reform forward. A Canadian study of high-performing health care organisations in different countries identified building capability for change and improvement as a key characteristic of the organisations studied (Baker et al., 2008), and in the next stage of reform the NHS needs to act on this finding.

In so doing, it is important not to repeat the mistakes of the past. In the first phase of NHS reform under the Blair government, the NHS Modernisation Agency was established with the role of supporting NHS organisations to undertake service improvement (see Chapter 3). Although the Agency did valuable work in a number of areas, it was superseded by the NHS Institute for Innovation and Improvement in 2005 because of a perception that it had grown too quickly and had taken away staff with expertise in service improvement from the very organisations they were intended to support. This suggests that priority should be given to ensuring that *every* NHS organisation builds its own capability for change and improvement rather than seeking external support. One of the reasons that this is important is the influence of local context on the ability of organisations to bring about change. Capability building that is located at the local level is likely to be better able to address variations in context in the pursuit of service improvement.

In emphasising the importance of building capability, the contribution that the introduction of general management has made to the NHS following the Griffiths Report of 1983 is worth remembering. Without a cadre of general managers able to take forward policies on targets and performance management, regulation and inspection, and the quasi market, the reform of the NHS would not have progressed as far as it has under the Blair and Brown governments. The experience of other health care systems – Canada is a good example – that are seeking to address many of the same challenges as the NHS but have found it much harder to make improvements on the same scale as England, lends support to this observation. Lacking the general management culture that is now firmly embedded in the NHS, and also the drive for reform that politicians have provided in England in the past decade, these systems serve as a timely reminder that the NHS has some of the leadership capability needed to bring about change and improvement, even if more needs to be done to develop the skills of frontline staff.

Moving forward

The lessons distilled in this chapter are not unique to the NHS. This much is clear from the writings of Peter Hyman who worked in 10 Downing

Street between 1997 and 2003, including a period as Head of the Prime Minister's Strategic Communications Unit, before becoming a school-teacher in north London. Hyman recounts from first-hand experience the approach taken by the Blair government to public service reform with the emphasis on demonstrating momentum and activism. This included launching a wide range of initiatives and seeking to manage the media at every opportunity. After his experience as a teacher, Hyman concluded that this approach was entirely the wrong one for convincing frontline professionals, or indeed for successful delivery:

> What the front line requires is a policy framework and goals, not hundreds of micro-announcements ... Now I realise that real 'delivery' is about the grind, not just the grand. It's about the combination of often small things that build over time, through individual relation-ships and genuine expertise and hard work. (Hyman, 2005, pp. 384–5)

Hyman's reference to the need for a policy framework and goals is a reminder that the argument for engaging frontline staff is not an argu-ment for government to abdicate its responsibilities. Rather it highlights the importance of finding a way of combining central direction with devo-lution to public sector organisations and frontline staff.

Of course, a major difficulty in acting on these insights, to return to lesson two, is the inexperience of politicians in leading large-scale change. Not only this, but also the depiction of the NHS in organisational charts as a hierarchical bureaucracy creates the misleading impression that ministers and their officials in Whitehall actually have control over how the system functions. One of the hardest and earliest lessons ministers learn is that the levers at their disposal are not always well connected to the delivery of care on the ground. As a consequence, while governments are able to make a real difference in some high priority areas, like cutting waiting times, their writ does not run across the full range of issues that matter to patients. The result is a Kubler-Ross-type cycle of anger and frustration at the failure of the NHS to take notice, followed by bargain-ing with officials to persuade them to connect the levers more effectively to care delivery, leading to depression that nothing seems to work (espe-cially halfway through when everything seems like a failure), and eventu-ally to acceptance and resignation that the NHS is probably unmanageable from Whitehall. The end result of one such cycle was Alan Milburn's decision to start the process of devolving power within the NHS through the development of NHS foundation trusts.

Again, it might be thought that civil servants could compensate for the inexperience of politicians, but recent history is not encouraging in this regard. On the one hand, civil servants, whose careers have been based in

Whitehall, are much better equipped to support ministers in developing policy, negotiating for resources in the spending reviews, and holding their own in discussions across government than in managing large-scale change. On the other hand, NHS managers who come into government are intuitively more inclined to engage with the challenge of change, but the pressure of the job and their lack of familiarity with relevant research evidence and experience in other sectors hampers their ability to advise ministers on what needs to be done. During my time in the DH, efforts were made to draw on the experience of people like David Simon from BP, who was working as an adviser in the Cabinet Office, and to engage with leading researchers of organisational change like Andrew Pettigrew, then of the University of Warwick. In truth, however, valuable as these efforts were, they were too intermittent to make a sustained impact on the DH's approach to reform, and in any case they were one step removed from the people who were driving reform, namely ministers and their special advisers.

In concluding this book, it is important to reiterate that improvement is possible, notwithstanding the many barriers to reform, both institutional and personal. To use a medical metaphor, having started the decade in intensive care, the NHS approaches its end in active rehabilitation, and through the final report of the NHS Next Stage Review, *High Quality Care for All*, has plotted a course to full recovery. Recognising that change is rarely linear, it would be a brave, or foolish, analyst who would predict smooth progress towards full recovery, particularly in the much more challenging financial climate that lies ahead. Nevertheless, the lessons brought together in this chapter offer guidance for future policy-makers on mistakes to be avoided and successes to be built on in taking forward the further transformation of the NHS.

Guide to Further Reading

Chapter 1

Further reading suggestions on the development of health services and health policy must necessarily be highly selective. Useful general accounts of the evolution of the welfare state in Britain are provided by Bruce (1968), Fraser (1973), Gilbert (1966, 1970) and Timmins (1995). Studies which look more specifically at the history of the medical profession and health services include those by Abel-Smith (1964), Cartwright (1971), Loudon et al. (1998), Porter (1997) and Stevens (1966). Eckstein (1958), Lindsey (1962) and Webster (1988, 1996) provide a wealth of material on the period before and after the creation of the National Health Service. Klein (2006) offers the best overview of the politics of health services in the period since 1939.

Chapter 2

The background to the Ministerial Review of the NHS is traced in Timmins (1995) and Butler (1992). A summary of the debate which took place during the Review is contained in Ham et al. (1990). The government's proposals were contained in three White Papers, *Working for Patients, Caring for People* and *Promoting Better Health* (Secretary of State for Health and others, 1989a, 1989b; Secretary of State for Social Services and others, 1987). Klein's account of the politics of the NHS (Klein, 2006) contains a highly readable analysis of the events which led up to the Review and the outcome. Ham (1997a) describes the implementation of the reforms, while Le Grand et al. (1998) review the evidence on the impact of the internal market. Ham (2000) analyses the politics of NHS reform in the late 1980s and 1990s from the perspective of health secretaries.

Chapter 3

The Blair government's original proposals were set out in a White Paper, *The New NHS* (Secretary of State for Health, 1997), a White Paper on public health, *Saving Lives: Our Healthier Nation* (Secretary of State for Health, 1999), and a consultation document on quality in the new NHS, *A First Class Service* (Secretary of State for Health, 1998b). Early commentaries on the government's plans were provided in Klein (1998) and Ham (1999). The government's reforms were taken forward in *The NHS Plan* (Secretary of State for Health, 2000), *Delivering the NHS Plan* (Secretary of State for Health, 2002), *The NHS Improvement Plan* (Secretary of State for Health, 2004a), and *High Quality Care for All* (Secretary of State for Health, 2008a). Assessments of the impact of the reforms can be found in Leatherman and Sutherland (2008), the Audit Commission and Health-care Commission (2008a), and the review led by Derek Wanless and others (2007) commissioned by the King's Fund.

Chapter 4

The Department of Health's annual reports are a useful source of information about NHS funding and current policy issues (DH, 2008a). Data on expenditure trends and the performance of the NHS since its establishment are contained in the compendium of statistics produced annually by the Office of Health Economics (2008). The Wanless review provides a good analysis and review of the issues involved in the long-term funding of the NHS (Wanless, 2001, 2002). Government policy on public health is set out in the series of White Papers and other policy documents referred to in Chapter 4, most recently *Choosing Health* (Secretary of State for Health, 2004b). The review of public health led by Derek Wanless (2004) and commissioned by the government describes progress in improving population health outcomes and risks for the future. An assessment of the government's response to this review, commissioned by the King's Fund and led by Wanless, can be found in Wanless et al. (2007).

Chapter 5

The Department of Health's website is a mine of information about current health policy issues and provides access to the White Papers and other policy documents discussed in Chapter 5. The website is not easy to navigate and documents can often be located most easily by using Google rather than the search facility on the website. Commentaries on government policies can be found in the reports of the Audit Commission and the Care Quality Commission (and its predecessor the Healthcare Commission), as well as in the reviews and inquiries undertaken by the Health Committee, the Public Accounts Committee and the National Audit Office. The websites of these organisations and committees provide access to their reports. The challenges of rationing in the NHS are explored in Klein et al. (1996), and have been brought to the fore through the work of NICE. The report of the Health Committee (2008b) into NICE summarises the issues raised by its work to date. Baggott (2007) provides an overview of health policy and is a useful introduction to the field.

Chapter 6

Jenkins (1978) examines policy analysis using a political and organisational perspective, and Parsons (1995) offers an overview of different perspectives on policy analysis. Beer (1969) provides an important interpretation of the evolution of politics in Britain. Norton (1981, 2005) discusses the role of the House of Commons and Richardson and Jordan (1979) focus on the part played by pressure groups in the policy process. Hennessy (1986, 1989, 1995, 2000) analyses the role of the Cabinet, civil service, Prime Minister and other institutions. Dunleavy and others (2006) assess recent developments in British politics and should be read alongside Rhodes (1997), Smith (1999), and Marsh et al. (2001). Fawcett and Gay (2005) offer a detailed account of recent changes to the centre of government. Deakin and Parry (2000) provide the best introduction to the role of the Treasury in relation to social policy. Seldon (2007) offers a comprehensive independent review of the changing face of Westminster and Whitehall under Tony Blair. Insider accounts of the Blair years can be found in Campbell (2007), Barber (2007) and Hyman (2005).

Chapter 7

Greer (2004) provides the best introduction to devolution and health policy through a comparative and historical political analysis of the dynamics of health policy-making in the four countries of the United Kingdom. Jervis (2007) describes the detailed development of health policy and the governance of the NHS in these countries in the period since 1999. The websites for the governments of Scotland (www.scotland.gov.uk), Wales (www.wales.gov.uk) and Northern Ireland (www.northernireland.gov.uk) contain reports and publications in relation to health and the NHS in these countries. Sutherland and Coyle (2009) bring together comparative data on health and health services in the United Kingdom.

Chapter 8

Brown (1975) has written a good, general account of the workings of the DHSS and the part it played in the management of the NHS, personal social services and social security until the mid-1970s. Day and Klein offer an assessment of changes in the 1980s and 1990s (Day and Klein, 1997) and should be read alongside the work of Greer and Jarman who bring the story up to date (2007). The Cabinet Office's capability review of the Department makes salutary reading (Cabinet Office, 2007). The author's analysis of the politics of NHS reform in the 1990s (Ham, 2000) analyses the role of health secretaries and the world in which they work. Smee's insider's account offers a detailed review of the many changes to the organisation of the DH and is particularly strong on the contribution of analysts and economists (Smee, 2005). Sheard and Donaldson (2006) focus on the role of doctors in government by examining the changing role of the chief medical officer.

Chapter 9

Brown (1975, 1979) discusses the historical relationship between the DHSS and health authorities, while Hunter (1980) explores the dynamics of policy-making in health authorities, and identifies a number of phases in centre–periphery relationships (Hunter, 1983). The author's own examination of policy-making in the NHS between 1948 and 1974 (Ham, 1981) covers similar territory. Klein's (2006) work on the politics of the NHS contains much that is relevant to the student of health policy implementation, as does the author's study of health authorities in the period 1981–85 (Ham, 1986). Harrison (1988, 1994) assesses the impact of the Griffiths Report on general management and the effect this had on the role of managers. McDonald (2002) reviews policy-making in health authorities in the 1990s. More recent developments are analysed by Blackler (2006), Greener and Powell (2003), Greener (2005) and Sheaff and colleagues (2003).

Chapter 10

Day and Klein (2001) discuss the role of the Audit Commission and the National Audit Office. Walshe (2003) offers a good introduction to regulation in the NHS. Smee (2005) and Smith (2005) review the evolution of performance indicators and performance management. The websites of the Audit Commission, the Care Quality Commission (and its predecessor the Healthcare Commission), the National Audit Office, the Health Committee and the Public Accounts Committee provide access to their reports on the performance of the NHS. Charlton and Murphy (1997) summarise the historical evidence on population health, and more recent trends can be found in Wheller et al. (2007) and in

Leatherman and Sutherland (2008). The Report of the Royal Commission on the NHS (Royal Commission, 1979) contains a general review of the impact of the NHS in its first 30 years. The RAWP report (DHSS, 1976a) describes the method used to allocate resources on an equitable geographical basis, while the Black Report, *Inequalities in Health* (1980), was the first systematic attempt to bring together information on social class differences in health and the use of health services. More recent evidence on health inequalities is reviewed by Dreyer and Whitehead (1997), the Acheson Report (1998), the Cross-Cutting Review (2002) and DH (2008f, 2008g). The series of inquiries into long-stay hospitals provide powerful evidence of client-group inequalities. Examples are the Ely and Normansfield reports (Ely Report, 1969; Normansfield Report, 1978). Martin (1984) has summarised the reports and has analysed the nature of the problems that exist in this area. Yates (1987, 1995) has examined waiting lists and the role of private practice.

Chapter 11

Pluralist ideas have been applied in the work of Eckstein (1960) and Willcocks (1967). The structuralist argument has been set out by Alford (1975a), and applied to the NHS by the author (Ham, 1981). The Marxist perspective has been most fully developed by Navarro (1976) and Doyal (1979). Stacey (1977) and Illsley (1977) review different concepts of health and the way these concepts have influenced service provision. Outside the health field, Saunders (1979) has written a major study of theories of power and the role of ideology which is of considerable relevance to the student attempting to understand the complexities of health policy-making. Smith's (1999) analysis examines the interplay between actors, institutions, context and structure. Harrison (1994) applies a range of theoretical perspectives to the study of health policy. Klein (2006) and Greener (2002) make the case for the use of a range of theories and perspectives in understanding health policy, echoing my own approach (Ham, 1980).

Chapter 12

The performance of the NHS in the international context is considered in a range of publications by the OECD and the WHO (see as an example WHO, 2000). The Commonwealth Fund's annual surveys offer comparisons of the United Kingdom and a number of other countries (see Davis et al., 2007, and www. cmwf.org). Coulter (2006) has drawn on these surveys to analyse the experience of patients in the United Kingdom compared with other countries. Changing attitudes to the NHS have been tracked in the British Social Attitudes' Survey (Appleby and Phillips, 2009) and trends in patient experiences in the NHS are reviewed by Richards and Coulter (2007). Pollock (2004) advances the argument that the NHS is being privatised and dismantled, while Le Grand (2007) reviews different approaches to NHS reform and argues for a bigger role for choice and competition. Tuohy (1999) provides a detailed historical and comparative analysis of the dynamics of health systems that helps to explain why market based reforms often have limited impact. The future funding of the NHS is discussed by various commentators (Bramley-Harker and Booer, 2006; Charlson et al., 2007; Farrington-Douglas and Coelho, 2008). The review of the funding of cancer drugs undertaken for the government by Mike Richards (2008) illustrates the complexities involved in determining the public/private mix of funding. Issues to do with health care rationing, both in the United Kingdom and elsewhere, are discussed by Coulter and Ham (2000) and Ham and Robert (2003).

Bibliography

Note: where no publisher is given, the author indicated is also the publisher.

Abel, L. A. and Lewin, W. (1959) 'Report on Hospital Building', *British Medical Journal Supplement*, (4 April): 109–14.

Abel-Smith, B. (1964) *The Hospitals 1800–1948* (Heinemann).

Acheson Report (1998) *Independent Inquiry into Inequalities and Health* (The Stationery Office).

Alderson, M. R. (1970) 'Social Class and the Health Service', *The Medical Officer*, (17 July): 50–2.

Alford, R. (1975a) *Health Care Politics* (University of Chicago Press).

Alford, R. (1975b) 'Paradigms of Relations between State and Society', in Lindberg, L. N., Alford, R., Crouch, C. and Offe, C. (eds), *Stress and Contradiction in Modern Capitalism* (Lexington Books).

Allen, D. (1979) *Hospital Planning* (Pitman Medical).

Allin, S., Masseria, C. and Mossialos, E. (2006) *Inequality in health care use among older people in the United Kingdom: an analysis of panel data* LSE Health Working Paper No.1/2006.

Allsop, J. and Mulcahy, L. (1996) *Regulating Medical Work* (Open University Press).

Alvarez-Rosete, A. and Mays, N. (2008) 'Reconciling Two Conflicting Tales of the English Health Policy Process Since 1997' *British Politics*, 3, 183–203.

Alvarez-Rosete, A., Bevan, G., Mays, N. and Dixon, J. (2005) 'Effect of Diverging Policy Across the NHS' *British Medical Journal*, 331, 946–50.

Alzheimer's Society (2007) *Dementia UK*.

Appleby Report (2005) *Independent Review of Health and Social Care Services in Northern Ireland* (Department of Health, Social Services and Public Safety).

Appleby, J. and Coote, A. (eds) (2002) *Five-year Health Check* (King's Fund).

Appleby, J. and Gregory, S. (2008) *NHS Spending. Local Variations in Priorities: An Update* (King's Fund).

Appleby, J. and Harrison, A. (2006) *Spending on Health Care: How Much is Enough?* (King's Fund).

Appleby, J. and Phillips, M. (2009) 'The NHS: Satisfied Now?' in Park, A., Curtice, J., Thomson, K., Phillips, M., Johnson, M. C. and Clery, E. (eds) *British Social Attitudes Survey: The 25th Report* (Sage).

Appleby, L. (2007) *Mental Health Ten Years On: Progress on Mental Health Reform* (DH).

Armesto, S., Lapetra, M. L. G., Wei, L., Kelley, E. and Members of the HCQI Expert Group (2007) *Health Care Quality Indicators 2006 Data Collection Update Report* (OECD).

Audit Commission (1997) *The Coming of Age* (The Stationery Office).

Audit Commission (2003) *Achieving the NHS Plan*.

Audit Commission (2005) *Governing Partnerships*.

Audit Commission (2008) *Are We There Yet?*

Audit Commission and Healthcare Commission (2008a) *Is the Treatment Working?*

Audit Commission and Healthcare Commission (2008b) *Are We Choosing Health?*

Bachrach, P. and Baratz, M. S. (1970) *Power and Poverty* (Oxford University Press).

Bagehot, W. (1963) [1867] *The English Constitution*, new edn (Fontana).

Baggott, R. (1986) 'Alcohol, Politics and Social Policy', *Journal of Social Policy*, 15(4): 467–88.

Baggott, R. (2007) *Understanding Health Policy* (The Policy Press).

Baggott, R., Allsop, J. and Jones, K. (2004) 'Representing the Repressed? Health Consumer Groups and the National Policy Process' *Policy and Politics,* **32**(3): 317–31.

Bajekal, M. and Prescott, A. (2003) *Disability. The Health Survey for England 2001* (The Stationery Office).

Baker, G. R., MacIntosh-Murray, A., Porcellato, C. et al. (2008) *High Performing Healthcare Systems* (Longwood).

Banks Review (1994) *Review of the Wider Department of Health* (DH).

Banting, K. (1979) *Poverty, Politics and Policy* (Palgrave Macmillan).

Barber, M. (2007) *Instruction to Deliver* (Methuen).

Barrett, S. and Fudge, C. (eds) (1981) *Policy and Action* (Methuen).

Bauld, L. and Judge, K. (eds) (2002) *Learning from Health Action Zones* (Aeneas Press).

Bebbington, A. and Darton, R. (1996) *Healthy Life Expectancy in England and Wales: Recent Evidence* (University of Kent).

Beecham Report (2006) *Beyond Boundaries* (Welsh Assembly Government).

Beer, S. H. (1969) *Modern British Politics*, 2nd edn (Faber).

Bevan, G. and Hamblin, R. (2009) 'Hitting and Missing Targets by Ambulance Services for Emergency Calls: Effects of Different Systems of Performance Measurement Within the UK' *Journal of the Royal Statistical Society*, **172**, 161–90.

Bevan, G. and Hood, C. (2006) 'Have Targets Improved Performance in the English NHS?' *British Medical Journal,* **332**, 419–22.

Bevan, G. and Robinson, R. (2005) 'The Interplay between Economic and Political Logics: Path Dependency in Health Care in England' *Journal of Health Politics, Policy and Law,* **30**, 53–78.

Bevan, H., Ham, C. J. and Plsek, P. (2008) *The Next Leg of the Journey: How Do We Make High Quality Care for All a Reality?* (NHS Institute for Innovation and Improvement).

Bevir, M. and Rhodes, R. A.W. (2003) *Interpreting British Governance* (Routledge).

Bevir, M. and Rhodes, R. (2006) 'Prime Ministers, Presidentialism and Westminster Smokescreens' *Political Studies* **54**, 671–90.

Black Report (1980) *Inequalities in Health* (DHSS).

Blackler, F. (2006) 'Chief Executives and the Modernization of the English National Health Service' *Leadership*, **2**(1): 5–30.

Bogdanor, V. (ed.) (2005) *Joined-Up Government* (Oxford University Press).

Boon, N., Norell, M., Hall, J., Jennings, K., Penny, L., Wilson, C., Chambers, J., and Weston, R. (2006) 'National Variations in the Provision of Cardiac Services in the United Kingdom: Second Report of the British Cardiac Society Working Group, 2005' *Heart*, **92**, 873–8.

Botting, B. (ed.) (1995) *The Health of Our Children* (HMSO).

Bottomley, V. (1995) *The NHS: Continuity and Change* (DH).

Bramley-Harker, E. and Booer, T. (2006) *Mind the Gap: Sustaining Improvements in the NHS Beyond 2008* (BUPA).

Brenner, H. (1979) 'Mortality and the National Economy', *The Lancet*, (15 September): 586–73.

Bridgen, P. and Lewis, J. (1999) *Elderly People and the Boundary between Health and Social Care 1946–91: Whose Responsibility?* (The Nuffield Trust).

Brown, G. (2003) *A Modern Agenda for Prosperity and Social Reform,* issued under cover of press release 12/03 by HM Treasury (www.hm-treasury.gov.uk).

Brown, R. G. S. (1975) *The Management of Welfare* (Fontana).

Brown, R. G. S. (1979) *Reorganising the National Health Service* (Blackwell & Robinson).

Bruce, M. (1968) *The Coming of the Welfare State*, 4th edn (Batsford).

Bunker, J. (2001) 'The Role of Medical Care in Contributing to Health Improvements within Societies', *International Journal of Epidemiology*, **30**, 1260–3.

Bunting, J. (1997) 'Morbidity and Health-related Behaviour of Adults – a Review', in Dreyer, F. and Whitehead, M. (eds) *Health Inequalities* (The Stationery Office).

Butler, J. (1992) *Patients, Policies and Politics* (Open University Press).

Butler, J. R. with Bevan, J. M. and Taylor, R. C. (1973) *Family Doctors and Public Policy* (Routledge & Kegan Paul).

Cabinet Office (2007) *Capability Review of the Department of Health*.

Cabinet Office Strategy Unit (2008) *Excellence and Fairness: Achieving World Class Public Services* (The Stationery Office).

Calman-Hine (1995) *A Policy Framework for Commissioning Cancer Services* (DH).

Campbell, A. (2007) *The Blair Years* (Hutchinson).

Cannon, G. (1984) 'The Cover-up that Kills', *The Times*, 12 June, p. 13.

Cartwright, F. (1971) *A Social History of Medicine* (Longman).

Castle, B. (1980) *The Castle Diaries 1974–76* (Weidenfeld & Nicolson).

Cawson, A. (1982) *Corporatism and Welfare* (Heinemann).

Central Health Services Council (1969) *The Functions of the District General Hospital* (HMSO).

Central Policy Review Staff (1975) *A Joint Framework for Social Policies* (HMSO).

Chancellor of the Exchequer (1998) *Modern Public Services in Britain*, Cm 4011 (The Stationery Office).

Charlson, P., Lees, C., and Sikora, K. (2007) *Free at the Point of Delivery – Reality or Political Mirage?* (Doctors for Reform).

Charlton, J. (1997) 'Trends in All-cause Mortality: 1841–1994', in Charlton and Murphy (eds) *The Health of Adult Britain 1841–1994*, Vol. 1 (The Stationery Office).

Charlton, J. and Murphy, M. (eds) (1997) *The Health of Adult Britain 1841–1994*, Vols 1 and 2 (The Stationery Office).

Charlton, J., Fraser, P. and Murphy, M. (1997) 'Medical Advances and Iatrogenesis', in Charlton and Murphy (eds), Vol. 1 (The Stationery Office).

CHI (Commission for Health Improvement) (2003) *Getting Better?* (The Stationery Office).

Chief Secretary to the Treasury (2003) *Every Child Matters* Cm 5860 (The Stationery Office).

Christensen, C., Grossman, J. and Hwang, J. (2009) *The Innovator's Prescription* (McGraw-Hill).

Clarke, C. (2008) *Achieving the Potential* (KPMG).

Cmnd 9058 (1983) *Financial Management in Government Departments* (HMSO).

Colin-Thome, D. (2004) *A Responsive and High-quality Local NHS. The Primary Care Progress Report 2004* (DH).

Committee on Standards in Public Life (2002) *Defining the Boundaries within the Executive: Ministers, Special Advisers and the Permanent Civil Service*.

Conservative Party (2008) *Delivering Some of the Best Health in Europe: Outcomes Not Targets*.

Coulter, A. (2006) *Engaging Patients in their Healthcare* (Picker Institute Europe).

Coulter, A. and Cleary, P. (2001) 'Patients' Experiences with Hospital Care in Five Countries', *Health Affairs*, 20, 244–52.

Coulter, A. and Ham, C. (eds) (2000) *The Global Challenge of Health Care Rationing* (Open University Press).

Coulter, A. and Magee, H. (eds) (2003) *The European Patient of the Future* (Open University Press).

Cowley, P. (2006) 'Making Parliament Matter?' in Dunleavy, P., Gamble, A., Hefferanan, R. and Peele, G. (eds) *Developments in British Politics,* 8th edn (Palgrave Macmillan).

Crisp, N. (2004) *National Standards, Local Action* (DH).

Crisp, N. (2005) *Commissioning a Patient-Led NHS* (DH).

Cross-Cutting Review (2002) *Tackling Health Inequalities* (DH and HM Treasury).

Crossman, R. H. S. (1963) Introduction to Bagehot, W. *The English Constitution* (Fontana).

Crossman, R. H. S. (1972) *A Politician's View of Health Service Planning* (University of Glasgow Press).

Crossman, R. H. S. (1975) *The Diaries of a Cabinet Minister:* Vol 1, *Minister of Housing 1964–66* (Hamilton & Cape).

Crossman, R. H. S. (1976) *The Diaries of a Cabinet Minister:* Vol 2, *Lord President of the Council and Leader of the House of Commons 1966–68* (Hamilton & Cape).

Crossman, R. H. S. (1977) *The Diaries of a Cabinet Minister:* Vol 3, *Secretary of State for Social Services 1968–70* (Hamilton & Cape).

Cutler, D. and McClellan, M. (2001) 'Is Technological Change in Medicine Worth It?', *Health Affairs,* **20**, 11–29.

Dahl, R. (1961) *Who Governs?* (Yale University Press).

Daniels, N. and Sabin, J. (1997) 'Limits to Health Care: Fair Procedures, Democratic Deliberation, and the Legitimacy Problem for Insurers' *Philosophy and Public Affairs,* **4**, 303–50.

Davey Smith, G., Gunnell, D. and Ben-Shlomo, Y. (2001) 'Life-course Approaches to Socio-economic Differentials in Cause-specific Mortality', in Leon, D. and Walt, G. (eds) *Poverty, Inequality and Health: An International Perspective* (Oxford University Press).

Davis, K., Schoen, C., Schoenbaum, S. et al. (2007) *Mirror, Mirror on the Wall: An International Update on the Comparative Performance of American Health Care* (The Commonwealth Fund).

Day, P. and Klein, R. (1983) 'The Mobilisation of Consent versus the Management of Conflict: Decoding the Griffiths Report', *British Medical Journal,* **287**, 1813–16.

Day, P. and Klein, R. (1997) *Steering but not Rowing?* (The Policy Press).

Day, P. and Klein, R. (2001) *Auditing the Auditors: Audit in the National Health Service* (The Stationery Office).

Deakin, N. and Parry, R. (2000) *The Treasury and Social Policy* (Palgrave Macmillan).

Deeming, C. (2004) 'Decentring the NHS: A Case Study of Resource Allocation Decisions within a Health District' *Social Policy and Administration,* **38**(1): 57–72.

Delamothe, T. (2008) 'NHS at 60: Founding Principles' *British Medical Journal,* **336**, 1216–18.

Department for Education and Skills and Department of Health (2004) *National Service Framework for Children, Young People and Maternity Services.*

DH (1991) The *Patient's Charter.*

DH (1994) *The Operation of the NHS Internal Market: Local Freedoms, National Responsibilities.*

DH (1997) *Statement of Responsibilities and Accountabilities.*

DH (1998a) *The Health of the Nation – a Policy Assessed* (The Stationery Office).

DH (1998b) *Partnership In Action.*

DH (1999) *A National Service Framework for Mental Health.*

DH (2000a) *Shaping the Future NHS: Long-term Planning for Hospitals and Related Services.*

DH (2000b) *The NHS Cancer Plan.*

DH (2000c) *National Service Framework for Coronary Heart Disease.*

DH (2001a) *Shifting the Balance of Power within the NHS – Securing Delivery.*

DH (2001b) *Valuing People: A New Strategy for Learning Disability for the 21st Century* Cm 5086 (The Stationery Office).

DH (2001c) *National Service Framework for Older People.*

DH (2003a) *Tackling Health Inequalities: A Programme for Action.*

DH (2003b) *Keeping the NHS Local.*

DH (2005) *Health Reform in England: Update and Next Steps.*

DH (2006a) *Health Reform in England: Update and Commissioning Framework.*

DH (2006b) *Departmental Report 2006* Cm 6814.

DH (2006c) *The Government's Response to the Health Committee's Report on Independent Sector Treatment Centres* Cm 6930 (The Stationery Office).

DH (2007a) *Cancer Reform Strategy.*

DH (2007b) *Valuing People Now: From Progress to Transformation.*

DH (2007c) *Putting People First.*

DH (2007d) *The NHS in England: the Operating Framework for 2008/09.*

DH (2007e) *Maternity Matters: Choice, Access and Continuity of Care in a Safe Service* (TSO).

DH (2008a) *Departmental Report 2008* Cm 7393.

DH (2008b) *The NHS Constitution.*

DH (2008c) *Raising the Profile of Long Term Conditions Care: A Compendium of Information.*

DH (2008d) *The Operating Framework for the NHS in England 2009/10.*

DH (2008e) *Developing the NHS Performance Regime.*

DH (2008f) *Tackling Health Inequalities: 2007 Status Report on the Programme for Action.*

DH (2008g) *Health Inequalities: Progress and Next Steps.*

DHSS (1971) *Better Services for the Mentally Handicapped,* Cmnd 4683 (HMSO).

DHSS (1972) *The Facilities and Services of Psychiatric Hospitals in England and Wales 1970,* Statistical and Research Report Series no. 2 (HMSO).

DHSS (1974) *The Facilities and Services of Mental Illness and Mental Handicap Hospitals in England and Wales 1972,* Statistical and Research Report Series no. 8 (HMSO).

DHSS (1975a) *Better Services for the Mentally Ill,* Cmnd 6223 (HMSO).

DHSS (1975b) *Draft Guide to Planning in the NHS.*

DHSS (1975c) *First Interim Report of the Resource Allocation Working Party.*

DHSS (1976a) *Sharing Resources for Health in England* (HMSO).

DHSS (1976b) *Priorities for Health and Personal Social Services in England* (HMSO).

DHSS (1976c) *The NHS Planning System.*

DHSS (1976d) *Prevention and Health: Everybody's Business* (HMSO).

DHSS (1977a) *Prevention and Health,* Cmnd 7047 (HMSO).

DHSS (1977b) *The Way Forward* (HMSO).

DHSS (1979) *Patients First* (HMSO).

DHSS (1980a) Health Circular (80) 8, *Health Service Development Structure and Management.*

DHSS (1980b) *Hospital Services: The Future Pattern of Hospital Provision in England.*

DHSS (1980c) *Mental Handicap: Progress, Problems and Priorities.*

DHSS (1981a) *Report of a Study on Community Care.*

DHSS (1981b) *Growing Older,* Cmnd 8173 (HMSO).

DHSS (1981c) *Care in Action* (HMSO).

DHSS (1981d) *Care in the Community.*

DHSS (1981e) *Report on a Study of the Acute Hospital Sector* (HMSO).

DHSS (1981f) *Report on a Study of the Respective Roles of the General Acute and Geriatric Sectors in Care of the Elderly Hospital Patient.*

DHSS (1983) *Health Care and its Cost* (HMSO).

Dixon, A. and Mossialos, E. (eds) (2002) *Health Care Systems in Eight Countries: Trends and Challenges* (LSE).

Dixon, A., Le Grand, J., Henderson, J., Murray, R. and Poteliakhoff, E. (2003) *Is the NHS Equitable? A Review of the Evidence* (LSE).

Doyal, L. and Epstein, S. (1983) *Cancer in Britain: The Politics of Prevention* (Pluto Press).

Doyal, L. with Pennell, I. (1979) *The Political Economy of Health* (Pluto Press).

Draper, P., Best, G. and Dennis, J. (1977) 'Health and Wealth', *Royal Society of Health Journal,* **97**, 65–70.

Dreyer, F. and Bunting, J. (1997) 'Patterns and Trends in Male Mortality', in Dreyer, F. and Whitehead, M. (eds), *Health Inequalities* (The Stationery Office).

Dreyer, F. and Whitehead, M. (eds) (1997) *Health Inequalities* (The Stationery Office).

Dunleavy, P. (1981) 'Professions and Policy Change: Notes Towards a Model of Ideological Corporatism', *Public Administration Bulletin,* **36**, 3–16.

Dunleavy, P. (2006) 'The Westminster Model and the Distinctiveness of British Politics' in Dunleavy, P., Gamble, A., Heffernanan, R. and Peele, G. (eds) *Developments in British Politics,* 8th edn (Palgrave Macmillan).

Dunnell, K. (1997) 'Are We Healthier?', in Charlton and Murphy (eds) *The Health of Adult Britain 1841–1994*, Vol. 2 (The Stationery Office).

Easton, D. (1953) *The Political System* (Knopf).

Eckstein, H. (1958) *The English Health Service* (Harvard University Press).

Eckstein, H. (1960) *Pressure Group Politics* (Allen & Unwin).

Edelman, M. (1971) *Politics as Symbolic Action* (Markham).

Edelman, M. (1977) *Political Language* (Academic Press).

Edwards, B. (2007) *An Independent NHS: A Review of the Options* (The Nuffield Trust).

Ellins, J., Ham, C. and Parker, H. (2008) *Choice and Competition in Primary Care: Much Ado About Nothing?* (Health Services Management Centre, University of Birmingham).

Ely Report (1969) *Report of the Committee of Enquiry into Allegations of Ill-treatment of Patients and Other Irregularities at the Ely Hospital, Cardiff*, Cmnd 3975 (HMSO).

Enthoven, A. (1985) *Reflections on the Management of the NHS* (Nuffield Provincial Hospitals Trusts).

Enthoven, A. and Tollen, L. (eds) (2004) *Towards a 21st Century Health System* (Jossey-Bass).

European Commission (2007) *Health and Long-term Care in the European Union*.

Expenditure Committee (1971) Employment and Social Services Sub-Committee, *Minutes of Evidence*, 31 March 1971, session 1970–1. HC 323ii (HMSO).

Expenditure Committee (1972) *Relationship of Expenditure to Needs*, eighth report from the Expenditure Committee, session 1971–2 (HMSO).

Farrington-Douglas, J. and Coelho, M. (2008) *Private Spending on Healthcare* (IPPR).

Fawcett, P. and Gay, O. (2005) *The Centre of Government – No.10, the Cabinet Office and HM Treasury* (House of Commons Library).

Fawcett, P. and Rhodes, R. (2007) 'Central Government' in Seldon, A. (ed.) *Blair's Britain 1997–2007* (Cambridge University Press).

Ferlie, E., Ashburner, L., Fitzgerald, L. and Pettigrew, A. (1996) *The New Public Management in Action* (Oxford University Press).

Ferri, E., Bynner, J. and Wadsworth, M. (2003) *Changing Britain, Changing Lives* (Institute of Education).

Flynn, R. (1991) 'Coping with Cutbacks and Managing Retrenchment in Health', *Journal of Social Policy*, 20(2): 215–36.

Foubister, T., Thomson, S., Mossialos, E. and McGuire, A. (2006) *Private Medical Insurance in the United Kingdom* (European Observatory on Health Systems and Policies).

Fowler, N. (1991) *Ministers Decide* (Chapman).

Fox, D. (1986) *Health Policies, Health Politics* (Princeton University Press).

Fraser, D. (1973) *The Evolution of the British Welfare State* (Palgrave Macmillan).

Freeman, R. (2000) *The Politics of Health in Europe* (Manchester University Press).

Friedrich, C. J. (1937) *Constitutional Government and Politics* (Harper).

Fries, J. F. (1980) 'Aging, Natural Death and the Compression of Morbidity', *New England Journal of Medicine*, 303, 130–5.

Gabbay, J. and le May, A. (2004) 'Evidence Based Guidelines or Collectively Constructed "Mindlines"? Ethnographic Study of Knowledge Management in Primary Care' *British Medical Journal*, 329, 1013–16.

Gaffney, D., Pollock, A., Price, D. and Shaoul, J. (1999) 'NHS Capital Expenditure and the Private Finance Initiative – Expansion or Contraction?' *British Medical Journal*, 319(3 July): 48–51.

Gilbert, B. B. (1966) *The Evolution of National Insurance in Great Britain* (Michael Joseph).

Gilbert, B. B. (1970) *British Social Policy 1914–39* (Batsford).

Glasby, J. and Littlechild, R. (2004) *The Health and Social Care Divide* (The Policy Press).

Glasby, J., Smith, J. and Dickinson, H. (2006) *Creating NHS Local: A New Relationship Between PCTs and Local Government* (Health Services Management Centre, University of Birmingham).

Godber, G. (1975) *The Health Service: Past, Present and Future* (Athlone Press).

Godber, G. (1981) 'Doctors in Government', *Health Trends*, **13**.

Gough, I. (1979) *The Political Economy of the Welfare State* (Palgrave Macmillan).

Government Office for Science (2007) *Tackling Obesities: Future Choices*, Project Report by Foresight.

Greener, I. (2002) 'Understanding NHS Reform: The Policy-Transfer, Social Learning and Path-Dependency Perspectives' *Governance*, **15**(2): 161–83.

Greener, I. (2005) 'Health Management as Strategic Behaviour' *Public Management Review*, **7**(1): 95–110.

Greener, I. and Powell, J. (2003) 'Health Authorities, Priority-setting and Resource Allocation: A Study in Decision-making in New Labour's NHS' *Social Policy and Administration*, **37**(1): 35–48.

Greer, S. (2003) 'Policy Divergence. Will it Change Something in Greenock?', in Hazell, R. (ed) *The State of the Nations 2003* (Imprint Academic).

Greer, S. (2004) *Territorial Politics and Health Policy* (Manchester University Press).

Greer, S. and Jarman, H. (2007) *The Department of Health and the Civil Service* (The Nuffield Trust).

Griffiths, C. and Brock, A. (2003) 'Twentieth Century Mortality Trends in England and Wales', *Health Statistics Quarterly*, **18**, 5–18.

Griffiths, R. (1992) 'Seven Years of Progress – General Management in the NHS', *Health Economics*, **1**(1): 61–70.

Griffiths Report (1983) *NHS Management Inquiry* (DHSS).

Griffiths Report (1988) *Community Care: Agenda for Action* (HMSO).

Guillebaud Committee (1956) *Report of the Committee of Enquiry into the Cost of the National Health Service*, Cmd 9663 (HMSO).

Hacker, J. (2004) 'Review Article: Dismantling the Health Care State? Political Institutions, Public Policies and the Comparative Politics of Health Reform' *British Journal of Political Science*, **34**, 693–724.

Halper, T. (1989) *The Misfortunes of Others: End-Stage Renal Disease in the United Kingdom* (Cambridge University Press).

Ham, C. J. (1977) 'Power, Patients and Pluralism', in Barnard, K. and Lee, K. (eds), *Conflicts in the NHS* (Croom Helm).

Ham, C. J. (1980) 'Approaches to the Study of Social Policy Making', *Policy and Politics*, (1): 55–71.

Ham, C. J. (1981) *Policy Making in the National Health Service* (Palgrave Macmillan).

Ham, C. J. (1986) *Managing Health Services* (School for Advanced Urban Studies, University of Bristol).

Ham, C. J. (1993) 'Priority Setting in the NHS: Reports from Six Districts', *British Medical Journal*, **367**, 435–8.

Ham, C. J. (1996) *Public, Private or Community? What Next for the NHS?* (DEMOS).

Ham, C. J. (1997a) *Management and Competition in the NHS* (Radcliffe Medical Press).

Ham, C. J. (1997b) 'Priority Setting in Health Care: Learning from International Experience' *Health Policy*, **42**, 49–66.

Ham, C. J. (1999) 'The Third Way in Health Care Reform: Does the Emperor Have Any Clothes?' *Journal of Health Services Research and Policy*, **4**(3): 1–6.

Ham, C. J. (2000) *The Politics of NHS Reform 1988–97* (King's Fund).

Ham, C. J. (2003a) *Betwixt and Between: Autonomization and Centralization of UK Hospitals*, in Preker, A. and Harding, A. (eds) *Innovations in Health Service Delivery* (The World Bank).

Ham, C. J. (2003b) 'Improving the Performance of Health Services: The Role of Clinical Leadership' *The Lancet*, **361**, 1978–80.

Ham, C. J. (2007a) *Increasing NHS Efficiency* (The Nuffield Trust).

Ham, C. J. (2007b) *When Politics and Markets Collide: Reforming the English National Health Service* (Health Services Management Centre, University of Birmingham).

Ham, C. J. (2008a) 'Gordon Brown's Agenda for the NHS' *British Medical Journal*, **336**, 53–4.

Ham, C. J. (2008b) 'World Class Commissioning: A Health Policy Chimera?' *Journal of Health Services Research and Policy*, **13**, 116–21.

Ham, C. J. (2008c) 'Competition and Integration in the English National Health Service' *British Medical Journal*, **336**, 805–7.

Ham, C. J. (2009) 'Chronic Care in the English National Health Service: Progress and Challenges' *Health Affairs*, **28**, 190–201.

Ham, C. J. and Coulter, A. (2001) 'Explicit and Implicit Rationing: Taking Responsibility and Avoiding Blame for Health Care Choices', *Journal of Health Services Research and Policy*, **6**, 163–9.

Ham, C. J. and McIver, S. (2000) *Contested Decisions* (King's Fund).

Ham, C. J. and Pickard, S. (1998) *Tragic Choices in Health Care* (King's Fund).

Ham, C. J. and Robert, G. (eds) (2003) *Reasonable Rationing* (Open University Press).

Ham, C. J., Kipping, R. and McLeod, H. (2003) 'Redesigning Work Processes in Health Care: Lessons from the National Health Service', *The Milbank Quarterly*, **81**(3): 415–39.

Ham, C. J., Robinson, R. and Benzeval, M. (1990) *Health Check* (King's Fund Institute).

Ham, C. J., Smith, J. and Temple, J. (1998) *Hubs, Spokes and Policy Cycles* (King's Fund).

Hampton, J. R. (1983) 'The End of Clinical Freedom', *British Medical Journal*, **287**, 1237–8.

Hansard (1986) 'NHS (General Managers)', written answers, 26 June, col. 298.

Harrison, S. (1988) *Managing the National Health Service* (Chapman & Hall).

Harrison, S. (1994) *National Health Service Management in the 1980s* (Avebury).

Hauck, K. and Street, A. (2007) 'Do Targets Matter? A Comparison of English and Welsh National Health Priorities' *Health Economics*, **16**, 275–90.

Haywood, S. and Alaszewski, A. (1980) *Crisis in the Health Service* (Croom Helm).

Haywood, S. and Hunter, D. (1982) 'Consultative Processes in Health Policy in the United Kingdom: A View from the Centre', *Public Administration*, **69**, 143–62.

Hazell, R. (ed.) (2003) *The State of the Nations 2003* (Imprint Academic).

Health Committee (2005) *NHS Continuing Care*. Sixth Report of Session 2004–05. HC 399-1 (The Stationery Office).

Health Committee (2006a) *NHS Charges*. Third Report of Session 2005–6. HC 815-1 (The Stationery Office).

Health Committee (2006b) *Independent Sector Treatment Centres*. Fourth Report of Session 2005–06. HC 934-1 (The Stationery Office).

Health Committee (2008a) *Dental Services*. Fifth Report of Session 2007–08. HC 289-1 (The Stationery Office).

Health Committee (2008b) *National Institute for Health and Clinical Excellence*. First Report of Session 2007–08. HC 27-1 (The Stationery Office).

Health Committee (2008c) *Foundation Trusts and Monitor*. Sixth Report of Session 2007–08. HC 833-1 (The Stationery Office).

Health Services Commissioner (2003) *NHS Funding for Long Term Care*. Second Report – Session 2002–2003. HC 399 (The Stationery Office).

Healthcare Commission (2005a) *Getting to the Heart of It. Coronary Heart Disease in England: A Review of Progress Towards the National Standards*.

Healthcare Commission (2005b) *Survey of Patients 2005. Stroke*.

Healthcare Commission (2007a) *Managing Diabetes*.

Healthcare Commission (2007b) *Independent Sector Treatment Centres*.

Healthcare Commission (2007c) *Stroke Patients in Wales More Likely to Die Than in England*.

Healthcare Commission (2008) *The Pathway to Recovery*.

Healthcare Commission (2008a) *Making a Difference? An Evaluation of the Performance of the Healthcare Commission 2004–08*.

Healthcare Commission (2008b) *State of Healthcare 2008*. HC 11 (The Stationery Office).

Heclo, H. (1974) *Modern Social Politics in Britain and Sweden* (Yale University Press).

Heclo, H. (1978) 'Issue Networks and the Executive Establishment', in King, A. (ed.) *The New American Political System* (American Enterprise Institute).

Hennessy, P. (1986) *Cabinet* (Basil Blackwell).

Hennessy, P. (1989) *Whitehall* (Secker & Warburg).

Hennessy, P. (1995) *The Hidden Wiring* (Victor Gollancz).

Hennessy, P. (2000) *The Prime Minister* (Penguin).

Hennessy, P. (2005) 'Rulers and Servants of the State: The Blair Style of Government 1997–2004 *Parliamentary Affairs*, 58(1): 6–16.

Hewitt, P. (2005) *Investment and Reform: Transforming Health and Healthcare* (LSE Annual Health and Social Care Lecture).

Hood, C. (1991) 'A Public Management for All Seasons', *Public Administration*, 69, 3–19.

Hood, C., Scott, C., James, O., Jones, G. and Travers, T. (1999) *Regulation Inside Government* (Oxford University Press).

Hunter, D. (1980) *Coping with Uncertainty* (Research Studies Press).

Hunter, D. (1983) 'Centre–Periphery Relations in the National Health Service: Facilitators or Inhibitors of Innovation?, in Young, K. (ed.) *National Interests and Local Governments* (Heinemann).

Hussey, P., Anderson, G., Osborn, R. et al. (2004) 'How Does the Quality of Care Compare in Five Countries?' *Health Affairs*, 23, 89–99.

Hyman, P. (2005) *1 out of 10* (Vintage).

Illsley, R. (1977) 'Everybody's Business? Concepts of Health and Illness', in Social Science Research Council, *Health and Health Policy Priorities for Research* (SSRC).

Irvine, D. (2003) *The Doctors' Tale: Professionalism and Public Trust* (Radcliffe Medical Press).

Jacobzone, S., Cambois, E. and Robine, J. (2000) *Is the Health of Older Persons in OECD Countries Improving Fast Enough to Compensate for Population Ageing?* (OECD).

Jenkins, W. I. (1978) *Policy Analysis* (Martin Robertson).

Jervis, P. (2007) *Devolution and Health* (The Nuffield Trust).

Jervis, P. and Plowden, W. (2003) *The Impact of Political Devolution on the UK's Health Services* (The Nuffield Trust).

Jha, A., Perlin, J., Kizer, K. et al. (2003) 'Effect of the Transformation of the Veterans Health Care System on the Quality of Care' *New England Journal of Medicine*, 348, 2218–27.

Jones, K. (1972) *A History of the Mental Health Services* (Routledge & Kegan Paul).

Joss, R. and Kogan, M. (1995) *Advancing Quality: Total Quality Management in the National Health Service* (Open University Press).

Judge, K., Mulligan, J. and New, B. (1997) 'The NHS: New Prescriptions Needed?' in Jowell, R., Curtice, J., Park, A. et al. (eds) *British Social Attitudes: The 14th Report* (Social and Community Planning Research).

Kanter, R. M. (1984) *The Change Masters* (Allen & Unwin).

Kavanagh, D. and Seldon, A. (1999) *The Powers Behind the Prime Minister* (HarperCollins).

Kelly, S. and Baker, A. (2000) 'Healthy Life Expectancy in Great Britain, 1980–96, and Its Use as an Indicator in United Kingdom Government Strategies', *Health Statistics Quarterly*, 07, 32–6.

Kennedy Report (2001) *The Report of the Public Inquiry into Children's Heart Surgery at the Bristol Royal Infirmary 1984–1995*, CM 5207 (1) (The Stationery Office).

Kingdon, J. W. (1995) *Agendas, Alternatives and Public Policies*, 2nd edn (HarperCollins).

King's Fund (2006) *Local Variations in NHS Spending Priorities*.

King's Fund Institute (1988) *Health Finance: Assessing the Options*.

Klein, R. (1995) *The New Politics of the NHS*, 3rd edn (Longman).

Klein, R. (1998) 'Why Britain is Reorganising its National Health Service – Yet Again', *Health Affairs*, **17**, 111–25.

Klein, R. (2006) *The New Politics of the NHS*, 5th edn (Radcliffe Publishing).

Klein, R., Day, P. and Redmayne, S. (1996) *Managing Scarcity* (Open University Press).

Lalonde, M. (1974) *A New Perspective on the Health of Canadians* (Government of Canada).

Laming Report (2003) *The Victoria Climbie Inquiry* (The Stationery Office).

Lawson, N. (1992) *The View from No. 11* (Bantam Press).

Le Grand, J. (1978) 'The Distribution of Public Expenditure: The Case of Health Care', *Economica*, **45**, 125–42.

Le Grand, J. (2002) 'The Labour Government and the National Health Service', *Oxford Review of Economic Policy*, **18**(2): 137–53.

Le Grand, J. (2003) *Motivation, Agency and Public Policy* (Oxford University Press).

Le Grand, J. (2007) *The Other Invisible Hand* (Princeton University Press).

Le Grand, J., Mays, N. and Mulligan, J. (eds) (1998) *Learning from the NHS Internal Market* (King's Fund).

Leatherman, S. and Sutherland, K. (2003) *The Quest for Quality in the NHS* (The Stationery Office).

Leatherman, S. and Sutherland, K. (2008) *The Quest for Quality: Refining the NHS Reforms* (The Nuffield Trust).

Lear, J. and Mossialos, E. (2008) 'EU law and Health Policy in Europe' *Euro Observer*, **10**, 1–3.

Lee-Potter, J. (1997) *A Damn Bad Business* (Gollancz).

Lewis, J. (1986) *What Price Community Medicine?* (Wheatsheaf Books).

Lindblom, C. E. (1965) *The Intelligence of Democracy* (The Free Press).

Lindblom. C. E. (1977) *Politics and Markets* (Basic Books).

Lindsey, A. (1962) *Socialized Medicine in England and Wales* (University of North Carolina Press).

Loudon, I., Horder, J. and Webster, C. (eds) (1998) *General Practice Under the National Health Service 1948–1997* (Oxford University Press).

Mackenbach, J. P. and Bakker, M. J. (2003) 'Tackling Socioeconomic Inequalities in Health: Analysis of European Experiences', *The Lancet*, **362**, 1409–14.

Mackintosh, J. P. (1974) *The Government and Politics of Britain*, 3rd revised edn (Hutchinson).

March, J. and Olsen, J. (1989) *Rediscovering Institutions: The Organisational Basis of Politics* (Free Press).

Marsh, D., Richards, D. and Smith, M. (2001) *Changing Patterns of Governance in the United Kingdom* (Palgrave – now Palgrave Macmillan).

Martin, J. P. (1984) *Hospitals in Trouble* (Blackwell).

Mays, N., Goodwin, N., Killoran, A. and Malbon, G. (1998) *Total Purchasing. A Step Towards Primary Care Groups* (King's Fund).

McCoy, D., Godden, S., Pollock, A. and Bianchessi (2007) 'Carrots and Sticks? The Community Care Act (2003 and the Effects of Financial Incentives on Delays in Discharge from Hospitals in England' *Journal of Public Health*, **29**(3): 281–7.

McDonald, R. (2002) *Using Health Economics in Health Services* (Open University Press).

McKeown. T. (1976) *The Role of Medicine* (Nuffield Provincial Hospitals Trust).

McKinsey Global Institute (1996) *Health Care Productivity*.

McNulty, T. and Ferlie, E. (2002) *Reengineering Health Care* (Oxford University Press).

Middlemas, K. (1979) *Politics in Industrial Society* (André Deutsch).

Ministry of Health (1946) *NHS Bill. Summary of the Proposed New Service*, Cmd 6761 (HMSO).

Ministry of Health (1967) *First Report of the Joint Working Party on the Organisation of Medical Work in Hospitals* (HMSO).

Mintzberg, H. (1983) *Structure in Fives: Designing Effective Organisations* (Prentice-Hall).

Moore, J. (1988) *Protecting the Nation's Health*, issued under cover of DHSS press release 88/97.

Moran, M. (1999) *Governing the Health Care State* (Manchester University Press).

Mossialos, E. and Palm, W. (2003) 'The European Court of Justice and the Free Movement of Patients in the European Union', *International Social Security Review*, **56**, 3–29.

Musgrove, P. (2003) 'Judging Health Systems: Reflections on WHO's Methods', *The Lancet*, **361**, 1817–20.

NAHA (National Association of Health Authorities) (1987) *Autumn Survey 1987* (NAHA).

Nairne, P. (1983) 'Managing the DHSS Elephant: Reflections on a Giant Department', *Political Quarterly*, 243–56.

National Assembly for Wales (2001) *Improving Health in Wales* (National Assembly for Wales).

National Audit Office (2005a) *The NHS Cancer Plan: A Progress Report HC 343 Session 2004–05* (The Stationery Office).

National Audit Office (2005b) *Reducing Brain Damage: Faster Access to Better Stroke Care HC 452 Session 2005–06* (The Stationery Office).

National Audit Office (2006) *The Provision of Out-of-Hours Care in England HC 1041 Session 2005–06* (The Stationery Office).

National Audit Office (2007) *Improving Services and Support for People with Dementia HC 604 Session 2006–07* (The Stationery Office).

National Audit Office (2008) *NHS Pay Modernisation: New Contracts for General Practice Services in England HC 307 Session 2007–08* (The Stationery Office).

National Audit Office and Audit Commission (2008) *Financial Management in the NHS: Report on the NHS Summarised Accounts 2007–08* HC 63-1 Session 2008–09 (The Stationery Office).

National Leadership Network (2006) *Strengthening Local Services: The Future of the Acute Hospital*.

Navarro, V. (1976) *Medicine Under Capitalism* (Prodist).

NHS Executive (1996) *Seeing the Wood, Sparing the Trees*.

Nixon, J. and Nixon, N. (1983) 'The Social Services Committee: A Forum for Policy Review and Policy Reform', *Journal of Social Policy*, **12**(3): 331–55.

Nolte, E. and McKeee, M. (2008) 'Measuring *The Health of Nations*: Updating An Earlier Analysis' *Health Affairs,* **27**(1): 58–71.

Normansfield Report (1978) *Report of the Committee of Inquiry into Normansfield Hospital*, Cmnd 7357 (HMSO).

North, N. (1995) 'Alford Revisited: The Professional Monopolisers, Corporate Rationalisers, Community and Markets' *Policy and Politics*, **23**(2): 115–25.

North, N. and Peckham, S. (2001) 'Analysing Structural Interests in Primary Care Groups, *Social Policy and Administration*, **35**(4): 426–40.

Northern Ireland Audit Office (2008) *The Performance of the Health Service in Northern Ireland* (The Stationery Office).

Norton, P. (1981) *The Commons in Perspective* (Martin Robertson).

Norton, P. (1997) 'Parliamentary Oversight', in Dunleavy, P., Gamble, A., Holliday, I. and Peele, G. (eds) *Developments in British Politics,* 5th edn (Palgrave Macmillan).

Norton, P. (2005) *Parliament in British Politics* (Palgrave Macmillan).

Nuffield Provincial Hospitals Trust (1946) *The Hospital Surveys: The Domesday Book of the Hospital Services* (Oxford University Press).

Oborne, P. (2007) *The Triumph of the Political Class* (Simon & Schuster).

O'Connor, J. (1973) *The Fiscal Crisis of the State* (St Martin's Press: also Macmillan, 1981).

OECD (2003) *A Disease-based Comparison of Health Systems* (OECD).

OECD (2008) *OECD Health Data 2008* (OECD).

Office of Health Economics (1989) *Compendium of Health Statistics*, 7th edn (OHE).

Office of Health Economics (2008) *Compendium of Health Statistics 2008* 19th edn (Radcliffe).

ONS (Office for National Statistics) (2006) *General Household Survey 2006.*

ONS (Office for National Statistics) (2008a) *Public Service Productivity.*

ONS (Office for National Statistics) (2008b) *United Kingdom Health Statistics* (Palgrave Macmillan).

Osmond, J. (2003) 'From Corporate Body to Virtual Parliament. The Metamorphosis of the National Assembly for Wales', in Hazell, R. (ed.) *The State of the Nations 2003* (Imprint Academic).

Owen, D. (1991) *Time to Declare* (Michael Joseph).

Packwood, T., Keen, J. and Buxton, M. (1991) *Hospitals in Transition* (Open University Press)

Paige, V. (1987) 'The Development of General Management within the NHS', *The Health Summary*, (June): 6–8.

Parsons, W. (1995) *Public Policy* (Edward Elgar).

Pater, J. E. (1981) *The Making of the NHS* (King's Fund).

Pettigrew, A., Ferlie, E. and McKee, L. (1992) *Shaping Strategic Change* (Sage).

Philp, I. (2004) *Better Health in Old Age* (DH).

Philp, I. (2006) *A New Ambition for Old Age: Next Steps in Implementing the National Service Framework for Older People* (DH).

Pickard, S., Sheaff, R. and Dowling, B. (2006) 'Exit, Voice, Governance and User-responsiveness: The Case of English Primary Care Trusts' *Social Science and Medicine*, 63, 373–83.

Pierson, P. (1994) *Dismantling the Welfare State?* (Cambridge University Press).

Pollock, A. (2004) *NHS plc* (Verso).

Pollock, A. and Godden, S. (2008) 'Independent Sector Treatment Centres: Evidence so Far' *British Medical Journal*, 336, 421–4.

Pollock, A. and Price, D. (2003) 'The BetterCare Judgment – A Challenge to Health Care', *British Medical Journal*, 326, 236–7.

Pollock, A., Dunnigan, M., Gaffney, D., Price, D. and Shaoul, J. (1999) 'Planning the "New" NHS: Downsizing for the 21st Century', *British Medical Journal*, 319(17 July): 179–84.

Popham, G. T. (1981) 'Government and Smoking: Policy Making and Pressure Groups', *Policy and Politics*, (3): 331–47.

Porter, M. and Teisberg, E. (2006) *Redefining Health Care* (Harvard Business School Press).

Porter, R. (1997) *The Greatest Benefit to Mankind* (HarperCollins).

Powell, J. E. (1966) *A New Look at Medicine and Politics* (Pitman).

Power, M. (1994) *The Audit Explosion* (DEMOS).

Propper, C. (1996) 'Market Structure and Prices: The Response of Hospitals in the UK National Health Service to Competition', *Journal of Public Economics*, 61, 307–35.

Propper, C. (1998) *Who Pays For and Who Gets Health Care?* (The Nuffield Trust).

Propper, C., Burgess, S. and Gossage, D. (2003) *Competition and Quality: Evidence from the NHS Internal Market 1991–1999* (University of Bristol).

Propper, C., Sutton, M., Whitnall, C. and Windmeijer, F. (2007) *Did 'Targets and Terror' Reduce English Waiting Times for Elective Hospital Care?* (CMPO, University of Bristol).

Public Accounts Committee (1977) *Ninth Report from the Public Accounts Committee Session 1976–77.* HC 532 (HMSO).

Public Accounts Committee (2008) *NHS Pay Modernisation: New Contracts for General Practice Services in England.* HC 463 (The Stationery Office).

Public Administration Committee (2001) *Fourth Report of the Select Committee on Public Administration 2000–01.* HC 293 (The Stationery Office).

Public Administration Committee (2007) *Politics and Administration: Ministers and Civil Servants. Third Report of Session 2006–07.* HC 122-1 (The Stationery Office).

Regen, E., Smith, J., Goodwin, N., McLeod, H. and Shapiro, J. (2001) *Passing on the Baton: Final Report of a National Evaluation of Primary Care Groups and Trusts* (University of Birmingham).

Regional Chairmen's Enquiry (1976) *Regional Chairmen's Enquiry into the Working of the DHSS in Relation to Regional Health Authorities* (DHSS).

Rhodes, R. A. W. (1979) 'Research into Central–Local Relations in Britain. A Framework for Analysis', appendix 1, in Social Science Research Council, *Central–Local Relationships* (SSRC).

Rhodes, R. A. W. (1997) *Understanding Governance* (Open University Press).

Richards, M. (2006) *Waiting Times for Cancer* (DH).

Richards, M. (2008) *Improving Access to Medicines for NHS Patients* (DH).

Richards, N. and Coulter, A. (2007) *Is the NHS Becoming More Patient-centred? Trends from the National Surveys of Patients in England, 2002–07* (Picker Institute Europe).

Richardson, J. J. and Jordan, A. G. (1979) *Governing under Pressure* (Martin Robertson).

Riddell, P. (2001) 'New Look Behind the Revolving Doors of Power', *The Times*, 13 June.

Robb, B. (ed.) (1967) *Sans Everything – A Case to Answer* (Nelson).

Roberts. J. (1990) 'Kenneth Clarke: Hatchet Man or Remoulder?' *British Medical Journal*, **301**, 1383–6.

Robinson, R. and Le Grand, J. (eds) (1994) *Evaluating the NHS Reforms* (King's Fund Institute).

Rosen, R., Smith, A. and Harrison, A. (2006) *Future Trends and Challenges for Cancer Services in England* (King's Fund).

Royal Commission on the National Health Service (1979) *Report*, Cmnd 7615 (HMSO).

Rundall, T., Starkweather, D. and Norrish, B. (1998) *After Restructuring* (Jossey-Bass).

Salter, B. (2007) 'Governing UK Medical Performance: A Struggle for Policy Dominance' *Health Policy*, **82**, 263–75.

Saltman, R. and von Otter, C. (eds) (1995) *Implementing Planned Markets in Health Care* (Open University Press).

Saunders, P. (1979) *Urban Politics* (Hutchinson).

Saunders, P. (1981) 'Notes on the Specificity of the Local State', in Boddy, M. and Fudge, C. (eds). *The Local State: Theory and Practice* (University of Bristol, School for Advanced Urban Studies).

Schoen, C., Osborn, R., Doty, M. M., Bishop, M., Peugh, J. and Murukutla, N. (2007) 'Towards Higher-Performance Health Systems: Adults' Health Care Experiences in Seven Countries 2007' *Health Affairs*, 26, w717–w734.

Schoen, C., Osborn, R., Huynh, P. T., Doty, M., Zapert, K., Peugh, J. and Davis, K. (2005) 'Taking the Pulse of Health Care Systems: Experiences of Patients with Health Problems in Six Countries' *Health Affairs*, w5–509–w5–525.

Schoen, C., Osborn, R., How, S. et al. (2009) 'In Chronic Condition: Experiences of Patients with Complex Health Care Needs, in Eight Countries, 2008' *Health Affairs*, **28**(1): w.1–w.16.

Scottish Executive (2000) *Our National Health* (The Stationery Office).

Scottish Executive (2001) *Rebuilding our National Health Service*.

Scottish Executive (2003) *Partnership for Care: Scotland's Health White Paper* (The Stationery Office).

Scottish Executive (2005a) *Building a Health Service Fit for the Future*.

Scottish Executive (2005b) *Delivering for Health*.

Scottish Government (2007) *Better Health, Better Care*.

Secretary of State for Children, Schools and Families (2007) *The Children's Plan*, Cm 7280 (The Stationery Office).

Secretary of State for Health (1992) *The Health of the Nation*, Cm 1986 (HMSO).

Secretary of State for Health (1996) *The National Health Service. A Service With Ambitions*, Cm 3425 (The Stationery Office).

Secretary of State for Health (1997) *The New NHS: Modern, Dependable* (The Stationery Office).

Secretary of State for Health (1998a) *Our Healthier Nation*, Cm 3852 (The Stationery Office).

Secretary of State for Health (1998b) *A First Class Service* (The Stationery Office).

Secretary of State for Health (1999) *Saving Lives: Our Healthier Nation*, Cm 4386 (The Stationery Office).

Secretary of State for Health (2000) *The NHS Plan*, Cm 4818-I (The Stationery Office).

Secretary of State for Health (2002) *Delivering the NHS Plan: A Plan for Investment, a Plan for Reform*, Cm 5503 (The Stationery Office).

Secretary of State for Health (2004a) *The NHS Improvement Plan*, Cm 6268 (The Stationery Office).

Secretary of State for Health (2004b) *Choosing Health*, Cm 6374 (The Stationery Office).

Secretary of State for Health (2006) *Our Health, Our Care, Our Say*, Cm 6737 (The Stationery Office).

Secretary of State for Health (2007a) *National Stroke Strategy* (DH).

Secretary of State for Health (2007b) *Trust, Assurance and Safety – The Regulation of Health Professionals in the 21st Century*, Cm 7013 (The Stationery Office).

Secretary of State for Health (2008a) *High Quality Care for All*, Cm 7432 (The Stationery Office).

Secretary of State for Health (2008b) *NHS Next Stage Review: Our Vision for Primary and Community Care* (DH).

Secretary of State for Health (2008c) *Pharmacy in England: Building on Strengths, Delivering the Future*, Cm 7341 (The Stationery Office).

Secretary of State for Health (2008d) *The Coronary Heart Disease National Service Framework: Building for the Future – Progress Report for 2007* (DH).

Secretary of State for Health and others (1989a) *Working for Patients* (HMSO).

Secretary of State for Health and others (1989b) *Caring for People* (HMSO).

Secretary of State for Health and Secretary of State for Children, Schools and Families (2008) *Healthy Weight, Healthy Lives: A Cross-Government Strategy for England*.

Secretary of State for Scotland (1997) *Designed to Care* (The Stationery Office).

Secretary of State for Social Services and others (1987) *Promoting Better Health* (HMSO).

Secretary of State for Wales (1998) *Putting Patients First*, Cm 3841 (The Stationery Office).

Seldon, A. (2007) *Blair Unbound* (Simon and Schuster).

Shaw, E. (2007) *Losing Labour's Soul* (Routledge).

Sheaff, R., Rogers, A., Pickard, S., Marshall, M. Campbell, S. et al. (2003) 'A Subtle Governance: "Soft" Medical Leadership in English Primary Care' *Sociology of Health and Illness,* 25(5): 408–28.

Sheard, S. and Donaldson, L. (2006) *The Nation's Doctor* (Radcliffe Publishing).

Shribman, S. (2007) *Children's Health, Our Future* (DH).

Smee, C. (1995) 'Self-governing Trusts and GP Fundholders: the British Experience', in Saltman, R. and von Otter, C. (eds) *Implementing Planned Markets in Health Care* (Open University Press).

Smee, C. (2005) *Speaking Truth to Power* (Radcliffe Publishing).

Smith, B. (1976) *Policy Making in British Government* (Martin Robertson).

Smith, J. and Goodwin, N. (2006) *Towards Managed Primary Care* (Ashgate).

Smith, M. (1993) *Pressure, Power and Policy* (Harvester Wheatsheaf).

Smith, M. (1999) *The Core Executive in Britain* (Palgrave Macmillan).

Smith, M., Edgar, G. and Groom, G. (2008) 'Health Expectancies in the United Kingdom, 2004–06' *Health Statistics Quarterly,* 40(winter): 77–80.

Smith, P. (2002) 'Performance Management in British Health Care: Will it Deliver?' *Health Affairs,* 21(3): 103–15.

Smith, P. (2005) 'Performance Measurement in Health Care: History, Challenges and Prospects' *Public Money and Management*, 213–20.

Smith, P. (2008) 'England: Intended and Unintended Effects' in Wismar, M., McKee, M., Ernst, K. et al. (eds) *Health Targets in Europe: Learning from Experience* (WHO Regional Office for Europe).

Smith, R. (1991) 'William Waldegrave: Thinking beyond the New NHS', *British Medical Journal*, 302, 711–14.

Social Services Committee (1980) *The Government's White Papers on Public Expenditure: The Social Services, Third Report from the Social Services Committee, Session 1979–80*, HC 701-2 (HMSO): vol. 1, *Report*; vol. 2 *Minutes of Evidence and Appendices*.

Social Services Committee (1984) *Griffiths NHS Management Inquiry Report, First Report from the Social Services Committee, Session 1983–4*, HC 209 (HMSO).

Social Services Committee (1990) *Public Expenditure on Health Matters, Session 1989–90*, HC 484 (HMSO).

Soderlund, N., Csaba, I., Gray, R., Milne, R. and Raftery, J. (1997) 'Impact of the NHS Reforms on English Hospital Productivity: An Analysis of the First Three Years', *British Medical Journal*, 315, 1126–9.

Solesbury, W. (1976) 'The Environmental Agenda', *Public Administration*, (winter): 379–97.

Stacey, M. (1977) 'Concepts of Health and Illness: A Working Paper on the Concepts and their Relevance for Research', in Social Science Research Council, *Health and Health Policy – Priorities for Research* (SSRC).

Stacey, M. (1992) *Regulating British Medicine* (John Wiley).

Starfield, B. (1992) *Primary Care: Concept, Evaluation and Policy* (Oxford University Press).

Stevens, R. (1966) *Medical Practice in Modern England* (Yale University Press).

Stowe, K. (1989) *On Caring for the National Health* (The Nuffield Provincial Hospitals Trust).

Sutherland, K. and Coyle N. (2009) *Quality of Healthcare in England, Wales, Scotland, Northern Ireland: An Intra-UK Chartbook* (The Health Foundation).

Sutherland Report (2008) *Independent Review of Free Personal and Nursing Care in Scotland* (Scottish Government).

Taylor, P. (1984) *The Smoke Ring* (The Bodley Head).

Thorlby, R., and Maybin, J. (2007) *Health and Ten Years of Labour Government* (King's Fund).

Thornton, S. (2004) 'It's Party Time' *Health Service Journal*, (7 October): 23.

Thwaites, B. (1987) *The NHS: The End of the Rainbow* (The Institute of Health Policy Studies, University of Southampton).

Timmins, N. (1995) *The Five Giants* (HarperCollins).

Timmins, N. (2007) 'Labour Policy Risks Boosting Private Medicine' *Financial Times* 15 November, 19.

Timmins, N. (ed.) (2008a) *Rejuvenate or Retire?* (The Nuffield Trust).

Timmins, N. (2008b) 'Patients Slow to Take Up Right on Choosing Hospital' *Financial Times* 2 October.

Titmuss, R. (1968) *Commitment to Welfare* (Allen & Unwin).

Tudor-Hart, J. (1971) 'The Inverse Care Law', *The Lancet*, (27 February): 405–12.

Tunstall-Pedoe, H., Vanuzzo, D., Hobbs, M., Mähönen, M., Cepaitis, Z., Kuulasmaa, K. and Keil, U. (2000) 'Estimation of Contribution of Changes in Coronary Care to Improving Survival, Event Rates, and Coronary Heart Disease Mortality Across the WHO MONICA Project Populations', *The Lancet*, 355, 688–700.

Tuohy, C. (1999) *Accidental Logics* (Oxford University Press).

Turner, A. (2002) *Health Strategy Review* (Cabinet Office) http://www.cabinetoffice.gov.uk/strategy/work_areas/health.aspx.

van Doorslaer, E., Rutten, F. and Wagstaff, A. (1993) *Equity in the Finance and Delivery of Health Care: An International Perspective* (Oxford University Press).

Wagstaff, A., van Doorslaer, E., van der Burg, H., Calonge, S., Christiansen, T. et al. (1999) 'Equity in the Finance of Health Care: Some Further International Comparisons', *Journal of Health Economics*, **18**, 263–90.

Walshe, K. (2003) *Regulating Healthcare* (Open University Press).

Walshe, K. (2008) 'Signed and Delivered: The Rules in Writing' *Health Service Journal*, (24 July): 14–15.

Wanless, D. (2001) *Securing Our Future Health: Taking a Long-Term View. Interim Report* (HM Treasury).

Wanless, D. (2002) *Securing Our Future Health: Taking a Long-Term View. Final Report* (HM Treasury).

Wanless, D. (2003a) *The Review of Health and Social Care in Wales* (Welsh Assembly Government).

Wanless, D. (2003b) *Securing Good Health for the Whole Population: Population Health Trends* (HMSO).

Wanless, D. (2004) *Securing Good Health for the Whole Population: Final Report* (HMSO).

Wanless, D. (2006) *Securing Good Care for Older People: Taking a Long-term View* (King's Fund).

Wanless, D., Appleby, J., Harrison, A. and Patel, D. (2007) *Our Future Health Secured?* (King's Fund).

Webster, C. (1988) *The Health Services Since the War*, Vol. 1 (HMSO).

Webster, C. (1996) *The Health Services Since The War*, Vol. 2 (The Stationery Office).

Webster, C. (1998) *The National Health Service: A Political History* (Oxford University Press).

Welsh Assembly Government (2005) *Designed for Life.*

Welsh Assembly Government (2007) *One Wales: A Progressive Agenda for Wales.*

Wheller, L., Baker, A., Griffiths, C. and Rooney, C. (2007) 'Trends in Avoidable Mortality in England and Wales, 1993–2005' *Health Statistics Quarterly*, **34**(summer): 6–25.

Whitehead, M. (1987) *The Health Divide* (Health Education Council).

WHO (World Health Organization) (2000) *The World Health Report 2000. Health Systems: Improving Performance.*

Wilding, P. (1982) *Professional Power and Social Welfare* (Routledge & Kegan Paul).

Wilkin, D., Coleman, A., Dowling, B. and Smith, K. (2002) *National Tracker Survey of Primary Care Groups and Trusts 2001/2002: Taking Responsibility?* (National Primary Care Research and Development Centre).

Willcocks, A. J. (1967) *The Creation of the National Health Service* (Routledge & Kegan Paul).

Wilsford, D. (1994) 'Path Dependency, or Why History Makes It Difficult but Not Impossible to Reform Health Care Systems in a Big Way' *Journal of Public Policy*, **14**(3): 251–83.

Wilsford, D. (1995) 'States Facing Interests: Struggles Over Health Care Policy in Advanced, Industrial Democracies' *Journal of Health Politics, Policy and Law* **20**, 571–613.

Woods, K. (2002) 'Health Policy and the NHS in the UK 1997–2002', in Adams, J. and Robinson, P. (eds) *Devolution in Practice* (IPPR and ESRC).

Woods, K. (2004) 'Political Devolution and the Health Services in Great Britain', *International Journal of Health Services*, **34**, 323–39.

Yates, J. (1987) *Why Are We Waiting?* (Oxford University Press).

Yates, J. (1995) *Private Eye, Heart and Hip* (Churchill Livingstone).

Young, H. (1989) *One of Us* (Pan Macmillan).

Young, H. and Sloman, A. (1982) *No, Minister* (BBC).

Index

347